THE CONFIDANTE

THE CONFIDANTE

CONDOLEEZZA RICE
AND
THE CREATION
OF THE
BUSH LEGACY

Glenn Kessler

ST. MARTIN'S PRESS
NEW YORK

www.stmartins.com

Book design by Mary A. Wirth

LIBRARY OF CONGRESS CATALOGING-IN-PUBLICATION DATA

Kessler, Glenn.
    The confidante : Condoleezza Rice and the creation of the Bush legacy
/ Glenn Kessler.—1st ed.
        p.   cm.
    Includes index and bibliographical references.
    ISBN-13: 978-0-312-36380-2
    ISBN-10: 0-312-36380-X
    1. Rice, Condoleezza, 1954–   2. Stateswomen—United States—
Biography.   3. Bush, George W. (George Walker), 1946– —Friends and
associates.   4. United States—Foreign relations—2001–   5. Women
cabinet officers—United States—Biography.   6. Cabinet officers—
United States—Biography.   7. African American women—Biography.
I. Title.

E840.8.R48 K475 2007
355'.033073092—dc22
[B]
                                                            2007020906

First Edition: September 2007

10 9 8 7 6 5 4 3 2 1

FOR CINDY

CONTENTS

KEY PERSONNEL   IX

INTRODUCTION: **FROM BIRMINGHAM TO BEIJING**   1

1. **REBIRTH IN PARIS**   20
2. **PASSAGE TO NEW DELHI**   48
3. **SHOWDOWN NEAR SEOUL**   65
4. **EXPOSED IN RIYADH**   88
5. **RUMBLE IN KHARTOUM**   102
6. **SLEEPLESS IN JERUSALEM**   120
7. **A QUESTION IN KIEV**   145
8. **DOUBLE DATES IN BAGHDAD**   158
9. **DIPLOMATIC WALTZ IN VIENNA**   181
10. **BLOWUP OVER BEIRUT**   206

CONCLUSION: **BACK TO BEIJING—AND BEYOND**   233

ACKNOWLEDGMENTS   245
NOTES   249
INDEX   275

KEY PERSONNEL

AT THE STATE DEPARTMENT

Condoleezza Rice, SECRETARY OF STATE

Robert B. Zoellick, DEPUTY SECRETARY OF STATE *(until July 2006)*

Philip D. Zelikow, COUNSELOR *(until January 2007)*

Jim Wilkinson, SENIOR ADVISOR *(until July 2006)*

Brian F. Gunderson, CHIEF OF STAFF

John B. Bellinger III, LEGAL ADVISER

R. Nicholas Burns, UNDERSECRETARY OF STATE FOR POLITICAL AFFAIRS

Robert Joseph, UNDERSECRETARY OF STATE FOR ARMS CONTROL AND INTERNATIONAL SECURITY *(until February 2007)*

Karen Hughes, UNDERSECRETARY OF STATE FOR PUBLIC DIPLOMACY

John R. Bolton, U.S. PERMANENT REPRESENTATIVE TO THE UNITED NATIONS *(until December 2006)*

Christopher R. Hill, ASSISTANT SECRETARY OF STATE FOR EAST ASIAN AND PACIFIC AFFAIRS

C. David Welch, ASSISTANT SECRETARY OF STATE FOR NEAR EASTERN AFFAIRS

Sean McCormack, ASSISTANT SECRETARY OF STATE FOR PUBLIC AFFAIRS

AT THE WHITE HOUSE AND PENTAGON

President George W. Bush

Vice President Richard B. Cheney

Donald H. Rumsfeld, SECRETARY OF DEFENSE *(until December 2006)*
Stephen R. Hadley, NATIONAL SECURITY ADVISOR
Elliott Abrams, DEPUTY NATIONAL SECURITY ADVISOR FOR GLOBAL DEMOCRACY STATEGY
Michael J. Green, SENIOR DIRECTOR FOR ASIA AFFAIRS *(until December 2005)*

OVERSEAS

Jack Straw, BRITISH FOREIGN SECRETARY *(until May 2006)*
Margaret Beckett, BRITISH FOREIGN SECRETARY *(after May 2006)*
Sergey Lavrov, RUSSIAN FOREIGN MINISTER
Philippe Douste-Blazy, FRENCH FOREIGN MINISTER
Tzipi Livni, ISRAELI FOREIGN MINISTER
Saud al-Faisal, SAUDI FOREIGN MINISTER
Ahmed Aboul Gheit, EGYPTIAN FOREIGN MINISTER
Tang Jiaxuan, CHINESE STATE COUNCILOR

THE CONFIDANTE

FROM BIRMINGHAM TO BEIJING

July 9, 2004

China's state councilor, Tang Jiaxuan, an austere and pompous Communist Party apparatchik, would not stop talking.

Condoleezza Rice watched the minutes pass with growing fury. It was July 2004, her final year as national security advisor, and she had traveled to Beijing as part of a solo trip to the region that many suspected was designed to burnish her diplomatic qualifications in case President Bush named her secretary of state after the election. Rice had been allotted one hour for her meeting with Tang, one of China's most senior officials, and then she was scheduled to meet with President Hu Jintao.

Reading from a stack of five-by-eight note cards, Tang launched into an angry blast at Taiwan, which China regards as a renegade province, and the administration's handling of the outspoken president of Taiwan, Chen Shui-bian. He did not appear to notice that during his harangue Rice sat very still, with her lips pursed. She didn't even look at Tang but stared at the corner of the coffee table.

Tang kept going. He denounced U.S. arms sales to Taiwan and warned that Taiwan was an obstacle to U.S.-China relations. In a veiled threat, he declared that Chinese officials "would not sit idly by" if arms sales to Taiwan continued. He even spent a long time describing Chen's lineage, alleging that the Taiwanese president descended from a family of pirates.

Finally, after using up nearly fifty-five minutes, Tang paused. "I have spoken too long," he said in mock apology.

"Yes, you have talked too long," Rice replied, with a sharpness that seemed to surprise Tang. "I have to go now to meet President Hu. But I'll leave you with this thought." She used the remaining five minutes to briefly and pointedly dissect his arguments before marching out of the room.

Eight months later, after Rice had been named secretary of state and was planning her first trip to Asia, it was time to make Tang sweat. Every time someone tried to insert a meeting with Tang on her schedule, Rice knocked it off. Not enough time for such a meeting, she said.

The Chinese government, especially the embassy in Washington, became apoplectic. So did many Asia hands at the State Department. Rice was scheduled to meet with the foreign minister, Li Zhaoxing, but in the Chinese system Tang outranked Li. If Rice saw Li but not Tang, then Tang, Li's predecessor as foreign minister, would lose face. The Chinese ambassador, convinced he would be fired over the snub, became increasingly desperate. Calls were made to the White House, and "friends of China" who knew Rice were enlisted—all in an effort to get her to change her mind. But she was firm. There was no time for Tang.

A meeting with Tang was still not on Rice's schedule when her plane landed in Beijing. After she entered her hotel suite, she unexpectedly received a vast smorgasbord of Chinese sweets, food, and wine. COMPLIMENTS OF STATE COUNCILOR TANG read the card accompanying the food.

As Rice and her aides began to devour the luscious delicacies, she mused out loud, knowing full well every word was being recorded by hidden Chinese listening devices. "What do you think?" she asked. "Should I see him?"

A meeting was finally scheduled. And State Councilor Tang turned out to be extremely solicitous and eager to hear Rice's views.[1]

"Present at the Creation," Part II

The confrontation with Tang—and how Rice bested him—demonstrates the essence of Rice's style as secretary of state. She has an instinct for the jugular. In public, she is almost always gracious and charming. Behind closed doors, she can be tough and direct, shocking foreign diplomats into action because they assume her words reflect the view of her very close friend, the president of the United States. Within months of taking up her post, she canceled a visit to Egypt and temporarily suspended $200 million in aid to signal displeasure with the arrest of a pro-reform politician. She also scrubbed a visit to Canada when it nixed participation in U.S. missile defense.

In a remarkably short period, Rice rose dramatically from ivory-tower

academic to presidential advisor. Now, by virtue of her talents and her close association with President Bush, she has emerged in Bush's second term as a powerful secretary of state. She has taken the helm of the U.S. foreign policy
establishment at one of the most perilous periods of U.S. history, a time of international tensions, conflict, and war.

Her close relationship with the president and her lack of family obligations
have freed her to become the most traveled secretary of state since Henry
Kissinger—in strong contrast to her predecessor, Colin L. Powell, the least traveled secretary in three decades. She is also strategic in the way she travels, deliberately skipping the long list of boring conferences that form the core of
international diplomacy in order to focus on trips where she can make a
difference—what she calls "transformational diplomacy."

But her options and opportunities as secretary of state are limited by one
deeply ironic fact: She was one of the weakest national security advisors in U.S.
history.

Her inexperience and her mistakes in that job have shaped the world and
colored the choices she must handle as secretary of state. The invasion of Iraq,
the missed opportunities with Iran, the breach in relations with Europe, the
North Korea nuclear breakout, the creation of secret CIA prisons in Europe,
the Arab anger at a perceived bias against the Palestinians—all of these problems were the direct result of decisions she helped make in the White House.
Now, as secretary of state, she has tried mightily—and with limited success—
to unravel the Gordian knots she tied in George W. Bush's first term.

Rice appears to have few illusions about the United States' fall from grace
throughout the world. But she believes that the mistakes the Bush administration has made will be forgotten as long as the big picture—such as transform-
ing the Middle East—is viewed as acceptable by historians.

Secretaries of state generally display on their office walls portraits of two of
their predecessors—Thomas Jefferson (who served under Washington) and
George C. Marshall (under Truman)—and Rice is no exception. But on her first
foreign trip as secretary of state, Rice suddenly called her office and asked them
to hang a third portrait: Dean Acheson, Truman's second secretary of state.[2]
Acheson, who titled his memoir *Present at the Creation,* was a prime architect of
much of the post–World War II foreign policy structures. When Rice was a
midlevel staffer in the administration of George H. W. Bush, working on the reunification of Germany and the coming collapse of the Soviet Union, she says
she thought she was merely reaping the fruits of Acheson's labors.

Rice gains solace from the fact that while the Truman period is now viewed
as a golden age of foreign policy, when they got everything right and every

response was perfect, Marshall and Acheson struggled with a series of calamities. The world, in fact, seemed pretty bleak at the time. The two men also worked for a president who was regarded as a know-nothing lightweight when he was commander in chief, but whose reputation has grown so significantly with the passage of time that he is now regarded as one of the great American leaders.

This book will focus largely on Rice's first two years as secretary of state, examining ten key issues that have defined her tenure. It is an insider's account, revealing many previously unreported discussions between Rice and her top aides, President Bush, and foreign officials as she sought to maneuver out of the problems created in Bush's first term.

During that period, U.S. foreign policy had two competing themes, framed by "realists" under former secretary of state Colin Powell, who sought pragmatic accommodation with the world on common goals, and "neoconservatives" at the Pentagon and Vice President Cheney's office, who had grand visions of remaking the world, even if it meant defying allies. In Bush's second term, Rice has charted a strategy that somewhat uncomfortably tries to square the circle—what one of her top aides calls "practical idealism."[3]

"Practical idealism" is a nonsensical term once previously advanced by none other than Al Gore in his losing presidential race with Bush, but at its heart it is an acknowledgment that the Bush administration badly bungled diplomacy in its first term. Rice's goal is to steer U.S. foreign policy so that Bush's objectives have a better chance of success. In essence, she is in a desperate race to save President Bush's foreign policy legacy—and her own. Despite her obvious skill and intelligence, the problems she helped create in the first term are so overwhelming that she will have great difficulty succeeding.

"Miss Rice Is Like My Sister"

Rice achieved rock-star status around the world shortly after taking office. This was no accident: She promptly put together a one-hundred-day plan, with important benchmarks and goals. She assembled a powerful personal staff. And she imported more than a dozen top officials from the White House, bringing a new level of media sophistication and attention to imagery to—and resentment inside—the State Department.

Rice's larger-than-life image has both its upside and its downside. She became such a public celebrity that the Museum of the American Cocktail named a drink after her: a vodka-and-sake concoction described as "100 percent rice, very clear, very cold, a little chilly at times."[4] (Actually, Rice, though a Russia specialist, can barely tolerate vodka.)

But the image-making backfired when she was on vacation in New York during Hurricane Katrina. Rice does foreign policy, not domestic policy. Although she privately told aides that she was appalled at the administration's bumbling response to the disaster in New Orleans, it was widely reported that she was booed by some audience members when she attended *Spamalot,* the Monty Python musical, and then accosted by a fellow shopper when she was spotted buying expensive shoes at the high-end Ferragamo store on Fifth Avenue. "How dare you shop for shoes while thousands are dying and homeless," the shopper reportedly yelled before being removed from the store.[5] African American filmmaker Spike Lee, who made a documentary about Katrina, said that this incident made him dislike Rice more than Bush. "The thing about it is she's gotten a free ride from black people. . . . I know you love your Ferragamo shoes, but come on."[6] But the reports were in fact an urban myth: Rice did go to Ferragamo, but she found the people there very polite.[7]

Rice's professional history has depended on strong male mentors and a sort of serendipity that has kept her moving from one top post to another. George W. Bush is only the latest in a series of strong father figures that has also included Josef Korbel (a professor who, in an oddity of history, was the father of one of Rice's predecessors, Madeleine Albright), former national security advisor Brent Scowcroft, former secretary of state George Shultz, and former Stanford president Gerhard Casper.

Bush is as proud of Rice's rise as any father. He once interrupted an interview with a French reporter to haul Rice into the room—and then he introduced her as "the most powerful woman in the history of the world."[8] But because the president is only slightly older than Rice—she was fifty at the beginning of his second term—he suggests he is more like her brother. Bush paved the way for her influence overseas by pointedly telling foreign leaders when they came to the Oval Office, "Miss Rice is like my sister." The message: Treat her well. Rice believes the president is also indicating that they grew up together, in terms of their approach to foreign policy.[9]

Whenever he can, Bush reinforces the idea that he and Rice are partners. In late 2006, nearly two years after he appointed Rice as secretary of state, Bush told a private gathering of U.S. diplomats at the United Nations that it is important for the president and the secretary of state "to be in synch, like a hand in a glove." With Rice standing at his side, he declared, "We are completely in synch. When she speaks, you know that she is speaking for me."[10]

Rice works hard to keep up the connection to Bush now that she is no longer in the White House. If a meeting is not planned that day, she will call him in the morning to check in. Usually she will call him on Saturday or Sunday to discuss the past week. And every night, she sends him a private written note, describing the diplomatic issues she had confronted that day—essentially a foreign policy version of the intelligence and military briefings the president regularly receives.[11]

Bush is endearingly protective of Rice. During one news conference, he skipped over prepared talking points concerning the horrors of Saddam Hussein's sons, what "Uday and Qusay Hussein do to their girlfriends, rape camps and torture," because, he confided, "I didn't want to say them in front of Condi."[12]

"The Rice-Bush Black Box"

Rice was Bush's foreign policy tutor in the 2000 campaign and at the start of his first term, watching carefully to make sure the foreign policy novice didn't stumble. By 2006, Rice stated that Bush has become "deeply conversant in these issues in a way that he was not when he came into office."[13]

She spent countless hours at the president's side—in the White House, at Camp David, and on his ranch in Crawford, Texas—forging a bond that has transcended the traditional position of national security advisor. Rice also became close to the first lady, Laura Bush, who on occasion has touted Rice as a possible president.

In front of other White House officials, Rice and President Bush developed almost a vaudeville routine as they discussed upcoming meetings with foreign leaders. The president would become petulant, asking why he had to have the meeting, and Rice would patiently explain its importance. Then when he would propose saying something undiplomatic, Rice would patiently reply that he could say that, but it could pose a problem. Bush would vent a little; Rice would remain calm. Ultimately, Bush, only half in jest, would shrug and say, "Miss Rice won't let me do that."[14]

But now, the pupil has become the teacher. To the puzzlement of many who knew her before she worked for George W. Bush, Rice has adopted, almost wholesale, Bush's moralistic and quasi-religious belief in the power of freedom and democracy. Aides say it is Bush who prods Rice to be bolder and take chances—the exact opposite of the relationship between Bush's father and his secretary of state, James A. Baker. Bush now appears to be the person with the big ideas, while, especially in his first term, Rice's role had previously been to provide the intellectual rationale for the president's thinking.

And while Rice was Bush's teacher, she was remarkably inexperienced for the job of national security advisor. She had no history of plotting grand strategy like

Kissinger or Zbigniew Brzezinski; she had been a popular teacher of comparative politics and an academic specialist of the military in the now-defunct Warsaw Pact. Moreover, her experience in the federal government was limited to a brief fellowship with the Joint Chiefs of Staff and a two-year stint as a midlevel aide on the National Security Council (NSC). Her senior-level managerial expertise consisted of six years as provost of Stanford University, an important post, particularly on budget issues, but a job with a relatively small staff that did not involve setting broad university strategy.

Even today, these deficiencies in her background are apparent. Rice, aides and associates say, is not good at either execution or following up on problems. She has good instincts and can master with aplomb the details of the problem at hand. But she loses focus after the crisis has passed, not always checking on whether the solution she reached is being properly implemented.

When Rice sat in the White House situation room during Bush's first term, she looked at a secretary of state who had been chairman of the Joint Chiefs of Staff and had held her job sixteen years earlier (Colin Powell); a defense secretary who had been a congressman, a White House chief of staff, and a defense secretary (Donald Rumsfeld); and a vice president who had been the number two Republican leader in the House of Representatives, White House chief of staff, and defense secretary (Dick Cheney). Cheney and Rumsfeld also had been the chief executives of Fortune 500 companies. And all three had once contemplated running for president.

As national security advisor, Rice was in the shadows. This was partly because of Bush's corporate-executive approach to governing, in which cabinet officials are line officers (the secretary of state is in charge of diplomacy, the defense secretary is in charge of war) while the White House staff are merely staff. Former Treasury secretary Paul O'Neill recounted how, during one important meeting, Bush ordered White House chief of staff Andrew Card to go out and rustle up a cheeseburger for him.[15]

In this staff role, Rice was often unable to resolve the fierce ideological battles within the administration. Unlike Rumsfeld or Cheney, she had not attracted legions of admirers or associates who were sprinkled throughout the government eager to fulfill her objectives. With the exception of a few former colleagues from Stanford, she was essentially alone.

During her White House years, Rice was careful not to tip her hand on her own policy recommendations. People who worked for Rice as national security advisor often use the same expression to describe the nature of her relationship with Bush: "the Rice-Bush black box." She would go behind closed doors with Bush, standing by his desk while he sat, and then emerge with an announcement that the president had made a decision. But it was impossible to tell whether the idea came from Bush or Rice.

Implementing those ideas was a huge problem. When she was national security advisor, decisions were made, but not executed—or decisions were deferred and never resolved. Decisions were also altered or reversed, and feuding advisors were emboldened to keep pressing their case or even ignore policy guidance in the hope of achieving final victory. She often attempted to meld incompatible approaches that later failed. The administration's 2002 national security strategy, for instance, tried to marry realism with neoconservativism when it oddly asserted the administration was pursuing "a balance of power that favors human freedom."[16]

Rice privately concedes that others have been better at the job of national security advisor, including her successor, Stephen Hadley. Now, Rice has a seat at the table and makes her voice known, and she is backed by a president who trusts her as a counselor, as a friend, and as a member of the family. As secretary of state, she has been liberated.

Rice set a new tone early in her tenure. Three weeks after taking office, she hosted Defense Secretary Rumsfeld and their Japanese counterparts at the State Department. When Rumsfeld began to speak, Rice gently cut him off. The message was clear: *I'll take the lead, Don.* The decisive nudge left a deep impression on the U.S. and Japanese officials in the room.[17]

Rice was lucky in that she became secretary just as the influence of Rumsfeld and Cheney was beginning to wane. Both men had tormented Powell in the first Bush term—though Rice thought Powell whined too much about his losses, rather than celebrating his wins.[18] Now, in the second term, Rumsfeld became bogged down in the war in Iraq. Cheney's chief of staff, I. Lewis "Scooter" Libby, had been crucial to Cheney's influence over U.S. foreign policy, but Libby was distracted by a criminal investigation that ultimately led to his indictment and departure from the administration. This was a blow to Cheney.

But, more than anything, the president's unflagging support is central to Rice's success. Powell did not enjoy the trust and confidence of the president, so foreign officials were never quite sure whether Powell was really selling U.S. policy or seeking allies in his own policy battles. Also, Rice is a more skillful one-on-one diplomat than Powell, who was miscast in the job and never appeared to understand the craft of diplomacy. Overseas, Powell leaned heavily on material prepared by the State Department professionals. On her Air Force plane, Rice will gather her closest aides in her private cabin and launch what amounts to a freewheeling college seminar on the issues she will face on the trip. She generally uses the briefings prepared by lower-level State Department officials only as reference material, allowing her to shape her message to meet the needs of the moment.[19]

Many diplomats say that Powell, even when angry, was always genial in his conversations, in contrast to Rice's style of calculated bluntness. "Being essentially a charming, well-behaved person by nature, when she does try to be more severe it is particularly impressive," said Wolfgang Ischinger, who as Germany's ambassador to Washington suffered through the depths of the U.S.-Germany relationship after the break over Iraq. "She never comes across as a rude person as many men are. When she is serious and really concerned, it makes a particularly strong impression."[20]

Her staff has noticed subtle clues to Rice's mood. When she is angry she will begin to scratch one of her hands; she will rub her face with a finger if she is tired and doesn't want to have another long meeting. But sometimes her feelings are raw and on the surface. Friends, aides, and diplomats speak in awe of "that look"—Rice's angry countenance when she feels she has been wronged. Her eyes narrow, her face becomes tight, her jaw is set, and she doesn't look away, but stares intently. There is even a Web site, Condiriceisangry.com, which features dozens of unflattering photographs of "that look."

Coit D. Blacker, a Stanford professor who is Rice's closest male friend, witnessed two occasions when Rice reacted with such venom that he actually felt sorry for the other person. Once, while shopping for jewelry, Rice asked to see some earrings and the clerk pulled out the costume jewelry. Rice said she wanted to see better items. When the clerk reacted negatively, whispering something she thought Rice couldn't hear, Rice tore her to shreds: "Let's get one thing straight. You're behind the counter because you have to work for the minimum wage. I'm on this side asking to see the good jewelry because I make considerably more." The manager rushed over to bring out the fine jewelry.

Another time, when Rice was Stanford's provost, minority students became angry after Rice suggested she would cut a subsidy for ethnic-group houses as part of an effort to balance the university's budget. The students, meeting in the Stanford Faculty Club, had worked themselves into a frenzy by the time she arrived to address them. Rice kept her cool as she answered questions for about an hour. But then a young white woman raised her hand and questioned Rice's commitment to equal opportunity. "I don't need a lecture from anyone on racial sensitivity," Rice shot back. "I've been black all my life." Some of the students applauded; others booed.[21]

"On Friends, She Goes Narrow and Deep"

I first met Rice in 1992, when I covered the Republican National Convention and she appeared as a surrogate for the campaign of President George H. W. Bush. I bumped into her after she appeared on a foreign policy panel and we ended up having a conversation about China policy. She expressed her disdain for Democratic candidate Bill Clinton's desire to link the U.S.-China relationship to China's progress on human rights. "What's going to happen the first time he needs China's help at the United Nations?" she asked. She said Clinton would quickly abandon the idea—and he did eighteen months after taking office. Her attitude was realpolitik at its best: You deal with states as they are, not how you hope they will become.

The encounter made a deep impression on me, so much so I can still remember every detail. She was poised and elegant, charming but forceful—and utterly sure of herself. In that vast sea of overstuffed, mostly male, almost all white faces that made up the crowd that year in the sweltering city of Houston, here was a rarity: a trim and attractive black woman.

All her life, Rice has made a formidable first impression. Her mother, Angelena Rice, dressed beautifully and told her daughter to "always remember, if you're overdressed it reflects badly on them; if you're underdressed, it reflects badly on you."[22] Rice appears to have inherited a steel core from her mother, who was capable of expressing great disdain, in contrast to her more genial father.

Blacker first met Rice when they were both junior faculty. He thought she was a unique combination of charm and toughness. "She was not diffident in conversation, but assertive in a pleasant way," he said. David Kennedy, associate dean of humanities when Rice joined Stanford as a freshly minted Ph.D., first met her in a backyard reception held at the home of Soviet scholar Alexander Dallin. On the spot, he thought, this is an "exceptional, poised, charming, motivated and distinctive individual. She had self-possession beyond her years, done with great charm."[23]

But beyond that surface of beauty and poise, few people ever feel they see, let alone know, the real Condoleezza Rice. She inspires intense loyalty from her closest aides and her friends, but she reveals little of herself. She has built a wall of privacy around herself that is never breached. As a child, she trained relentlessly to be a figure skater and a pianist, two skills that demand poise and grace even when you make mistakes. She's still that kind of performer, the ice skater who grins and keeps going even after she has fallen on her bottom.

In both the United States and overseas, Rice's lack of a male companion and her rise to power has resulted in nasty attacks on her sexuality—attacks that would never be made against a single man. The cartoon *Boondocks* jeered, "Maybe if there was a man in the world who Condoleezza truly loved, she wouldn't be so hell-bent to destroy it."[24] A Russian politician crudely declared that world tensions would decline if Rice had a man—actually, a barracks of men—to keep her satisfied.[25] A highly popular movie in Egypt in 2006, *The Night Baghdad Fell,* included a fantasy sex scene in which one of the main characters overcomes impotence by sleeping with Rice.[26]

The only time Rice publicly speaks of love is when she describes her academic interest in Russia and the Russian language. Rice was once asked by a television reporter whether she regretted never getting married, as this might be an issue if she ever decided to run for elective office. Rice said she had never rejected marriage, but "life has unfolded the way life has unfolded, and I'm awfully glad that it's unfolded this particular way."[27] She has also been very career-focused and does not appear to ever have had much interest in having children. She told another interviewer that she never really wanted to raise a family. "I think maybe it's because I'm an only child," she said. "I like children, but especially when they're eighteen."[28]

Friends such as Blacker and Randy Bean, her closest female friend, say that Rice is remarkably at ease with herself when she is surrounded by people she has known for decades. After she became secretary of state, she came to a party at Blacker's house, kicked off her shoes, and began dancing through the night to rock and roll. Blacker, who is gay, wanted to show his partner how tight her behind is; he postulated that if he aimed a quarter at her butt, it would bounce off like a rocket. He was right. Rice, who was dancing, didn't realize what he had done until everyone began laughing hysterically. She was flattered—and proud.

Blacker is a Democrat who served in the Clinton administration and advised Gore in the 2000 campaign, while Bean, a blond-haired documentary filmmaker at Stanford, describes herself as a liberal progressive. They would seem to have little in common with Rice. Yet the three have formed a long and lasting bond since they met at Stanford in the early 1980s. In Bean's words, they became "a second family" who took annual trips together and spent New Year's together. "On friends, she goes narrow and deep," Bean said, meaning Rice does not have a lot of friends but the relationships are intense.

Bean and Rice, both the daughters of ministers, became close friends in 1985 when Bean was between house-sitting stints and Rice let her sleep on the floor of her apartment for four months. Rice's mother had just died, and Bean helped Rice through the emotional trauma. "Emotions don't come to surface easily with her, but she later told me, 'You saved my life,'" Bean said.

Bean later went through her own difficult emotional period, going bankrupt as a result of medical bills. "I was stone broke," Bean said, and Rice insisted on providing financial assistance in this period of challenge and difficulty. Bean said she did not want help, and did not want to be in a friend's debt, but Rice was firm. Bean said Rice's intervention was an important motivator in rebuilding her life, both because she knew she had a friend who believed in her and because Rice was not someone you could easily cross.[29]

Real estate records show that in 1998 Rice (along with Blacker) helped buy the two-bedroom, pale blue clapboard house that Bean lives in. In 2003, Blacker sold his one-third share to Rice and Bean. In 2005, Bean and Rice signed documents that gave them a $50,000 line of credit on the house, which apparently was used for home maintenance such as painting and landscaping. In 2006, the house was assessed at nearly $670,000.[30]

"We are more family now than anything. She would throw herself under a bus for me," Bean said, though she half-ruefully adds, "I wonder if she will be out of the country when I need her under that bus."

"I Should've Gotten to Where I Am"

Rice has milked her upbringing in the South in many of her speeches overseas, using it as an example of how even democracy in the United States is not perfect. There are three main periods to her life that have influenced her performance as secretary: her childhood, her intellectual transformation after she became interested in Soviet studies, and her exposure to high-level decision making in the George H. W. Bush administration and at Stanford.

Rice's accounting of her early years sometimes leaves some listeners with the impression that she struggled to move ahead in American society. But the real story is more complicated. Her teenage years and adult life have been mostly spent in the West, in Colorado and California. "She is not from the South; she is from the West," said Michael McFaul, a former student and now Stanford professor, citing her informal style and distaste for hierarchy.[31]

She was born in Alabama in 1954, six months after the landmark *Brown v. Board of Education of Topeka, Kansas* ruling by the Supreme Court that desegregated schools. But she only lived in the Birmingham area until she was eleven, and by virtue of her temperament and her upbringing, the civil rights movement largely passed her by. She grew up in Titusville, a solidly middle-class African American enclave of neat brick houses occupied by educators, physicians, and government workers; it was originally created after the end of slavery by so-called house slaves, many of whom were the descendants of children born from illicit relations between slaves and slave owners. She was raised to be different, with rigorous lessons in French (which she hated), ice skating, and piano. "My family is third-generation college-educated," Rice defiantly told an interviewer. "I should've gotten to where I am."[32]

Rice's name does not have black roots, but was invented by her mother from an Italian phrase. As Rice explained in the earliest major profile written on her, a *Boston Globe* article in 1984, her mother liked the sound of musical terms. "But she said 'andante' was kind of slow and she didn't want that, and 'allegro' was fast, she certainly didn't want that. So she looked at 'con dolce,' which means 'with sweetness.'" Her mother experimented with different endings before selecting *e*'s and *z*'s to create the name.[33]

Her father, John Rice, was a Presbyterian minister at a church his father founded—and where Rice lived for her first three years—and also a guidance counselor at Ullman High School. When her mother was pregnant, Rice's father had no doubt that she would deliver a boy who would be a fine middle linebacker. He coached a high school football team. Rice tagged along to be able to spend time with her daddy, and either the exposure to the game or her desire to please her father gave her an intense love of football. As secretary of state, Rice leaped at a chance to have lunch with New York Giants running back Tiki Barber, quizzing him in detail on the NFL draft and his fitness routine.[34]

Segregation was a part of life, but Rice's parents did their best to shield her from it. They would not let her drink from blacks-only water fountains but told her to wait till she got home if she was thirsty. When a white department store saleslady tried to make seven-year-old Rice try on a dress in the storage closet, her mother curtly informed her that either Rice would use the whites-only dressing room or the salesclerk would lose the commission. The threat worked and the nervous saleswoman stood guard, worried for her job if other customers noticed.[35]

In one of the seminal moments in the civil rights movement, white supremacists bombed Birmingham's Sixteenth Street Baptist Church in 1964, killing four black girls, ages eleven to fourteen. Rice felt the explosion rattle the ground, "like a freight train or something had come." She knew one of the girls who was killed—there is a photo of her father presenting a Sunday school certificate to pretty Denise McNair, dressed in white—but according to Rice she was not a playmate, as McNair is sometimes described.[36]

In the aftermath, Rice's father patrolled Titusville with a shotgun. He did not let her watch the protests spawned by the bombing. Her mother bought up her entire allotment of Girl Scout cookies so she would not have to walk door-to-door to sell them. But her parents' efforts to protect her did not end there. Rice's family left Birmingham shortly after the bombing, first for Tuscaloosa, where Rice's father became dean of students at Stillman College, and then for the University of Denver, where he eventually became associate vice chancellor.[37]

One commentator suggested Rice was her parents' own civil rights movement. Rice dismisses the notion that she had a sheltered life as "ridiculous," saying, "I would have had to have been living under a rock, not to know what was going on in Birmingham."[38]

In Denver, Rice attended an integrated school for the first time—and also encountered a guidance counselor who, shockingly, said she was not college material. But she shrugged off the warning and, having skipped first and seventh grades, headed to the University of Denver at the age of fifteen. In one of her freshman classes, where she was one of two or three blacks in a lecture hall of 250 students, a professor embraced the theory that whites were genetically superior to blacks in intelligence. Rice stood up and protested. "I'm the one that speaks French. I'm the one who plays Beethoven. I'm better at your culture than you are. This can be taught."[39]

These experiences with racism taught Rice that the United States has its flaws, a theme she now regularly evokes in speeches overseas. "You are less arrogant about the United States itself if you are a member of a minority—you are more understanding that all societies have skeletons," Rice said more than twenty years ago, in words that are echoed in her rhetoric today. "I know that even this experiment has had a lot of problems—the treatment of minorities, the treatment of women, the treatment of American Indians—and there I am less arrogant about what we have achieved and more tolerant of others trying to achieve it."[40]

Rice intended to major in music, but she realized that she would never be in the top leagues and instead "might end up teaching thirteen-year-olds to murder Beethoven." In her junior year, she decided to look for another major; this was difficult news to break to her parents who had purchased her a $13,000 Steinway grand piano. She found her new calling when she took a class with Josef Korbel, a gregarious but autocratic professor who was a refugee from communism and saw the United States as a moral beacon to the world. For Rice, Korbel's introduction to Russia, Soviet studies, and international relations was "like love at first sight."[41]

With Korbel's encouragement and guidance, Rice became so enthralled that after graduating from college at nineteen, she decided to become a professor in a highly specialized field, Eastern Europe, writing her dissertation on the relationship between the Soviet and Czech armies. As Rice put it, "I was attracted to the Byzantine nature of Soviet politics, and by power: how it operates, how it's used."[42]

Rice became an admirer, and teacher, of the works of Hans Morgenthau, a towering figure in international relations. Morgenthau, regarded as one of the fathers of the realist school of foreign policy, advocated a balance of power among states as a way to ensure world order and peace. In his landmark work, *Politics Among Nations,* published in 1948, he defined six principles of political realism, in which he stressed a rational and unemotional approach to policymaking. "The statesman must think in terms of the national interest, conceived as power among other powers," he wrote. "The popular mind, unaware of the fine distinctions of the statesman's thinking, reasons more often than not in the simple moralistic and legalistic terms of absolute good and absolute evil."[43]

"I Thought You Needed to Be a Full Professor"

At Stanford, where she joined the faculty in 1981 at the age of twenty-six, Rice proved to be a dynamic and popular instructor, winning teaching awards. She quickly demomstrated an unusual facility for communication. She never used a text, but would give seamless lectures armed with only a few scribbles on a notepad. Even today, Rice has difficulty reading a speech well and only comes alive when she takes questions from the audience, allowing her to speak extemporaneously. Her first book, on the Czechoslovakian military, was dedicated to Korbel and to her parents.

She stood out as a Republican on the largely liberal campus, and within the obscure field of Eastern bloc military studies, she stood out for being black, female, and hawkish. Her father had registered Republican because the Jim Crow Democrats made it all but impossible for blacks to vote. She had voted for Jimmy Carter in 1976 but became disgusted at what she thought was Carter's naive reaction to the Soviet invasion of Afghanistan. In her telling, that's when she became a Republican, voting for Ronald Reagan in 1980. But she was intrigued by Gary Hart's proposals on military reform in 1984. (Blacker, her close friend, had been a congressional aide to the Colorado Democrat.) And Rice, as an academic, disapproved of Reagan's confrontational, moralistic approach to the Soviet Union, according to her friend Dennis Ross, who was a Soviet scholar at the University of California at Berkeley at the time.[44]

"A lot of us thought Reagan was pursuing a high-risk strategy toward the Soviet Union, that the Soviets would simply harden their policies if presented with a challenge," Rice said in 1988.[45] Even then, Rice had more than a purely academic interest in policy. She considered running for Congress as a moderate Republican in the mid-1980s, according to Ross and others. "You had a sense that this person would not be content to be part of the political science faculty," McFaul said.[46]

When George H. W. Bush was elected president, Ross became director of policy planning at the State Department and tried to hire Rice as his deputy in 1989. But he made the mistake of mentioning the idea to Scowcroft, the president's national security advisor. Scowcroft had had his eye on Rice ever since he was taken by this "slip of a girl" at a dreary academic meeting five years earlier, when she forcefully challenged some of his assumptions. He snapped her up for the National Security Council (NSC) staff before Ross could seal the deal for State.

Scowcroft, as national security advisor, was very cautious, and Rice in her two years at the NSC reflected his approach. In the dynamic of that administration, it was Baker's State Department that put its foot on the gas on such issues as German reunification, while it was Scowcoft's NSC that tried to put on the brakes. "They tended to more cautious, we tended to be more ambitious," Ross said. In the internal debates on how strongly to support Soviet leader Mikhail Gorbachev, Rice did not make a strong intellectual mark, seemingly comfortable with the arguments of both hawks and doves.[47]

Years later, Rice would concede that perhaps the George H. W. Bush administration might have been too slow to react to the rapid changes in the Soviet empire. But she said it was better for the United States to be careful. "When you have so much power, you have to be careful not to get in the way of historical events that are going your way. Too heavy a hand by the United States might have provoked a counter reaction."[48]

Rice was well liked in the administration—and she formed a strong bond with the president—but colleagues say there was little sense that they were working with a future secretary of state. She made it clear she would only stay two years before going home to California. She was seen as a promising professor in her field, someone who simply wanted to get a grounding in policymaking.

The collapse of the Soviet Union and the crumbling of Eastern Europe made a deep impression on an academic who had confidently predicted a few years earlier that the Soviet Union would never give up its empire because "states, especially great powers, do not behave in this way."[49] When Rice returned to Stanford in 1991, she told Bean that no matter what happened in the rest of her life, she would never again work in a period when the world changed so dramatically.

Shortly after returning to Stanford, Rice was unexpectedly tapped, at the young age of thirty-eight, to become provost, the second-ranking post at the university. It is a relatively powerful position, compared to the provost at most other universities: She presided over the deans of Stanford's seven schools and handled the budget while the president focused on raising money and setting policy. She had impressed Stanford's new president, Gerhard Casper, when she was part of the presidential search committee, and he wanted to make an impact by hiring someone who was so young and a minority.[50]

When Casper selected her, Rice was still only an associate professor, technically a disqualification that was quickly fixed. After David Kennedy, the former dean, heard she had been appointed, he was puzzled, telling a colleague, "I thought you needed to be a full professor." He was told, "She is, as of today."[51]

Rice had never had any managerial role—she had not been a dean, the traditional stepping-stone to provost, let alone a department chair. When Blacker heard she had been offered the job, he warned her she would need to develop her own decision-making style. Rice didn't waste any time, quickly making a mark as a decisive and controversial executive. Universities thrive on consensus and discussion, but Rice showed she had little patience for the traditional give-and-take of the academic world. In order to balance the budget, she laid people off and cut services and programs, prompting protests and anger. When she eliminated the job of the highest-ranking Latino administrator, acting over spring break when the campus was empty, students even began a hunger strike.[52]

Rice, who had advanced quickly in part because she was a minority, particularly upset students and faculty by arguing that affirmative action should not have a role in tenure decisions. She said racial considerations were only appropriate in the initial hiring, to get a foot in the door, but the guaranteed job security and higher pay that came with tenure should be based on actual performance. She faced down her critics in a stormy meeting of the faculty senate in 1998, telling opponents that as long as she was "chief academic officer," women and minorities would not get preference in all-important tenure decisions, which go a long way to defining the future of an institution.

Kennedy once told her he admired the fact that she didn't flinch. "When you have to talk to the Ukrainians on nuclear weapons, this is child's play," Rice responded.[53]

Rice was provost for six years, a relatively long time. She left the post to become a presidential campaign advisor to George W. Bush, whom she had impressed after a meeting arranged by another one of her patrons, former secretary of state George Shultz. (Shultz also paved the way for Rice to serve on major corporate boards, such as Chevron, which later named an oil tanker after her.) When she stepped down, she remarked at her going-away party, with a bit of humor in her voice, that if she had to do the job over again, maybe she would have been "a little less forceful" as provost.

The admission was surprising to her friends, since Rice rarely betrays any second thoughts or likes to show any weaknesses. "It was one of the few times she was able to revisit things in a fairly critical manner," Blacker said. As Bean puts it, "Condi is the least reflective person I know."[54]

"She Was Tough and Realistic—and Then She Was Not"

One of the mysteries of Condoleezza Rice is the intellectual transformation that she has undergone during the Bush presidency.

For her entire academic career, she was a realist in the tradition of her hero, Hans Morgenthau, and her mentor, Brent Scowcroft. During the 2000 campaign, when she openly described herself as a realpolitiker, she wrote an article for *Foreign Affairs* on the foreign policy of the future Bush administration that is a hallmark of realism. "Power matters," she wrote, focusing on Great Power relations and making no mention of the threat from terrorist groups like al-Qaeda. "There is nothing wrong with doing something that benefits all humanity, but that is, in a sense, a second-order effect." At another point, she wrote, "American values are universal [but] it is simply not possible to ignore and isolate other powerful states that do not share those values."[55]

Now, Rice argues the opposite, especially when she pushes for democracy in the Middle East on the grounds that the current system only provides a false sense of stability. Rice insists that everything changed after the attacks of September 11. But that seems more of an excuse than an explanation. "She was tough and realistic—and then she was not," said Kennedy, still puzzled by the transformation.[56]

Traditional realists, such as Scowcroft and Brzezinski, opposed the invasion of Iraq, believing it was an unnecessary diversion. A sober, realistic view of 9/11 might have said it was a tragedy, but it did not threaten the vitality of the United States or call into question the current international system. A realist would have demanded a sustained crackdown on al-Qaeda, but not against terrorism in general. Just as Rice in 1992 was so scornful of Clinton's effort to force China to change its system if it wanted better trade with the United States, a realist would not have pushed close allies like Egypt and Saudi Arabia to introduce elections and change their political systems.

Friends and associates point to two possible explanations for Rice's shift, neither quite satisfactory. One explanation points to her deep religious background; the other suggests that Rice is simply a political opportunist.

People who support the second explanation say that Rice has been extraordinarily ambitious and thus she was willing to shift with the winds in order to obtain greater glory. Under this theory, Rice in government carefully avoided being associated with either of the warring camps of the Republican Party, the realists or the moralists, in order to preserve her political options.

One Stanford colleague recalls being shocked by Rice's highly partisan speech at the 2000 Republican National Convention, in which she harshly attacked Democrats. "I was quite unsettled by it," he said. "I was quite angry at it. This was not the Condi Rice I had known. It seemed like she was abandoning her moorings."[57]

"Dr. Rice made a decision," said Lawrence Wilkerson, chief of staff to Colin Powell, who emerged as a harsh critic of Rice for her failure to support Powell in the first Bush term. "She made a decision that she would side with the president to build her intimacy with the president."[58]

The more charitable explanation for Rice's shift goes like this: Rice is not a casual Presbyterian but a Calvinist. She believes deeply in the notion of predetermination: A person may not have access to God's plan but he has a plan for each person—and that plan will slowly be revealed to you.[59]

For Rice, it would not have been a strange coincidence that she would work for one president and then, through that connection, would work for his son, who would become president even though he lost the popular vote—and that they would both be in the White House when the terrorists attacked the World Trade Center and the Pentagon on September 11. In her mind, this would all have been part of God's plan.

In California, Rice attended a conservative church in Menlo Park, and she has always had a deeply religious, moralistic streak. Most political scientists are realists; that's what they need to do to get ahead. But her defenders say that when faced with the greatest crisis of her life—the second time in her life when she went to Washington and, overnight, the world changed—she reached back to the faith that had sustained her throughout her life. It is this faith, friends say, that has allowed Rice to plunge forward and forcefully defend the administration and its handling of Iraq and other foreign policy mistakes.

"Condi always had the capacity to see the world she wants to see—as opposed to the world that actually exists," Blacker said.[60]

REBIRTH IN PARIS

February 9, 2005

At the Conservatoire Hector Berlioz in Paris, an eager group of sixteen French youngsters were learning to read music when they received a special visitor: a secretary of state on a mission to reshape American diplomacy—and her own image.

Rice was accompanied by more than two dozen aides, reporters, and other officials, including the mayor of Paris. They squeezed into the small classroom, but that did not seem to faze the businesslike teacher, who continued to lead the children through their paces. Rice, tapping her toes to keep time, soon joined in a French music comprehension refrain with the children, singing softly, "Fa-do-sol-si-re-la-sol."

"I remember this," she said, telling the children through an interpreter that she learned to read music from her grandmother when she was three, even before she learned to read. "It takes a lot of work to learn to read music," she said. "You have to practice and practice and practice." She didn't mention that after years of study, in college she had abruptly abandoned her ambition to become a concert pianist, shifting to Soviet studies instead, when she realized she would never be in the top ranks.

As reporters watched the initially stilted conversation, one of her aides, Jim Wilkinson—who, more than anyone, was the impresario of the event—circulated among them, quietly making sure they understood how "cute" the staged event looked.[1]

Rice was nearing the end of her first overseas trip, which began just days after she had been confirmed by the Senate. Almost every moment had been meticulously planned for weeks by Rice and her top aides, starting from the day President Bush announced that she would be his nominee for secretary of state in his second term. The State Department traditionally prides itself on being worried about the policy, not the politics, but Rice and her team had brought a White House sensitivity to images and message discipline. The overriding goal of the trip was to signal to Europeans that the Bush administration was serious about repairing relations ruptured by the Iraq War. But there was also a deeper, more personal mission at stake: eliminating the stereotype of Rice as a cold and bloodless White House staffer and catapulting her into a world figure with possible political aspirations.

No detail was too small, especially for Wilkinson, a hyperactive former Capitol Hill staffer whom Rice had brought to the National Security Council for his savvy at shaping media images. He had commissioned studies from the State Department historian's office. He wanted to know what makes the difference between a good secretary of state and a bad one. Proximity to the president, the historian responded. That conclusion made Wilkinson feel better about Rice's chances.

Wilkinson also wrote down a list of negative questions about Rice, a clear-eyed exercise designed to think seriously about the concerns of the media and the State Department. Once he had that list down, he could then look for ways to answer them—or at least neutralize them. Among the questions were these:

- Hadn't she been a bad national security advisor?
- Didn't she have disdain for the Foreign Service?
- Isn't she part of the neoconservative cabal that doesn't care about diplomacy?
- Isn't she cold and unfriendly?

To counter the notion that Rice was cold, Wilkinson decreed that almost no pictures should be allowed of Rice alone after she moved to the State Department; instead she should always be photographed with other people in an effort to warm her up. On her first day on the job, for instance, he arranged for a crowd of people to stand around her when she addressed State Department workers from a staircase in the building's main entrance. In another subtle switch, he decided that massive podiums were to be avoided for speeches because she has such a slim frame and stands just five feet, six inches tall.[2]

To show Rice cared about diplomacy, he wanted Americans to see that their secretary of state was at work overseas. He arranged a series of cultural expeditions, such as the trip to the Paris conservatory, each scrupulously chosen to suggest Rice's appreciation for the local culture. Of course, he loved the photographs that then would be printed in the newspapers back home. He would stuff the drawers of his small office, just outside Rice's suite, with positive press clippings of Rice, especially photographs that captured exactly the image he had wanted to convey.

In Washington, Wilkinson decided to move Rice's news conferences with foreign officials upstairs to the ornate rooms of the seventh and eighth floors of the State Department. Rice would be photographed sitting in front of a fireplace or walking fifty feet to a microphone, evoking the spirit of presidential sessions in the White House. Powell, by contrast, had always escorted visitors to the front door of the State Department and then would speak to reporters in front of the glass doors as other people walked in and out of the building. During the transition, Wilkinson had watched a Powell news conference and to his horror saw a man speaking loudly on his cell phone in the background during the entire news conference. The whole thing seemed undignified and unprofessional. The "walk-outs," as the Powell sessions were called, were banned; the Rice news conferences were henceforth known as "walk-ups."

To make sure the Paris visit came off without a hitch, Wilkinson even borrowed Nina Bishop from the White House advance team. The most iconic image of the Bush presidency came amid the smoldering ruins of the World Trade Center. Surrounded by firemen, Bush appeared to spontaneously grab a bullhorn to help extort the firemen and the entire nation to stand firm. It was Bishop who had arranged that trip—and had even handed Bush that bullhorn.

"I Do the Hiring Here"

When Bush won reelection in 2004, Rice was ready to go back to California. She hadn't expected to be national security advisor in the first place. She told friends she hadn't even wanted that job because her father had been terribly ill during Bush's first campaign. Though she had been Bush's foreign policy advisor in the 2000 campaign, she wanted to return to California to be with her dad. But Bush persisted, and Rice finally said yes. Randy Bean had begun to explore installing a webcam system and other ways for Rice to keep in touch with her father when he died just four days after she was named national security advisor. "That was his gift to her," Bean said. "He freed her to go to Washington, unburdened."

Now, with the first term nearly finished, Rice really was desperate to return to Stanford. But Bush had other plans. Two days after the November 3 election, on a Thursday, she flew up to Camp David with the president, the first lady, and the chief of staff, Andrew Card. The president met with her privately on Friday morning, November 6, and got quickly to the point: Powell was out, and he wanted Rice to be secretary of state.[3]

"I would have to think about that," Rice replied. She noted that she had planned to go home and it had been four really long years—actually five years, when you count her year as his campaign advisor. She suggested Bush should consider sweeping away the whole foreign policy team so he could start fresh in the second term. The current crew had gone through the September 11 attacks, two wars, and many other difficult issues.

"I think you may need a new national security team," Rice said.

"I do the hiring here," Bush replied.

Bush and Rice discussed the job periodically over the next three days, for a total of about two hours. She was exhausted from the campaign, and spent most of her time at Camp David sleeping or watching football in her cabin, not thinking about the job. She felt very comfortable with the president. She certainly didn't need assurances of access or other guarantees if she took the job, though she was wondering how they would retain their unique close relationship if she were no longer in the same building but in different parts of Washington.

"We've been very close, down the hall," Rice told Bush. "I see you eight times a day, and I don't want to lose that connection."

But she did want to know Bush's feelings on one issue. Would he be willing to support the creation of a Palestinian state in his second term? This was critical for Rice. With long-term Palestinian leader Yasir Arafat on his deathbed, she wanted to know how far Bush would go to support the Palestinian cause. The president assured her he was on the same wavelength.

There was one other concern for Rice: the travel the job would require. From outside appearances, Rice might appear to be a model of brains and polish, a high achiever who is comfortable spending endless hours on the road, going from banquet to banquet. Beneath the public image, however, is a woman who hates to travel. She thinks of herself as a "nester," and doesn't enjoy sightseeing or long trips away from home. Powell didn't like travel, either, and had been heavily criticized for his reliance on "telephone diplomacy." Rice understood that in this age of instant communication, Powell's approach had been wrong—lengthy dinners, lunches, and meetings with foreign officials overseas were now even more essential. But she didn't savor that part of the position.

She wouldn't commit to the job that weekend, even as Bush teased her every so often, asking, "Have you made up your mind yet?" She called her Aunt G, Genoa McPhatter, her closest relative, who said she was pleased for her. She called a few other relatives and also Coit Blacker.

"No shit," Blacker replied. "I thought you were coming back home." Blacker had been arranging a spot for her at Stanford, and he knew she had been planning to begin packing the next week so she could be back at Palo Alto in January.

"I thought I was coming home, too," Rice replied. Blacker asked how Bush was convincing her, and Rice said he had big plans for the second term and wanted to build a foreign policy foundation for the future.

By Monday, Rice was excited about the opportunity. Before they left Camp David, she told Bush she would accept the job.

On Friday, Bush sent Rice a powerful signal that he would listen closely to her. "I believe we've got a great chance to establish a Palestinian state, and I intend to use the next four years to spend the capital of the United States on such a state," he said during an East Room news conference with Prime Minister Tony Blair of Britain. "I believe it is in the interest of the world that a truly free state develop." Never had the president so publicly committed himself to set such a date for action.[4]

The following Monday, Powell's resignation was announced.

"Don't Brief Down"

Rice asked Wilkinson and John B. Bellinger, her legal advisor, to cochair her transition team, essentially reprising the roles they had had when Rice had to appear before the commission investigating the September 11 attacks in the first term. Wilkinson would handle communications and Bellinger would focus on preparing for the confirmation hearings.

Bellinger viewed the transition as akin to the friendly takeover of a company. But he also knew that the State Department was in near terror over Rice's arrival, in part because his deputy at the NSC, a foreign service officer, bluntly told him about the fear spreading through Foggy Bottom, as the department's headquarters are sometimes called by careerists. Though Powell has been a lonely figure in the upper echelons of power in the Bush administration, he was beloved by the bureaucracy. State Department workers thought he was an inspiring leader who had won long-needed funds from Congress and who listened to their ideas. Powell publicly said he saw his role as bringing the State Department's voice to the interagency debate; Rice, it was believed, was planning to impose the White House's voice on the State Department.

Wilkinson felt a chill as he walked through the State Department parking garage the first time and spotted many bumper stickers supporting John Kerry for president. One assistant secretary of state was even reported to have held a staff meeting in her office to bemoan Kerry's defeat. Rice knew she needed to take some steps to reassure her new troops. She thought every move sent a signal. She took pains not to appear to be shoving Powell aside, since he was still secretary until the end of January. In fact, she and her aides decided they would not set foot in the secretary's office until the day after Powell left. She also ordered her staff never to make comparisons between her and Powell, even off the record.

Rice was scheduled to receive management briefings, twice a week for two hours, from the undersecretaries and assistant secretaries, in a windowless room on the first floor of the State Department. She deliberately asked that the first briefing be given by Grant Green, the outgoing undersecretary of state for management, in an effort to show the State Department that she cared about the inner workings of the agency.

The briefings gave Rice a sense of the quality of the troops she would inherit. William Burns, the assistant secretary of state for Near Eastern affairs, gave a brilliant overview of the situation in the Middle East; he would later be given the plum post of U.S. ambassador to Russia. But she and her staff felt a number of the assistant secretaries, particularly Elizabeth Jones (Europe), Roger Noriega (Western Hemisphere), and Connie Newman (Africa), gave mediocre presentations.[5] Rice would end up replacing all of the regional assistant secretaries. But while Powell had a mix of political appointees and foreign service officers in those posts, Rice decided to use mostly foreign service officers again, in an effort to reassure the building.[6]

The State Department, which proudly regards itself as the first cabinet department, is a vast organization of 57,000 people, many located in 264 embassies, consulates, and other missions overseas. The United States has diplomatic relations with 188 countries, few of which can command the full attention of the secretary of state for an extended period of time. Each secretary must figure out how he or she will interact with the 19,000 civil servants and foreign service officers who implement and manage U.S. policy on a day-to-day basis, including the 8,000 employees located in the sprawling State Department building in downtown Washington. Rice looked at the memoirs of every recent secretary of state and read carefully the sections on how they managed their transitions. George Shultz, who served under Ronald Reagan for six years, also organized a dinner at the Army-Navy Club which every living secretary of state (except an ailing Warren M. Christopher) attended to give Rice tips and instructive war stories.

One of a secretary's first decisions is how he or she will organize what is known in the building as "the seventh floor"—the place where Rice and her top aides would work. In the past two decades, there have been three basic approaches to managing the building: the James Baker model, the Colin Powell model, and the George Shultz model. Baker had a very strong seventh floor that essentially ignored the rest of the State Department; he and a handful of aides made the policy, to the resentment of the career staff. The polar opposite to the Baker approach was Powell, who ran the State Department like a military organization, allowing each section to do its tasks and so permitting ideas to bubble up from the ranks; this made him a popular leader. Shultz's approach was something of hybrid; he ran the building, but he was also respected by it.

Rice and her aides claimed they chose the Shultz model, but in reality she adopted Baker's style. She was not going to let the building run her. Baker, after all, is regarded as one of the most successful secretaries of state, while Powell—at least in initial postmortems—is considered a failure.

But after the respect Powell paid to lower-level officials, Rice's approach was resented. Powell could be instantly reached by e-mail and would often respond quickly, though he had his favorites in the department. Rice doesn't use e-mail and prefers formal meetings, even with assistant secretaries.

Under Rice, secrecy is paramount. On sensitive issues, in fact, Rice will warn other officials, "Don't brief down," meaning don't tell lower-level aides about the discussions. So, for example, people would be ordered to send cables overseas without understanding why the cables were being sent. With so little communication between the seventh floor and the other levels, even senior officials were left puzzling over the policy, looking for clues in Rice's public statements—which were often deliberately obtuse. A midlevel State Department official overseeing Syria, Lebanon, Egypt, and Jordan, for instance, quit in 2006 after telling colleagues he only knew what the United States was doing in one of those countries (Jordan) because Rice didn't care about it.[7]

Rice is obsessed with leaks. Lower-level officials who, under Powell, regularly briefed the press were told they could no longer return reporters' phone calls. The press aides in each bureau—who varied in quality under Powell—were given access to less and less information, so even the real professionals could barely do their jobs. The drafts of the secretary's speeches used to be circulated widely through the building so different bureaus could react to them; this practice was stopped under Rice. Often, her speeches overseas are completed on the plane, and reviewed only by a small circle.

Two weeks after taking office, Rice became furious over a newspaper article on U.S. policy toward North Korea that appeared the morning she was to meet with the South Korean foreign minister. She gathered together lower-level aides working on the issue to express her displeasure. "I don't like leaks," she said, banging the table for emphasis.[8] A chill quickly went through the building.

"We Look Like Six Monkeys"

Having decided to assemble a strong seventh floor, Rice then needed a formidable group of advisors at her side.

In putting together her team, Rice was not afraid of big egos or clashing personalities, or even the occasional outsider; however, she expected and wanted absolute loyalty. She welcomed disagreement and debate over policy, but she would not tolerate disloyalty to the overall project: This was Team Rice. Within days of becoming secretary, she fired the assistant secretary of state for law enforcement and narcotics, Robert Charles, because she discovered that Charles—a former aide to House Speaker Dennis Hastert—had tried to drum up support on the Hill for a position he was advocating on Afghanistan. Rice felt Charles was trying to box her in—and his abrupt dismissal was intended to send a message.[9]

Each key player on Team Rice had a distinct role to play, and, like a skilled football coach, Rice put together an initial lineup that was impressive for its diversity and cohesiveness. She set up the staff so no one person had complete authority. She worked closely with Dina Powell, then head of White House personnel, going over a list of names almost every day in her apartment. She ended up offering a key post to Powell as well.

Many of her top aides had long histories working with each other. Wilkinson, Powell, and the chief of staff, Brian Gunderson, had worked for former House majority leader Richard Armey. Gunderson had been chief of staff for Robert B. Zoellick, the new deputy secretary of state, in the first term when Zoellick had served as U.S. trade representative. Zoellick, in turn, had been a senior aide to Secretary of State Baker during the administration of Bush's father, working closely with Rice and the incoming counselor, Philip Zelikow, on the reunification of Germany. And the new undersecretary of state for political affairs, R. Nicholas Burns, had been a special assistant to Zoellick during that period—and then was Rice's deputy at the NSC.

Wilkinson, at thirty-four, was the youngest and possibly oddest member of Rice's inner circle. A self-described Texas conservative, opposed to abortion rights and a supporter of the National Rifle Association, Wilkinson hailed from a small East Texas town of a thousand people and had once considered becoming a mortician. The baby-faced Wilkinson was full of nervous energy, often irritating but in an endearing sort of way. At senior staff meetings, when most people are polite and cautious, Wilkinson would burst in and declare, "We look like six monkeys trying to fuck a football." That certainly got people's attention. (One senior official once asked Wilkinson what he meant by that remark, and Wilkinson said if the official didn't understand it, he couldn't explain it.)

Wilkinson was skilled at the art of political warfare. During the 2000 presidential campaign, he helped promote the notion that Al Gore claimed to have "invented the Internet"—which was not quite true but made Gore a subject of ridicule.[10] During the invasion of Iraq, he was the brains behind the vast media center erected in Qatar, where many reporters covering the war came to loathe him. In *Control Room,* a documentary about Al Jazeera's coverage during the war, Wilkinson makes a brief appearance that captures his relentless, grinding manner. He is shown repeating the same banal talking point to a network correspondent before the camera turns on, as the camera is running, and then even as the correspondent is removing the microphone from Wilkinson's suit jacket.

At the White House, Rice had given Wilkinson the grand title of deputy national security advisor for communications, but in reality he spent a lot of time spinning reporters. Many top officials couldn't understand at first what Rice saw in Wilkinson, but ultimately concluded she liked his forceful, direct way of saying there was a problem—and then working actively to fix it. She also valued his instincts about handling the media—and the politics of decisions. At the State Department, he thought nothing of throwing his weight around and quickly antagonized career professionals with his demands and his refusal to follow tradition.

Wilkinson dearly wanted to be chief of staff. He was tired of being pegged as media handler and wanted to be more involved in the mechanics of policy-making. Rice first indicated she wanted to offer the job of chief of staff to Bellinger, but he told her he wanted a position with line authority. She said she understood and made Bellinger legal advisor, an important senior-level post. Then she turned to Gunderson, forty-three, even though she had never worked with him before. She broke the news gently to Wilkinson, going out of her way to walk to his office to tell him about her decision to hire someone else.

Each secretary of state re-creates the job of chief of staff to suit his or her own needs, and Rice had decided to divide it in two. Wilkinson would be in charge of planning, strategy, and communications, with the title of "senior advisor," while Gunderson would focus on personnel and congressional relations. Both would report directly to her, meaning that political operatives—not State Department officials—controlled her schedule. Gunderson also had close ties with the conservative wing of the Republican Party, and so had the essential job of protecting her vulnerable right flank. Dialing around Washington, he kept in close touch with Karl Rove, the political guru at the White House, and key conservatives throughout Washington, making sure no one thought that Rice was straying too far from the fold.

Wilkinson knew Gunderson well and so couldn't feel too down about not getting the job.[11] Gunderson, for his part, was shocked that she had reached outside her circle for such a critical position. Others in the inner circle were surprised by the choice and felt the taciturn Gunderson was too quiet at first. Rice tried to reassure Gunderson before she departed on her first trip, telling him with a note of relief in her voice, "I think this is going to work well."

For the crucial role of spokesman, Rice chose loyalty over State Department tradition. She named Sean McCormack, a relatively low-level foreign service officer who had been spokesman for the National Security Council during Bush's first term. The NSC spokesman is often a foreign service officer, but never had one returned to State as an assistant secretary of state. McCormack had served two brief tours overseas, in Turkey and Algeria, and had been among the junior staff who traveled with Madeleine Albright before landing at the White House. His elevation greatly angered traditionalists at State, not to mention other, more experienced public-affairs specialists around the building. (The complaints grew even louder when Rice permitted three other former NSC aides to leapfrog over more experienced foreign service colleagues, prompting the president of the American Foreign Service Association to publicly complain about the "damaging impact of this controversy on professionalism, morale and esprit de corps" because loyalty seemed to be the main criterion for promotion.)[12]

McCormack also had the misfortune of following the legendary Richard Boucher, the longest-serving spokesman in department history, having served Baker, Christopher, Albright, Powell, and then, briefly, Rice while McCormack awaited Senate confirmation. Boucher had made an art form out of the 12:30 P.M. daily briefing; the entire department would stop and listen to Boucher's daily remarks in order to craft their conversations later that afternoon with embassies and foreign officials. McCormack, an affable man married to a journalist, had a rough start trying to follow Boucher's footsteps. Frequently, McCormack would simply refer reporters' questions to previous statements by Rice, rather than try to move the policy forward with his own words. The department began to tune out the briefings. McCormack improved as the months passed, but his selection showed that Rice intended to be her own spokesman.

"The Best of the Best"

For the three key policy-making positions, Rice in effect re-created the team—Zoellick, Zelikow, and Burns—that had spearheaded, with her, the reunification of Germany in the George H. W. Bush administration sixteen years earlier.[13] That underscored the breadth of her ambition of wanting to reshape the Middle East and Asia. Many State Department officials who worked with Rice's top aides were struck by the audacity of their goals—which grew from a deeply held belief that they had ended the cold war and changed Europe, and thus were uniquely prepared to reshape the rest of the world. One official remarked that if you put a lie detector on Zelikow and asked him if he personally unified Germany, he would pass.

"We got lucky enough to be at the end of one great historical transition," Rice told the three men, referring to the end of the cold war. "I guess our payment for that is to be at the beginning of another great historical transition."[14]

Rice's clout as secretary was demonstrated when she decided to hire Zoellick to be her deputy—and got him to accept it. As U.S. trade representative, Zoellick was a cabinet member, and he had already been told he had been penciled in to be Bush's choice for World Bank president. That would have been the dream job for Zoellick. He is known as one of the smartest policy makers in Washington—and has a big enough ego to let everyone know that he thinks he has few peers in both the realms of economics and foreign policy. Zoellick, the ultimate policy wonk, is especially skilled at difficult negotiations that require both a broad feel for strategy and a narrow knowledge of the smallest details. Zoellick's ability to learn so much about a particular issue—and his tendency to talk at length about it—at times irritated Bush, who once turned to the Pakistani trade minister and said, in front of a group of aides, "He's a smart guy, but isn't Zoellick a pain in the ass?"

But Rice felt she needed Zoellick, a tall, gangly man with a shock of reddish hair that he keeps combed over bald areas. He had been critical to the success of Baker's State Department—and Baker's stint as Treasury secretary—and he had also been part of the Vulcans, the core group of Bush foreign policy advisors in the 2000 campaign. He would fill Rice's knowledge gap in economics and dealings with Congress. At key moments during the first term, Rice had relied on Zoellick's insights. Zoellick watched her prepare for the difficult 9/11 Commission hearings and helped shape her answers. Rice asked him to play a similar role as she prepared for her confirmation hearings, in what are called the "murder boards"—mock question-and-answer sessions. Zoellick would stop her after she gave an answer, quiz her on what she was trying to say, and then offer more precise alternatives.

The fifty-one-year-old Zoellick was traveling in Africa when he got the call from the White House about Rice's interest. He wasn't eager to accept the job—he detested the State Department bureaucracy, but he felt he had no choice if he wanted a better position down the road. (The World Bank post eventually went to Deputy Defense Secretary Paul Wolfowitz.) Even Cheney, who never forgot Zoellick's role as Baker's top aide during the Florida recount battle after the 2000 election, weighed in and urged him to accept the subcabinet post. Zoellick would leave after only eighteen months to join a Wall Street firm, but his loyalty was rewarded when he was named World Bank president in May 2007 after Wolfowitz was ousted after two years.

Though Rice and Zoellick appeared to have little in common personally, he was essential to her fast start, imposing a discipline on policymaking that had been lacking at Powell's State Department. Zoellick was shocked at how flabby much of the thinking was at State, almost as if people had been trained not to have ideas. When one lower-level official suggested sending a démarche (official complaint) to the European Union, Zoellick snapped that that wasn't a policy. "What you need to do is figure out what you want the Europeans to do, and then decide how you are going to get them to do it," he lectured. When aides arrived Monday morning, the workaholic Zoellick usually had already read all the weekend cables, and marked each one up with questions and marching orders.

Unless Rice brought Zoellick into an issue, he essentially ran his own mini–State Department. He acquired his own portfolio of issues, such as Sudan, China, and Latin America,[15] but eventually he began to regard them as the dregs in which Rice had little interest. Anything really important, he believed, eventually would need to be handled by the secretary herself. Zoellick also played almost no role in running the department, leading some of the assistant secretaries to believe he wasn't willing to support them in interagency disputes and only cared about his own pet projects. On his office wall, Zoellick kept a framed copy of a trade deal he had negotiated, telling visitors that it was from a period in his life when he still did something productive.

In a first for a deputy secretary of state, Zoellick would often travel overseas with reporters on board his plane. For reporters, Zoellick was a relief after spending so much time with the on-message, image-conscious Rice. He would emerge from meetings with foreign leaders and usually just flip through his notes, written on yellow legal pads in a tiny script, and report exactly what was said. He believed that informed reporters were less likely to make mistakes. The energy and attention that Rice and her staff spent on packaging the news mystified him.

Rice added to the intellectual firepower of her team when she selected Zelikow to be her counselor. This had been a legendary senior-level position at

State that once required Senate confirmation, but the Clinton administration had taken the slot and turned it into a new and very different job: undersecretary for global affairs. Powell didn't even bother to fill the post of counselor, essentially a minister without portfolio. But it was ideal for Zelikow, a fifty-year-old deep thinker with limited interpersonal skills.

Zelikow, a professor at the University of Virginia, had worked closely with Rice on European affairs at the National Security Council in the senior Bush administration. They started at the White House on the same day in 1989 and left within twenty-four hours of each other in 1991. They were both deputies to Robert D. Blackwill, who had once bragged to President George H. W. Bush that he had hired people smarter than he was.

After leaving the White House, Zelikow wrote a book about U.S. policy during the tumultuous period of German reunification, generously giving Rice coauthorship, though he wrote most of the manuscript and she appeared to have mainly reworked a few chapters.[16] The book is well-written, extremely detailed, and exhaustively footnoted, much like the 9/11 Commission report. Just prior to joining Rice at State, in fact, Zelikow had been executive director of the commission. Rice didn't seem to hold that against Zelikow, even though the commission's report repeatedly faulted Rice, and its demand for her public testimony was one of her most uncomfortable moments during Bush's first term.

Zelikow had assisted Rice in setting up the national security staff at the start of the George W. Bush administration, but he was not offered a position at the NSC. Still, Rice relied on Zelikow to ghostwrite the administration's initial national security strategy after the September 11 attacks, in which the idea of preemptive war as a key tool in foreign policy was first outlined. (That section would later be seen as a rationale for the Iraq War when the strategy was released in September 2002, but Zelikow had written it months earlier, not even thinking of Iraq.)

One of the criticisms sometimes made of Powell's State Department was that it rarely had any new ideas. This is a problem in any large bureaucracy, where fresh thoughts from the lower levels eventually are vitiated or erased altogether as they make their way up the chain of command. With Zelikow at her side, Rice felt she had an all-purpose think tank available to her at all times—and simply cut out the bureaucracy.[17] Many people found him pompous, arrogant, and abrasive—he was always demanding two- or three-hour meetings with Rice—but he had a remarkable ability for synthesizing an argument or coming up with an out-of-box solution while the rest of the group was still rehashing old concepts. Rice felt Zelikow was a kindred spirit philosophically, but with a tendency toward hyperbole that she had learned to discount. When Zelikow thought he was making a particularly salient point, he would unconsciously smooth back his hair.

The counselor position was dead when Rice resurrected it, but Zelikow delighted in learning more about its history. During the Taft and Wilson administrations, he would note, the counselor had been second in command to the secretary of state. He gathered up the photographs of his predecessors and arranged them outside his small office, just like the offices of Senate-confirmed spots. But he was there by the grace of the secretary, not the approval of the Senate. During a meeting of top officials to discuss the line of succession in case Washington was struck by a devastating terrorist attack, other Rice aides watched with amusement as Zelikow rapidly flipped through the long list of names to find his near the bottom.

For a career foreign service officer the top position is generally the undersecretary for political affairs, who oversees the regional bureaus and thus is in charge of the heart of the department. Here, again, Rice turned to a longtime colleague—the forty-nine-year-old Burns. He had been Zoellick's assistant at State and then Rice's deputy at the NSC during the George H. W. Bush administration, but he had also risen fast during the Clinton administration. He had been a key aide to President Clinton on Russia and other parts of the former Soviet Union and a spokesman for Christopher and Albright.

Burns was considered a closet Democrat, and probably would have ended up with the same job if John Kerry had won the presidency in 2004. This made him instantly suspect in conservative circles; any moderation on the part of Rice was attributed to Burns's machinations. "His influence on Secretary of State Condoleezza Rice is so surprising that critics use the word Svengali," fumed columnist Robert Novak.[18] In an editorial complaining about Rice's policies titled "John Kerry's State Department," *The New York Sun* harshly attacked Burns, archly noting: "Mr. Burns has impeccable credentials for a Kerry administration official. He studied in France, earning the Certificat Pratique de Langue Française from the Sorbonne, and speaks French, Arabic, and Greek."[19]

In reality, Burns was intensely loyal to Rice and took his orders from her. He never forgot that when he worked for her in the first Bush administration, Rice delayed her vacation so he could take a month off and witness the birth of his third child, having missed the first two births because he was working so hard.

Burns is an extraordinarily smooth diplomat and, drawing on his service as a spokesman, eagerly courts the media without ever veering from the party line. In fact, he was often too smooth for many reporters, who grew to dislike his briefings while traveling on the road with Rice because he provided little information and tended to put the most upbeat spin on whatever had transpired. Some reporters even cited examples of when they felt Burns had deliberately misled them. With great glee on one trip, reporters did not tell Burns they had secretly overheard a tense luncheon conversation between Rice and the Russian foreign minister, Sergey Lavrov, until after Burns had told them that it had gone swimmingly.

This lineup was impressive, stronger than the team Powell had put in place, and the diplomatic community immediately took notice. In the words of one senior foreign official, it "was the best of the best."[20] But it was also unbalanced. With the exception of Zoellick, none of the top policy makers had much experience outside of Europe (Burns, for instance, had been ambassador to Greece and to NATO, though early in his foreign service, in the 1980s, he briefly worked in Africa and the Middle East.) Even Rice's choice for assistant secretary of state for East Asia was essentially a Europeanist; within a year, many of the top officials with long experience in East Asia and Near East bureaus departed.

European officials were thrilled, but diplomats outside Europe, especially in Asia, despaired over the lack of Asian experience among Rice and her top advisors. Both in Asia and in the State Department, people sensed that Rice didn't like Asians, such as the Chinese, in part because they stick to their talking points too long. Rice clearly felt more comfortable with European interlocutors. Rice handed almost the entire China portfolio to Zoellick and, in her first year, she blew off the annual meeting of Southeast Asian countries that every secretary in the previous two decades had attended.

Moreover, she was an African American woman who surrounded herself with a bunch of middle-aged white men.

"Oh My God"

Beyond this core team, Rice later made two other personnel choices that were both bold and controversial.

The first was John R. Bolton as UN ambassador. The sharply conservative Bolton had been undersecretary of state for arms control in the first term, giving Powell fits as he pushed policies that reflected the viewpoints of Cheney and Rumsfeld. Powell and Bolton always made sure they had witnesses in meetings with each other because neither felt he could trust the other to report accurately what was said. Bolton, a smart, tough bureaucratic infighter, is often misidentified as a neoconservative, when in fact he is simply a hawkish realist who wants to advance U.S. interests and power overseas, rather than a starry-eyed believer that freedom and liberty will cure the ills of the world. Bolton was also known as a caustic critic of the United Nations, making him an unusual choice for ambassador.

But Rice knew she had to find a role for Bolton, who enjoyed the backing of Cheney. More important, Bolton has a strong base of supporters, especially among the pro-Israel lobby, and that base of support is critically important to Bush. Bolton's name was immediately floated as deputy secretary of state, but that was too much for Rice. She directed Wilkinson to knock down the rumor—hard—as soon as it appeared in news reports. Eventually, to the surprise of her staff, she went to Bush and pitched Bolton's name as UN ambassador. Bush liked the idea. When Rice called Senator Joseph Biden, the ranking Democrat on the Senate Foreign Relations Committee, Biden burst out laughing. Kofi Annan, the UN secretary-general, had an even more pungent reaction when Rice gave him the news: "Oh my God."

Bolton's demanding personality became an issue in his confirmation, but that did not deter Rice. When Rice was Stanford provost, if a department worried that a qualified candidate for tenure might not mesh with the department's culture, Rice always had a standard answer: "Are you telling me that if you were the music department you wouldn't hire Mozart because he would be a difficult colleague?" She took the same approach at State, focusing less on personal chemistry than on expertise—and Bolton was an expert in international law and UN resolutions. He had especially impressed her when he negotiated an agreement with Russia on nonproliferation.

There were other reasons why choosing Bolton made sense for Rice. He had played a key role in shaping hard-line policies on North Korea, on Iran, and even on India's nuclear program—all policies that Rice wanted to change. If Bolton had gone to the Pentagon or the White House, he would have been a difficult—and possibly successful—opponent. The UN ambassadorship was prestigious, thus pleasing Bolton's supporters. But at the United Nations, Bolton would be implementing orders from Rice, not shaping policy. Bolton knew how the game was played; he was convinced Rice made the offer to get rid of him.

The second unusual choice was Karen Hughes as undersecretary of state for public diplomacy. Rice had outlined public diplomacy—the promotion of the United States overseas—as a key priority, but the job in the past had suffered through a series of uninspired appointments. The office the undersecretary headed had resulted from an awkward merger of State and the U.S. Information Agency, and no one had figured out how to make it work. A series of commissions had issued numerous reports, but few of the recommendations had ever been implemented.

Dina Powell had first thought of Hughes, who had been one of Bush's closest aides at the start of the administration but had returned to Texas because
her son was homesick.

"How about Karen Hughes?" Powell asked Rice as they sat in Rice's apartment, considering the empty space for public diplomacy on the organizational
chart. Rice had said she wanted someone special for the job.

"You mean someone *like* Karen Hughes?" Rice replied.

"No. I mean Karen Hughes," Powell said, noting that Hughes's son would
soon go to college and she might therefore be open to returning to Washington.
Powell's instincts were right, and Rice's hiring of Bush's alter ego was considered another sign of her clout. (Powell, who was born in Egypt and immigrated
to the United States at age four, became Hughes's deputy.)

Hughes suffered a rough beginning. She was ill-prepared for her first trip to
the Middle East in September 2005, even though she brought along a plane-
load of reporters, including representatives of all five U.S. television networks,
one from Al Arabiya television, and a writer from *GQ* magazine. She had barely
read her briefing papers and was ridiculed for a series of inane statements she
made on the road, demonstrating her lack of depth in foreign policy. But her connection to Bush proved invaluable when it came to fighting bureaucratic wars.
She regularly had lunch or dinner with Bush to update him on her progress—a
level of access highly unusual for a cabinet secretary, let alone a third-level undersecretary. Hughes quickly began implementing many of the think-tank and
blue-ribbon commission recommendations that had long been ignored, the
equivalent of throwing spaghetti against the wall and seeing what stuck.[21] She
became an important advisor to Rice, even on policy issues.

Finally, Rice's former deputy at the NSC, Steve Hadley, was named her replacement as national security advisor, giving her the kind of ally at the White
House that Powell never found. Hadley, a mild-mannered man not known for
grand strategy, would often come to the State Department for meetings that
Rice chaired—and he would let her sit in her old chair when she came to meetings held in his White House office. Both foreign diplomats and U.S. officials
noted the power dynamics, giving rise to the joke that Rice had three deputies—
Zoellick, Zelikow, and Hadley.

"The Time for Diplomacy Is Now"

During the transition, Rice would regularly invite her closest advisors to her
apartment, where they would munch on a variety of cheeses—Rice's favorite
finger food—and drink Coca-Cola as they pondered how Rice could make an

immediate impression as secretary of state.[22] The group contemplated the key issues they were inheriting from Powell and how they might be tackled. Wilkinson put together a color-coded master calendar for each of the first hundred days, noting the days she would travel and who she would meet. The calendar also laid out targets for the first six months, but its core focus was on the first hundred days—which, not by coincidence, is the period in which new presidents have been judged ever since Franklin D. Roosevelt's blitz after he took office in 1933.

The hundred-day plan also outlined a series of "firsts"—the first overseas trip, the first cable to the State Department, the first foreign leaders Rice would meet, and so forth. The team also assembled a list of tasks that she could accomplish quickly, such as faster visa processing or more educational exchanges, to demonstrate that the change in secretaries had made a difference. To soothe feelings on Capitol Hill, she unearthed a complex but important issue involving Russian nuclear weapons that concerned Senator Richard Lugar of Indiana, the committee chairman, which she could easily fix.

Rice and her team had a sense of urgency. They feared that in the second term, it would be harder to score achievements if they didn't move quickly. Wilkinson and Gunderson, as former Hill staffers, had been involved in the Republican takeover of Congress. The Contract with America promoted by then House Speaker Newt Gingrich had promised a series of votes in the first hundred days. They worried that for Rice, the first hundred days would also be seen as an important benchmark by the media. Wilkinson had a battle cry: "No wasted motion." (To the surprise of Rice's aides, almost no reporters did hundred-day stories.)

The drafting of Rice's statement at her confirmation hearings was mostly in the hands of Michael Anton, an NSC speechwriter, but Wilkinson thought it would be useful for the State Department speechwriting team to meet with Rice. The three speechwriters came over to the White House Situation Room, not sure if they would keep their jobs. The conversation meandered and seemed uninspired, and Rice shot an irritated look at Wilkinson for wasting her time. Then, the youngest and most junior of the speechwriters, twenty-five-year-old Christian D. Brose, shyly raised his hand and offered a suggestion that, for Rice, crystallized her foreign policy themes. He noted that diplomacy had always been governed by state-to-state relations. But now, in the wake of September 11, the challenge is to focus on what happens within states, not between them.

"Who is that young red-haired kid?" Rice asked Wilkinson as they left the room. "Let's keep an eye on him." Despite his youth, Brose would soon become Rice's chief speechwriter.

Rice's confirmation hearings began on January 18 and lasted the better part of two days. Democrats were eager to make her nomination a referendum on the administration's policies on Iraq, but she handled the pointed questions with aplomb. Rice's aides were ecstatic when the Democratic senator they feared the most, Barbara Boxer of California, released to the press her line of attack a few days before the hearings started. They couldn't believe their good luck. Another antagonist was the recently defeated Kerry, who kept questioning Rice long into the night, after many of the other senators had departed. Rice coolly dispatched his ponderous queries, leaving Kerry looking like a sore loser.

Rice's opening statement was a familiar defense of the administration's positions, providing little hint of how she planned to radically change some of them. But there was one sentence that stood out, signaling something new: "We must use American diplomacy to help create a balance of power in the world that favors freedom," Rice said. "And the time for diplomacy is now."[23]

Her statement about the "time for diplomacy" had been Zoellick's idea. It was controversial at the White House and annoyed Powell and his aides because it seemed to suggest that the administration had not practiced diplomacy during Bush's first four years. Rice's staff, in fact, was very worried that the line might generate a backlash in the press. As national security advisor, Rice had allowed relations with Europe to become frayed over the Iraq War, global warming, and other issues. But Rice loved Zoellick's suggestion because she wanted to signal that she was going to break with the past and actually work to restore relations with the United States' allies. She had been greatly influenced by an essay in *Foreign Affairs* by a good friend, Yale historian John Lewis Gaddis, titled "Grand Strategy in the Second Term."

Gaddis said that, as the world's sole superpower, the United States could easily think it didn't matter what other nations thought of it, but this was a mistake. "Influence, to be sustained, requires not just power but also the absence of resistance," Gaddis wrote. "Anyone who has ever operated a vehicle knows the need for lubrication, without which the vehicle will sooner or later grind to a halt. This is what was missing during the first Bush administration: a proper amount of attention to the equivalent of lubrication in strategy, which is persuasion."

Gaddis argued for a policy of reassurance, an effort to reach out and demonstrate that the United States valued the opinion of others. "Muscles are not brains," he said. "It is never a good idea to insult potential allies, however outrageous their behavior may have been. Nor is it wise to regard consultation as the endorsement of a course already set."[24]

Rice's first trip overseas was designed to showcase this new approach. Rice and her staff had endless discussions about where she should go. To generate ideas, Wilkinson asked the State Department historian to produce a memo on the travels of previous secretaries. In the end, they decided to focus on Europe—with a twist.

Almost every moment of the trip was choreographed to send a message to Europe: "Let's get past our disagreements and work together." Rice would go first to Britain, the oldest U.S. ally, and then to Germany, where relations had been damaged by the war. At one point, she would detour to Israel and the Palestinian territories, where she would appoint a U.S. general to work with the two sides on coordinating Israel's departure from the Gaza Strip. Then she would return to Europe, giving a speech in Paris—the center of American opposition to the invasion of Iraq—and then end the trip by attending a European Union meeting in Luxembourg.

The detour to Israel was a shrewd gambit. Europeans have long complained that the Bush administration paid little attention to the Israeli-Palestinian conflict—and had consulted too little with Europe about it. In one stroke, Rice intended to show that she cared about the Palestinian issue, and even more important, she was reporting back to Europe about what she had done there. In particular, she wanted to convince the Europeans that the Israeli prime minister's plan to withdraw from Gaza made sense. The Europeans didn't trust Sharon, but the Bush administration had helped shape the plan and was intellectually invested in it.

The message to the Europeans would be clear and direct. Wolfgang Ischinger, the German ambassador, said that during the first term he felt he had to be a detective, searching for little pieces of evidence in order to understand U.S. policy. In 2004 he was invited by the White House protocol office to attend a speech by Bush, and he nearly didn't go, thinking he would be just one of two hundred ambassadors. He arrived and found a seat in the back. As he puzzled about why he didn't see other ambassadors, he was suddenly ushered to the center of the front row, where he was placed amid a bevy of American officials. Then to his total shock, Bush thanked him in the introductory remarks for being there (although he mispronounced Ischinger's name). For Ischinger, it was the first signal that there might be a thaw in U.S.-German relations. But no one had even given a hint that his presence at the speech might be important.

With Rice's move to the State Department, the quality of the relationship improved quickly. "One morning I woke up and I discovered there had been a foreign policy revolution in Washington," Ischinger recalled. "All of a sudden

Europe is being discovered. We found ourselves discussing issues which we had been dying to discuss with the Americans."[25]

With that first trip, Wilkinson imposed a discipline on the State Department that had been lacking in the past. Powell hated to travel, but when he did, he sometimes seemed to roam the earth with no real purpose in mind. Before Wilkinson would approve any overseas trip, he asked basic questions: What are you trying to accomplish? What are the policy objectives? He was not going to waste Rice's time just because some State Department official thought it would be nice for her to attend a conference. He required that every action she took must be tied to an objective. Before any trip, he argued, Rice had to be able to explain what she planned to accomplish—and when she returned, she had to show what she did. Some officials were taken aback by Wilkinson's simple questions, and because they had no real answer, they responded with diplomatic gobbledygook. "What the fuck does that mean?" Wilkinson demanded. He ended up removing from Rice's schedule a bunch of alphabet-soup diplomatic meetings that most of her predecessors, out of habit, had regularly attended.[26]

"The Question Is Simply Not on the Agenda"

Rice flew to Europe the day after President Bush's 2005 State of the Union address, where for the first time she sat in the front row in the cavernous House chamber as a Senate-confirmed member of the cabinet. Democrats had briefly delayed Rice's confirmation in order to force a debate about Iraq, and she was confirmed by a vote of 85-to-13, the most negative votes cast against a nominee for secretary of state in 180 years. Before departure, Rice tried to make light of the tension, telling her aides that the point of the first trip was to show the world she could get off the plane without falling down the stairs.

Powell traditionally traveled with a maximum of eleven or twelve reporters, who followed a strict rotation that sometimes meant *The Washington Post* or *The New York Times* didn't get a seat. So be it, no favorites, was the way Powell's people saw it. Wilkinson thought that was crazy, and he constantly bent the rules to make sure leading news organizations had a seat on the plane if they wanted it. For Rice's first trip, an unprecedented nineteen reporters were given seats, which meant eight State Department officials (including the medical doctor, who normally travels with the secretary of state) were kicked off the plane and told to stay home or catch up with Rice by commercial flights. Wilkinson thought extensive news coverage was more essential than State Department tradition or bruised feelings. At one point, Wilkinson even removed a spare pilot to make room for a reporter.

Many reporters find that traveling with the secretary of state is much different than covering the U.S. president on an overseas trip. Hundreds of reporters follow the president in a press charter, so they almost never see him except in tightly controlled settings. The relationship often turns testy. By contrast, on the secretary's plane the small group of reporters mingles frequently with her and her staff—and reporters get instant feedback on their articles. (Rice never seems to hold a grudge about a negative story, but might sweetly ask why the reporter seemed so cynical that day.) The constant conversation reduces the adversarial tension so common between government officials and reporters. Many State Department correspondents are former White House reporters who are interested in focusing less on politics and polls and more on policy issues.

Rice wanted to give the reporters a gift, and her staff debated what would be most appropriate. Wilkinson suggested some sort of bag with classical music CDs, but McCormack came up with the idea of a small portable atlas, each individually inscribed by Rice. "We're going to travel a lot, and I wouldn't want anybody to feel lost," she announced at the end of her first plane briefing, describing it as "a little memento of our first trip together."[27]

The briefing had actually been somewhat contentious, as Rice repeatedly ducked questions about whether the United States was interested in regime change in Iran. Rice answered with a well-worn refrain that didn't directly answer the question: "I don't think anybody thinks that the unelected Mullahs who run that regime are a good thing, for either the Iranian people or for the region. The region is going in a quite different direction, and the President last night again said that the Iranian people deserved better."

Each attempt by reporters to get Rice to clarify her answer resulted in the same sort of nonanswer, such as, "What we support is that the Iranian people should have a chance to determine their own future, and right now under this regime they have no opportunity to determine their own future."[28] It was the sort of dodge that had worked as national security advisor, but now she was secretary of state. Her words boomeranged around the world, and soon the European press was filled with stories that Iran was the next country in the crosshairs of the American military machine.

Rice and her staff reeled. They hadn't realized how carefully every word she uttered would be scrutinized. Rice had thought the trip would be dominated by questions on Iraq, but now because of a few sharp questions and some poorly worded answers, Iran was the main topic. The questions came at a sensitive point: Britain, France, and Germany were negotiating with Iran over its nuclear program, but the talks had not made much progress in the absence of explicit

U.S. backing. At Rice's first news conference in London, one reporter noted that Powell's deputy, Richard Armitage, had publicly said a year earlier the United States did not believe in regime change in Iran and now the policy seemed to have shifted. Another reporter directly asked if the United States would consider attacking Iran. "The question is simply not on the agenda at this point in time," Rice said.[29]

Ironically, Rice was saved by German chancellor Gerhard Schroeder, one of the strongest critics of the Iraq War, who had won reelection on an anti-Bush platform. By the time Rice had arrived in Germany, the Iran issue had turned into a feeding frenzy. Dozens of cameras were set up for the news conference with Schroeder, and Rice's aides held their breath as they awaited his answer to the inevitable question: Was he concerned about Rice's remarks, and did he think it would have a negative effect on the negotiations between Iran and the three European nations?

"Not at all, if you don't mind me saying. No, no, absolutely not," Schroeder said. "What we are, indeed, discussing is the fact, what tools should we ideally use to get to this desired state of having democratic circumstances in a country. So I do not fear that there could be any kind of negative effect on the European Three. Far rather, I think it's an important move, and the right one."[30]

"Condi, You Hit a Home Run"

Schroeder's comments calmed the furor, which had threatened to sink Rice's tour of Europe just one day after she began it. Now the focus would return to what was to be the centerpiece of her trip: a speech at Institut d'Études Politiques de Paris, popularly known as Science Po, the distinguished political academy and the alma mater of French president Jacques Chirac and the French elite.

Rice planned to go to the heart of anti-Americanism—what her aides called "the belly of the beast"—and extend a hand of friendship. The speech would be the first in a series of speeches around the world in Rice's first six months, an effort to provide an intellectual foundation for her approach to diplomacy. Powell, to the frustration of some of his advisors, did not like to give such speeches. But Rice, the onetime political scientist, felt it was important.

Wearing a superbly cut navy blue suit and a large strand of white pearls, Rice was obviously nervous the first few minutes of her speech. But she slowly gained her confidence and was able to firmly deliver the key message of the day.

"We have had our disagreements. But it is time to turn away from the disagreements of the past. It is time to open a new chapter in our relationship, and a new chapter in our alliance," Rice said. "America stands ready to work with Europe on our common agenda—and Europe must stand ready to work with America. After all, history will surely judge us not by our old disagreements, but by our new achievements."[31]

In terms of oratory, the speech was merely adequate, but it covered the bases, saying what Europeans wanted to hear and soft-pedalling areas of disagreement. Rice even managed to work a reference to the French national motto, "Liberté, Egalité, Fraternité," into her speech, though she did it with a heavy American accent. (Rice understands French but cannot really speak it; she was a reluctant French student as a child because her lessons were scheduled for Saturday afternoons, when she would have preferred to play with friends.) The French ambassador, Jean-David Levitte, told Rice after her speech, "Condi, you hit a home run."

The speech was only one part of her charm offensive. She spent two days in Paris, rather than just flying in and out, and Wilkinson had planned a series of events to demonstrate her appreciation of French culture. Rice met with a group of prominent intellectuals—an important signal in a nation where intellectuals are celebrities, and where every president is expected to have written a serious book before he can be elected. She also visited the music conservatory to talk about the importance of music in life—which to the French seemed highly unusual but quite civilized, coming from an American diplomat. The newspapers were filled with articles about Rice's background and her clout. When Levitte arrived in Paris, he was struck by the fact that "everyone was determined to fall in love with Condi Rice."[32]

During the meeting with intellectuals, Rice engaged in a debate that left some shaking their head at her ideological zeal. She told them that Iran was a "totalitarian state," and she refused to back down even when some French participants gaped in protest. Rice said she would have called Iran "authoritarian" a year earlier, but the recent parliamentary elections had changed her mind. (Election lists had been purged of liberal candidates, resulting in a conservative victory.) She added that the West was wrong to accept the Soviet Union on its terms during the cold war, and now the same mistake should not be made with Iran. One of the French participants, who thought she clearly didn't understand Iran, condemned her remarks as scary.[33]

But U.S. officials felt just the fact that she would engage with the French on their turf would be seen as a plus in the minds of Europeans. In the words of one aide, "She can speak European." Chirac had argued for a "multipolar" world as a way to counteract American influence. Rice didn't try to argue that multipolarity was a bad idea. Instead she noted its roots in classic international relations theory and then argued that it had no relevance to today's world—that, in fact, it was intellectually incoherent. Her goal was to challenge the Europeans on their own terms in a way that was deeply unsettling.[34]

The combination of the speech and Wilkinson's well-planned events paid off. The overall impression in Europe was extremely positive. The French newspaper *Le Figaro* declared, "With an impeccable silhouette, she put the 'la' back in the new diplomacy."[35]

The reporters traveling with Rice also noticed a change. The whole feel of the trip was different than a Powell trip. With Powell, Boucher would sometimes wander to the back of the plane to try to calm the reporters if he sensed they were going off on the wrong tack. But that was a rare event. Now there was a constant stream of officials, sometimes four at a time (led by Wilkinson), making sure that the reporters got the message of the day—or even the hour. And, almost overnight, Rice had changed, too. She was amazingly on message, using the word "freedom" at least 106 times in her news conferences and interviews in Europe.[36] After the Paris speech, she no longer seemed to be a rather predictable and cautious White House official. The production values, the clothes, and the ambitious effort to start fresh with Europe all suggested that something new was going on. Rice's years in the White House as a staff aide had obscured the fact that she was at heart a performer—that the little girl who would get up early every day to practice figure skating and who yearned to be a pianist had finally found a stage big enough for her talents.

There was one more neardisaster, once again involving Iran. The day after her Paris speech, James Rosen of Fox News needled her about whether there was "unity of message" in dealing with Iran. Rice took the bait, and just after offering an olive branch to the Europeans, she upbraided them for not bluntly telling the Iranians that they faced action in the UN Security Council. "I don't know that anyone has said that as clearly as they should to the Iranians," Rice said. "They need to hear that the discussions that they're in with the Europeans are not going to be a kind of way station where they're allowed to continue their activities, that there's going to be an end to this, and that they're going to end up in the Security Council."[37]

The wire services ran with the story, especially Agence France-Presse, which said the day "seemed destined to go sour" until Rice (and her anxious aides) pulled back the statement later in the day.[38] Rice's fatigue was showing as she yet again tried to put the issue to rest, putting the onus back on Iran, not Europe. "I said yesterday, or the day before or the day before that—I really can't remember which day—that the Iranians should take the opportunity that the

Europeans are giving them to live up to their obligations," Rice said with exasperation during a news conference at NATO's Brussels headquarters.

"I Never Wanted to Run for Anything"

The reporters' questions about Iran had an impact on Rice. She returned to Washington realizing that the issue threatened to cause yet another breach with Europe. Whereas Europe and the United States should have been united on Iran, she began to understand that the United States was somehow viewed as the problem, not Iran. This would have been obvious to most people outside the White House bubble, but for the first time, Rice was directly exposed to the problem. In the first Bush term, the administration had never really backed the European negotiations with Iran; its enthusiasm for talks was so wan that the Europeans were convinced the administration wanted them to fail.

Rice quickly won Bush's approval for a shift in tactics—which was privately communicated just a couple of weeks later when he, accompanied by Rice, made his own trip to Europe. Bush became the first president to visit the headquarters of the European Union, a symbolic act of great importance to many Europeans. In meetings, Bush sought reassurances from Chirac and Schroeder that they were committed to punishing Iran if the negotiations did not succeed. When they said yes, he told them he would help them by explicitly offering American "carrots"—lifting opposition to Iran joining the World Trade Organization and selling Boeing spare parts to Iran for their aging aircraft—if that would move the negotiations along and perhaps increase the chances for success.[39]

While Rice delivered on Iran, she also showed the Europeans she was no pushover. The European Union was primed to lift an arms embargo on China stemming from the Tiananmen Square massacre in 1989. The issue was entirely symbolic—the ban had no practical legal effect—but it was important to the Chinese and the Europeans. Rice was skeptical. On her first trip to Europe, she told diplomats they would rue the day if U.S. troops ever faced European-armed Chinese soldiers across the Taiwan Strait. Luxembourg foreign minister Jean Asselborn, whose country then held the rotating European Union presidency, was so startled by her tough talk that he spilled his coffee in the lap of the European foreign policy chief, Javier Solana. The Europeans kept pressing, but on her return visit with Bush, she met with Straw and was absolutely firm: yes on Iran, no on China. The European Union reluctantly shelved the idea.[40]

During that trip, Rice put on a dramatic outfit when she arrived at a military base in Germany to introduce Bush before a speech. She was wearing a black skirt that hit just above the knee, along with a black coat with seven gold buttons that fell to midcalf—and the coat hung open to reveal sexy, knee-high boots. With one arm stretched out, she looked like a cross between Mussolini and Liza Minnelli. Though the president was overseas, it was this photograph of Rice that appeared on the front pages of the nation's newspapers. In some ways, it violated Wilkinson's dictum about her not being photographed solo— except that dozens of soldiers could be seen behind Rice, cheering and shouting their approval.

Robin Givhan, the fashion writer of *The Washington Post,* devoted an entire article to the outfit. "Rice's appearance at Wiesbaden—a military base with all of its attendant images of machismo, strength and power—was striking because she walked out draped in a banner of authority, power and toughness," Givhan wrote. "She was not hiding behind matronliness, androgyny or the stereotype of the steel magnolia. Rice brought her full self to the world stage—and that included her sexuality. It was not overt or inappropriate. If it was distracting, it is only because it is so rare."[41]

Ischinger and other European diplomats took notice, too. They were impressed that Rice had so quickly convinced Bush to change the administration's position on the Iran talks. But this was something different than diplomacy. "That is when we first thought she is really more than the national security advisor or the secretary of state," he said. "She was acquiring elements of political leadership and charisma, and making a big splash here."[42]

In a conversation with Wilkinson, Rice professed to be puzzled about the fuss. She asked him why the media wrote articles about her boots. Wilkinson at first demurred, saying he didn't feel comfortable explaining the reason.

"Oh, Jim, you're like my little brother," Rice said. "Tell me."

Wilkinson hemmed and hawed but finally answered: "Men like these."

Rice leaned over and whispered: "We know that."[43]

The boots photograph appeared in the press on February 25; Rice had only arrived at the State Department on January 27. The transformation was nearly complete, but Wilkinson had one more trick up his sleeve.

On March 11, Rice sat down for an interview with the editorial board of *The Washington Times.* Wilkinson slipped a note to the editorial page editor, Tony Blankley, whom he had known for years; they had both worked on Capitol Hill for the Republican House leadership. The note suggested the *Times* ask her if she would consider running for president. It was an audacious proposal. She had only been on the job a month, but such speculation helped bolster the idea that Rice was a strong leader. As it happened, then White House reporter

Bill Sammon was already prepared to ask what he called the "fun political stuff."[44] Rice exclaimed "Jeez" before she gave a classic nonanswer.

"I never wanted to run for anything. I don't think I even ran for class anything when I was in school," Rice said. "However, I have enormous respect for people who do run for office. It's really hard for me to imagine myself in that role."[45]

Her remarks generated banner headlines and immediate speculation about a "Condi versus Hillary" race in 2008.

Wilkinson could rest easy: A star was born.

CHAPTER 2

PASSAGE TO NEW DELHI

March 15, 2005

Humayun's Tomb is an oasis in the sprawling and traffic-plagued Indian capital of New Delhi, a magnificent red and white mausoleum surrounded by green grass, water channels, and fountains. This is where the Mughal dynasty fell, when the last of the emperors sought sanctuary from the British in 1857 before he was arrested. It also inspired the more famous Taj Mahal, about 125 miles to the south. For a diplomat with little time to spare, a trip here is the most expedient way to get a taste of India.

Rushing from one meeting to another to see the full cacophony of senior officials in India's vibrant democracy, Rice managed to squeeze in a pilgrimage to Humayun's Tomb. She strolled through the gardens and climbed up the stairs, her every step watched through the telephoto zoom lenses of photographers and cameramen kept at the edge of the gardens. In the peaceful still of the spring air, Rice paused and closed her eyes as she stood in front of the tomb, breathing in its history.

It was only a twenty-minute stop in a visit to India that lasted less than eighteen hours. But the photographs and news footage of her brief tour reverberated across the subcontinent, appearing in newspapers and on television news programs across India and eventually around the world. Rice was making a statement of respect for India's past. She also wanted to demonstrate that, unlike Powell—who was notorious for rushing from government buildings to the airport in his motorcade without a glance out his window—she would take time to experience the cultures of countries she visited. This was partly the inspiration of Jim Wilkinson, a publicity device he (along with John Bellinger) had concocted during the transition so the pictures of Rice overseas would have more impact than the usual boring stand-ups at news conferences.[1] In India, Wilkinson made sure to shoo the reporters away whenever it seemed they might end up in camera range and spoil shots of Rice walking in front of the towering monument.

Just as the visit to Humayun's Tomb paid rich dividends despite its brevity, Rice's trip to Delhi was far more important than suggested by her brief period on the ground. She arrived in India on March 15, 2005, barely one and a half months after becoming secretary, and set in motion one of the boldest initiatives ever launched by a secretary of state. It was nothing less than a repudiation of three decades of U.S. policy on nuclear weapons—and a gambit to secure India, long an antagonist of the United States, as one of its closest allies. Her willingness to make this gamble—and Bush's willingness to back her—demonstrated an unusual confidence early in her tenure.

Beyond the invasion of Iraq, few of Bush's decisions have as much potential to shake the international order as the opening to India. For three decades the United States had treated India as a pariah in the nuclear sphere because it used a civilian nuclear program to produce fissile material for weapons. (India had violated a commitment to use a research reactor only for peaceful purposes when in 1974 it used plutonium produced in that reactor for a nuclear test. It claimed this was a "peaceful nuclear explosion.") When Rice arrived in India, the administration was officially still dedicated to an incremental easing of the nuclear rules regarding India. Within four months, that long-standing policy would be abandoned. With Rice's encouragement, Bush decided that India would be able to buy foreign-made nuclear reactors if it opened its civilian facilities to international inspections—and did not put any constraints on its ability to produce materials for nuclear weapons.

The push with India reveals a hallmark of Rice's State Department: a penchant for secrecy, with key decisions made by Rice and a handful of close aides. Rice's India initiative took the State Department bureaucracy by surprise, especially those who had dedicated decades to preventing the spread of nuclear weapons. Many people felt completely cut out of the loop.

Rice's aides argue that is why career professionals need to be kept uninformed—because they would have tried to kill the idea before it was ever considered. In their view, major diplomatic turning points, such as Nixon's historic decision to open relations with China, must be first conducted in secret because established bureaucracies tend to resist new ideas. But the failure to win support within the bureaucracy—or even consult with Congress—would make it much more difficult to win support for the agreement. And Congress has a very important role that could not be easily discounted: Laws that prohibited the sale of nuclear technology to India needed to be changed before any of Rice's grand plans could take effect.

"These Nagging Nannies Were Alive and Well"

During the 2000 presidential campaign, Rice had made clear her interest in broadening ties with India. In her article in *Foreign Affairs,* she said that "India is not a great power yet, but it has the potential to emerge as one" and pointedly noted that "India is an element in China's calculation, and it should be in America's, too."[2]

By the time Rice was nominated as secretary of state, she had decided that early on she should pursue a nuclear deal with India. When she was national security advisor, she was struck by a comment by her Indian counterpart, Brajesh Mishra, who had bluntly told her that someday the United States would need to let India get out of the nuclear netherworld. But she only told Steve Hadley, her NSC deputy, and Robert G. Joseph, the NSC nonproliferation expert, of her plans before she became secretary.[3]

The new approach actually was spurred on by an unrelated event: Bush, in a December 2004 Oval Office meeting with Pakistani president Pervez Musharraf, had secretly agreed to sell F-16 fighter jets to Pakistan, in an effort to inoculate Musharraf from a requested crackdown on Islamic fighters in the northwest territories of his country.[4] As required by U.S. law, a previous sale had been canceled by Bush's father in 1990 after concerns were heightened about Pakistan's nuclear activities. The strategic implications of the F-16 sale were enormous for India, since New Delhi worried the aircraft could be used to deliver nuclear weapons.

Shortly after settling in his office as deputy secretary, Zoellick was shocked to learn that the State Department bureaucracy was about to announce the F-16 deal with Pakistan. Rice was overseas with Bush in Europe, and Zoellick—long a proponent of closer ties with India—cabled her and Hadley on the plane to warn that an announcement without preparing the Indian government would badly damage the broader strategic goal of making India a U.S. partner. Rice agreed to hold up the announcement and assigned Zoellick and Philip Zelikow to come up with a way to break the news to New Delhi.

They decided to make lemonade out of lemons. They ignored the incremental plans and ideas developed by lower-level officials in State's South Asia bureau. The sale of F-16s should not have been handled in isolation, they concluded, but instead it should be considered as part of a broader reevaluation of the future of U.S.–South Asian relations. In other words, the moment was ripe for a dramatic rethinking of U.S.-India ties.[5]

These discussions built on ideas that had long been pushed—without much success—by Robert D. Blackwill, who had hired both Rice and Zelikow on his staff when he handled the European portfolio for the National Security Council under Bush's father. Blackwill had been one of the Vulcans during the 2000 presidential campaign, and was sent to India as ambassador early in Bush's first term. He was notorious in his contempt for the State Department bureaucracy, believing he reported directly to the White House. As early as October 2001, he cabled Washington urging a rethinking of nuclear policy toward India.[6] Those cables were ignored by Powell, who detested Blackwill.

"During the first year of the Bush presidency, I vividly recall receiving routine instructions in New Delhi from the State Department that contained all of the counterproductive language from the Clinton administration's approach to India's nuclear weapons program," Blackwill recounted. "These nagging nannies were alive and well in that State Department labyrinth. I, of course, did not implement those instructions. It took me many months and many calls to finally cut off the head of this snake back home."[7]

Powell had been eager to build ties with India, but unlike Rice he listened closely to concerns of the nuclear experts in the State Department. As Powell put it in 2003, in defending an incremental approach, "We also have to protect certain red lines that we have with respect to proliferation."[8]

Toward the end of the first term, Blackwill became one of Rice's top deputies on the National Security Council. He ended up having an important impact on Rice's thinking about India. Blackwill, who became a lobbyist for India after Bush's reelection, also spoke to Zoellick about India during the transition between the Powell and Rice eras at State. The emerging strategy—and its willingness to ignore nuclear orthodoxy—tracked his deeply held beliefs.

Zelikow shared Blackwill's frustration that the relationship with India had not developed as fast as officials had hoped during Bush's first term. The 2002 national security strategy that Zelikow had largely drafted at Rice's behest included language that pointed to the possibilities of a broader partnership with India and a willingness to downplay the nuclear issue: "Differences remain, including over the development of India's nuclear and missile programs, and the pace of India's economic reforms. But while in the past these concerns may have dominated our thinking about India, today we start with a view of India as a growing world power with which we have common strategic interests."[9]

In 2004, the administration had adopted an incremental easing of the rules regarding nuclear sales to India, known by the unwieldy name Next Steps in Strategic Partnership (NSSP), a process largely overseen by Hadley. But it had gone forward at a grindingly slow pace and offered little prospect for immediate success, in part because it took the Indians two years to enact export control laws, which still did not fully meet the commitments they had made up front.

The irony was that India's nuclear program had helped define the course of U.S. nonproliferation policy. After China detonated its first nuclear weapon in 1964, U.S. officials briefly considered arming India with nuclear weapons as a counterweight, according to the declassified records of the Gilpatric Committee, appointed by President Johnson to consider policy options.[10] But ultimately the United States decided to halt the spread of nuclear weapons through the 1968 nuclear Non-Proliferation Treaty (NPT). At the time, there were predictions that there would be twenty to thirty states with nuclear weapons within a few decades. Yet the nonproliferation programs successfully limited this spread to less than a handful, including India, which rejected the treaty as discriminatory because it defined India as a non-nuclear-weapon state, potentially leaving it forever outside the nuclear club.

In 1974, when India conducted what it called a "peaceful nuclear explosion," it was clear that the NPT alone could not halt the spread of nuclear weapons. The United States and others developed an international consortium known as the Nuclear Suppliers Group to close the loopholes in the export control regime that had allowed India to advance its weapons program through supposedly peaceful nuclear cooperation. The effect was to limit nuclear cooperation with India and other states that sought to develop nuclear weapons. As a result, India's nuclear program has since then been largely homegrown, cut off from international markets. This has hobbled India's use of nuclear power, which provides only about 3 percent of installed electricity capacity. Meanwhile, India was desperate for energy as its population and economic output have soared.

"The biggest constraint on India's economic growth is energy," explained Ronen Sen, India's ambassador to the United States. "We can't address issues of poverty, illiteracy, health care and very basic fundamental needs of our people without energy."[11]

Of course, it was India's choice to remain an outsider that led to its nuclear ostracism—and there are other sources of electricity besides nuclear power. But India's complaint had a favorable reception in Washington. Rice herself thought it was an "accident of history" that India was not grandfathered in as a nuclear state under the NPT.[12]

The problem, as Rice and her aides began to see it, is that India's status outside the nonproliferation regime created unique problems. Since it had never signed the nuclear nonproliferation treaty, but it had a nuclear power program, it was trapped in a halfway house. Any approach to India was handicapped by this reality. This, then, was the conundrum: The Bush administration wanted to make India a great power, but officials thought India could never join the great powers when it was outside such a crucial part of the international system.

The key was to bring India into the system, in effect to forgive it for its sins even though the system had worked remarkably well in limiting India's ability to benefit from its refusal to play by international rules. Rice and Zelikow tend to view international events through the prism of Europe, and fervently believe they are remaking the post-9/11 world much as President Harry Truman remade the post–World War II world.

A bold move toward India was increasingly seen as part of that strategy, much like building relations with former adversaries Germany and Japan after World War II was so critical to the system created by Truman. Zelikow saw the concerns about nuclear proliferation in India as parallel to the worries in the 1950s about rearming West Germany as part of its entry into NATO. In Zelikow's view, there was criticism then, just as there would be criticism now, but rearming Germany had been critical to binding it to the West. It was a gamble that had stood the test of time. (Some might argue that the analogy was misleading: With Germany, the United States was trying to create a new international regime in order to integrate it into a new world order. With India, the Bush administration was essentially dismantling a major element of the international regime to accommodate India.)

Rice also believed it was time to delink Pakistan and India. For too long, she thought, policy makers in the region and in the United States had looked at the relationship as a zero-sum game—what was good for India was bad for Pakistan, and vice versa. She wanted to let the Indians know that no matter what Pakistan got in terms of military hardware, the relationship between the United States and India would stand on its own terms. In her inelegant phrase, she wanted to "de-hyphenate the relationship."[13]

Rice and her staff discussed at length how to approach the Indians. Should the ambassador be directed to deliver a message? Should Zoellick go? But as Zoellick and Zelikow became bolder in their proposals, Zoellick told Rice that she should make the pitch to the Indians—that the impact of the message would be far greater if it came from the secretary of state. Rice agreed. She wanted to get a feel for how receptive the Indians would be to a deal before she tried to line up support within the U.S. government. But she made sure to let President Bush in on her plans before she left.

"We are going to have to do something about the nuclear issue with India," she told the president.

"I know," Bush said.[14]

The trip to India became the first stop of a long round-the-world tour in March that also took her to Pakistan, Afghanistan, Japan, South Korea, and China.

"You Have to Treat India as a Partner"

As Rice flew to India, she dropped a few hints to reporters about what she was thinking, but she couched it in such bland language that they failed to pick up on the cues. "With India we clearly have a broader and deeper relationship than we've ever had, and I look forward to having a chance to talk with the Indians about continuing to broaden and deepen that relationship," Rice said. "I think there are many more opportunities—economic, in terms of security, in terms of energy cooperation—that we can pursue with India."[15] Not a single reporter followed up, focusing questions instead on such obvious targets as China and North Korea. They missed the story so badly that her aides started to whisper that she really was planning something big with India, including possibly the sale of nuclear reactors.

It was so early in Rice's tenure that reporters still found it hard to discern the spin from the news. Some reporters sprinkled references to nuclear reactors in their stories, but by and large they got sidetracked by other issues—such as rumors of the pending sale of F-16 jets to Pakistan (which Rice declined to confirm, saying she was planning no announcements on the trip) and U.S. objections to an India-Iran natural gas pipeline deal. Rice, for her part, continued to disguise the India initiative behind language that offered little in terms of news.

"The president wanted me to have a chance to come to India early in my tenure as secretary of state and early in his second term because this is a relationship that has transformed in recent years from one that had great potential into one that is really now realizing that potential," she said at a news conference with Foreign Minister Natwar Singh.[16] It just seemed like routine "nice to visit New Delhi" diplobabble.

In private conversations with Indian officials, however, Rice made it clear that she was thinking in very bold terms. Rice's presentation, while still vague about the specifics, sent shock waves through the Indian government. She took Indian officials into her confidence and disclosed the pending F-16 sale to

Pakistan—adding that India could also buy advanced weapons. She also told Prime Minister Manmohan Singh that Bush had decided to go beyond the NSSP and explore cooperation on civil nuclear energy. She suggested that the United States would accommodate India as a great power—in contrast to the usual approach (from the Indian perspective) of restraining India. Few Indian officials had expected such an expansive presentation from the novice secretary of state.[17]

From the Indian perspective, the partnership Rice suggested offered a way to finally remove the nuclear impediment to closer ties with the United States. "If you are going to be looking at India as a partner, then you have to treat India as a partner and not as a target," Foreign Secretary Shyam Saran recalled. "Both these things cannot be done together."[18]

At the end of the trip, as Rice was flying back to Washington from Beijing, she called Zelikow into her cabin on the Boeing 757 jet. She was struck by her impressions of the stop in India—the spirit of the Indian officials, their sense of their goals and the future of India, the incredible dynamism and economic potential of the country. She was also taken with their insatiable need for energy. Bottom line, she liked working with the Indians. She began to dictate the outlines of a South Asian strategy to Zelikow, which formed the basis for a six-page, single-spaced memo that Rice sent to Bush a few weeks later.

The memo proposed that the administration end the incremental approach on nuclear issues with India, and simply go for broke and cut a broad deal. The incremental approach would require congressional approval eventually, and might be just as difficult to achieve as the "Big Bang," as one of Rice's aides ironically dubbed the idea. While nuclear orthodoxy would be swept away, the broader strategic goal was simple: position India to become one of the United States' two or three closest partners.

The memo also laid out a strategy for dealing with other parts of the region, including recommending a reorganization of the Soviet Asia bureau to include Central Asia countries that had once been part of the Soviet Union (and thus were still part of the European bureau). The memo outlined ways to make sure that Pakistan held real elections in 2007 and did not end up with another failed democracy. (During her stop in Pakistan, Rice repeatedly side-stepped questions about whether she had pressed Musharraf, who had taken power in 1999 in a bloodless coup, on when he would give up his army uniform.) The memo noted that if the administration wanted to have leverage with India by 2007 on such issues as the border dispute with Pakistan in Kashmir—in order to encourage the democratic process in Pakistan—then the time to build relations with India was now. While some supporters of a deal viewed a more powerful India as a counterweight to China, the memo did not explicitly make that case, except that it suggested that the influence of India and its democratic values could spread toward East Asia.[19]

The memo did not offer any other options for a broader relationship with India short of cutting a deal on the nuclear issue. Rice wasn't interested in halfway steps. She thought the nuclear issue was weighing down the relationship with India—and so in her mind it was simply the right thing to do.[20]

"You and I Need to Talk Civilian Nukes"

Ten days after Rice went to Delhi, the White House announced the sale of F-16s to Pakistan. Bush called Prime Minister Singh and urged him not to make too big a deal out of the announcement, that India had the potential of gaining much more out of the new partnership. Singh got the message: The Indian government's reaction to the sale was surprisingly muted.

At the State Department, Zelikow, White House Asia Advisor Michael J. Green, and Assistant Secretary of State Christina Rocca held a background briefing for reporters on the new strategy for South Asia. Zelikow, identified in the transcript as "administration official number one," gave a presentation that roughly mirrored the memo he had drafted for Rice, surprising Green and Rocca because his remarks far exceeded the talking points that had been prepared for the session.[21] But as time passed, it was clear his bolder pronouncement reflected the administration's emerging position.

Only a few days before Rice had spoken publicly of looking forward to completing the NSSP, but it was suddenly being viewed as inadequate. "The president and the secretary developed the outline for a decisively broader strategic relationship" with India, Zelikow announced. "Secretary Rice presented that outline last week to Prime Minister Singh. Its goal is to help India become a major world power in the twenty-first century. We understand fully the implications, including military implications, of that statement."[22]

Rice had invited Singh to come to Washington in July for a meeting with Bush. Now she decided the administration should try to cut a deal in time for that session—an idea that met with opposition within the government. Opponents hoped to slow down the initiative as a way of killing it. She believed that it could only succeed if it was placed on a fast track.

Behind the scenes, Bush was an enthusiastic backer of Rice's plans. In mid-April, Foreign Minister Singh visited Washington and met with Bush and Rice. The president spoke of making India a global power and the challenge it faced in the energy field. He also went beyond using vague generalities about nuclear energy cooperation and actually raised with Singh the idea of selling nuclear reactors to India.[23]

Despite the president's interest, bureaucratic obstacles remained. At this critical junction, Rice created her own luck. A week before leaving for India, she had nominated one of the leading skeptics of a nuclear deal with India—John R. Bolton, the undersecretary of state for arms control—to be UN ambassador. That took the legendary bureaucratic infighter out of the picture. (Even before the announcement, Bolton had felt marginalized on India discussions, as Zelikow sent out cables without seeking clearance from Bolton.)[24] The long battle over his appointment delayed confirmation of his replacement, NSC proliferation expert Robert Joseph, until May 26. Other key posts in the nonproliferation ranks were unfilled, leaving officials in that area thinking they had no voice in the debate. Joseph then oversaw a botched merger of the arms control and nonproliferation bureaus, leading to an exodus of top officials.[25]

The Pentagon was a traditional ally of the nonproliferation hawks on such issues as Iran and North Korea. But, in this case, Pentagon officials fully backed closer relations with India, in part because of the potential for military cooperation and also because they viewed a stronger India as a strategically important counterweight to China.

Hadley was more receptive to the concerns of nonproliferation specialists, so while he supported the general idea of stronger ties with India, he was less certain about how and when the administration should make its move. His staff also was divided, though on balance they were against Rice's approach. Joseph, when he came on board on June 1, also wasn't happy about a fast-track process, but by then it was getting late in the game. Rice had already assigned the undersecretary for political affairs, Nick Burns, to begin negotiations with India, working mainly with his counterpart, Foreign Secretary Saran. The concerns of government nonproliferation experts were represented by Joseph, working with John D. Rood, his successor and counterpart at the National Security Council.

Career professionals at the State Department, feeling increasingly cut out of the process, sought to structure an agreement that would not completely undercut long-held U.S. nonproliferation doctrine. One key goal, they thought, was to convince India to agree to limit production of plutonium to a level that ensured the minimal deterrent capability it sought. They also wanted India to place all of its electricity-producing reactors under permanent safeguards to be monitored by UN inspectors. Such an arrangement would ensure, in accordance with U.S. law, that any American technology going to India would not be used for its weapons program. Moreover, they thought that without a limit on fissile-material production, the deal could allow India to make many more weapons than it needed. Some skeptics in the administration were also concerned about rewarding a country that had built nuclear weapons in secret, much like North Korea and Iran. They argued that the deal would hurt U.S. efforts to pressure those countries on their programs.[26]

But during talks in June, Saran and other Indian officials made it clear to Burns that they were not interested in outside influence over India's nuclear weapons program. And time was running short for an agreement: Singh was due to arrive at the White House on July 18. Under Rice's game plan, sketched in May, the deal would be reached at that summit meeting—and then the details of implementation would be achieved in time for Bush's planned visit to India in early 2006.

Rice's timetable was news to the Indians, few of whom expected a breakthrough during the Bush-Singh meeting in July; in fact, Singh had promised the left-wing parties in his coalition he would not cut a deal. The Indians, in fact, seemed more focused on getting fuel supply for U.S.-built reactors at Tarapur, not the kind of broad-based nuclear cooperation Rice was seeking.[27] But Bush, under Rice's influence, already had reached the conclusion that the nuclear concerns carried less weight than the enormous benefits that a broad partnership with a large and friendly democracy could bring.

During a ceremony at the end of May in Moscow to mark the sixtieth anniversary of the end of World War II, Bush introduced Prime Minister Singh to Laura Bush and quickly launched into a minitutorial about India's growth and energy needs, as well as its diverse citizenry, which includes the world's second-largest Muslim population. "You and I need to talk civilian nukes," Bush told Singh.[28]

Burns called Saran and suggested he come a few days early, ahead of Singh's trip, so they could try to reach an agreement. Saran arrived on Friday, July 15, and intensive negotiations were held during the weekend. Joseph, however, did not participate in those talks. Instead, he went first to Vienna to brief the International Atomic Energy Agency (IAEA) on Iran's nuclear program, and then to Libya. Joseph stayed in touch with Washington by phone, but his absence left the relatively young Rood as the lone nonproliferation voice on a negotiating team stacked with officials determined to clinch a deal.

"We're Not Going to Give Up"

From the start, the negotiations were tense as it became clear that the U.S. goals were not what India was hoping to hear. One by one, Indian negotiators balked at requests, indicating they would walk away before accepting conditions for inspections and other safeguards.

Burns and Saran negotiated for nearly three straight days. Then Rice went to Foreign Minister Singh's suite in the Willard Hotel on Sunday, July 17, to provide a final push. At 6 P.M., after an hour and half of bargaining, she and Burns thought they had an agreement, and so went off to dinner. But then Saran called Burns at 9:30 P.M., saying the deal was off—it was too much politically for the Indian government to swallow all at once. Burns called Rice and told her the agreement had collapsed. Rice went to bed, thinking the two sides would have to issue a statement saying they would continue to work on an agreement.

When Rice woke up the next morning, she decided it would be a mistake to miss this moment. It would only get harder to reach a deal. She called Burns at 5 A.M. "We're not going to give up," she told him. "I think we ought to make one more run at this."

Prime Minister Singh was due to meet with Bush that day. At 8 A.M., Rice rushed over the Blair House, where the prime minister was staying, and persuaded him to let the negotiators try again.[29] India stood to gain the most from a deal on nuclear cooperation, but at every turn it was the United States that appeared to push hardest for an agreement.

Thus, before Bush and Singh met one-on-one in the Oval Office, their closest aides, including Rice, Hadley, Burns, and Rood, were closeted in the Roosevelt Room furiously scribbling out the text of a deal in a frenzied two-hour stretch. Just as the two leaders were due to meet, a proposed text was delivered. When they emerged an hour and a half later, only one word had not been decided.

In essence, India wanted the coveted status of an official nuclear state, a recognition that would get it into the most exclusive club in the world. Under the Non-Proliferation Treaty, only the United States, Russia, China, France, and Britain are weapons states. All other countries, except for Pakistan, India, and Israel, signed on to the agreement, promising to forgo nuclear weapons in exchange for civilian nuclear technology. Now India wanted the technology, wanted to remain outside the treaty, and wanted membership in the club. The final text fudged the issue. The agreement at one point hung on a single phrase—whether to use the word "voluntary" or "voluntarily" and where to place it—which the U.S. side worried could give India a way to avoid international inspections of its civil facilities.[30] That issue took nearly an hour to resolve, with Rice and Prime Minister Singh finally settling it during lunch at the State Department.

With the details still being haggled, the news conference that Bush and Singh held at noon gave little hint of the announcement that would come later in the day, shocking nuclear specialists in both countries. The final text, which was reached at 1 P.M., was so closely held before being released to the media that lower-level Indian officials from the Atomic Energy Commission chased after White House staffer Michael Green in the White House complex to see it. Reporters noticed that the nuclear section of the agreement was squeezed into the joint statement in single-space format, suggesting it had been a last-minute addition.

That night, Bush toasted Singh at an elaborate dinner in the White House State Dining Room that featured elephant-shaped flower arrangements. "India and the United States are separated by half the globe," Bush declared. "Yet to-day our two nations are closer than ever before."[31]

The Indians viewed Rice as the linchpin of the deal. Rice's "tremendous ef-fort and amount of energy" was critical to reaching an agreement, Saran said. Rice and her team "had a very clear picture in their mind about where they wanted to go, and they made every effort possible to get there."[32]

Rice had achieved a significant victory, but the rushed conclusion of the July agreement also began to undermine it. Lawmakers in Congress were stunned. There had been little or no consultation with key members on any as-pect of the deal before it was announced—and, in fact, in a written statement Rice had assured Congress during her confirmation process six months earlier that no plans for India would require changes to U.S. law. Rice's desire for se-crecy had outweighed any interest in informing Congress, even though lower-level State Department officials had warned that it was essential to bring Congress on board before an agreement was reached. A midlevel nonprolifera-tion civil servant had written a memo early in 2005 warning about the legal ob-stacles and bluntly saying that Congress would cause problems unless its prerogatives were respected.[33]

Rice saw the memo but did not heed its warnings because she was reluctant to provide briefings on a deal that had not yet been concluded. In retrospect, Rice realized the failure to keep Congress in the loop might have been a costly mistake.[34]

As secretary, Rice heavily promoted the idea of "transformational diplo-macy," which meant reshaping the State Department for the modern era, in-cluding shifting resources from Europe to hot spots in the Middle East and Africa. But among the career professionals the term became the subject of deri-sion as they felt increasingly out of the loop on issues such as the unexpected deal with India. "Transformational diplomacy means you don't have to listen to contrary ideas," said one bitter State Department official who had spent years trying to prevent the spread of nuclear weapons.[35]

"These Are Big and Important Issues"

With Congress pressing for more answers, Indian and American negotiators also began a months-long debate between the two countries about what the words in the agreement actually meant. The frantic last-minute negotiations had papered over many disagreements on the meaning of such words as "voluntary," "separation," and even "agrees," leading to protracted negotiations.

The agreement was also controversial in India, where close association with the United States is viewed with suspicion. "I would say it is not only an act of statesmanship but an act of faith," said Sen, the Indian ambassador. "Both our countries were departing from something which has been well engrained in the mind-sets of most of our people. We knew there was going to be significant opposition to change. Change is always viewed with suspicion and often viewed as subversive."[36]

The key to the agreement was India separating its nuclear facilities, including twenty-two nuclear power plants either in operation or under construction as well as a number of research reactors and breeder reactors, from the fuel cycle facilities associated with all of these reactors. India had agreed to make such a separation "in a phased manner," and to "voluntarily" place the civilian plants under "safeguards"—inspection and other verification measures—by the International Atomic Energy Agency. India, which has a broad definition of its "strategic program," claimed it would be a costly undertaking because its nuclear complex is so intertwined, with plants producing electricity also aiding the strategic program.

In September, the United States, via the U.S. embassy, submitted to India what diplomats call a "nonpaper"—an unofficial communication—which shared with Indian officials a U.S. proposal that India place all its existing and future nuclear power plants on the civilian side of the ledger. The document was intended to show the Indian government some of the internal U.S. discussion, but the Indian government rejected it, saying the discussion of separation was up to India, not the United States.[37]

Under the NPT, the United States was obligated as a nuclear-weapon state never to aid a state like India with its nuclear weapons program. Bush administration officials assured Congress that India would present a separation plan that was "credible" and "defensible" from a nonproliferation standpoint.

Six Indian plants—two of which are under construction—are already under international "safeguards" to verify that nuclear material is not diverted for weapons. Indian officials suspected the United States really wanted a total of sixteen to eighteen plants under safeguards, though Burns in his discussions with Saran avoided a specific number, simply suggesting "a majority" of nuclear plants. In December, India offered to add four plants to the list, for a total of ten, but that was not enough for the Americans.

The Indians countered with twelve plants, and then finally offered fourteen plants. While fourteen out of twenty-two is almost two-thirds, in reality it meant that India was only adding half (eight plants) of those not already under safeguards—and some U.S. officials suspected that India would only name plants that were still under construction. That meant that India's indigenous reactors that are supplying electricity could now openly be used for producing the material for nuclear weapons. But U.S. officials made the calculation that what was most important was that India not use any of the new nuclear fuel, facilities, and technologies it would acquire to assist in its weapons programs.

In February 2006, the administration held what is known as a deputies committee meeting—one level below cabinet head—to review the status of the talks. At that meeting, officials decided that the key issue was not the number of nuclear plants under safeguards but whether safeguards would remain "in perpetuity" once imposed.

This was a bitter pill for the Indians, who were concerned about making a permanent commitment to inspection without a permanent commitment by the United States to supply fuel to those plants. The five original nuclear-weapon states—the United States, Russia, China, France, and Britain—are able to add or remove plants from safeguards at will. The issue regarding "voluntarily" had turned on this same issue: The Bush administration was willing to bend a lot for India, but it did not want to officially give India the same status as a nuclear-weapon state.[38]

Yet, in a speech to Parliament, Singh laid down a tough negotiating stance and essentially said this is how he interpreted the agreement. "A change is now discernible in the international system," he said. "The understandings reflected in the Joint Statement will give India its due place in the global nuclear order. The existence of our strategic program is being acknowledged even while we are being invited to become a full partner in international civil nuclear energy cooperation."[39]

In March 2006, as Bush flew to Delhi for his meeting with Singh, Rice, in an interview with reporters on Air Force One, consciously signaled that Bush wanted to be sure that the safeguards on nuclear plants would remain permanent. Bush had told aides that if they could not get permanent safeguards, there would be no deal. "These are big and important issues," Rice said. "And the one thing that is absolutely necessary is that any agreement would assure that once India has decided to put reactors under safeguards, it remains permanently under safe-guards."[40]

Before Bush arrived in India, Singh had little support in his cabinet for reaching a final accord on implementing the agreement. But when Bush landed, he took Singh aside on the airport tarmac and told him he was eager to strike an agreement.[41] The negotiating came down to the last hour, but an imple-mentation deal was finally reached.

Nuclear specialists in the U.S. government complained that their concerns once again were overridden in the final negotiating rounds. The implementa-tion plan specified that fourteen of India's twenty-two nuclear plants would be subject to international inspections. But the country's eight other reactors, and any future ones for military purposes, would be off-limits—and these were the reactors most likely to produce nuclear weapons material. And although the Bush administration originally wanted a pact that would let India continue producing material for six to ten weapons each year, the plan in theory would allow it enough fissile material for as many as fifty bombs annually, though such an increase is currently constrained by the operating level of India's few uranium mines. Some outside experts predicted the agreement would unleash a dangerous arms race between China and India. Moreover, while India commit-ted to continue its moratorium on nuclear weapons testing, it did not agree to sign the Comprehensive Test Ban Treaty.

Burns, as the chief negotiator, was defensive about the criticism. He felt he had listened to the nonproliferation experts inside the administration—and be-lieved he had gotten a good deal. The focus on the number of nuclear plants was misplaced because as more civilian plants were built, they would be covered by the agreement. He also belittled the idea that India would use the agreement to build up its nuclear weapons stockpile. India, with 300 million people in the middle class and 700 million in poverty, was desperate for energy and thus had little motivation to expand its small deterrent force. But he also privately con-ceded that opponents had one pretty good argument—the deal would compli-cate the administration's efforts to prop up the nonproliferation treaty.[42]

Some critics suggested that if the administration had not been in such a rush, it could have achieved a much better result. India, for instance, was facing a uranium shortage at the time of the talks, so if the administration had held back, India might have been forced to make bigger concessions simply to ob-tain the uranium. But once the United States struck its agreement, Russia rushed in with a uranium sale, and that moment of leverage was lost.

By moving as fast as she did, Rice changed the dynamics. Congress could no longer entertain the question of whether the United States should abandon its previous policy. Instead, lawmakers were forced to consider whether rejecting the agreement—or even trying to modify it—would set back closer ties between the United States and India for years. Ironically, the squeeze play was never on India; it was always on the State Department bureaucracy and Congress.[43] Rice's penchant for strategy, secrecy, and surprise had allowed her to achieve a breakthrough that had eluded other policy makers for years, but at great cost to her relations with Congress and with unknown and potentially serious consequences for the ability of the United States to discourage the spread of nuclear weapons.

CHAPTER 3

SHOWDOWN NEAR SEOUL

Command Post Tango, the nerve center for a possible war between the United States and North Korea, is located deep inside a small mountain. No secretary of state had ever visited the top-secret facility, let alone reporters. Yet, on her first official visit to South Korea, Rice and her entourage boarded Black Hawk helicopters immediately after landing in Seoul and flew to the underground bunker—just as twenty thousand U.S. and South Korean troops were conducting semi-annual war games.

When reporters got off the helicopters and walked up to the entrance, carved into the side of the mountain, some felt they were walking onto the set of a James Bond movie. Inside, the bunker—reinforced with concrete shielding— had the utilitarian feel of many military installations. The reporters were kept outside the war room, sitting in a steel gray stairwell, while Rice received a classified briefing on the war games. The room, with about one hundred soldiers sitting at desks with computer terminals, was dominated by a twenty-foot-high computer-driven video display dubbed the "knowledge wall," featuring maps, satellite photos, and troop formations. The scenario is always the same: North Korea suddenly attacks South Korea, and U.S. and South Korean troops defeat it.[1]

After reporters entered the war room, Rice spoke to the troops, thanking them for being on what she called the "front lines of freedom."

"I know that you face a close-in threat every day," Rice said. "I know that you face also the fact that the Republic of Korea, a great democracy now, faces the threat across the divide of a state that is not democratic, that is not free, and that does not have the best interests of its people at heart."[2]

Just hours before, Rice had sent an entirely different message to the reclusive government in Pyongyang. "No one denies that North Korea is a sovereign state," Rice said in a major speech on Asia policy that she gave at Sophia University in Tokyo. "We have said repeatedly that we have no intention of attacking or invading North Korea."[3]

American reporters missed the importance entirely, but Korean reporters had jumped on the story—the recognition of North Korea as a "sovereign state" was a major diplomatic concession intended to lure the prickly government back to six-nation nuclear disarmament talks that it had boycotted for nearly a year.

Rice's mixed signals were typical of the administration's often schizophrenic approach to one of the most dangerous issues it faced: North Korea's nuclear-weapons programs. This was yet another problem that Rice had let fester during the Bush administration's first term, allowing the policy to meander while conservatives who wanted to topple the North Korean dictatorship and regional specialists who wanted to negotiate a solution constantly undercut each other. The administration's policy was a muddled mess, with each side in the policy battle convinced Bush secretly backed them.

As secretary, Rice had already made the diplomatic impasse worse with a rookie misstep during her confirmation hearings, when she referred to North Korea as an "outpost of tyranny" just as North Korea was looking for a signal of respect. Using the word "sovereign" was an attempt to find a way out of the diplomatic box.

The trip to Command Post Tango had been controversial among Rice's aides. It had come about because Rice had wanted to meet with troops who had served in Iraq. General Leon J. LaPorte, commander of U.S. forces on the Korean peninsula, had suggested meeting troops actually doing their job in the region because Rice's schedule happened to bring her to the country in the middle of a war game. Phil Zelikow thought the visit would help balance the "sovereign" statement, but Michael J. Green, the National Security Council staffer for Asia, was against it, thinking it would be too provocative. Christopher R. Hill, the U.S. ambassador to South Korea who had just been confirmed as assistant secretary of state for East Asia, thought it would not be a problem. Rice's team argued the pros and cons but Jim Wilkinson loved the imagery of going into the bunker. That cinched it.[4] Wilkinson would later brag to reporters that it was quite a coup to get permission to bring them inside the top-secret facility.

The Odd Man Out

North Korea's pursuit of nuclear weapons is one of most difficult foreign policy challenges of our era, but there is little doubt that the Bush administration's failure in the first term to produce a coherent policy made the problem much worse. Under Bush's watch, North Korea's nuclear program, once estimated by the CIA to have produced enough material for perhaps one or two nuclear devices, had broken free. North Korea now has enough material for perhaps ten bombs—and the weapons-grade plutonium it possesses increases by about a bomb a year. Having collected that pile of plutonium, North Korea in 2006 then took the alarming step of conducting its first nuclear test.

The Clinton administration reached an understanding in 1994 freezing North Korea's nuclear facility in Yongbyon, launching a process that was supposed to lead to the facility's dismantlement. Conservatives had long been skeptical of the deal, known as the Agreed Framework, in part because it called for building two light-water nuclear reactors (largely funded by the Japanese and South Koreans). Some Clinton advisors thought when they made the deal that the North Korean regime would collapse before that commitment needed to be fulfilled, but that turned out to be a bad bet. By the 2000 election, Clinton's policy had moved on to the point that many of his advisors thought North Korea appeared on the verge of a major breakthrough in relations with its longtime antagonist—and Clinton seriously considered making the first presidential visit to Pyongyang in the waning days of his presidency. But when Bush became president, his top foreign policy advisors still believed the 1994 agreement had been a mistake.

Only days after the disputed 2000 election was decided, Powell had invited a group of Clinton State Department officials to his home in McLean to brief Rice and him on the status of talks with North Korea. Powell brought them into his dining room—and, because Rice was running late, met privately with them for nearly an hour. The officials left with the sense that Powell was impressed with the progress, but they could get no reading of Rice's feelings.[5]

Powell, as usual, was the odd man out. Bush clearly sided with his more hawkish advisors on North Korea, even publicly humiliating Powell when he suggested the new administration would pick up where Clinton left off. In private meetings with his aides, Bush focused on the horrific human rights situation in North Korea and chafed at efforts to make his language about the Pyongyang government more diplomatic.[6] Powell was further surprised when, during the 2002 State of the Union address, Bush labeled North Korea part of an "axis of evil" that included Iran and Iraq.[7] Some of Bush's advisors secretly searched for ways to kill the Agreed Framework, since soon the concrete for the reactors would be poured and in a couple of years the key nuclear components inside would be delivered.[8]

A year and a half after Bush took office, the administration still had not arranged its first meeting with the North Koreans. U.S. officials had finally reached consensus that representatives of the two countries should meet when, in July 2002, U.S. intelligence analysts concluded that the North Korean government had a clandestine program to enrich uranium. Clinton administration officials had seen signs of such a program, but had decided to watch and wait, believing it would be better to improve relations and then handle the matter quietly, when they thought North Korea would believe it had more to lose from a confrontation.

The hard-liners in the Bush administration now had their opportunity and pushed for a simple declaration that the Agreed Framework was dead. (There are some signs that the intelligence finding was hyped—particularly the prediction that Pyongyang would have an operating uranium-enrichment facility within two years. In 2007, the administration began to retreat from its earlier claims.)

In October 2002, Assistant Secretary of State James Kelly was dispatched to confront the North Koreans about the evidence of the secret program, at a meeting that the North Koreans thought was intended to launch a wide-ranging discussion of a new relationship with the United States. U.S. officials assumed North Korea would deny the program and then the administration would have an excuse not to pursue serious discussions with Pyongyang. But after Kelly accused the North Koreans of violating the Agreed Framework, they unexpectedly appeared to confirm it, handing the administration a new crisis just as the White House was preoccupied with its plans for an invasion of Iraq.

Because of divisions within the administration over the next steps—and the distraction over the impending Iraq War—the White House handled its response poorly. A little diplomacy might have averted a complete break with North Korea, but instead the two sides quickly escalated the confrontation. The administration pressed to cut off fuel oil deliveries that had been promised under the 1994 agreement—the one tangible benefit that North Korea had regularly received from the deal. Indeed, under the agreement, North Korea's freeze of its plutonium reactor was directly linked to the deliveries of heavy fuel oil.

By December, North Korea had kicked out international inspectors, disabled inspection equipment, and restarted the nuclear facility. Within months, the North Koreans took spent fuel rods—which, under the 1994 agreement, had been under constant surveillance in a cooling pond—and began repro-cessing them into weapons-grade plutonium. (Plutonium is a different route to making a weapon than highly enriched uranium.) Meanwhile, the Bush ad-ministration, hampered by internal disputes, struggled to fashion a diplomatic effort to confront North Korea. Some top officials were dazzled by a CIA report from a single defector that North Korean leader Kim Jong Il's grip on power was increasingly fragile. The report was later withdrawn as unreliable.

The shadow of Clinton's efforts hung heavily over everything. Clinton's team had held extensive bilateral negotiations, so that was unacceptable. Bush, with Rice's prodding, settled on multilateral talks involving other countries in the region. Bush especially wanted China at the table, so Powell arranged for a three-way meeting.

"The Failure of Condi Rice"

The three-nation talks, held in Beijing in April 2003, were a disaster. Before Kelly left Washington, he had tried to secure permission to talk directly to the North Korean delegation, but his efforts resulted in strict orders from Rice that he could not engage in bilateral talks. But some State Department officials had previously dropped hints to the Chinese that once the North Koreans showed up, the Chinese could leave the room and bilateral talks could commence. Af-ter an opening session with all three parties, the North Koreans refused to at-tend any more meetings until they were granted a private audience. Kelly sent Powell an e-mail pleading for a bilateral meeting—and the Chinese ambassador made a personal appeal to Rice—but the White House held firm. Even Powell felt Kelly's request went too far. In a brief encounter with Kelly, however, a North Korean official declared that North Korea already had a nuclear weapon and might test it.[9]

Some members of the U.S. delegation were furious when they discovered that shortly before the talks North Korean diplomats in New York had in-formed two State Department officials that they had begun reprocessing the fuel rods. The officials had immediately informed Kelly about the disclosure, but Powell and his deputy, Richard Armitage, decided to keep the information secret from others in the government.[10] When North Korea appeared to restate this claim in a radio broadcast just before the talks were to begin, the State De-partment claimed it was a faulty translation.

The reason for this deception is clear: Under the delegation's instructions, the talks were supposed to cease immediately if North Korea admitted to repro-cessing the rods, so they likely would have never taken place if hawkish officials realized North Korea had already admitted it had begun to transform the rods into nuclear-weapons fuel. After that, Powell's State Department, especially the East Asia bureau, was kept on a very tight leash. Even at talks with the Japanese and South Koreans, Kelly, who had a plodding demeanor, was frequently required to read from a script that had been vetted by Rice's National Security Council staff.

Bush's refusal to let his negotiators sit down with the North Koreans one-on-one would make the diplomacy much harder. The East Asia bureau constantly pressed for it, believing it was the only way to resolve the dispute. Other nations in the region frequently met bilaterally with the North Koreans. But Rice and Bush were convinced that if the United States permitted bilateral negotiations, once again the problem would be viewed as a U.S.– North Korea dispute, not a matter of regional concern.

The crisis thus went into a slow stall as North Korea merrily built up its nuclear arsenal with material from the plutonium reactor—and U.S. officials refused to discuss any deal unless Pyongyang first admitted to the alleged uranium program. The next round of disarmament talks, in August 2003, was expanded to include Japan, South Korea, and Russia. But the bar on bilateral contacts was maintained, except for a brief meeting in the corner of the room; Kelly batted away any questions from the North Koreans by telling them to reread the statement he made at the plenary session. During the second meeting of the six nations, in February 2004, Bush, influenced by Cheney, very nearly pulled the plug on the whole process.[11]

Only in June 2004, under pressure from Japan, its closest ally on the issue, did the Bush administration produce the barest outline of an idea to resolve the impasse. Under the proposal, the United States said it would give North Korea no rewards until it fully disclosed its nuclear programs and allowed independent verification of its report within three months. The administration's offer only vaguely hinted at what might follow if North Korea was cooperative—and included no penalties for failing to negotiate seriously. It was a flimsy attempt at an opening bid, disappointing allies who felt the North Koreans would only give up their weapons with tangible up-front assurances of economic and energy aid. Diplomats noted that only two of the delegations were so powerless that they had to constantly wait for instructions from their capitals during the talks—the United States and North Korea.

The impasse over North Korean policy within the administration was deeply frustrating to all players in the debate. They blamed the same person: Rice. Asked in late 2003 what the history of the administration's North Korea policy should be called, a hawkish administration official quickly answered: "The failure of Condi Rice." His stark assessment was shared by administration officials on all sides of the North Korean debate. Officials believed that Rice, as national security advisor, failed to push the administration to settle on a coherent policy, and then was unable to ensure that decisions, once made, were actually carried out.[12] This was true on a number of issues, but it seemed particularly acute on North Korea. Part of the problem is that there were actually two separate policy-making tracks on North Korean nukes, one headed by Kelly at the State Department and one headed by Robert Joseph, the nonproliferation chief at the NSC. Officials from one camp rarely attended meetings run by the other camp—and Rice never fused the two approaches into a coherent policy.

"Outposts of Tyranny"

By the time Rice became secretary of state, the dispute over North Korea's nuclear program had lasted more than two years, and yet there had been only four meetings to settle it that included both North Koreans and the United States at the table. The six-party talks were so cumbersome and slow, hampered by the need to translate so many languages, that they rarely progressed beyond prearranged talking points. The 1994 deal was reached only after dozens of bilateral meetings between U.S. and North Korean diplomats. The Bush administration supposedly was looking for more than another Band-Aid fix. But it supported a process that was designed to fail.

North Korea, which had never officially responded to the U.S. proposal, rooted for John Kerry to win the 2004 presidential election because Kerry had said he would immediately begin bilateral negotiations with Pyongyang. In discussions with U.S. officials, North Korean officials would urge them to consider Kerry's "wise counsel." KCNA, the propaganda news service of North Korea, would frequently praise Kerry's call for direct dialogue. After the June 2004 meeting, and during the final stretch of the presidential campaign, North Korea hedged its bets and hoped for Bush's defeat, refusing to return to another round of talks.

Once Bush was reelected, however, the North Korean government told visitors that it was looking for signs that in the second term Bush would end his "hostile policy," citing the tone of the State of the Union address as especially important (perhaps because Bush first referred to the "axis of evil" in the 2002 State of the Union). The White House got the message and the president was uncharactistically restrained in his remarks about North Korea.

But North Korea, ever eager to perceive a slight, instead focused on a throwaway line in Rice's confirmation hearings. In her opening statement, Rice had listed six countries as "outposts of tyranny:" Belarus, Burma, Cuba, Iran, North Korea, and Zimbabwe. It was a silly expression, barely noticed by the media, and she never again repeated it. But a few days later, in his inaugural speech, Bush declared he would push to eliminate tyranny around the world. The North Koreans linked the two statements and decided the administration was committed to toppling the regime. On February 10, just days after Rice became secretary, North Korea announced it was a nuclear power and would permanently withdraw from the six-nation talks. The North Korean statement referred repeatedly to Rice's "outpost of tyranny" remark, demanding an apology before it would ever consider returning to the talks.

If the North Koreans had focused less on Rice's statements and more on her personnel choices, they would have realized that she was interested in resolving the standoff. In December, she had selected Chris Hill to replace Kelly as assistant secretary and chief negotiator at the six-party talks. Hill, who has a dry wit and an easy manner, is a career foreign service officer with a reputation for making deals—and sometimes stretching his instructions in order to get them. If Kerry had won and former UN ambassador Richard Holbrooke had become secretary of state, he probably would have selected Hill for the same job. Holbrooke, a master at dealing with reporters, had been Hill's patron and tutor. Hill had learned Holbrooke's lessons well: Unlike Kelly, who fled from dealing with reporters, Hill loved to talk to the media. (Holbrooke also felt it was necessary to sometimes liberally interpret his instructions.)

During the Clinton administration, Hill was a key negotiator in the Dayton Peace Accords that ended the Bosnian war, and he played an important role in the crisis over Kosovo. He was ambassador to Macedonia when protestors attacked the U.S. embassy in 1999 over NATO air strikes in Yugoslavia. He came to President Bush's attention when the president of Poland lavishly praised Hill's performance as ambassador there and requested that Hill stay on. Hill later lobbied to become ambassador to South Korea, though he only served eight months before Rice plucked him for the assistant secretary job.

In Seoul, Hill had charmed the South Korean public by repeatedly visiting universities and other hotbeds of anti-Americanism to give speeches and have debates. He established a cyber chatroom and personally answered questions from Koreans under the name "Ambassador." He caused a stir by paying respects at a memorial for thousands of civilians who were fired upon by the then military government in a 1980 massacre. Many Koreans suspected that the U.S. government had backed the attack, and no senior U.S. official had ever before visited the cemetery in Gwangju.

Though Hill had no experience negotiating with the North Koreans he was the epitome of a creative diplomat, someone willing to take chances and push the envelope. Rice knew what she was getting when she hired Hill. His selection excited Korean specialists, who had despaired of the administration ever getting serious about resolving the dispute with Pyongyang.

Hill found out he was being considered for the job when, in December 2004, he was on a regular ambassadorial visit to Washington and scheduled a meeting with the incoming national security advisor, Steve Hadley. He wanted to tell Hadley that the administration needed to get a deal with North Korea, and the way to do it was to show more flexibility in the diplomacy.

Hill was surprised when Rice joined the meeting and began to ask broader questions about Asia policy. She used a football metaphor, saying that in the National Football League they draft athletes, not positions—meaning the administration needed its best diplomats for the second term after fighting two wars during its first four years. It became clear she was thinking of offering him the job. Hill later sent her a memo suggesting that the administration put together an overall package of incentives and then sell it to the Chinese, who in turn would sell it to North Korea—just as he had used Serbian leader Slobodan Milosevic to sell ideas to the Bosnian Serbs during the Dayton talks.[13]

"We'll Get Killed"

North Korea's announcement that it was leaving the talks upended those plans. Instead, Rice and Hill had to figure out ways to get North Korea back to the negotiating table. China, which provides much of North Korea's energy and food and had boosted trade with Pyongyang by 20 percent from 2004 to 2005, was a source of continuing frustration. The Chinese had been the host of the six-party talks but to U.S. officials it was clear China viewed itself merely as a facilitator.

While China supported the goal of preventing North Korea from having nuclear weapons, it valued North Korea as a buffer state that prevented U.S. forces from being on its border. China also prized stability, not conflict. The Chinese appeared to have joined the talks in part because they feared the Bush administration, left to its own instincts, would blunder into a war. But, bottom line, China wanted the United States to resolve the problem itself. During the six-party talks, Chinese officials would frequently display a schoolmarm's attitude, lecturing the Americans to be more flexible.

In March 2005, after her visit to the bunker in the mountain and discussions with South Korean officials in Seoul, Rice flew to Beijing, where she held extensive talks on how to get North Korea back to the negotiating table. Publicly, she raised the idea of imposing economic or political penalties against North Korea, what she called "other options in the international system."[14] But it was an empty threat. Neither the Chinese nor the South Koreans would accept such a solution. Increasingly, it was the United States, not North Korea, that seemed isolated.

The Chinese indicated they were not even willing to increase pressure on North Korea. (In the past, they had lured the North Koreans back to the talks with monetary rewards.) Chinese officials expressed some sympathy for North Korea's concern over the "outpost of tyranny" remark, suggesting that a pullback of that statement would set a positive tone for the talks. They also proposed that the United States make concessions in its June 2004 offer, such as joining Japan and South Korea in offering fuel oil as soon as North Korea agreed to give up its weapons. None of these suggestions were acceptable to the Americans.[15]

On one visit to Beijing, Hill tried a different tack, asking Chinese officials to consider a "technical" interruption of North Korea's supply of oil as a way of pressuring the government to return to disarmament talks. (North Korea imports all the oil it consumes.) But the Chinese rejected the idea, offering the lame excuse that stopping the oil flow would damage their pipeline. When Hill's discussion with the Chinese became public, the Chinese were furious, believing incorrectly that he had purposely leaked the story.[16]

Hill, ever the negotiator, just wanted to get into the game. He had dealt with the Bosnian Serbs, and he thought the North Koreans were chumps, no match for the Serbs. (Hill's staff eventually began to roll their eyes at his constant references to his Yugoslavian triumph.) During the March trip to Asia, he told Michael Green that bilateral talks with North Korea were necessary but Green warned him that Rice wasn't prepared to take that step. Nonetheless, Hill floated the idea of holding bilateral talks with the North Koreans in a conversation with Rice and some aides. Rice hesitated.

"You can't do that," Wilkinson blurted out. "We'll get killed."

Rice looked at Hill and said, "Maybe you'll get your chance to go to Pyongyang, Chris, but they have to earn it."[17]

Rice understood that bilateral negotiations would be a big prize for the North Koreans, but wanted to know the quid pro quo before she would agree to it. In any case, she was willing to let Hill meet with the North Koreans bilaterally as long as the meeting took place in the context of the six-party talks—giving him far more flexibility than Kelly ever had. She agreed that all the previous machinations, such as meeting in the corner of a room, had been a little crazy. She just didn't want the six-nation talks to become a façade for a U.S.–North Korea negotiation.

The North Korean government sometimes has a shrewd sense of timing. For several weeks in the spring, there were feverish reports in the media that North Korea appeared on the verge of conducting a nuclear test. Then, just as the six-party talks appeared on the verge of irrelevancy—and Pentagon officials eagerly began to suggest it was time to give up on the talks and go to the UN Security Council—the North Koreans suddenly decided they needed to shift tactics. In May, the North Koreans indicated through diplomatic channels that they wanted a senior official to attend a seminar held in New York being organized by Donald Zagoria, a professor who arranges so-called Track II sessions, which are unofficial diplomatic meetings. If a U.S. official would meet with the North Korean envoy on the sidelines of the seminar, then North Korea suggested it might return to the talks. Hill urged Rice to let the North Koreans have visas in order to see what would happen. The move helped break the ice.

After the visas were issued, Hill's deputy negotiator, Joseph DeTrani, went to New York separately on June 6 to meet with North Korean diplomats at the United Nations. DeTrani reached Hill that evening while he was at a baseball game at RFK Stadium with some news: North Korea was willing to come back to the talks, but would not commit to a date. But if Hill would meet with the North Koreans, then concurrently with that meeting North Korea would announce the date of the next round of talks.

Rice was planning another trip to Asia in July, so Hill proposed he meet with the North Koreans on the date she was to arrive in Beijing. Originally, Hill wanted the talks to begin the next day, but Rice suggested it would be better if the talks began a couple of weeks after the announcement so the administration could settle on its negotiating strategy.

In the meantime, Rice encouraged the South Korean government to make an extraordinary offer to North Korea—a proposal that would provide energy-starved North Korea with electrical output equivalent to the two unfinished nuclear plants promised in the 1994 deal. South Korea also would immediately give the North a large infusion of aid, including 500,000 tons of rice as well as raw material for shoes, clothing, and soap. This electricity offer went far beyond the vague promise to study North Korea's energy needs contained in the U.S. proposal offered in June 2004.

The North Koreans are extremely sensitive to language. So, in order not to spoil the tenuous mood, Bush even modified his undiplomatic language about North Korea, referring at one point to "Mr. Kim" instead of using his usual phrase: "dictator."

"You Don't Show Up"

The deal now seemed set. On July 9, Hill would meet with the North Koreans and the Chinese for dinner as Rice was flying to Beijing. The announcement that the talks would start the week of July 25 would be made shortly after her plane touched down in Beijing. But nothing is ever simple when dealing with the North Koreans—and the choreography of the moment would have been lost if Hill had not had an extremely flexible attitude about his instructions.

On the morning of July 9, Hill was walking on the Great Wall of China when one of his aides received a call on his cell phone. The North Koreans had decided they would not come to the meeting if the Chinese were present. Hill's instructions were firm: no Chinese, no meeting. Hill, speaking on the phone as he walked on the Great Wall, stated that the Chinese had to be there. The embassy's deputy chief of mission also called the Chinese. They thought they had an agreement.

Some U.S. officials believe the Chinese knew Hill was so eager to begin negotiating that they took advantage of him. At 6 P.M., Hill went to the meeting location selected by the Chinese—the gleaming St. Regis Hotel, which is actually owned by the Chinese government. Rice was in the air and Hill wasn't sure if the Chinese would show up. He could have called Rice on the plane, but he chose not to do so.

Twenty minutes later, neither the Chinese nor the North Koreans had shown up. Hill asked his aide to call the North Koreans, who then asked if the Chinese were there. When Hill's aide asked what they should say, Hill made a snap judgment. He wanted to have the meeting and he didn't want to lose this opportunity, so he would deal with the consequences later. The North Koreans were told the Chinese had not shown up, and fifteen minutes later Hill was sitting down with his North Korean counterpart, North Korean deputy foreign minister Kim Gye Gwan.

Kim began by asking about U.S. attitudes about North Korean sovereignty. Hill repeated the statement Rice had made in Tokyo in March—that "no one denies that North Korea is a sovereign state." Then Kim began to ask about the administration's "hostile policy," but Hill decided to throw back the question and ask about North Korea's "hostile policy" toward the United States. That did the trick: Kim informed Hill that North Korea would announce that night they were returning to the talks the week of July 25. They adjourned the meeting, moved on to dinner, and spent the next couple of hours discussing how the talks would unfold.

Hill was cheered by the fact that Kim earnestly told him that it was the "dying wish" of Kim Il Sung, the father of North Korean leader Kim Jong Il, that North Korea give up its nuclear programs. Kim Il Sung ruled the communist state from its founding in 1948 until his death in 1994, shortly before the deal with Clinton was set. Every North Korean official at the meal was wearing the obligatory button bearing the likeness of Kim Il Sung.

North Korea officially decided that Rice's statement about sovereignty was an apology for her ill-chosen words about tyranny. "The U.S. side clarified its official stand to recognize the DPRK as a sovereign state, not to invade it and hold bilateral talks within the framework of the six-party talks," the statement announcing the talks said, using the initials for the Democratic People's Republic of Korea. "The DPRK side interpreted the U.S. side's expression of its stand as a retraction of its remark designating the former as an 'outpost of tyranny' and decided to return to the six-party talks."[18]

Now Hill had to explain to his boss what had happened. After Rice's plane landed in Beijing, he met her in her hotel suite and told her he had some good news and some bad news. "The bad news is the Chinese did not show up, but the good news is the North Koreans have agreed to come back to the talks and have announced that in Pyongyang," Hill announced.

Rice crinkled her nose—not a good sign. "I thought we had an understanding on that," she said. Hill felt on the spot with his new boss but put on a good show of bravado. Just about everyone else in the room was convinced he had played a game of wink-wink-nod-nod with the Chinese.

It was now near midnight. Downstairs in the press room, reporters were getting ready to turn off their computers and head to bed when they started to see wire bulletins about the North Korean announcement. Sean McCormack came downstairs and confirmed it, and tried very hard to dance around the fact that Hill had just violated the sacrosanct rule of the Bush administration by meeting with the North Koreans without any minders present.

The next morning, when Rice met with Foreign Minister Li Zhaoxing, she sternly told him that she had expected the Chinese to be at the meal and was not happy with the process.

"You were supposed to host the dinner, but then you don't show up," she complained, making it clear that she thought the Chinese behavior was not straightforward. Li made no excuses, but told her she should focus on the outcome, not the process.[19]

On the trip, Rice unexpectedly had included in her entourage Richard Lawless, Hill's counterpart on Asia policy at the Defense Department. Powell almost never included policy experts from the hated Pentagon, but Lawless's presence on the plane was an interesting maneuver. Just a month earlier, he had infuriated Rice when, speaking anonymously to reporters traveling with Rumsfeld in Asia, he had hinted that the United States would soon bring a sanctions resolution against North Korea at the Security Council. When Hill briefed reporters on the plane about his meeting with Kim after Rice left Beijing, Lawless stood behind him with a noticeably skeptical look. The policy war over Korea in the administration was in a new phase, his face seemed to say—but it was not over yet.

"The President Has an Obligation"

In her meetings with Chinese president Hu Jintao in both March and July, Rice warned that the United States would need to take measures to protect itself from North Korea's illegal activities. She explained that she understood the premium that China placed on stability in the region. But North Korea's criminal actions were creating a situation that was inherently unstable, and the United States and allies would have to take defensive measures.

"The North Koreans are counterfeiting our money," Rice told Hu. "The president has an obligation to deal with the counterfeiting of our money."

It was a cryptic reference to a policy initiative that was ready to be launched— and would end up obliterating Hill's efforts to reach an agreement. Hu took the message seriously, in part because his finance ministry had already been working closely with the Americans on the issue.

North Korea, by its very nature, is a criminal state and makes little pretense of following international rules and regulations. The Congressional Research Service estimated that North Korea nets $500 million a year from counterfeiting, drug smuggling, and other illegal activities, while gross revenues exceed $1 billion.[20] It was well known that the government had become adept at counterfeiting currency, making expert copies of the money issued by each of the other countries at the six-party talks. But only the United States decided to make an issue of it.

At the beginning, that was not the intent. Early in the Bush administration, the Secret Service had approached White House officials with a request: Could they quietly ask the North Koreans to stop counterfeiting our money? But at a time when Powell's State Department was under attack for not being tough enough on North Korea, officials there seized on the idea of countering North Korea's illicit activities as a way of proving their conservative bona fides.

An interagency group was formed to track North Korea's counterfeiting and other criminal operations and then figure out ways to cut them off. The group made slow progress for two years. Then, on the counterfeiting front, the group had just finished its work when Rice headed to Beijing in July. The Treasury Department told officials it was ready to target a bank in Macao called Banco Delta Asia, which it had identified as the main conduit for bringing North Korean–made counterfeit bills into the international system.

The U.S. government had already seized more than $45 million in highly deceptive counterfeit $100 notes produced in North Korea, known as super notes; officials believed they were produced with the approval and supervision of top North Korean officials. The Treasury Department had determined that senior officials at the Macao bank accepted large deposits of cash, including the super notes, and agreed to place the bogus money into circulation. Treasury officials also believed the bank accepted multimillion-dollar wire transfers from North Korean front companies that were deeply involved in criminal activities.[21]

But the Justice Department had a problem. In August, they were planning to spring a major sting operation, called "Smoking Dragon and Royal Charm," which involved alleged conspiracies to peddle more than $4 million in counterfeit notes, counterfeit cigarettes, Ecstasy pills, crystal meth, and arms in the United States—and which would yield dozens of possible suspects. Justice Department officials feared any move on the Macao bank would affect their investigation. So the administration's top Korea policy makers proposed that the announcement by Treasury regarding Banco Delta Asia be delayed until after the Justice Department bust.

That would put the announcement off until September. By coincidence, that was just at the point Hill was poised to finally convince North Korea to sign a document that committed it to give up its nuclear programs. Many on Hill's staff were opposed to any move against North Korea's counterfeiting operations, fearing it would spoil the delicate mood. Hill was also concerned, believing that it was important to focus solely on illicit activities and not do anything that would affect North Korea's legal businesses. He knew some administration officials thought the whole country was illegitimate, but that was not how other members of the six-party talks saw it. Hill, who worked especially closely with his South Korean counterpart (they had both been posted in Poland at the same time), didn't want to break up the tenuous unity at the negotiating table.

Bush would not be deterred. He decided he was not going to pull punches on North Korea's criminal activities just to keep diplomats happy. But officials also realized that an announcement before the talks could kill them while an announcement after the talks could torpedo any deal. It was decided that the Treasury Department action would not appear in the *Federal Register* until the

North Koreans were deep in negotiations; the White House figured the Chinese would not let the North Koreans walk out in the middle of the talks. The crackdown on North Korea's illicit activities thus was a ticking time bomb.[22]

"It's Not Exactly a Showstopper Issue"

The talks that Hill had secured during his meal in Beijing began at the end of July, lasted a couple of weeks, took a five-week pause, and then restarted in earnest in September. The tone that Hill set, under Rice's direction, was completely different than the moribund sessions that Kelly had attended. Hill gave the impression that the handcuffs were off, that he was free to meet with North Koreans as often as he wanted, and that he had tremendous negotiating flexibility. The bar on bilateral contacts seemed to have been lifted, winning applause from observers for Rice's willingness to show new initiative in the negotiations. In the tart expression of Richard Armitage, Powell's deputy, the previous approach had been ridiculous: "We were looking, at least to my mind, like something out of the old Soviet days, where there were watchers watching the watchers who were watching the principals."[23]

It was partly an illusion. Hill still had to contend with hard-liners back in Washington, but he constantly briefed the media, giving the impression that he was in charge. Given the time differences, every day after the talks ended he would go to the embassy and call Rice on a secure line, giving her a summary of the day's negotiations. Rice then would deal directly with Hadley and Bush, and sometimes Cheney, discussing even miniscule aspects of the text. But other members of the delegation would call back to Washington, giving their own reports to their own superiors, and Hill would be reined in if officials felt he was going too far off the reservation. Hill was the public face of North Korean diplomacy, but he was only one member of Rice's inner circle on the issue—as would be clear later, when everything had fallen apart.

Hill's colleagues on the U.S. delegation, in fact, thought he focused too much on the handling of the press and not enough time on figuring out a negotiating strategy or building consensus back in Washington. They also faulted him for relying too much on the Chinese to deliver the North Koreans. One top aide contrasted him with Holbrooke, saying Hill lacked sufficient Washington experience to understand the power dynamics back home.

Hill's main objective was to secure a "statement of principles"—a document that would lay out the negotiating map. North Korea would formally commit to giving up its weapons in the document and then the other nations at the table would detail the possible incentives available to North Korea as it eliminated its weapons programs. The hard work of determining the sequencing of dismantlement and rewards would come later, but in theory the text would commit Pyongyang to end its programs and Washington to finally admit it should be rewarded for doing so.

J. D. Crouch, the deputy national security advisor who was highly skeptical of North Korean intentions, ran the committee that reviewed the text during the negotiations. It was largely stacked up against Hill, though his ace in the hole was his direct line to Rice. On one early call, Hill had to listen to a cabal of core conservatives criticize his proposals—Crouch, Pentagon undersecretary Douglas Feith, State nonproliferation chief Robert Joseph, and vice presidential chief of staff I. Lewis "Scooter" Libby.[24] Nick Burns, the undersecretary of state for political affairs, eventually became part of that group, usually being the only one to stick up for Hill's positions. The group would come up with recommendations on how Hill should negotiate. Hill would never quite get what they wanted, though the outcome generally remained in the realm of the reasonable—until he decided that the only way to get a deal was to seriously consider North Korea's demand in the negotiations that it must be able to one day obtain light-water reactors.

It was the conservatives' worst nightmare—Clinton's Agreed Framework all over again.[25]

The battle over the issue had started even before Hill returned to the second session. The North Koreans had shrewdly decided Rice's acknowledgment of their sovereignty meant that they had a right to peaceful nuclear power; one way the United States could demonstrate that it respects North Korea's sovereignty was to support that right. Hill told the North Koreans they had "Agreed Framework nostalgia," but privately he felt it was no big deal. The issue of whether North Korea has a theoretical right to peaceful nuclear energy is not as important as the main question: whether an agreement to eliminate North Korea's nuclear programs could be reached in the first place. Moreover, he believed, even if North Korea wanted to build a civilian nuclear program, none of the countries now at the table would be willing to fund it. He even went public with his position: "If you ask me, it's not exactly a showstopper issue," Hill said, referring to North Korea's right to develop peaceful nuclear energy. "The real issue is getting rid of all their nuclear programs."[26]

Hill clearly had not been a contestant in the ideological battles that had characterized the administration's debates over North Korea in the first term; the notion that the Bush administration could even hint that North Korea could one day generate nuclear energy was almost unbelievable. Ever since the crisis began in 2002, the Bush administration had insisted on what in diplomatic parlance was known as "CVID"—complete, verifiable, irreversible dismantle-ment of nuclear programs. It was the holy grail of some conservatives, even though the concept of "irreversibility" was on its face a logical impossibility.

The Chinese came up with several drafts of a proposed joint statement, and the fourth draft was acceptable, with minor modifications, to the Russians, the South Koreans, and the Japanese. Hill's State Department colleagues recom-mended that it be accepted as well, believing it would isolate Pyongyang.

But Hill could not convince Washington, which was concerned about the language on "bilateral dialogue" and other issues.[27] The Chinese added pres-sure, suggesting they were willing to announce the talks had failed and would let the media decide who was at fault. The unstated threat was that the United States would get the blame. U.S. officials blanched and said they wanted to keep going—and the extra innings allowed the North Koreans to once again insist on a nuclear reactor in the fifth draft. (The fourth draft, by contrast, only made a cryptic reference to peaceful nuclear use.)[28]

"Exist Peacefully Together"

The final statement, announced by China on September 19, was a masterpiece of diplomatic ambiguity. North Korea said it would "abandon" its weapons and programs—not "dismantle"—in exchange for a laundry list of possible incentives. The uranium program that had started the crisis was not men-tioned, though there was a reference to "existing nuclear programs." The agreement contained no clear time line for when North Korea would give up its nuclear programs, or how, or in what sequence, though it said the steps would take place under the principle of "commitment for commitment, ac-tion for action."

Minutes before the statement was announced at a news conference, as the negotiators were relaxing and thinking their work was done, Hill got a call from Rice on his cell phone. He went outside the room to talk to her, and the avid sports fan first asked her the question at the top of his mind: Had the New England Patriots football team won? (The Patriots had lost.) Rice and Hill chatted a little bit about football, and then Hill asked, "Are we okay?" To his surprise, the answer was no.

Rice told him she had a huge problem with the statement because it men-tioned "peaceful coexistence" between the United States and North Korea. The phrase raised the hackles of the former Sovietologist. "Peaceful coexistence" had been a communist term that described relations between communist and capi-talist states and had been used in communiqués such as a 1954 trade agreement between China and India. Even more troubling, the term might be politically explosive for Bush's conservative base.

"Peaceful coexistence" had been in the previous drafts, and Hill had shrugged off the occasional complaints from hard-liners on the negotiating team about it. Now it had come to his boss's attention—and she told him that she wanted that phrase removed.

Hill huddled with the Chinese delegation to get the problem fixed. The other delegations thought Rice's intervention was ridiculous, but after a tense discussion, the English version of the document was changed to "exist peacefully together." The other versions were not changed; Chinese officials pointed out that in their language the characters were the same for either phrasing.[29]

On the critical question of the light-water reactor, the statement left much open to interpretation: "The DPRK stated that it has the right to peaceful uses of nuclear energy. The other parties expressed their respect and agreed to discuss at an appropriate time the subject of the provision of light-water reactors to the DPRK."

Before the statement was announced, Rice spoke to her counterparts from China, Russia, South Korea, and Japan to urge that they issue their own statements making it clear that North Korea would not get a light-water reactor anytime soon. In her mind, she thought North Korea could only begin this theoretical discussion of obtaining a light-water reactor in the distant future—when it had proved it was a good international citizen. But she was concerned the final statement was too vague on this point, potentially giving North Korea an opening to raise it early in the process. The Chinese were not happy with this development, believing individual interpretations would undermine the ambiguity of the statement. They told Rice that as chair of the meeting, their only comment should be the joint statement.

The Chinese fears had merit. A few hours after the news conference announcing the agreement, Hill read a tough statement, drafted largely by the neoconservatives, which appeared to undercut some of the diplomatic wiggle room in the joint statement.

The situation had been ripe for mischief. The deal had been struck, the hard work had been done, and Rice and Hadley began to tune out. White House official Michael Green—not a hard-liner—was off at a birthday party in St. Michaels, Maryland, a waterfront village on the Chesapeake Bay, and had poor reception on his cell phone. He could barely hear the draft statement when it was read to him. It sounded okay, and he was having such a good time he didn't check back for the final version. (Rice only received an oral readout of elements in the statement.)

Back in Washington, Crouch and White House nonproliferation chief John Rood were distressed with the concessions Hill had made. They took Hill's closing statement and inserted language dear to the hearts of the nonproliferation community, but which were gratuitous in the wake of the fragile agreement. For instance, it laid down stern conditions for North Korea to get a reactor—and noted the U.S. intention to kill the previous project under the Agreed Framework to build nuclear reactors. The twelve-hour time difference between Washington and Beijing played a role—it was nearly morning in Beijing and the statement needed to be transmitted back to the delegation. With few eyes looking it over, the tone of the statement turned pretty sharp.

Hill had been distracted by Rice's problem with "peaceful coexistence," and he was not happy with the statement that arrived from Washington. Jim Foster, the delegation's Korea expert, told him that as the negotiator he was under no obligation to read it. (Some people in Washington also figured that Hill would ignore the statement.) Hill thought he'd gotten what he had wanted in the negotiations and the statement would not mean that much in the long run. Accounts differ on whether Hill actually read the entire statement out loud to the other delegations, but in any case the full text was officially released.[30]

The statement ghostwritten by the hawks probably was just one part of the myriad of things that crippled the talks, but it likely played an important role. Rice's push to get the other parties to issue statements on the light-water reactor also was a factor. It appears North Korea's foreign ministry had oversold the deal back home as a rebirth of the Agreed Framework, and the blizzard of statements (from all but China) undercut that argument. After Hill made his statement, the North Korean foreign ministry issued its own statement, declaring nothing would ever happen until the United States built a light-water reactor: "The U.S. should not even dream of the issue of the DPRK's dismantlement of its nuclear deterrent before providing LWRs, a physical guarantee for confidence-building."[31]

"How About If I Gave Kim a Peace Treaty?"

Meanwhile, four days before the deal was set, Treasury had formally announced the action to designate the Macao bank as a money-laundering concern, essentially a warning to U.S. banks not to do business with it.

"Holy shit," Hill thought when he saw the notice.

He had completely forgotten that was coming. But he figured the administration was on high ground because Rice had warned the Chinese earlier in the year of the need for "defensive measures." However, no one, not even Treasury officials, realized how effective the action would be—or how quickly it would poison the atmosphere of the talks.

North Korea's criminal activities are estimated to account for as much as 40 percent of its exports and a much higher percentage of its total cash earnings.[32] Banco Delta Asia (one of the smallest banks in Macao) also was reputed to have handled the infamous personal "Bureau 39" accounts of Kim and his family. Within days after the Treasury announcement, the bank teetered on the edge of collapse. Much to the delight of U.S. officials, other banks around the world began to curtail their dealings with North Korean companies because they feared becoming the target of Treasury as well. In the eyes of the hardliners, the Banco Delta Asia action had been a striking blow against North Korea, making it difficult for the government to engage in international trade.

Hill wanted to keep up the momentum of the September talks with his own visit to Pyongyang, thereby once and for all shattering the bilateral taboo. He had been hinting for months he would seek permission to make such a trip, and thought he had covered his right flank by arranging to bring along Jay Lefkowitz, Bush's special envoy for North Korean human rights. He had hoped to slip into North Korea unannounced during a long trip to Asia in November, just before the next round of talks was set to begin. Hill wanted to get inside North Korea in part to gain access to other players in the North Korea system, particularly the military, which he sensed was reluctant to give up its nuclear weapons. It was also clear that Kim Gye Gwan, his North Korean counterpart, had only limited negotiating authority. Going to Pyongyang seemed the logical step in trying to get the negotiations to the next level.

But Hill's idea was met with deep skepticism inside the administration, even by Rice. She thought it was too early to go to Pyongyang; North Korea still needed to earn such a trip. Hill told aides that Cheney's office insisted that the North needed to shut down its nuclear reactor at Yongbyon as a show of good faith, but that may have been intended to deflect attention from his boss. Rice made it clear that she thought Hill had virtually no chance of getting to Pyongyang—though she was amused by the idea of Lefkowitz going there— and in the end Hill never officially asked to go forward with the trip. The North Koreans refused to turn off the reactor. The moment was lost.[33]

Requiring North Korea to shut down the reactor was a defensible position, and it also reflected a distrust of Hill and his style among some in the administration. But an administration determined to negotiate a solution probably would not have set such conditions. (Hill's trip, for instance, could have been set up so North Korea would agree to shut down the reactor by the time he finished his visit.)

When Hill showed up for the next round of six-party talks, the North Koreans were in a foul mood because of the Treasury crackdown. Hill told them he had no control over the Treasury Department, but he would be happy to arrange a briefing on the matter. The talks ended within days, though the North Koreans believed Hill's offer of a briefing meant they had secured an agreement to have bilateral talks in the United States on the Treasury matter—and maybe more. North Korea's announcement that there would be bilateral talks further undercut Hill's credibility with conservatives, though he insisted he had made no such agreement. A stalemate would persist for months, and Hill darkly suspected his administration rivals were pleased.

As Hill shuttled back and forth to Asia in a vain effort to prod North Korea back to the negotiating table, Rice and her top advisors were intrigued with the idea of reshaping the security structures of East Asia. They had jointly unified Germany and reshaped Europe, and privately they suggested they could do the same for Asia—though neither Rice nor Zelikow had much expertise in the region. Zelikow wrote a number of memos for Rice, which some officials interpreted as a quixotic effort to re-create the "four plus two" process that unified Germany and apply it to the Korean peninsula, even though the situations were historically and culturally different.

The elements of the grand bargain envisioned by Rice and Zelikow were contained in the September agreement negotiated by Hill. For months after that agreement, Rice and her aides labored to fashion a plan, centered on the idea of reaching a peace treaty with North Korea. Bush was intrigued, and Rice kept trying to smooth out the differences, but officials could never reach a consensus on how to translate the bold ideas into an operational plan and negotiating process. The same old battle continued: Do you get North Korea to change by squeezing it as hard as you can or by opening it up to the outside world?

Oddly, while this debate was still raging at the staff level, Bush raised the idea himself over lunch with Hu Jintao when the Chinese president visited Washington in April 2006. The lunch was held in the East Room of the White House, with some two hundred guests from the worlds of diplomacy, business, and entertainment. With Olympic figure skater Michelle Kwan on his left side, Bush turned to Hu and asked whether Kim Jong Il could be convinced to undertake economic reforms like Chinese leader Deng Xiaoping in the 1970s. Hu replied that Deng was able to tackle such difficult internal reforms because his external concerns had been solved through President Richard Nixon's opening to China. Hu implied that the external situation for Kim was not as benign.

"How about if I gave Kim a peace treaty?" Bush asked.[34]

Hu agreed to have an emissary take a message back to North Korea that

Bush was interested in a breakthrough. But by then it was too late. North Korea was on its own trajectory. On July 4, 2006, it tested ballistic missiles, brushing aside Chinese pleas to not raise tensions. Even the Chinese supported a UN Security Council resolution condemning the test. A few months later, on October 9, North Korea announced it had conducted its first-ever nuclear test, earning an apparent spot in the world's most exclusive club—nations that possess atomic weapons.

Some top U.S. officials had privately hoped North Korea would take the precipitous step, even though it ran the risk of destabilizing Asia, because they thought it would end the struggle within the administration over whether to isolate or engage North Korea. "Thank God for Kim Jong Il," one conservative administration official gleefully said the night of Pyongyang's test.

Such hopes by conservatives were soon dashed. The North Korean nuclear test was such a shock to the region—and the White House—that just months later, Hill was given permission to strike a first-stage implementation deal with North Korea. To the horror of conservatives, the Bush administration committed itself to resolve the Banco Delta Asia matter even before Pyongyang was required to freeze its plutonium reactor. (The alleged uranium enrichment program that had sparked the crisis four years earlier was conveniently minimized.) Even so, allowing North Korea to stockpile enough plutonium for nearly a dozen weapons and then conduct a nuclear test can only be considered a failure of diplomacy. Rice, distracted by Iraq, allowed the situation to spiral out of control as national security advisor and then missed an opportunity as secretary of state to resolve the dispute before North Korean ever detonated a nuclear weapon. Throughout the impasse over North Korea's nuclear ambitions, she never seemed able to decide whether isolation or engagement was the right policy—and thus she allowed the U.S. approach to remain incoherent.

CHAPTER 4

EXPOSED IN RIYADH

June 20, 2005

Rice's jet landed in Riyadh as the sun was setting, the final stop on one of the most exhausting days likely ever scheduled for a secretary of state. Her day had begun before 5 A.M. and would end well past midnight. She had flown to four cities in three countries and held two long one-on-one meetings with heads of state.

In the middle of that hectic day, in Cairo, she gave what was perhaps the defining speech of her tenure as secretary of state—a plea for greater democracy in the Middle East, including full rights for women.

Rice emerged from the aircraft in Saudi Arabia wearing a spectacular outfit of subtle gold pinstripes on luxurious white silk—shimmering and pale, almost as if it was designed to match the flowing white robes of the Saudi men who had gathered to meet her. Her female predecessor, Madeleine Albright, had always worn a hat on her trips to the desert kingdom in deference to the modesty demanded of women, but Rice had no head covering. The Saudis gathered around her and then the group—led by Rice and the foreign minister, Saud al-Faisal—slowly walked across the tarmac to the waiting motorcade.

Crown Prince Abdullah, the de facto ruler and a tough old man who has a bedouin sense of honor, had arranged for all of his half brothers to meet with Rice over dinner—a collection of royals designed to show his respect for her and the power she represented as one of Bush's closest advisors. Behind closed doors, he also gave Rice a gift: an abaya, the head-to-toe black covering that every woman in Saudi Arabia must wear while in public. It was beautifully hand-sewn, and Rice thought it was a sweet gesture, offered in a generous and kind way.

But the abaya also has a certain symbolism in Saudi Arabia. Abdullah's gift was oddly inappropriate yet also a fitting symbol for the challenges ahead—a cold splash of water on the day.[1]

"A Precondition for Security, Stability, and Prosperity"

The Bush administration's push for greater democracy in the Middle East was born in the aftermath of the September 11 attacks, but it has its roots in the debates over policy toward the Soviet Union in the 1970s. Some of the neoconservatives who in the 1970s had pressed for greater freedoms in the Soviet sphere and more attention to Soviet dissidents, and then witnessed the Soviet Union collapse in 1991, saw the opportunity for a similar approach in the Middle East after 9/11. Within the administration, they began to press for a sustained U.S. effort to change the character of the autocratic regimes and to empower dissidents, possibly modeling the effort on the Helsinki process that neoconservatives believed had helped lead to the demise of communism in eastern Europe.[2]

The 1975 Helsinki Accords were designed to recognize disputed post–World War II borders and establish a mechanism for settling other disagreements. But human rights and fundamental freedoms became key parts of the treaty, giving the West leverage to promote and protect dissident groups in the Soviet bloc and urge greater freedoms for its residents. One of the former Soviet dissidents, Natan Sharansky, became a sort of evangelist for democracy promotion in the Middle East; his book *The Case for Democracy: The Power of Freedom to Overcome Tyranny and Terror* was required reading for top Bush administration officials.

Other key figures, such as Deputy Defense Secretary Paul Wolfowitz, drew from other lessons of history. Wolfowitz had been a senior State Department official responsible for Asia policy in the Reagan administration when Reagan decided to abandon Philippine strongman Ferdinand Marcos in favor of democracy-minded Corazon Aquino—a move that Wolfowitz felt ushered in a wave of greater freedoms across the region.[3] The invasion of Iraq, in his mind, flowed naturally from that historical analogy—a sudden flowering of democracy that would reverberate and change a region forever.

Bush and his top aides became convinced that the United States' traditional reliance on autocratic leaders who suppressed freedoms and democracy had helped spawn Islamic radicalism; without democracy, the only way to battle repression was through extremism. Bush came to believe that the bipartisan tradition of working with rulers like Abdullah of Saudi Arabia and President Hosni Mubarak—who generally supported U.S. interests—had resulted in decades of false stability. For a president strongly committed to Israel, the idea of spreading democracy in the Middle East also conveniently minimized the question of whether the festering Israeli-Palestinian conflict might have inspired anger at the United States in the Arab world.

But, despite high-flying rhetoric by Bush in a series of speeches promoting the idea, the effort to promote democratic institutions in the Middle East was largely stillborn during Bush's first term. The State Department under Powell was never especially interested in pushing it. Arab leaders angrily rejected anything along the Helsinki lines, and were also distressed that Bush insisted on lumping Afghanistan in what he called the "greater Middle East." A watered-down plan was launched, haltingly, at the Group of Eight (G-8) summit hosted by Bush in 2004 in Sea Island, Georgia. But the meeting really had a different purpose—it was an effort to find some common ground with the Europeans, still angry with the conduct of the war in Iraq, during the election year.

In his second inaugural address, Bush relaunched the idea and even raised the stakes, making democracy in the Middle East and around the world the central purpose of his final term. Using the words "free," "freedom," or "liberty" forty-nine times in a twenty-one-minute address, Bush declared that relations with "every ruler and every nation" would be based on how they treated their citizens. "All who live in tyranny and hopelessness can know the United States will not ignore your oppression or excuse your oppressors," Bush said, adding that "it is the policy of the United States to seek and support the growth of democratic movements and institutions in every nation and culture, with the ultimate goal of ending tyranny in our world." He even quoted from Sharansky's book as a reflection of his own views on the importance of expanding democracy in the world.[4]

Though Bush is generally regarded as the most pro-Israel president in history, the Israeli government was noticeably cool to the idea of Arab democracy. At an April 2005 meeting in Crawford, Texas, Prime Minister Sharon was unenthusiastic when Bush told him that democratization in the region was "a precondition for security, stability, and prosperity since only a democracy would want to halt terrorism." The Israelis had been able to build stable ties with Arab autocrats, and they feared elections would only bring to power groups hostile to Israel. Sharansky, the toast of Washington, admitted that in Israel "they see me as a lunatic from a Soviet prison, disconnected from the harsh realties of the Middle East."[5]

Bush's speech, rhetorically at least, represented a major shift in U.S. policy—and immediately exposed tremendous contradictions between the stated goals of his administration and its actual practices. The war on terrorism, in fact, had forced the administration to become even cozier with undemocratic regimes such as Egypt, Saudi Arabia, Pakistan, and Uzbekistan, which the State Department ranked as among the worst human rights abusers. Up to that point, Bush had been largely silent about Russian president Vladimir Putin's dismantling of democratic institutions, and had played down human rights concerns in China because he needed Beijing as an ally in the effort to restrain North Korea's nuclear ambitions. On the other side of the ledger, countries such as Venezuela and Iran had some level of democratic activity, much more than such friendly autocrats as the Saudis, but the Bush administration heaped scorn on countries it viewed as unfriendly. The policy was muddled by such contradictions, and it would be up to the new secretary of state to try to make sense of it.

Perhaps no one appeared to be a more fervent believer in the president's message than Rice. During the administration of George H. W. Bush, when she worked for Brent Scowcroft, Rice had appeared to be a hard-headed realist, and sometimes as secretary she would take a pragmatic, even nonideological approach if she thought it would provide a solution. But on this issue, she was as starry-eyed as the most avid neoconservative.

The September 11 attacks had had a profound effect on Condoleezza Rice. She looked at the Middle East and decided the absence of political space and dialogue had left the societies increasingly unhealthy, as if malignant cells were crowding out healthy ones, killing the body. The former Soviet scholar also began to reexamine the cold war and the struggle with the Soviet Union through a different prism. Key U.S. decisions, such as demanding democracy in West Germany and imposing a democratic charter on Japan, began to loom larger and more important to the ultimate collapse of the Soviet Union decades later.[6]

Her "realist" colleagues from the G. W. H. Bush days, such as Robert Zoellick, Robert Blackwill, and Brent Scowcroft, wondered at the transformation and sometimes privately resorted to pop psychology to explain what had happened to Rice. They didn't view it merely as a cynical shift made to please her new boss. They thought that something deep inside her had been drawn out by the current president, perhaps something to do with her Christian faith or experience with racism in the Deep South that she had had to repress when she was the lone black woman working in the arms control and security field.

They wondered if she felt, as a young scholar, that she had to play tough to prove herself with the boys and now she was able to truly express herself.

Scowcroft, in particular, was stunned by Rice's "evangelical tone" and archly noted to interviewers that Rice's expertise was in the Soviet Union, not the Middle East.[7] He thought the whole concept of a "false stability" was ridiculous. "We've had fifty years of peace," he said.[8]

"They Couldn't Have Picked a Worse Time"

Within the State Department, the longtime experts on the Middle East also thought that blind faith in the power of elections and democracy was delusional. They were convinced that the only winners would be Islamic extremists, not American interests. Rice made it clear that such an attitude would not be acceptable, and career officials got the message. One political appointee who served under both Powell and Rice noticed a stark difference when the talking points were prepared for the secretary before meetings with Arab leaders. Under Powell, democracy was usually eighth or ninth on the list and then often dropped off altogether before the meeting; with Rice, democracy was often one of the first three points, if not the first.[9]

As soon as Rice became secretary she also took some highly visible steps to demonstrate that she was serious. When Egyptian foreign minister Ahmed Aboul Gheit visited Washington in February, she seized on the jailing of Egyptian opposition candidate Amyan Nour to make a point. Nour was jailed just nine days after Bush's inaugural address, giving Rice an opening. "They couldn't have picked a worse time to do this," Rice told Elliott Abrams, the key point person on democracy and the Middle East at the National Security Council. She directed the State Department spokesman to make a tough public statement about Nour's plight.[10]

The statement caught the attention of Cairo. Before he arrived in Washington, Aboul Gheit privately met with C. David Welch, then the U.S. ambassador to Egypt and Rice's choice to be assistant secretary of state for Near Eastern affairs, to try to figure out a way to avoid a clash with Rice. Aboul Gheit felt he was in a difficult position because he had no authority over such a domestic issue.

At the end of Aboul Gheit's meeting at the State Department, Rice ordered everyone to leave the room except for one aide, Aboul Gheit, and the Egyptian ambassador to the United States. She warned that if Nour was not released, she might cancel a planned trip to Egypt in March. Aboul Gheit said the case was part of the Egyptian legal system and there was not much more that could be done. He pleaded with her not to mention Nour's name at the news conference they planned to hold after the meeting. Rice didn't mention the name, but she leaped at the chance to send a diplomatic blow when a reporter asked about the case.

"Oh, on—yes, right," Rice replied, as a visibly shaken Aboul Gheit stood next to her. "Yes, I did raise our concerns, our very strong concerns about this case. I did talk at some length about the importance of this issue to the United States, to the American administration, to the American Congress, to the American people. And I expressed our very strong hope that there will be a resolution of this very soon."[11]

A couple of weeks later, Nour was still in jail and, over the strong objections of the Near East bureau, Rice scrubbed the trip to Egypt. When the State Department press office tried to suggest that the case had nothing to do with the trip cancellation, Jim Wilkinson unofficially spread the word that it had everything to do with Nour. The next morning Mubarak announced that he would allow competitive presidential elections. There is little indication that the announcement was caused by her trip cancellation—U.S. officials knew Mubarak's plan was under discussion—but it suddenly appeared as if the democracy effort was bringing results.

Rice also played an active role in the wake of the assassination of former Lebanese prime minister Rafik Hariri on February 14, which led to the so-called Cedar revolution and the removal of Syrian troops from that troubled country. The death of longtime Palestinian leader Yasir Arafat shortly before she became secretary, and the election of Mahmoud Abbas as his successor, also suggested democracy was stirring in the Palestinian territories. It was in this heady period—even Nour had been released from jail—that Rice went to the Middle East in June to deliver her speech on democracy in the Middle East.

"Do You Want Eleven-Dollar-a-Gallon Gasoline?"

As usual, Rice's speech would read much better than she delivered it. She was stilted and pedantic, and only came alive during the question-and-answer session. But it is difficult to overstate its importance. No previous secretary of state had gone to the Middle East and publicly told the most important U.S. allies in the region that they had to open up their societies and end emergency decrees, grant voting rights, and free people arbitrarily charged for treason for merely raising questions about government policies. Of course, words are one thing and actions are another—and the administration's leverage over these countries would become increasingly limited in the coming months because of its own blunders. Arab diplomats now greet mention of Rice's speech with a smirk. But words are an important start. Rice, to her credit, began a conversation that other secretaries had long avoided.

The speech was largely written by Rice's increasingly favorite speechwriter, twenty-five-year-old Christian Brose. Less than two weeks before the speech was to be delivered, Brose received a typically effusive e-mail from Wilkinson that left him with virtually no guidance on what to write. Nearly half of the e-mail focused on logistics, not content: Rice wanted the venue for giving the speech to "be symbolic . . . she was not excited at all about the American University . . . she said it 'needs to be evocative.'" (Rice's staff considered the pyramids as a speech location but learned it would get too hot in the middle of the day, so in the end they reluctantly accepted the university.)

Rice "thinks this will be seen as one of the biggest speeches of her tenure," Wilkinson added. "Needs to be dramatic . . . needs to be respectful but issue a 'strong challenge.' . . . definitely needs to address the rights of women." Brose's challenge was further compounded by a series of bad ideas proposed by other Rice aides, such as Phil Zelikow's suggestion that Rice announce an initiative to translate great Western works of literature into Arabic.

On the trip, Rice had also brought along Bush's favorite wordsmith, Michael Gerson, a powerful administration figure who had become a senior White House policy advisor, focusing especially on democracy promotion. Wilkinson had seated Brose next to Gerson on the flight, hoping the younger man could pick up some tips from the master. On the morning of the speech, Gerson sat in a hotel restaurant in Amman, Jordan, with a copy, making notes in the margins. By then, the speech was already on its ninth or tenth draft. Brose had delivered a rough version as Rice's plane took off from Andrews Air Force Base. Rice and her top aides gathered in her tiny cabin and worked through it line by line for several hours as the jet flew to the first refueling stop in Shannon, Ireland. The first version was very tough—Brose liked to put Rice out on a limb as far as possible so the more experienced experts could pull her language back.

In one section of the speech, Brose would have had Rice publicly name three dissidents in Saudi jails—a case that was already a sore point in U.S.–Saudi Arabia relations. Rice's aides had a long and serious discussion about whether the names should stay in the speech. Does it help the United States or help the dissidents? How would Abdullah react? Wilkinson, as usual, put the matter succinctly when he argued that adding the names would go too far: "Do you want eleven-dollar-a-gallon gasoline?"

Rice decided she could more successfully press the case by raising it but not personalizing it. The names were removed.[12]

Before Rice arrived in Cairo, she had to stop in Sharm el-Sheikh, the Egyptian resort on the Sinai peninsula, so she could pay her respects to President Mubarak. He wasn't planning to be anywhere near Cairo when she gave her speech.

In her private conversations about democracy with autocrats like Mubarak, Rice does not try a frontal approach. She backs into the conversation, asking the leader to describe the course of political reform in the country. "Reform is necessary," Rice will say. "Making more political space for legitimate political activity is necessary. Now tell me how you think you're going to get there."

Sometimes, such as with the Russians, Rice might try to describe what she sees happening in the country and then use that to force a conversation. "Let me tell what I see," Rice said in private conversations with Russian officials. "I see overconcentration of power in the Kremlin, with no countervailing institutions. That's a danger because even if you have the most benign president in the Kremlin, at some point it might not be a benign president. Then you have all this power concentrated in one place, and that's a danger to democracy. So how do you think about that?"

Rice found that often this indirect approach would elicit more revealing answers than if she simply came into the meeting with a list of steps that needed to be taken by the other government. Yes, she would be told that the political system is not that mature and some things need to be addressed. She tried not to fall into the trap of suggesting that any path, no matter how slow, would be fine. She would prod and push for certain steps to be taken now, such as reducing central authority, allowing a free press, adding constitutional protections—or else, she would say, reform won't happen at all. Rice also tried to appeal to the individual vanity of the leaders or the countries. The Egyptians, for instance, loved her repeated references to their traditional role as a pacesetter in the Middle East.[13]

"They Will Be So, I Assure You"

After meeting at length with Mubarak, Rice held a news conference with Aboul Gheit, who had been criticized in Egypt for failing to stand up to Rice when she blasted Egypt over the Nour case. Aboul Gheit is a slick customer who oozes charm and can't seem to keep his hands off Rice. She seems to scare him, so he overcompensates by bantering with her and interrupting her repeatedly, grabbing her elbow. Now, Aboul Gheit seemed to be desperately trying to make up for the humiliation he had experienced during his February visit to Washington.

Rice was asked if she had been satisfied that the upcoming presidential elections announced by Mubarak would be "open, free, and fair." Aboul Gheit broke in to declare, almost like Yul Brynner, who played the Egyptian pharaoh in *The Ten Commandments,* that it will be done.

"Who would object to fair, transparent elections? Everybody wants a fair, transparent election, and they will be so, I assure you," Aboul Gheit almost shouted.

Suddenly, as if on cue, a huge television light stand came crashing down, as if God himself was ready to smite Aboul Gheit. Reporters had immediately noticed that Aboul Gheit did not mention the word "free." Saul Hudson of Reuters called him on that lapse, asking whether it was deliberate.

"No, no, no, no, no, no, no," Aboul Gheit backpedaled emphatically. "Free, fair, and transparent. And there are lots of legislations that are being enacted these days to ensure that particular issue." (None of that turned out to be true.)

Hudson also got to the nub of the issue with Rice, asking about U.S. credibility in the region. "Many people in the Arab world actually question whether the United States has the moral authority to be passing judgment, given the treatment of U.S. soldiers of detainees and, some people say, the United States applies a double standard when it criticizes governments it doesn't like but goes soft on governments that it does," he noted.

Rice completely ignored the question about a double standard—dangerous territory for the administration—but she passionately, and even eloquently, addressed the credibility gap.

"Democracy does not guarantee that people will not do bad things; sometimes, people will do bad things," she said, using the Abu Ghraib prison scandal as an example of the importance of the free press. "But what democracy guarantees is that they will be openly and transparently debated." (The irony that some Bush administration officials had harshly criticized the news coverage of Abu Ghraib as bordering on unpatriotic was not mentioned.)

Rice added a personal note: "We also have to be humble about the fact that it has taken us a long time to live up to those values. After all, the United States was born as a slave-owning state. And it took us almost one hundred years to end that . . . that tragic condition. Americans were only completely guaranteed the right to vote in my lifetime, with the Voting Rights Act of 1965."

Aboul Gheit saw an opening for a jab at Rice, allowing for a rare public display of the tension of the moment as the news conference descended into a game of diplomatic oneupmanship.

"You recall, Secretary, that I told you also in the car that there is anger in the region. And there is anger in the region. And we have to control that anger," Aboul Gheit said.

Rice responded: "And we recognize that the situation in this region is one that cannot continue to persist. When people strap suicide bombs onto themselves to blow up innocent people or drive airplanes into buildings, something is wrong. And that's what we together are trying to address."

Aboul Gheit, still playing for the local media, tried to get in the last word: "And, if I may, finding a settlement for the Palestinian problem. That is crucial."

"That's what we're working on," Rice snapped coldly, ending the news conference and sweeping out of the room to get on her plane. Only the day before, Rice had announced a breakthrough in the negotiations over Israel's withdrawal from Gaza, so Aboul Gheit's last comment seemed to be particularly ungracious to Rice.[14]

Back on the plane, Rice's aides were so excited about Rice's answer to Hudson—"she hit it out of the park"—that Brose was given instructions to work some of her language into the final version of the speech. Zelikow thought the news conference was extraordinary, showing how wobbly and uncertain the Egyptians were about the American enterprise and how hard it was for Egyptian officials like Aboul Gheit to keep their balance.

"Democracy Is Never Imposed"

After arriving in Cairo, Rice's motorcade caused monumental traffic jams because Egyptian authorities had sealed off the route; Rice's aides were flummoxed to see people stuck in traffic, angrily shouting and waving their fists at the long line of black sedans and minivans speeding through the streets. At the American University, Rice spoke in a rather drab auditorium that was filled to the rafters with an invitation-only audience of six hundred government officials, academics, and diplomats. The twenty-five-minute speech, which mixed tough-minded rhetoric with assurances that the Bush administration was not planning to impose democracy, earned no applause until it was completed. Rice then took questions for another forty minutes.

Parts of the speech were stirring, even eloquent. It was a quintessential American moment—uplifting yet impossibly naive.

"Throughout the Middle East, the fear of free choices can no longer justify the denial of liberty," Rice said. "It is time to abandon the excuses that are made to avoid the hard work of democracy. There are those who say that democracy is being imposed. In fact, the opposite is true: Democracy is never imposed. It is tyranny that must be imposed. People choose democracy freely."

Of course, in the Arab world, the Iraq invasion is seen as an American attempt to impose democracy. Rice skipped lightly over that fact, saying "ordinary Iraqis are displaying great personal courage and remarkable resolve."

The United States, she said in the section quickly added on the plane, "has no cause for false pride and we have every reason for humility," because of its history of slavery and racism. "The moral worth of my ancestors, it was thought, should be valued by the demands of the market, not by the dignity of their souls."

Rice also demanded equal treatment for women: "Half a democracy is not a democracy."

Rice offered mild praise for Mubarak, who has ruled with an iron fist since 1981, for having "unlocked the door for change" by agreeing for the first time to allow an opposition candidate to run against him. The move was "encouraging," she said, but now "the Egyptian government must put its faith in its own people." She called on Mubarak to end violent attacks on pro-democracy demonstrators, stop "arbitrary justice," and lift emergency decrees allowing the police to break up gatherings of more than five people.

Rice's language was in part an attempt to make up for damage done by her boss's wife. Standing amid the pyramids while on a goodwill visit to Egypt the previous month, Laura Bush had described Mubarak's election gambit as a "very bold step." Opposition groups that regarded the election as a sham were infuriated. Rice's carefully calibrated message was designed to mitigate the criticism of the first lady's remarks.

On Saudi Arabia, Rice noted that three people who petitioned the monarchy to adopt a constitutional system had been jailed on charges of trying to encourage dissent. "That should not be a crime in any country," she said, not naming the three individuals.

"For sixty years, my country, the United States, pursued stability at the expense of democracy in this region here in the Middle East—and we achieved neither," Rice declared. "Now, we are taking a different course. We are supporting the democratic aspirations of all people."

But then Rice opened the door to charges of hypocrisy. She was much tougher on Iran and Syria—two countries often in disagreement with the United States—than she was on Egypt and Saudi Arabia, two U.S. allies. She denounced the "organized cruelty of Iran's theocratic state" and called on Syria "to make the strategic choice to join the progress all around it."[15]

This is the kind of statement that weakens U.S. credibility in the region.

The United States has differences with Syria and Iran, but as police states go, they are essentially at the same level as Egypt and Saudi Arabia.

After the speech Rice spent an hour meeting with some opposition leaders, including Ayman Nour, whose case she had championed. The session was closed to the press, except for brief opening remarks, and Nour passed her a note thanking her. Yet Rice drew the line at meeting with representatives of the Muslim Brotherhood, Egypt's largest opposition party, which had been banned from political activity for five decades. The Egyptian government has outlawed Islamic parties, and Rice said she would respect the laws of Egypt. It was a strange diplomatic straddle—some U.S. diplomats in years past had quietly met with Muslim Brotherhood activists—that left reporters scratching their heads.

When it was later pointed out that she had met with outlawed dissidents from Belarus and that President Bush had recently invited a defector from North Korea into the Oval Office, Rice replied, "I hardly think the Egyptian government is either the North Korean government or the Belarusian government."[16]

Rice was skating on thin ice here. Freedom House, a U.S.-based human rights group, annually ranks countries by the political rights and civil liberties afforded their citizens. At the time that Rice made her speech, Egypt had one of the worst combined ratings: equal to Belarus, Iran, and Zimbabwe, three countries on her list of six "outposts of tyranny" she had named in her confirmation hearings. Saudi Arabia was ranked even lower, as one of the world's most repressive governments—along with Burma, North Korea, and Cuba, the other three "outposts of tyranny." Syria was listed as the equal of Saudi Arabia. The official State Department human rights reports also document in vast detail the cruelty and repression of Egypt and Saudi Arabia. Rice's straddle indicated the limits of the administration's democracy campaign: U.S. friends in the region will be given a bit of a break, while its enemies will not.

ABC News's Jonathan Karl pressed her on these points in a contentious interview he had with her after the speech. Rice was on quite a high, and she seemed taken aback by Karl's persistent, probing questioning. If Rice dislikes a question, she will frequently insert the reporter's name into the answer. It isn't clear if this is an unconscious habit or an effort to let the readers of the transcript within the administration know who was asking such a nasty question. (Of course, as reporters came to realize this, they were thrilled if they jabbed Rice hard enough to get their name in the answer.) In this case, Rice used "Jon" on the first difficult question and then proceeded to answer virtually every question with "Jonathan." By the end, if she had known Karl's middle name, she probably would have used that as well.[17]

"I'm Afraid I Haven't Read It, to My Eternal Shame"

Rice then flew to Riyadh for the final leg of her lengthy day. Crown Prince Abdullah, who within weeks would become king when the long-ailing Fahd died, arranged for a lavish dinner attended by all of his brothers. For Rice and her aides, the most vivid example of the Saudi propensity for over-the-top excess was a pond that was placed in the middle of the dining room—complete with a twelve-foot glass bridge that also served as a shark tank, holding one shark that swam back and forth inside the bridge during the meal. Reporters waited in the Palace Conference Center, an all-marble edifice that appears stuck in a 1960s time warp. It looked as if it had been furnished by the Long Island mob—tacky and overstuffed, reflecting the taste of people who had just struck it rich.[18]

It wasn't until after midnight that Rice and Prince Saud emerged to meet reporters for their news conference. Saud, who has been foreign minister for thirty years, going back to the days of Henry Kissinger, shrewdly opened with a long list of issues that form the core of the bilateral relationship: the Israeli-Palestinian peace process, the war in Iraq, the crisis in Lebanon. He didn't need to mention oil. The implication was clear: This relationship will survive the current American silliness.

Saudi officials also strategically placed three female journalists in the front row. They were dressed head to toe in abayas, just like the one the crown prince had privately given to Rice. One, a reporter for Saudi television, wore open-toed shoes that revealed sparkling nail polish. Saud made a point of asking the female reporters to ask the first and last questions, saying, "We have to do the ladies." Rice, somewhat naively, told reporters later she was pleased to see the female Saudi journalists at the news conference.

At the news conference, the obvious question was asked: What did Saud think about Rice's demand about three prisoners, who had been imprisoned for nearly one and a half years? "I told the secretary that they have broken a law," Saud airily replied. "They are in the hands of the court." (Seven weeks later, in one of Abdullah's first acts after he became king, they were pardoned and released—a small Saudi tribute to Rice—though Saudi officials suggest the pardons would have happened earlier if the administration had not made the case an issue.)

And what did Saud think of Rice's speech, which had been widely reported across the Middle East all day? Saud showed why he is a master of the game, able to hide an insult in a compliment. "I'm afraid I haven't read it, to my eternal shame," he said.[19]

During the long meal and endless meetings, in fact, the Saudis never asked a single question about Rice's speech—didn't even mention it—but Welch and other Rice aides were certain Saud had read it very closely before Rice had arrived. No Saudi official, in fact, would ever mention the speech to Rice, even months later. But the Saudis clearly were not pleased.

"I think the word 'democracy' has become a religious icon in the United States," the Saudi ambassador to the United States, Prince Turki al-Faisal, sarcastically told a private gathering in Washington in 2006. "If you don't espouse it, you are considered an infidel or an apostate. If you espouse it, you have entry into the faith. We have similar views about Islam in Saudi Arabia."[20]

As Rice left the Middle East the next day, flying to a conference on Iraq in Brussels, she again signaled there were limits to her democracy campaign. Jon Karl asked her why, as a woman, she didn't make more of an issue about the fact that women can't drive in Saudi Arabia. "It's just a line that I have not wanted to cross," Rice said.

She argued that Saudi women needed broader political rights to challenge and possibly change the political and cultural calculus of their nation. Women do not have the right to vote, but the Saudi government had made vague statements about hoping to eventually grant women voting rights. "I am quite certain that when women are able to express their aspirations and their views in the political system . . . that we will see what is really custom and what really does matter to Saudi women," Rice said.[21]

Rice's answer hinted at the core tenet of the administration's thinking—a belief, perhaps naive, that people make the right choices once they have the right to vote. Elections equal freedom. The hard work of establishing parties, enforcing the rule of law, creating civil society, and building the institutions of democracy never quite received the same attention.

Strikingly, when Rice had met with a group of Saudi journalists for the roundtable discussion, there were almost no questions on her democracy speech. Finally, one asked if Rice understood the consequences of sudden democracy in the region—that Islamist parties would come to power. Rice acknowledged that reform involves more than elections, but expressed hope that once extremist parties run for office, they wouldn't do very well because voters would care more about the practical aspects of governing—like working sewers—than jihad. "I think there's at least a very, very good chance that the extremists would not do very well," she said.[22]

Within months, her prediction would be proved very wrong.

CHAPTER 5

RUMBLE IN KHARTOUM

July 21, 2005

Rice settled down in her chair in the imposing presidential residence of Lieutenant General Omar Hassan Bashir, Sudan's ruler, and noticed something strange. Her translator was missing. None of her other aides were in the room, either. Not the assistant secretary of state for African affairs. Not her other policy advisors. Not Raymond Odierno, the three-star general from the Pentagon who attends key meetings. No one except for Liz Lineberry, her personal assistant, who normally never attends such high-level meetings. Bashir speaks no English and Rice speaks no Arabic. They sat in awkward silence as the minutes ticked away.

Outside, there was mayhem.

Bashir's secret police, manning the palace entrance, had blocked many of Rice's key aides, and reporters accompanying her, from entering the building, which stands on the bank of the Nile. Jim Wilkinson had briefly been in the room with Rice but went out to find the others. One security officer shoved Wilkinson against a wall. "If you touch me again, I'll knock you on your ass," he yelled at the guard.

Rice's interpreter, Gemal Helal, cursed the guards in Arabic before they finally relented and let him in. General Odierno, a bullet-headed, towering figure who had commanded the division in Iraq that captured Saddam Hussein, literally pushed away the smaller Sudanese to make his way into the palace. Eventually, after furious complaints and a lot more shoving, the rest of Rice's entourage joined her in the meeting.

Bashir began to make a pitch for lifting U.S. sanctions, even though his government was conducting what the United States called genocide in his western province of Darfur. He argued that he needed significant financial support for peace to be achieved. Rice told Bashir he needed to disarm the government-backed militias responsible for much of the violence in Darfur. Bashir airily replied, without a hint of irony, that if only one side in the conflict was disarmed, "the result is going to be genocide." Rice shot back that the Sudanese government was responsible for security in the region.[1]

The scene outside the room wasn't going any better than the meeting. Rice's press corps had finally squeezed inside the front door, but the U.S. reporters were forcefully pushed away by the guards when it came time for photographs and television footage of the meeting. The guards only permitted Sudanese journalists to enter. Wilkinson, increasingly angry, decided to go on the record with his complaints so the wire services could begin to file news reports about the melee from their BlackBerrys and cell phones. "Diplomacy 101 says you don't rough your guests up," he fumed as he and Sean McCormack demanded access for the American reporters.

As it began to dawn on the Sudanese that they might have a problem, several officials suddenly showed up and offered apologies. "It is not our intention in any way to bar the media from doing its job," the Sudanese ambassador to the United States said, noting that he too had received the same treatment from the guards and had also arrived late to the meeting.

Reporters continued to press for access, and the Sudanese finally agreed to let the U.S. reporters in for television footage at the end of the meeting. But they made it clear that this was only a "camera spray"—meaning no questions. Ordinarily, this is the kind of request that reporters might have honored, since they generally play by the rules. But Bashir is rarely available even for shouted questions—a camera spray with the secretary of state was most unusual—and after being roughed up by Bashir's goons, no one was in a mood for accommodation.

McCormack and Wilkinson knew this and, out of earshot of the Sudanese, all but urged the traveling press to break decorum. The Sudanese officials repeated over and over that no one was allowed to ever ask Bashir any questions. McCormack said he understood that, but he had no control over reporters' actions. "Sir, I will pass along your request on behalf of the Sudanese government," McCormack said, respectful but firm. "But that is all I will do."

McCormack then pointed at the U.S. reporters. "Sir, this is a free press, sir," he said.

"No, no, that is not a free press," the Sudanese press officer stammered.

Amazingly, the guards again tried to block the access of reporters when it was time for the camera spray. The journalists started pushing their way past the guards, chanting, "Cameras do not go in without writers." As they entered, Bashir was overheard bragging to Rice about the historical significance of his ancestral home, including the claim that the town had had a university there two thousand years before Christ. "Amazing," Rice replied with mock politeness.

The reporters awkwardly looked at each other, wondering who would speak first, when NBC's Andrea Mitchell decided to take the plunge: "Mr. President, tell us why is the violence continuing?" One of the Sudanese officials started shouting, "No, no, no." "Why should Americans believe your promises" regarding Darfur, she continued in her best shouted television voice, when "your government is still supporting the militias?"

Bashir, with a smile frozen on his face, snapped at the guards in Arabic, "Don't let her." Mitchell kept yelling her questions. Bashir, looking increasingly upset, gestured with his arms. "Finished," he shouted.[2]

The guards pounced, dragging Mitchell away by twisting her arms as Wilkinson shouted, "Get your hands off her!" When Mitchell started getting teary-eyed, one of the Sudanese officials smirked and loudly declared that she was drunk (which is how the official Sudanese news agency portrayed the incident). Then they hustled the rest of the reporters out of the room.

Wilkinson was so worried that he might get in trouble for the fracas that he rushed to Rice's limo and made sure she understood he thought the Sudanese behavior was outrageous. His pitch worked. When Rice arrived at the airport— she was planning to visit a camp in Darfur—she was furious.

"They are worse than the Saudis," she said to her staff as she got on board.[3]

She then wandered back to the press section, determined to make an international incident out of the matter. She told the reporters she had demanded an apology from the government, and expected one before the plane landed an hour later. "It makes me very angry to be sitting there with their president and have this happen," she said. "They have no right to push and shove."

Later, as the plane left Sudan, Rice told reporters with a playful look, "I'm going to have Bob handle Sudan from now on."

"Let's Finish It"

"Bob" was Robert Zoellick. By the time Rice had arrived in Sudan in mid-July, Zoellick had already made three trips to Sudan in just four months. In the partnership between Rice and Zoellick, Sudan and the tragedy of Darfur was largely his project. He had known virtually nothing about the issue when he made his first trip in April, except that it was a presidential and congressional priority. But he quickly absorbed the vast and difficult history of Africa's largest country, able to spout off with ease the name of any tribal leader or government official who could possibly play a role in ending the conflict.

While the problems of Africa generally do not hold much interest for Americans—or U.S. policy makers—Sudan was different. The country had known little but civil conflict since its independence fifty years ago, especially between the largely Arab, Islamic northern part of the country and the largely animist and Christian African south. Khartoum controlled much of the country's wealth (especially its oil riches) and had imposed sharia law. The north-south conflict had lasted more than two decades, leaving two million people dead, primarily from famine and disease, and four million homeless.

Some of the southern rebels professed to be Christian, attracting the support and attention of evangelical Christians in the United States. This made Sudan critical to Bush's largest base of political support. In fact, it even struck close to home: Churches in Midland, Texas, had joined together to form an alliance to keep Sudan at the top of the administration's agenda. Early in his first term, Bush appointed a special envoy, former Republican senator John Danforth, to push for a comprehensive peace plan that would end the war in the south.

Sudan was ready to make a deal. The Bush administration's aggressive response to the 9/11 attacks terrified the government of Sudan, which had once harbored Osama bin Laden. Khartoum suddenly made available its vast intelligence files on al-Qaeda in an effort to demonstrate that it was a willing partner in the war on terrorism.

But the administration's determination to end the conflict made it blind to grievances in other parts of the country. With the Iraq War raging, Bush wanted nothing more than a formal peace signing on the White House lawn. Powell was dispatched in October 2003 to visit the talks, being held in a lovely lakeside resort in Naivasha, Kenya, and dangle the prospect of a presidential invitation if a deal were reached by the end of the year. Bashir and the southern rebel leader, John Garang, were offered coveted seats in the gallery next to the first lady during the State of the Union address. Powell also suggested that sanctions against Sudan would be lifted and full diplomatic relations would be restored.

"Now that we've come this far, let's finish it, let's kick it in, let's throw it into high gear," Powell told reporters as he flew into Kenya for his meetings.[4]

It turned out to be a huge mistake. Khartoum concluded that the Americans were so desperate for a peace agreement that it would probably have a free hand to brutally put down a budding rebel movement in the western part of the country, known as Darfur—an area the size of France. In February 2003, eight months before Powell's trip to Kenya, two African rebel groups had attacked police stations and military outposts in Darfur. They also wanted greater control over their own affairs—though, unlike the southern Sudanese, they were largely Muslim—and were worried that the deal between Khartoum and the south would still leave Darfur marginalized.

. With senior U.S. officials so focused on the north-south agreement, they were largely ignorant of the problems in Darfur. And Khartoum had become adept at manipulating local conflicts to suit its own ends. Arab herders and African farmers had long coexisted uneasily in Darfur, and it was relatively easy for Khartoum to recruit local militiamen, called the Janjaweed, to crush the rebellion. In a catastrophic reign of terror, two thousand villages were burned, more than two million people were made homeless, and as many as four hundred fifty thousand died from conflict or disease. Women were especially targeted for rape.

The result was a policy disaster.[5] Only eleven months after dangling goodies before the Sudanese government, Powell accused it of committing genocide in Darfur, undoubtedly aware that his own government was not prepared to pursue the measures outlined for signatories to the UN Genocide Conventions. In one of his last acts as secretary of state, in January 2005, he attended the signing ceremony of the North-South Comprehensive Peace Agreement, which was held in Nairobi, not Washington. (Bashir, having been accused of genocide, was no longer welcome at State of the Union addresses.) Under brilliant sunshine, in a soccer stadium, Powell was joined by African leaders, diplomats, and thousands of dancing and chanting Sudanese refugees. It was a bittersweet moment for the secretary of state because the agreement he had sought for so long was terribly tainted. Not only was the Darfur conflict raging, but the prospects that the north-south deal would hold together seemed tenuous. The peace plan was intended to keep Sudan intact for six years, after which a referendum on independence would be held. In a carefully negotiated compromise, an autonomous government was to emerge in the south while new national institutions were created. But the Sudanese refugees attending the ceremony said they believed the peace deal meant that in six years their part of Sudan would become an independent nation known as South Sudan.

The best the Americans could hope for was that, with the charismatic Garang brought into the government (he was to become vice president), the former rebel leader had the potential to negotiate peace in Darfur. Powell left office two weeks later, leaving the seemingly intractable problems of Sudan in Rice's lap.

Rice first broke an impasse within the administration. Pressure had been building overseas for the United Nations to authorize the International Criminal

Court to undertake a war crimes investigation of the Darfur atrocities. But hard-liners in the administration, who had convinced President Bush to withdraw the U.S. signature from the treaty establishing the court, had been opposed to any actions that would be seen as giving the nascent body legitimacy.

Rice concluded that the U.S. position of declaring genocide but blocking an international criminal investigation made no sense. But she also did not want to set a precedent that would undermine the administration's opposition to the court. So shortly after becoming secretary, Rice pressed inside the government for a change in policy—and then called her French and British counterparts to win agreement on a UN Security Council resolution that would allow the United States to abstain. The compromise allowed the court to finally begin its work.[6]

Having struck that deal, Rice then handed the Sudan portfolio to Zoellick. She had become disturbed about the policy during her initial briefings as secretary, decided it was a complete mess, and so asked Zoellick to sort it out. They both decided that the State Department had invested a huge amount of time in the north-south agreement but had never figured out how to reconcile that process with the tragedy in Darfur, especially after Powell had declared that genocide was taking place there.[7]

"The Run of the Place"

In April 2005, Zoellick flew off for his first trip to Sudan with a handful of reporters. It was clear he was new to the subject, but he had done voracious reading. He even handed out copies of an article in an obscure publication known as the *Boston Review,* written by a Sudan specialist named Alex de Waal, which he said was far better than any of the stuff he had gotten from the State Department.[8] Zoellick had done a lot of thinking about Darfur and had come up with a plan to pressure the Sudanese government.

He first headed to Oslo, where a donors' conference was being held to fund the north-south deal. Zoellick came with a huge pledge of U.S. support—as much as $2 billion—but he strongly suggested that it was tied to progress on Darfur. He also met with the two key players on the agreement, Garang and Sudan's first vice president, Ali Uthman Muhammad Taha. Ordinarily, this would have been it—the usual exchange of talking points before heading home. At least that's what Powell would have done. But Zoellick had cleverly decided to speed up the pace of diplomatic discussion. He had the meetings, took a side trip to Iraq—and then showed up in Khartoum two days later, ready to spring some ideas.

In Oslo, for instance, Taha had complained it was difficult to provide security for Darfur. This was a routine statement from the Sudanese government.
When Zoellick arrived in Khartoum, he told Taha he had a solution for his
problem: Sudan should permit NATO to airlift a huge increase in African
Union peacekeepers, tripling the size of the force to about seven thousand.
Taha blanched, but agreed.[9] (Rice and Zoellick formed a tag team on this initiative. With Taha's agreement in hand, a week later Rice raised the issue at
a NATO meeting in Lithuania. Her NATO counterparts were surprised at
first—and the French grumbled—but NATO soon agreed to undertake its first
mission ever in Africa. UN Secretary-General Kofi Annan also played an important role in this effort.)

But Taha, arguably the main power player in Sudan, also knew how to send
his own signals. Zoellick is a history buff. Taha made sure to show him the
stone staircase where the renowned British general Charles Gordon was killed
and beheaded when he tried to end an Islamic rebellion over British efforts to
end the slave trade of black Africans. The message wasn't subtle: This is what
happens to westerners who don't understand Sudan.

Jonathan Karl of ABC News got a firsthand look at the bizarre complexity
of Sudan when he managed to secure an interview with Sheikh Musa Hilal, re-
putedly the most ruthless of the Janjaweed leaders and a top candidate for a war
crimes indictment. Late that night, after Zoellick's meetings, Karl met Hilal
while he was having dinner. Karl was stunned to see that Hilal's dinner companions were leaders of the Fur tribe—the very people Janjaweed were accused
of terrorizing—and that the dinner was being held at a social club for police
officers. "Far from fearing arrest, the man called a war criminal by the United
States seemed to have the run of the place," Karl recalled.[10]

Before making an obligatory stop in Darfur, Zoellick flew in a noisy pro-
peller plane to see Garang at his headquarters in Rumbek. He landed on the
red dirt landing strip and was greeted by a quaint color guard of fifty rebel soldiers and a twenty-man military band in bright red uniforms, playing off-key
martial music. The divide between north and south was suddenly clear: It felt
like Africa, in contrast to the desert surrounding Khartoum. An aid worker said
the normally bare-breasted women—who ululated for Zoellick—had worn
shirts for his visit. Potholed tracks also had been graded in the past month in
anticipation of Zoellick's arrival. But the nearest paved road was five hundred
miles away, and Rumbek had no electricity, running water, or telephone service. Sudan is rich in natural resources, especially oil, but little of those riches
had trickled outside the central power in Khartoum.

Garang, a large man with grand schemes who had studied at Grinnell College in Iowa, was determined to turn his hometown into the capital of southern Sudan, to the dismay of U.S. officials, who felt that the largest city in the region—Juba—was more appropriate. Rumbek certainly had the feel of a boomtown, with scores of thatch-roofed huts under construction.[11] When Zoellick and Garang met in Garang's ramshackle one-story headquarters, Zoellick pressed Garang to use his influence with the Darfur rebels to end the violence. Garang nodded but made no promises. Though Garang had heard Zoellick pledge $2 billion in aid two days earlier, he boldly asked for an immediate infusion of $30 million. "I don't carry that much on me," Zoellick quipped.

Garang then requested a private one-on-one meeting with Zoellick, where he outlined a startling proposal. Garang noted that Israel and Iraq were both U.S. assets in the Middle East. He wanted to offer South Sudan as the third leg of a "strategic triad"—presumably meaning military bases. Zoellick could only marvel at Garang's brazen vision for his desperately poor region.

"Marhab, Marhab, Ya Condoleezza"

By the time Rice arrived in Sudan three months later, the administration's efforts appeared to be having an effect. The additional African Union forces were being flown into Darfur with NATO's help. The Sudanese government also appeared to be cooperating, though there continued to be hints that it was cooperating with the Janjaweed as well. The level of violence in Darfur had fallen, though there were few villages left to burn. Zoellick had made two more trips to Sudan, pushing the north-south accord along and traveling throughout Darfur. He had crafted a plan to end the rapes of women when they left the camps to forage for firewood, and Khartoum had accepted it. Garang had moved to Khartoum, becoming first vice president in the new national unity government, a position in theory second only to Bashir.

Rice had come to Sudan with four television correspondents—an unusually high number—intending to telegraph to audiences in the United States that U.S. policies were making a difference. But the fracas with Bashir's security guards, which ended up dominating the coverage, was a sign that nothing is ever secure in Sudan, that tragedy and heartbreak is always lurking.

Before leaving Sudan, Rice flew to see the showpiece camp in Darfur, Abu Shouk. From the air, Darfur looks like a moonscape, bleak and lifeless and punctuated only by the charred remains of abandoned villages. While there were more than one hundred camps for displaced people across Darfur—and in neighboring Chad—somehow Abu Shouk had earned a coveted spot on the diplomatic circuit, the main place where international dignitaries could demonstrate their concern for the benefit of television cameras. Abu Shouk received so many visitors that a small tableau of ersatz camp life had been created in a compound of seven thatched huts, where women can demonstrate that they have learned pasta making (on Italian machines) and small classes of children and adults are taught folklore. The runway at El Fasher could easily accommodate Rice's Boeing 757 jet. A sign on the gate informed visitors that it was for "Very Important Persons Only."

Powell had come here briefly in June 2004, and Zoellick had followed in April. (To his credit, he went to different camps on later trips.) Now it was Rice's turn. She spent ninety minutes in the camp (compared to Powell's twenty minutes), though twenty-five minutes was spent in an exhausting series of interviews, under blazing heat, with each television correspondent, a National Public Radio reporter, and print reporters.

Dozens of children greeted her with welcoming chants of "Marhab, marhab, ya Condoleezza," but other camp residents were kept outside the compound of demonstration huts. When Powell had visited, the camp held about forty thousand people in makeshift tents. Now, a year later, it contained about double that number and appeared more like a small village. The tents had evolved into neat rows of mud-brick homes, numbered streets, bicycles, and dozens of donkeys and other animals.

In one of the huts, Rice met with about fifteen women who had been raped. As they told their stories, Rice became teary-eyed and the men in her entourage became so uncomfortable that one by one they left, leaving only Rice and her translator. Rice was composed when she left the hut, but she refused to talk about what she had heard. Only months later would the experience of hearing "the personal stories of rape, of beatings, and of other unspeakable horrors" slowly creep into her public statements, a few more details at a time.[12]

"In Abu Shouk, I met privately with a small group of women, who spoke of their rape, and the rape of their daughters," Rice said more than a year later. "Their stories were harrowing and heartbreaking, but what was most chilling was the matter-of-fact way in which they spoke of their despair, as if it were a painful but unavoidable fact of their daily lives."[13]

For Rice, seeing Darfur was not the most memorable part of the trip. The onetime political scientist was most struck by the image of Garang sitting in his office in the presidential palace, the triumphant achievement of a former rebel leader who had waged war for two decades.[14]

It was a desert mirage. Ten days after Rice left Sudan, Garang was killed in a helicopter crash as he flew back to Sudan in stormy weather after a meeting with the president of Uganda.

"Your People Are Dying"

Garang's death was a crushing blow because he had held the movement together and his deputies did not have the experience or clout to deal with Khartoum. Every investigation suggested the crash was nothing but an accident, but
many in southern Sudan became convinced Khartoum had orchestrated it.
Within months, U.S. policy in Sudan would once again be teetering on the
edge of failure.

The Sudanese government kept virtually none of its promises, and the violence in Darfur had only been increasing, demonstrating that the African
Union force—with a limited mandate—was incapable of handling the task,
even with seven thousand troops. Baba Gana Kingibe, a senior AU official, said
in October that the government clearly coordinated offensive operations with
the Janjaweed. In one case, four hundred militiamen on camels and horses ram-
paged through several villages, killing thirty-two people and burning eighty
homes and shelters, while Sudanese helicopter gunships hovered overhead.[15]

Yet the administration kept offering inducements to Sudan. To the outrage
of some members of Congress, the State Department waived rules that prevented Sudan from hiring a Washington lobbyist and then removed it from the
list of the worst offenders of human trafficking. The reason given for improving Sudan's status was because the Sudanese government presented Rice with
the plan to end sexual violence against women. It was a cynical gesture. The
plan had been conceived by Zoellick, who presented it to the government two
weeks before Rice's trip. All the government had done was hand it back to
Rice.

In November, Zoellick made yet another trip to Sudan, but several undiplomatic outbursts made apparent the increasing frustrations of his assignment.
The Darfur rebel movement had split, and the animosity was so great that the
rebel leaders refused to come together to meet Zoellick, leaving him visibly annoyed and sitting alone at the negotiating table in a fancy Nairobi hotel.

"I'm the historic and present leader," said Abdel Wahid al-Nur, a founder
of the Sudanese Liberation Army. "I can't sit with the others who say they are
the SLM."

"Let him sit as a member, not as a leader," said a spokesman for Minni
Arko Minnawi, who had won elections (or staged a coup, depending on the
version of events) and had in effect ousted Nur.[16]

After a half hour, the rebels walked back in, but one leader said he would
only read a statement and then walk out again. Zoellick lost it: "While you are
bickering, your people are dying."

Later on the trip, Zoellick had a full-scale blowup, captured by television cameras, when he visited a camp in Darfur and insisted that a Sudanese government official not accompany him when he went to talk to victims of an attack that had left eighty-one people dead. Zoellick stuck his finger in the official's face and yelled, "Out! Out!" The official yelled back, "Not out!" Bashir later issued a statement saying, "We don't need Zoellick to resolve our internal problems."[17]

The rebel forces were not saints, either. Increasingly they fought each other—and attacked and killed African Union forces and aid workers. The situation in Darfur was getting desperate.

Zoellick had arrived at the camp wearing a blue plastic bracelet bearing the slogan NOT ON OUR WATCH. But he was growing exasperated. "If people are determined to kill each other," he said, "there's not a lot the United States can do."[18]

"A Binary Choice"

In early 2006, the administration concluded that only a large UN force, with an expanded mandate, could bring peace to Darfur. This was a reversal from 2004, when Powell repeatedly said a large force was not necessary and could not police such a large area—and that the African Union should take the lead. Under the administration's plan, there would now be a force of twenty thousand with substantial NATO involvement. But Khartoum was adamantly opposed, believing it would be an infringement of its sovereignty. Zoellick even called John Bolton, the U.S. ambassador to the United Nations, to urge him to try to get approval for the force when the United States held the rotating presidency of the Security Council. Bolton was stunned by the call; Zoellick barely communicated with him.[19] But UN officials, and many potential troop contributors, were aware of the political and logistical obstacles to accomplishing this in the absence of a peace agreement, and the Americans failed to push through a resolution during their Security Council presidency.

Zoellick then decided that the long-running Darfur peace talks in Abuja, Nigeria's capital, were the best way to resolve the conflict.[20] He had no illusions about the rebel groups, thinking they were mostly thugs, but Khartoum indicated that it might accept the UN force if a peace agreement were reached—and the UN force was needed to bring peace to the region. The media paid little attention to the talks, which had dragged on for two years under the mediation of the African Union. A former prime minister of Tanzania, Salim Ahmed Salim, oversaw the negotiations but with the fragmentation on the rebel side and important sectors of the Darfur population absent from the process, progress was stalled. A 2004 cease-fire had been broken almost as soon as it had been reached. The rebel groups and the government would meet and talk past each other, simply restating positions.

Zoellick flew to Europe in March to try to prod the talks forward, meeting with European Union foreign policy chief Javier Solana and Taha in Brussels and then flying to Paris for a long talk with Salim, where he tried to instill him with enough confidence to put forward a draft text of a peace agreement. Zoellick emphasized that the United States would back Salim fully and not leave him out on a limb.

Salim originally wanted to put forward an enhanced humanitarian cease-fire, but Zoellick kept pressing for a full agreement. Taha had met with rebel leaders in Tripoli after his meeting with Zoellick, and Zoellick sensed from their discussions that both sides were willing to consider something more ambitious. An agreement needed to cover security issues—dismantling the Janjaweed and the rebel forces—and also address how wealth and power would be shared between Darfur and Khartoum. Salim and his team drafted an eighty-five-page document that attempted to split the difference between the two sides, but several key issues were not resolved or left deliberately vague. Salim set a deadline for acceptance: April 30, a Sunday.

As the deadline approached, under pressure from all sides, the government accepted the agreement. But Taha made clear Khartoum had deep misgivings about parts of it. Pushing first for government acceptance turned out to be a tactical error because the rebel groups became suspicious. The rebels did not have an organized political power structure, operating almost like a loose semitribal network, and the document was difficult for them to digest in the first place. But the fact that Khartoum said it was acceptable instantly made it unacceptable for the rebels. Zoellick was convinced some rebel leaders never read it, since throughout the process some would demand things that were already in the text.

Meanwhile, back in Washington, Zoellick was getting regular updates from Cameron Hume, the U.S. chargé d'affaires in Khartoum who was attending the Abuja talks. Hume, who focused especially on the security issues, sensed the rebel groups would not come together in time and convinced Salim to extend the deadline by forty-eight hours. Zoellick was due to receive an award from Columbia University's business school that Monday, so he arrived at work with two suitcases—one with a tuxedo for New York and one with enough clothes for five days in Abuja.

Salim requested that Zoellick come to Abuja. Hume told Zoellick the odds of success were in the single digits but it was important enough to give it a shot.

That was enough for Zoellick, who told Rice he was going to Nigeria. He then videotaped his speech for Columbia University before taking a small government jet to Africa, arriving at 9:30 A.M. Tuesday in Abuja.

The talks were being held in a rundown hotel on the outskirts of Abuja, one of the most isolated and least attractive capitals in the world. The Americans could barely stand to use the toilets at the Chida International Hotel and were convinced every mosquito carried malaria and every bit of food held the potential for disease. The hotel, with barely functioning air-conditioning in the stifling heat, was prone to power shortages, especially at night, forcing work to be conducted by the light of cell phones and BlackBerries.

Zoellick met first with Salim and the AU mediation team, who were adamant that it would be a mistake to reopen the text. But they had also run out of ideas. Then he spent the day meeting with the rebel leaders and Sudanese government officials. Taha, who had been in Abuja for three weeks, had left before Zoellick arrived, a complication that so concerned Washington that Bush called Bashir and urged him to let Taha return to the talks. Taha never returned, and, despite Sudanese promises, Zoellick even had trouble reaching him by phone.

Zoellick listened to the rebel concerns, trying to show empathy but also emphasizing that this was crunch time. The deadline was extended another forty-eight hours, until Thursday. That night, lying awake in bed, he decided the best approach was to force what he called a "binary choice," a yes-or-no option. This was a technique he had used as a trade representative in World Trade Organization negotiations involving 148 countries: You listened to everyone's concerns and put together a balanced package of amendments to address those concerns— but then you refuse to alter the amendments. Otherwise, if you change it for one party, then everyone will try to nickel-and-dime the package to death.

Zoellick made sure to call Rice once a day, giving her an update. But she gave him complete freedom; it was his show.

The Americans had been joined in Abuja by a cast of international mediators, including British development minister Hilary Benn, Pekka Haavisto, a European Union representative, and Allan Rock, the Canadian ambassador to the United Nations. Benn took the lead in developing the nonsecurity package of amendments, while Zoellick handled the security side. The talks were dominated by shifting alliances and rumors of hidden payoffs and shady deals. Zoellick assigned U.S. diplomats to shadow the rebel groups, trying to keep track of their moods and concerns.

Another key player was the flamboyant president of Nigeria, Olusegun Obasanjo, who seemed to thrive in the atmosphere of pressure and intrigue. Obasanjo, who as host officially oversaw the talks, immediately bought into

Zoellick's plan to pressure the parties. One consistent rumor was that Libya was bribing rebels not to sign. Obasanjo confronted Ali Treiki, the Libyan envoy to the talks, and demanded an explanation from the flustered diplomat. Obasanjo yelled at the diplomat that he had "better fix it now" or else Obasanjo would "tell the world." Treiki denied the rumors but dashed out of the room.

"I Am a Fearsome Enemy"

Minnawi, by now the leader of the largest Darfur rebel faction, had given Zoellick a document with a detailed set of security demands promising him that if Zoellick could win the government's agreement, he would support the deal. The Americans knew it was too much for the government to swallow. But during the swirl of meetings, Zoellick managed to befriend a Sudanese general who had trained at Fort Knox and quietly got an unofficial sense of what elements of Minnawi's paper the government could accept.

The original AU plan had only a vague requirement for the government to come up with a plan to demobilize the Janjaweed. Those requirements were toughened with specific instructions. The amendments also detailed that five thousand rebel forces would be folded into the army and police forces. But the government and rebels had vastly different estimates of the size of the rebel forces. Minnawi, who had the most troops on the ground, was concerned that his rival, Nur, whom Minnawi had ousted in the fall, would suddenly show up with more troops than expected. So provisions were added that several thousand more troops would receive education and other training.

When Zoellick outlined the draft proposals Wednesday night to the rebel groups, he thought the initial response was positive from both Minnawi and Nur. Minnawi said he didn't really care about the nonsecurity provisions but wanted a few tweaks to the security side. Only a small splinter group, JEM, seemed to be a problem, but most of their leaders lived in Europe and they had already been quoted in the press as saying they didn't want a peace agreement.

Zoellick had a more difficult time with the government, particularly over the nonsecurity positions, but his unspoken alliance with the Sudanese general seemed to win acceptance for the security plan. He finally reached Taha by phone and had a pleasant conversation with him. The government can live with the proposals, Zoellick told Taha. The whole thing seemed to fall into place when Minnawi came to see Zoellick at 7:30 P.M. Thursday night and told him he would accept the amendments. He was more concerned about Nur and the possibility he would claim to have more fighters than were apparent on the ground. So Zoellick produced a side letter, promising that U.S. soldiers would help count the number of rebel forces.

As the midnight deadline neared, the talks moved to Obasanjo's presidential compound, where African Union and Arab League officials were gathering. The original plan had been for Nur to give his response first, but fresh from his meeting with Minnawi, Zoellick urged Obasanjo to let Minnawi go first. "I got Minni lined up," he said confidently, and told Obasanjo that Minnawi's acceptance will pressure Nur to sign onto the plan. Then, hearing Nur was outside in the parking lot, Zoellick went outside to try to browbeat Nur into accepting the deal.

Zoellick was pressing Nur, saying this was the moment to cut a deal, when Chris Padilla, his chief of staff, came rushing out. "Sir, you need to come back in," Padilla said. Zoellick said okay, but kept talking to Nur. Padilla came out again. "Sir, you must come back in—now," he emphasized. "Somebody got to Minni."

Inside, Minnawi was speaking, suddenly raising objections to the nonsecurity provisions that he had previously said didn't mean much to him. Now he wanted a few more seats in the regional legislature, an almost useless entity that would have discretion over no more than $3 million in funds. Zoellick was furious and decided to let his anger show.

"I'm disappointed in you. You let me down. I expect people to keep their word," Zoellick icily told Minnawi in full view of the African leaders and negotiators. "I cannot believe you are dropping peace for the sake of a few more seats." Zoellick didn't shout, but his tone showed that he had lost his patience. "Let me be clear," he concluded. "I can be a very good friend, but I am a fearsome enemy."[21]

When it was Nur's turn, it was clear that Zoellick's talk in the parking lot had not made much of an impression. Nur began by giving the history of Darfur, asserting it had been an independent country in 1916. Zoellick told him this was a time to decide.

"We are seeking self-determination," Nur said.

"You are seeking self-determination, but your people are in camps and dying," Zoellick shot back. "If you decide for peace, my country will stand with you to help you. If you pass up this opportunity, there will not be another one. It is finished."

When Nur said his people were the victims, Zoellick replied, "You said you are the victims; you are going to remain the victims."[22]

The day before, to win support, Zoellick had given each of the three rebel leaders—and President Bashir—an individually tailored letter from President Bush. The letter from Bush to Bashir held out the prospect of improved bilateral relations if peace was achieved in Sudan. Zoellick began to read from Bush's letter to Nur, saying it showed he had guarantees.

Obasanjo also kept up the pressure. Though not a large man, Obasanjo has an imposing presence, and he repeatedly pressed the rebels to accept the amendments through a mixture of cajoling, bullying, and flattering. "I am not a rebel," the former army general told the rebel groups. "I fought against rebels in the Biafra war. And we defeated rebels. But at the end of the day we still had to talk."

At one point, Obasanjo thrust his fist in Nur's face, yelling, "You let me down, and you betrayed me." He then grabbed him by the collar and dragged him into another room for more tongue-lashing.

The discussions dragged through the night. Minnawi came back at around 4 A.M. and asked for more time for a decision. Obasanjo sarcastically said, "You say you coming back soon. In the Bible it says Jesus is coming back soon and it's been two thousand years. I don't know what that means." But at 5:30 A.M., he agreed to adjourn until 9 A.M. so Minnawi could give a final answer.

Alex de Waal, a fellow at Harvard University's Global Equity Initiative who was advising the African Union during the talks, encountered Minnawi talking to a few of his rebel commanders in a coffee shop. Minnawi looked drawn and worn-out. De Waal decided to pander to Minnawi's ego, asking him how he made decisions when he was in the middle of a battle. Minnawi replied that he made the decisions alone. De Waal told him he had to act the same way on the political battlefield—you consult but you also make the final decisions alone. They embraced, and Minnawi said he would accept. But de Waal did not sense any conviction.

At 9:15 A.M., Minnawi came back to the compound. Obasanjo demanded, "What have you got for me?" No one knew what his answer would be, and de Waal convinced himself all was lost. Nur had given his word to Solana in a phone call that he would sign, but had since reneged on the deal. Haavisto was certain Minnawi would answer no as well. A drawn and exhausted Minnawi replied that he accepted the document with reservations. Obasanjo replied that such concerns could be handled during the implementation talks. Once at least one rebel group had accepted the deal, Khartoum had little choice but to go along.

But the drama wasn't over yet. The signing ceremony was delayed when an electrical fire started in the hotel after officials tried to print out the agreement using two printers at once. During the delays in producing the signing document, Minnawi learned that his brother had been killed in Darfur. Minnawi disappeared, wondering if the government had done it—or if angry colleagues were sending a message. Obasanjo showed little sympathy but kept up the pressure.

He told Minnawi that maybe his brother's death would not have happened if he had signed the deal two days earlier.

The Sudanese government suddenly wanted to fly Bashir to the ceremony, but Obasanjo would not risk any delays. As the negotiators discussed the Sudanese request, Obasanjo pulled a banana off the table, peeled it, split it in two, and rubbed both parts in the dirt, saying that in Nigeria if you give a monkey a banana it will do that so you do not take the banana back.

"This is my banana, and I'm not letting you take it back," he told the Sudanese envoy.

Failure After Success

The Darfur peace agreement was a rare diplomatic achievement—but it was also tenuous. Zoellick flew back to Washington, where he and Rice flanked Bush as the president hailed the agreement and said he would ask Rice to push for a Security Council resolution mandating the UN force. The Bush administration was generally reluctant to sit down and negotiate with regimes it found distasteful, such as Iran, Syria, and North Korea, but in the case of Sudan, the influence of the Christian right made it imperative for the administration to push as hard as it could to achieve results. Zoellick thought the agreement he had negotiated demonstrated that the administration could achieve results with odious regimes if it was just willing to sit down and talk.

Zoellick realized the Darfur agreement needed to be carefully implemented and monitored. But it was his last hurrah. Zoellick quit as deputy secretary to join a Wall Street investment house shortly afterward. Most of his advisors departed as well, leaving the State Department's widest gap in Sudan expertise in a decade. Over at the White House, another key player on Sudan—Michael Gerson, a critical link to evangelical groups—also resigned. U.S. policy drifted over the summer of 2006, as Assistant Secretary of State Jendayi Frazer, now freed from Zoellick's dominating influence, fought against any attempt to appoint a special envoy for Sudan.

The Darfur agreement further splintered the rebel groups and was soon in tatters. It became clear that Nur and Minnawi were such bitter rivals that if one accepted the agreement, the other would refuse. Minnawi won himself a White House visit with Bush. But the Americans had placed their bet on the wrong horse. Minnawi was a member of a minority ethnic group, the Zaghawa, representing only 8 percent of the population in Darfur, so his acceptance (and subsequent appointment to a high position in the Khartoum unity government) made the deal suspect to the majority Fur tribe. Soon the rebel groups were fighting each other again, this time with some of the worst atrocities committed by Minnawi's forces. The Sudanese government readied its forces for a decisive military defeat of the rebels.

In late April, the deputy chief of the political/economic section of the U.S. embassy in Khartoum had warned in a cable to Washington that an Abuja peace accord would be unlikely to stop the violence and might actually ignite even worse fighting. "Stopping the violence in Darfur will require a military force with first world leadership, first world assets, and first world experience," Ron Capps wrote, saying such a force would require the United States to take a lead role.

He acknowledged that the Sudanese government would resist and Security Council members would be skeptical. "Yes, it will be hard," he wrote. "But being hard should not deter us from doing what is right. This is genocide. If we are serious about stopping it, this is what it will take. Otherwise, which American president will be the one to apologize to the dead of Darfur?"[23]

In August the UN Security Council finally passed a resolution demanding that Sudan accept a UN peacekeeping force, despite repeated warnings by the Sudanese government that it would reject UN troops and allow only the African Union to command troops on the ground. And under pressure from Congress, in September Bush appointed a special envoy—former USAID director Andrew Natsios. But it was too late. Sudan was no longer fearful of the United States, which was trapped in a war in Iraq, and with dwindling international clout, there was little appetite or available military units to lead a peacekeeping effort. Sudan remained unmoved even as the administration for months threatened new sanctions. Khartoum now had its protectors: China, with the veto power of a permanent member of the UN Security Council, had become a huge investor in Sudanese oil, while the Arab League agreed that Sudan was in a valiant fight against potential colonial occupiers. For her part, Rice never appeared directly engaged in the issue, preferring to hand it off first to Zoellick and then to Natsios, while she grappled with the administration's other foreign policy headaches. She never seemed willing to invest the prestige of her office or demonstrate a personal commitment to ending the conflict.

Three years after Powell had first declared that genocide was taking place in Sudan, hundreds of people every month continued to die in the camps of Darfur—mute evidence of the policies that failed to save them.

CHAPTER 6

SLEEPLESS IN JERUSALEM

After Rice landed in Tel Aviv and her motorcade sped toward Jerusalem, it was clear she was not happy.

It was the last stop of a difficult weeklong tour of the Middle East. A day earlier, she had been in Bahrain, where a meeting designed to showcase democratic reforms in the Middle East had collapsed in embarrassment. Egypt had refused to sign a final declaration unless Arab governments were guaranteed the right to decide which pro-democracy groups would receive aid from a new fund promoted by the Americans. It had been an astonishing rebuff on one of Rice's signature issues—and from a close U.S. ally that received more than $2 billion in annual aid from the United States.

Officially, the British and the Bahrainis were cohosts of the conference, known as the Forum for the Future, but of course the Americans had a hidden and heavy hand in the development of the ill-fated statement.[1] Moreover, there had been a flap over Elizabeth Cheney, the vice president's daughter and the principal deputy assistant secretary of state for Near East policy. Cheney was in charge of democracy promotion in the Middle East, so the Forum for the Future was her responsibility. But she arrived late because she had decided she wanted to join Rice, who was scheduled to make an unannounced trip to Baghdad just before the Bahrain meeting.

Cheney desperately wanted to see with her own eyes the outcome of the war promoted by her father. She had pestered Jim Wilkinson before the trip, and he told her there were no more seats available on the helicopters that would fly the staff from the airport to Iraq's Green Zone, the protected enclave for U.S. personnel in central Baghdad. But after Rice's plane took off for the Middle East, Cheney kept pressing, telling Wilkinson that she had received permission from the female Secret Service agent who accompanied her everywhere. (As the vice president's daughter, Cheney merited her own Secret Service detail.) Wilkinson questioned the agent, who seemed rather young and inexperienced, but she confirmed that she had approved Cheney's request. Space suddenly became available for Cheney and her agent.

When Rice's Boeing 757 jet landed in Bahrain so the staff could transfer to the military aircraft that would fly Rice to Iraq, a team of Secret Service agents was waiting to escort Cheney to the conference. Rice's trip was secret to all but a handful of people so the Secret Service had no inkling of what was going to happen. The agents were stunned when Cheney told them that everything had been arranged for her to go with Rice to Baghdad. She and her agent slipped onto the military jet.

The visit to Iraq was uneventful, but when Rice returned to Bahrain, Cheney's Secret Service detail was still at the airport, ready to shoot someone. They were furious at Cheney, at Wilkinson, at Cheney's young agent, at everyone on Rice's team, because the vice president's daughter had gone into the war-torn country, even under the protection of the U.S. military. Cheney's parents were also rather surprised to learn she had visited Iraq when she called from Bahrain to let them know of her adventure.

Sean McCormack remarked on the dark humor of the moment. "Am I the only one who sees the irony of this?" he was overheard to ask.[2]

Then, to top it off, the Bahrain conference turned into a public relations nightmare.

Now Rice faced another potential disaster. She had planned to make a quick trip to Israel and the Palestinian territories before flying halfway around the world to an Asian economic summit in South Korea. She had hoped to announce an important development in the Israeli-Palestinian conflict: The Israelis had left the Gaza Strip in the summer of 2005, and after months of negotiations the Palestinians were finally supposed to be given control of their own border crossing, near the town of Rafah on the Egyptian border.

But when Rice got in her limousine, her two top aides on the Middle East—Assistant Secretary C. David Welch and Deputy National Security Advisor Elliott Abrams—told her there was no deal on the border crossing. When she had left Washington days earlier, she was told a deal was "very close," and now it was still "very close." Every day, it was very close. Rice laced into both men in frustration. Again, not enough groundwork had been done.

She ran down the list of issues blocking an accord. "Why had this not been accomplished?" she asked. "Where do we stand on that?" She worried out loud that the special representative for the Gaza withdrawal, former World Bank president James R. Wolfensohn, had shrewdly set up the situation so that if an accord was not reached, the United States would get the blame—not the Israelis and the Palestinians.

"Why won't this succeed? It's because the Israelis and the Palestinians do not want to reach an agreement," Rice said.

Welch wondered if this was Rice's first taste of the huge frustrations that diplomats working in the region had experienced for more than three decades. But Welch and Abrams knew she was right, both on Wolfensohn's gambit and on the actual substance of the agreement. Welch pulled out his cell phone and told his aides that they needed to begin to draft a document that the United States could present to the two parties.

Abrams and Welch also had a new weapon: Rice's direct involvement. Be flexible, they told the Israelis and the Palestinians, or you will damage the credibility of a great friend. "Don't be the one who causes this not to work," Abrams delighted in telling both sides. "She won't like that."[3]

"I'm Still in a War Mode"

Bush's promise to Rice that he was willing to back a sustained effort to create a Palestinian state in his second term was one of the main reasons she agreed to become secretary of state. Yet paradoxically, the goal of finally resolving the Israeli-Palestinian conflict now seems further away than ever, in part because of decisions she and the president made in the first term and since Rice's tenure as secretary of state.

To some extent, it is unfair to blame American officials for the failures of Israelis and Palestinians. But the United States plays a critical role in managing the conflict. The Bush administration disengaged at critical moments and often appeared to tilt too strongly to Israel, leaving intense anger in the Arab world at U.S. policy. The administration's stated goal was to build Palestinian institutions and remove leaders with terrorist links. Yet as a result of U.S. policies, the militant group Hamas has won legislative elections and the Palestinian Authority has become a shell on the verge of collapse.

Bush came into office highly skeptical of President Clinton's sustained engagement in the peace process. Clinton had struggled to achieve a peace accord in his final days in office, but it collapsed in a wave of Palestinian attacks known as the second intifada. Bush, in fact, showed little interest in the details of the complex disputes in the region and was wary of intervening deeply in the negotiating process. The president often has a visceral negative reaction when officials try to delve deeply into such subjects as the final borders of Israel and a Palestinian state or the status of Jerusalem—issues that are central to the conflict. At the end of his term Clinton debated those questions at length with Israelis and Palestinians, but Bush dismissed them as "all those old issues." In comments that struck some aides as naive, Bush would say the Israelis are wasting their money on expanding settlements in the West Bank because ultimately those projects will become housing developments for Palestinians.

The result is that Bush would make statements, such as announcing in a speech to the United Nations after the September 11 attacks that he believed in the goal of a Palestinian state, but would offer no real path for achieving that outcome. Throughout the first term, the administration followed a pattern of engagement and disengagement—a burst of publicity about new initiatives or special envoys, followed by policy drift and an unwillingness to push either side, especially the Israelis, to take big steps toward improvement. Eventually, the effort went dormant, sometimes for months, until yet another approach was crafted. Clinton had clearly been working on creating a Palestinian state and stated that in his waning days in office. Bush, to his credit, dispensed with the diplomatic mumbo-jumbo and forthrightly declared it was U.S. policy that there should be a Palestinian state. But there is a huge difference between merely making a declaration and actually working to achieve a goal.

Bush's personal relations with Middle East leaders also affected his approach. He quickly grew to dislike Palestinian leader Yasir Arafat, whom Clinton had repeatedly invited to the White House in a vain effort to make Arafat a peacemaker. (Bush spoke to Arafat twice by telephone but never met him.) After 9/11, Bush began to believe that Arafat was too linked to terrorism to have any role in the peace process.

Meanwhile, Bush embraced Israeli prime minister Ariel Sharon as a soul mate in the war on terror. Bush called Sharon a "man of peace" in 2002, infuriating Arabs angry over the Israeli army's attacks against Palestinians in the West Bank.[4] The administration increasingly relied on Sharon's ideas and vision to guide its policy.

After a trip to the region in March 2002, Vice President Cheney concluded that peace could never be achieved as long as Arafat remained in power. He felt that dealing with Arafat was inconsistent with the administration's war against terrorism. Cheney's view became a central tenet of a speech the president delivered on June 24 of that year, in which he cut off relations with Arafat and envisioned a Palestinian state by 2005 if the Palestinians built a democracy and halted attacks on Israelis. As appeared so often, Powell had been blindsided by the shift; only a couple of weeks before he had talked about convening an international conference with all the players, including Arafat.[5]

Arafat "is a loser," Bush privately told Jordan's King Abdullah. "I'm not going to spend my political capital on losers, only winners. I'm still in a war mode, and the war is terrorism. If people don't fight terrorism, I am not going to deal with them."[6]

European, UN, and Arab diplomats believed that isolating Arafat was a fundamental mistake. In their view, Arafat, with all his flaws, was the only Palestinian leader with enough clout to strike a lasting deal with Israel. Bush's decision to cut off Arafat left U.S. policy stalled for months, since there was no one in charge on the Palestinian side who could meet with senior U.S. officials.

For a quarter century Sharon had railed against making deals with the terrorists, so Bush's speech was one of the most important moments of his life. "For Sharon it was like the coming of the messiah," said Dov (Dubi) Weissglas, his chief of staff and longtime friend, who watched the speech on CNN with Sharon. "In all the years I knew him, I never saw him so touched and excited. It was like a vision that came true."[7]

By Powell's account, Rice was a frequent and nagging drag on any of his efforts to make progress in the Middle East during Bush's first term. In 2001, an "anxious" Rice called to tell him that Bush "just wonders whether you really need to give" a speech on the Israeli-Palestinian conflict.[8] When Powell was ordered to go on a ten-day Middle East trip in 2002 during the worst outbreak of violence, Rice called him "constantly" while he was on the road, with "her admonitions, sometimes approaching actual dressings-down . . . worrying that Powell was going too far and telling him to hold back."[9]

In fact, Rice had secretly taken over the Israeli-Palestinian account in 2002, establishing a direct link with Sharon through Weissglas in order to micromanage the policy. For the rest of the first term, Powell's State Department largely became irrelevant to U.S.-Israel relations as Rice and Weissglas dealt directly with each other at the behest of Bush and Sharon.[10]

Weissglas vividly remembers when Rice confronted him in September 2002, as Israeli tanks surrounded Arafat in his government compound in Ramullah, demanding Arafat turn over individuals suspected of terrorism. For ten days, Arafat was trapped as Israeli forces methodically destroyed much of the compound. Weissglas had flown to Washington with a forty-five-minute defense of Israeli actions, carefully crafted with Sharon. But Rice cut him off after just ten minutes.

Weissglas, who calls Rice "a magician in the art of language," said she did not yell, but pointedly noted that the administration was in a sensitive situation with the Arab world as it prepared to go to war with Iraq.

"This effort, if it happens, it will be a strategic relief to Israel," Rice said. "It is more important than Arafat. What you are doing now is an obstruction." She said that Bush was probably the greatest friend of Israel since its creation, and now Israel was creating a problem.

"The United States will never restrain you against any action which is needed to protect your people and stop terror, even if takes place in the worst political context," Rice added. "This is not the case. Arafat is not a ticking bomb. To me, he is not important."

Weissglas could see she was annoyed. "Okay, I gotcha," he said. Shaken, he left the White House and called Sharon on his cell phone from the Cosi sandwich shop across the street. "Arik, I think we should better get the hell out of there," he said. A day later, Sharon decided to end the siege.[11]

When Bush made his June 24 speech, the administration had not produced a detailed plan for enacting the president's vision, largely because of objections by the Israelis, who were closely consulted on Bush's remarks. Only under pressure from Arab and European leaders did the administration support the "road map," a detailed "performance-based," three-phase peace plan largely drafted by diplomats from the European Union, Russia, and the United Nations— which, along with the United States, formed a diplomatic group known as the Quartet.[12] Internal debates within the administration kept the plan bottled up for months, and it was only released on the eve of the Iraq War after the personal intervention of Britain's prime minister, Tony Blair.

In June 2003, Bush held two back-to-back summits in Sharm el-Sheikh, Egypt, and Aqaba, Jordan, to inaugurate the road map process. Arafat had yielded to pressure to create a prime minister's post, which in theory diluted his power. Mahmoud Abbas, a longtime Arafat aide who abhorred violence, was selected for the job and embraced by Bush as the new face of Palestinian leadership. Bush also announced that Rice, then his national security advisor, would take a leading role in implementing the road map. Bush appointed a special envoy, John S. Wolf, to monitor progress on the peace plan.

But Rice would make only one trip to the region, a month later, and very quickly the process fell apart. By September, Abbas had quit, claiming the Americans and Israelis had not backed him fully, and the road map was essentially dead only months after being launched.

With the collapse of the peace plan, Rice had a confidential conversation with Weissglas. "The road map is at best a marginal plan. It doesn't work," she said. She noted that as long as it was in office, the Bush administration would stand behind the process, which put the onus on the Palestinians to end terrorism first. But in a year there would be a presidential election and Bush might lose. The Europeans were also adding pressure to stop the incremental peace process and leapfrog immediately to final-status negotiations. She told Weissglas to go home and think of "a move of significance"—something that would regain the initiative and help the United States say, "Look at what Israel has done; now the Palestinians have to do something."[13]

By year's end, on Weissglas's recommendation, Sharon would offer a new gambit: In the absence of any Palestinian partner, he would undertake a unilateral withdrawal from Jewish settlements on the Gaza Strip, essentially a Palestinian slum of 1.3 million people squeezed into a narrow coastal area. The twenty-one settlements and areas controlled by the Israeli military made up 20 percent of the Gaza Strip, including much of its fertile land and all of the southern seashore.[14]

Sharon had shrewdly calculated that because of long-standing American opposition to Israeli settlements Bush and Rice would actively promote his Gaza plan, which he labeled "disengagement." But Rice also had a secret role in the idea, pushing the Israelis to think boldly. Originally, Weissglas returned with a proposal to withdraw from three to five settlements. Rice told him the United States would praise any such announcement, "but it is not any sort of political breakthrough. If you want a different reality, it has to be Gaza in its entirety. Then we will be able to respond loudly and clearly."[15]

With the road map now moribund, Rice decided that Israel's withdrawal from any of the Palestinian territories represented progress. But many experts thought Sharon would simply withdraw from Gaza, which was ungovernable, and then hold on to much of the West Bank, essentially dictating the boundaries of the Palestinian entity. (The administration pressed Sharon to also withdraw from settlements on the West Bank in order to counter that criticism.)[16]

For instance, Brent Scowcroft, Rice's former mentor, thought Bush was "mesmerized" by Sharon, who "just has him wrapped around his little finger." Over dinner at the end of 2003, Scowcroft and Rice had what he described as a "terrible fight" over the Gaza plan.

"At least there's some good news," Rice said.

"That's terrible news," Scowcroft bluntly replied. "For Sharon this is not the first move, this is the last move. He's getting out of Gaza because he can't sustain eight thousand settlers with half his army protecting them. Then, when he's out, he will have an Israel that he can control and a Palestinian state atomized enough that it can't be a problem."[17]

The administration tried to negotiate terms with Sharon that would make that scenario less likely. But Sharon also drove a hard bargain. Weissglas told Rice that the plan would be difficult to sell to the Israeli public because it was unilateral, meaning the government could not point to any concessions from the Palestinians. Israel needed something from the United States. "In the absence of the Palestinians, it is you guys," he told Rice.[18]

In early 2004, Bush gave Sharon a carefully negotiated letter that suggested the administration supported the Israeli position on retaining major settlement blocks and refusing the Palestinian right to return to Israel. Any peace deal would likely include those elements, but only after the result of negotiations between the two parties (and with compensation to the Palestinians for accepting those two points). Bush's deal with Sharon greatly angered Arab world. The perceived tilt toward Israel, combined with the invasion and occupation of Iraq, undermined U.S. credibility in the region.

When Rice became secretary of state, the Israeli portfolio followed her back to Foggy Bottom—and the Palestinian issue was now officially her burden.

"Your Job Is to Shoot Them—the More Dead the Better"

In a stroke of good fortune, Arafat died in December 2004, between Rice's nomination and her confirmation as secretary. Abbas was back, having been elected to replace Arafat as Palestinian president. The Israelis were preparing to leave Gaza over the summer. There was a sense of new possibilities and new opportunities.

Rice approached the issue carefully. Her most immediate goal was ensuring that the Israeli withdrawal from Gaza was successful. She felt it held great potential to change the game in the Middle East. The Europeans thought Arafat's death should reinvigorate the road map and negotiations should begin soon on final-status issues to create a Palestinian state. But Rice did not understand the fears of anxious Europeans that the Israelis needed to negotiate with the Palestinians before Israel left Palestinian territories. In fact, she thought it was odd that after years of telling the Israelis to withdraw, now the Europeans wanted to put up roadblocks. She focused on convincing the Europeans that Sharon's withdrawal from Gaza was not the end of a process, but a beginning that should be embraced. She argued, somewhat disingenuously, that the Gaza withdrawal would jump-start the road map plan, even though it had nothing to do with it.

Rice also wanted to protect Sharon. She felt the venerable Israeli prime minister was taking a tremendous gamble, potentially breaking up the Likud Party, which he had helped form (though she thought this would not necessarily be a bad thing). Rice did not hesitate to bluntly question Sharon about some Israeli activities, particularly the route of a security barrier that struck this child of the South as a land grab akin to segregation. But Sharon liked Rice and was very candid with her about his plans. He wanted to be sure that the United States did not do anything that would potentially harm his project.

This left the Palestinians with the short end of the stick. Sharon had conceived his plan when Arafat was the Palestinian leader, and he had seen no need to work with the Palestinian government. This was a "unilateral" action. There was nothing to negotiate. But the Palestinians thought that now that Mahmoud Abbas had been elected, circumstances had changed. Abbas, who customarily wears suits, making him look more like a banker than a revolutionary, needed to be involved in the Gaza withdrawal so he could claim some credit for it and bolster his standing with the Palestinian people.

Rice suggested to the Israelis they might seek ways to "coordinate" with the Palestinians. The Israelis were reluctant—and demanded that the new Palestinian government demonstrate that they could take action against the militant groups operating openly in the territories.

As a sign of Rice's caution, she announced on her first trip to Israel and the Palestinian territories that she had appointed a U.S. general to assist the Palestinian Authority as it rebuilt its security forces. Much of the Palestinian security infrastructure—funded by $50 million from the CIA in the 1990s—had been destroyed by the Israelis during the second intifada. But Lieutenant General William Ward was specifically told not to intervene in discussions between the two sides or act as any sort of mediator. The process would be left to the parties, even though history has shown that they frequently need the firm hand of the United States to strike a deal. The deputy secretary, Robert Zoellick, was not directly involved in Israeli-Palestinian issues, but he watched the Ward mission with concern. He didn't think the effort was real—that Rice, having announced the appointment, was just letting it meander inconclusively.[19]

Rice's two closest aides on the Israeli-Palestinian dispute are Abrams and Welch, who became the Mutt and Jeff of the peace process. Essentially, Abrams handled the Israelis and Welch the Arabs, though they were largely inseparable, frequently traveling together to the region.

A fiercely pro-Israel neoconservative, Elliott Abrams had never really known Rice before he joined the National Security Council staff in 2001 as director for human rights and democracy. He is a classic Washington insider. He had once worked for Senator Daniel Patrick Moynihan (D-N.Y.), but then moved sharply to the right during the Reagan years. In 1991, as part of the Iran-contra affair, he was indicted for giving false testimony before Congress; he pleaded guilty to withholding information from Congress (and was later pardoned by President George H. W. Bush). Rice valued his perspective on Israel, so much so that even when he had the human rights portfolio she would check in with him on potential initiatives to anticipate the Israeli reaction. He eventually took over the entire Middle East account at the NSC. When Rice became secretary, she discussed a variety of jobs for him at State. But he had been an assistant secretary of state three times already—and likely would have trouble getting confirmed—and he had no interest in a post like policy planning. Steve Hadley offered to elevate Abrams to deputy national security advisor, so Rice struck a deal: Anytime she went to the Middle East, she would take Abrams with her.

Welch, in contrast to the more ideological Abrams, was a classic State Department Arabist. Before becoming assistant secretary for Near Eastern affairs, Welch had been ambassador to Egypt, chargé d'affaires in Saudi Arabia, and a political officer in Jordan and Syria; in between those stints overseas he had handled U.S. policy toward the region from a desk in Washington. (He overlapped with Rice on the National Security Council staff in 1989–1991.) Welch, whose wife is also a State Department officer, is often cool and collected even during the most turbulent periods. He demonstrated those traits in his first overseas post, when a mob attacked and burned the U.S. embassy in Islamabad, Pakistan, killing four staff members. Welch attracted notice for his calm under fire. He even managed to work well with Abrams—a feat that his predecessor, William Burns, was unable to accomplish during the Powell years.[20]

The Palestinians thought that Rice's fervent support of the Israeli approach to the Gaza plan was largely because Abrams was intellectually and ideologically invested in it. Abrams had worked closely with Sharon's government as the plan was being developed—indeed, Sharon had briefed Abrams on the idea during a meeting in Rome before announcing it—so the Palestinians felt they could never get an even break from the Bush administration. Abbas wanted the release of thousands of political prisoners, a reduction in the Israeli checkpoints and roadblocks that were a daily humiliation to the Palestinian people, and real engagement with Sharon and his government.[21]

The Americans instead offered money. Bush announced in his 2005 State of the Union address that he would seek $200 million to encourage Palestinian reforms, though $50 million was actually earmarked for Israel to build terminals for people and goods at checkpoints surrounding Palestinian areas. When

Abbas visited Washington in May, Bush announced he would provide $50 million in direct aid to build housing, schools, roads, water facilities, and health clinics in Gaza to help ease the transition as the Israelis left the Gaza Strip. In a public statement in the Rose Garden, Bush also tried to mitigate the effect of his 2004 letter to Sharon saying Israel could expect to keep large settlement blocks. "Changes to the 1949 armistice lines must be mutually agreed to," Bush said, though he notably did not give Abbas his own letter to balance out the concessions to the Israelis.[22] Abbas emphasized in his meeting with Bush that he did not want a repeat of 2003; he needed to be empowered.

While words and money were nice, Abbas wanted bullets and rifles. The Americans and the Israelis demanded Abbas confront Hamas, but the Israelis blocked the transfer of rifles, fearing the weapons would be turned on them if there was another outbreak of violence. Abbas called Ward and Welch, and pleaded that the Palestinian Authority be given something that would give him the upper hand.

The Americans were not very sympathetic to the complaints, believing Abbas and the Palestinian Authority were a perpetual disappointment. In their view, Abbas never had the will to act. You don't get something for nothing, Rice thought. Abbas was supposed to reform Fatah, his corrupt and aged political party, and overhaul the security services in order to face Hamas. But from Rice's perspective, nothing seemed to be happening except complaints. She thought Abbas was a nice man but ineffective, and she soon became frustrated because he seemed to make little progress. The United States had invested in him, she thought, and he seemed incapable of delivering.[23]

At one point, when some militants took potshots at Abbas in July, Welch called him and demanded that he had to take action to show the Palestinians he was boss. "Your job is to shoot them—the more dead the better," Welch said, adding in Arabic, "Fuck them."

Abbas deployed a few forces, but he did not have a taste for confrontation. He believed in trying to co-opt Hamas. He had engineered a cease-fire in attacks on Israelis—he felt this was a substantial accomplishment—and then he invited Hamas to participate in legislative elections. He thought they would win some seats, and then the new Palestinian government would seek to dismantle the militias.

Just as Sharon had taken advantage of Bush's ideological fervor for the war on terror, Abbas exploited the administration's zeal for democracy in the Arab world, arguing that his plan for dealing with Hamas would be an important step in Bush's grand goal of bringing democracy to the Middle East.[24] The pitch was compelling to Rice and her aides, but it required the administration to essentially accept the idea that a militant group could participate in politics before it gave up its weapons. The administration was already turning a blind eye to the militias springing up alongside the political parties in Iraq, but Hamas was a well-established group that had long been listed as a terrorist organization by the State Department.

The plan had a fatal flaw: It assumed that Abbas and Fatah would win the elections planned for January 2006. No one imagined that Hamas, which claimed credit for dozens of suicide bombings and called for the elimination of Israel, would do well in its first effort at electoral politics. "Unfortunately, they opted to follow our cue," said one top Palestinian official months later, after Fatah had lost.

The Israelis pulled out of Gaza in August, ending its thirty-eight-year occupation, a feat accomplished quickly and efficiently and with little bloodshed. Rice made two trips to the region in the two months before the pullout, trying to prod both sides to coordinate better. She helped broker one accord on demolishing Israeli housing in Gaza, but in the end there was little cooperation.

The Quarter, an international peace-monitoring group, had appointed Wolfensohn, the former World Bank president, to assist on economic reconstruction of Gaza, and he repeatedly tried to push the Israelis and the Palestinians to work together, to little avail. Months were spent trying to negotiate just an understanding on about a thousand acres of Israeli greenhouses in Gaza that provided employment for about four thousand Palestinian workers. The Israelis planned to destroy the computerized irrigation systems in the greenhouses if they were not compensated, making them useless, but the Palestinians did not want U.S. aid money intended for Palestinians to go to departing Israeli settlers. In the end, Wolfensohn had to dig into his own pocket—and the pockets of some rich Jewish friends—to raise the $14 million needed to preserve the greenhouse systems.[25]

When the Israelis left Gaza, which is a stronghold of Hamas, the militant group strung a huge banner declaring, THREE YEARS OF INTIFADA BEAT TEN YEARS OF NEGOTIATIONS. Abbas and his aides seethed, thinking they had been let down by the Israelis and the Americans. They found it hard to compete with Hamas's logic, since they could not claim that they had much to do with the departure from Gaza.[26]

Rice did not understand the complaints. There was plenty to celebrate by the Palestinians. They were rid of the Israelis, they had the land and the greenhouses. The world was standing ready to make Gaza an economic success. She thought a lot of this was marketing—how you frame it—and in the end

Hamas beat Fatah to the punch. Hamas was able to spin the Israeli departure from Gaza to its advantage. It was a harbinger of things to come.[27]

"I'm Not Going to Be Treated This Way"

By the time Rice had arrived in Jerusalem in November 2005, relations between the Israelis and the Palestinians were tense. Sharon had cut off contact with Abbas because the Israeli leader felt the Palestinian was refusing to crack down on militant groups. The accord on border crossings hung perpetually unresolved, leaving the Gaza Strip mostly sealed off from the outside world. The greenhouses that Wolfensohn had saved were bursting with produce, but there was no way to transport the persiable food outside Gaza. The Palestinian legislative elections were due to take place in two months—and Fatah, led by Abbas, had little tangible to show the Palestinian people.

After Welch and Abrams had pressed the parties to show flexibility, Rice decided she could reach a deal that would open the Rafah crossing on Gaza's border with Egypt. On November 14, she flew quickly to Jordan to express condolences for a terrorist bombing, returned to Jerusalem, and decided to delay her departure for the Asian economic summit. Rice's decision to stay had happened so quickly that reporters had no fresh clothes, as their luggage had already been stored on the plane for the flight to South Korea.

It was also Rice's fifty-first birthday. Amid the helpings of birthday cake, one Palestinian official gave her a bag of Gaza bell peppers as a gift—and a symbol of the produce that could flow out of Gaza with an accord.

From her ninth-floor suite—named for slain Israeli peacemaker Yitzhak Rabin—in the David Citadel Hotel, Rice launched an all-night session, often negotiating the fine details of the text herself—bus convoys, inspections, and video monitors—line by line, word by word. The Israelis and the Palestinians were huddled in other parts of the hotel—the Palestinians were placed in a banquet room in the basement with enough food for a wedding—and Javier Solana, the EU foreign policy chief, was in another hotel. (The Europeans were to help monitor the crossing.) As the issues became more difficult and more political, senior ministers began to arrive in the middle of the night to negotiate directly with Rice. Even Weissglas, who had been the lead negotiator, eventually said, "I can't agree anymore. This is now a cabinet member level issue."[28] Eventually, the parties began passing around a laptop computer with the draft text, suggesting changes. Rice herself only got two hours of sleep before a deal was cinched in the morning.

"She was very pleasant, very polite, but very firm," Weissglas said. "She is a terrific drafter and very creative in terms of the solutions she may offer." He marveled that she never seemed tired, and that when she emerged from her early-morning nap, "she looked great."[29]

The key issue was the complete lack of trust on both sides about security. The Israelis wanted guarantees that the long border with Gaza would not become a sieve for weapons and militants that would threaten the Jewish state. The Palestinians wanted control over the movement of people and goods in and out of a territory they were now in charge of managing.

Rice focused especially on Mohammed Dahlan, the Palestinian Authority's civil affairs minister, but in effect Fatah's boss in Gaza, because Abbas would never agree to a deal unless Dahlan gave his approval. On the Israeli side, she had to press Shaul Mofaz, the defense minister, and Yuval Diskin, the head of Shein Beit, the Israeli internal security department. The Israelis wanted the right to decide who could or could not enter and leave the Gaza Strip but gave that up while retaining the right to watch the passage via camera.

At a critical moment, Rice decided on her own that the United States would commit to a crucial third-party role to resolve differences between the parties. She made the decision without checking back with Washington or gathering input from other agencies, believing she knew Bush's instincts well enough that he would have no problem with her decision.[30]

One key player was stewing over Rice's sudden intervention: Wolfensohn. He confronted Abrams in the hotel and told him he was going to resign. "I've been here, working day after day," he said. "Since Rice arrived, you've met with the Israelis and with the Palestinians. But I have not been involved nor have you asked to consult with me. I've never been treated this way in seventy-two years. I'm not going to be treated this way."[31] Abrams thought little of Wolfensohn, believing he was a blowhard who actually spent too much time at his grand homes around the world rather than worrying about the Palestinians. He gleefully interrupted a meeting Welch was having with the Palestinians to recount Wolfensohn's harangue.

Wolfensohn went public that night with his frustrations, announcing he was ready to quit. "If you want to blow each other up, I have a nice house in Wyoming and in New York and in Australia, and I will watch with sadness as you do it," he said at a conference.[32] Amid all the negotiations, Rice had to calm Wolfensohn down and convince him no slight was intended. He would later graciously say at the news conference announcing the accord that a secretary of state has significant clout and "to push it over the edge, one needs not envoys, but secretaries of state."[33]

The complex agreement involved not just the Rafah crossing but also a crossing known as Karni, through which the produce trucks from the greenhouses needed to pass in order to get to Israeli markets. The agreement called for a minimum number of truckloads to pass through each day, with the number increasing substantially by the end of 2006. There was also language committing to the eventual rebuilding of the Palestinian airport and seaport.

The deal was a substantial personal achievement for Rice, demonstrating her talent at getting to the heart of an issue and managing to find a solution that satisfied participants with little trust in each other. She took some risk, putting her prestige on the line when there was no guarantee an agreement could be reached.

But the episode also demonstrates what even a number of Rice's aides describe as her weakness at implementation and follow-up. She got on the plane to Asia—and within weeks, the carefully negotiated deadlines and agreements had fallen apart. The strawberries, tomatoes, peppers, and other produce rotted in the greenhouses, which lost millions of dollars, because the Karni crossing agreements were not implemented.[34] Rice had moved on to the next crisis, but the Palestinians and the Israelis were once again arguing among themselves without the firm hand of the Americans. The stumbling implementation of the Rafah agreement would soon influence the Palestinian elections.

"Don't Have an Election If You Think You Will Lose"

By December, the Americans began to realize that there might be a problem with the elections: Hamas could actually do better than expected.

The Israelis had begun to raise serious concerns about Hamas's participation in the election, with Sharon at one point threatening to block them. Tzipi Livni, a rising star in Israeli politics and then the justice minister, flew to the United States and met with Rice, Abrams, and others to express her concerns. She had looked at the constitutions of dozens of countries and had studied the transition to power in Northern Ireland, Afghanistan, and other hot spots. Armed militias were always required to give up their arms before they could participate in the political process. "Don't let Hamas run," Livni pleaded.

Livni got the same message everywhere she went in Washington: Don't worry, Hamas won't win. And, U.S. officials added, if Hamas gains some seats, look at Lebanon, where Hezbollah appears to be acting like a responsible political party. The Americans said it was important to get Hamas into the political system and then they would disarm.[35]

"This was a blunder, no question," Weissglas said. "This belief in democracy by itself should not be blamed. But it was too simplistic. An election by itself is not sufficient to create a democracy."[36]

Rice's attitude was heavily influenced by Abbas, who came to Washington in October to meet with Bush. Over dinner with Rice, he made an impressive and articulate presentation about the first election in more than a decade for the Palestinian parliament. "If we don't let them participate, my vision will be tainted," Abbas said. "I can't be a legitimate leader. They will say we were afraid of them. It would seem like a typical Arab election." He argued that a frontal conflict will create a civil war and only by bringing Hamas into the mainstream could they be moderated.

The Americans were persuaded. Bush had faith in elections, which he was certain would change the character of the Islamists. But he had one piece of advice when Abbas came to see him in the Oval Office: "Don't have an election if you think you will lose." Abbas and his aides thought that was laughable. Only in the worst-case scenario, they thought, could Hamas garner as much as 35 percent of the vote.[37]

For months, Rice and her aides had been trying to persuade Abbas to learn the art of communicating to the Palestinians about Fatah's accomplishments. She had dispatched Jim Wilkinson in August to work with the Palestinians to create media centers in Gaza and on the West Bank and to organize Abbas's office, using $1.2 million in U.S. funds. The Palestinians were happy to take the money, but did not take Wilkinson too seriously because he seemed to have little understanding of the issues. Abbas and his aides made little use of the facilities provided by Wilkinson and shrugged off his suggestions that Abbas participate in public events like planting trees.

Another Rice aide who puzzled the Palestinians was Karen Hughes, Rice's czar for public diplomacy. Hughes had made a well-publicized trip to the Middle East in September, earning derision in the Arab media for some of her comments. When she met with Abbas's top aides in October, before Abbas traveled to Washington to meet with Bush, she shocked them by indicating that until she visited the Middle East she didn't realize there was so much interest in the Palestinian cause in the Arab street.

Then, within minutes, Bush's former political advisor managed to secure a meeting with President Bush for Abbas's delegation. They had a very pleasant thirty-minute conversation with the president, who asked what it meant to be in Fatah. Ghaith al-Omari, an Abbas political advisor, told Bush that Palestine could be the first democracy in the Middle East. Bush interrupted, "No, Iraq and Palestine will be the first." When the Palestinians suggested that Israeli settlement expansion might make a Palestinian state impossible to achieve, Bush replied: "Don't worry. I have some political sway with Israel and will use it if need be."[38]

Welch and Abrams went to the Palestinian territories in December to get a feel for the situation. Welch asked the Palestinians if the elections should be postponed, offering four possible rationales: The Israelis block Palestinian voting in East Jerusalem, Sharon had suffered a stroke, security concerns, or Hamas might win. Abbas said he wanted to go forward. There was only one discordant note: Welch and Abrams visited the home of Hanan Ashrawi, a former Palestinian peace negotiator who had formed an independent party with finance minister Salam Fayyad. "Watch out," she told them. "I can feel it. These guys may win."[39]

"We've Got a Surprise on Our Hands"

The elections were held on January 25, 2006. Earlier in the month, Sharon had suffered a second, massive stroke that left him permanently incapacitated. His deputy, Ehud Olmert, became the interim prime minister and effective head of Kadima, a new centrist political party Sharon had established in the wake of the wrenching Israeli debate over the Gaza withdrawal. Sharon wanted to pull back from much of the West Bank, which would define much of the contours of the Palestinian state (though on Israeli terms). Rice's bet on Sharon's vision appeared to be finally paying off. On their own, it appeared as if the Israelis would leave many of the settlements.

At the last minute, the administration began spending about $2 million in foreign aid money to increase the popularity of the Palestinian Authority—and by extension Fatah, which had long controlled it. The $50 million in aid that Bush had given Abbas in May for Gaza had not been spent yet, so the burst of spending (without logos to identify the American source) was designed to showcase projects in lieu of other accomplishments. The program dwarfed the campaign budgets of Fatah and Hamas and included such projects as a street-cleaning campaign, free food and water for Palestinians at border crossings, computers for community centers, and sponsorship of a national youth soccer tournament.[40]

Rice was monitoring the elections from her office. The initial reports and exit polls showed that Fatah was in the lead but Hamas was doing better than expected. Just before she left the office at around 8 P.M., the numbers looked tight but it seemed clear Fatah would win. But then she saw Liz Cheney, who cautioned: "You know, there's one thing I want to say about these numbers. The exit polls are notoriously wrong and the people doing the polls are nervous even sharing the numbers with us. Some people on the ground think Hamas may be doing better than these numbers show."[41]

The next morning, Rice got up before 5 A.M. and glanced at the newspaper headline: Fatah appeared to have won; Hamas was unexpectedly strong. No surprise there, so she went upstairs to the little gym she had installed in her apartment in the Watergate, complete with an elliptical and treadmill. She turned on the television news. As she began working out, she noted a headline crawl across the bottom of the screen that said, "Palestinian cabinet resigns in wake of Hamas victory." Well, that's wrong, she thought as she kept working out. Then, she saw the crawl again and began to get concerned. She called the State Department operations center and asked for the final story on the Palestinian elections. "Hamas won," she was told.

Rice quickly placed a call to Jacob Walles, who as U.S. consul general in Jerusalem dealt with the Palestinians. "Is this right?" she asked.

"There is a lot of confusion, but it appears Hamas won," Walles said.

Welch, in the meantime, had been woken by a call from the operations center, alerting him to the fact that the numbers had gone the wrong way. During the conversation, Rice interrupted with her own call. "Have you heard the news?" she asked. "We've got a surprise on our hands."

Rice also spoke to Bush. "That's the democratic process," Bush said when she told him the election result. Rice and Bush agreed to say the election was free and fair, and now Hamas has an obligation to govern.

Rice decided it was going to be a long day. She got back on the treadmill to finish exercising before she went into work.[42]

"The Line Is That This Is a Free Election"

That morning in her office, Rice gathered her top staff and asked how they could have so badly misjudged the outcome. Clearly, they did not have enough understanding about what was happening in the Palestinian territories. (It later became clear that Fatah also had been so disorganized that it ran multiple candidates in many districts, splitting the vote and handing a victory to the sole Hamas candidate.)

Rice called Livni, who had become Israel's foreign minister; Abbas; Solana; and the UN secretary-general, Kofi Annan. She was relatively blunt with Abbas, saying that "this is not such a significant result after ten years of errors by Fatah." She told him he needed to clarify the powers of the president and see what powers he had versus the legislature and the cabinet. She also promised to keep in touch. Over time, Rice's dismay at Abbas's failure as a leader would grow. He had been handed an opportunity for Palestinian self-government and had utterly failed.

On the other calls and in conversations with her staff, she quickly established what would become the mantra of the Bush administration. "The line is that this is a free election," she said. "They voted for a change of party, against corruption and for change. But there is no path to statehood through violence and terrorism. We are not going to deal with or work with Hamas. To govern is to choose and now they have to choose. They have to recognize the right to existence of its negotiating partner."[43]

Rice's quick turn on a dime was impressive, but it belied the devastating effect the Hamas victory would have on her dreams for a Palestinian state or democracy in the Middle East. Suddenly, aid would have to be cut for the Palestinian cause and once again there would be no negotiating partner for Israel. Meanwhile, the rise of Hamas would vindicate the warnings of the autocrats in Cairo and Riyadh about the dangers of democracy. Over the course of a year, her decisions had helped shape this outcome—the first time since the prophet Muhammad that there was a democratically elected Islamic state in the Arab world.

The administration had rhetorically backed Abbas and poured hundreds of millions of dollars to fund public works projects. But it failed to back him when he asked for concrete help, especially in his dealings with the Israelis— problems compounded by Abbas's own failures in leadership. The administration was highly attuned to the shifts of Israeli politics but tone-deaf to the upheaval in Palestinian society. It was so focused on facilitating Israel's withdrawal from the Gaza Strip that it did not press Israel to end settlement expansion, release additional prisoners, or take other measures that might have reduced Palestinian indignation. Finally, despite deep Israeli misgivings, the administration abandoned its own standards on terror groups and decided Hamas could participate in the elections even though it had not disarmed its militia.

"We're Being Betrayed by the Americans"

The Hamas victory brought the campaign to establish a Palestinian state to a dead stop. The Bush administration once again disengaged. Abbas and his aides became worried about Hamas's growing clout in the Palestinian territories and were convinced that isolating Hamas would not work. They pleaded with U.S. officials for leeway in dealing with Hamas, but the answer was always the same—no, Hamas is a terrorist group. Hamas's victory also affected the push for democracy in the Middle East, as doubts began to grow about the wisdom of the administration's approach both in Washington and abroad.

Two weeks after the election, Rice appeared before the House International Relations Committee to discuss the proposed budget for the State Department. The committee chairman, Henry Hyde of Illinois, is a rock-solid Republican who had a habit of using the annual session on the budget to make important points on foreign policy. This year, he decided to say out loud what many mainstream Republicans privately thought about the administration's democracy effort—that it was a disaster.

Hyde warned against what he called "the golden theory" about the "magic elixir of democracy." He said that the notion that democracy and freedom always produce "beneficial results" rests on "a misinterpretation of cause and effect in our history." He argued that democracy returned to Europe after World War II and spread in East Asia largely because of a massive U.S. military presence in those countries. "Democracy is more than a single election, or even a succession of them," he said, contending that "implanting democracy in large areas would require that we possess an unbounded power and undertake an open-ended commitment of time and resources, which we cannot and will not do."

Hyde also warned that "a broad and energetic promotion of democracy may produce not peace and stability but revolution," and that "there is no evidence that we or anyone can guide from afar revolutions we have set in motion." He heaped scorn on the idea that democracy could be easily implanted in societies where historically it is alien. "It may, in fact, constitute an uncontrollable experiment with an outcome akin to that faced by the Sorcerer's Apprentice," Hyde concluded.[44]

The committee hearing room became completely silent as Hyde's booming voice bounced off the walls and he methodically knocked over the intellectual pillars that held up the administration's policy. Rice, clearly taken aback, responded with her usual talking points that tyranny is imposed, not democracy. "It is a difficult course and there have been setbacks along that course," she said. Rice never had good relations with Congress, but after this public confrontation there was a distinctive chill in her relationship with Hyde.

A week later, Rice flew to Cairo and Riyadh on a trip that provided a sobering counterpoint to her June visit, when the administration's grand ambitions were first outlined (described in Chapter 4). She had spent a year prodding unelected Middle Eastern leaders to give more aid to the Palestinians and to open up their political systems. She now was headed on a mission designed to argue exactly the opposite. She planned to urge caution in supporting a Palestinian

legislature that came to power in an election she had hailed as free and fair—
while seeking the support of autocratic governments that she had recently demanded become freer.

The United States was determined to halt all but humanitarian aid to the
Palestinians until Hamas accepted Israel's existence, ended violence, and ac-
knowledged previous agreements between the Palestinian Authority and Israel.
For Arab governments, even ones that agreed with that notion, the answer
would be simple: Have patience and keep supporting the Palestinians. The
Saudis may detest Hamas, but in public, at least, a tightly controlled Islamic
state has to applaud any organization that vows to bring Islamic rule to the
Palestinian territories.

Rice's first stop was Cairo, and she went directly from the plane to a meeting with Egypt's intelligence chief, Omar Suleiman—a signal that the rules had
changed. Suleiman is a brilliant and talented survivor of years of Middle East
intrigue, and effectively the prime minister of Egypt. He had played a key role
in brokering many agreements between Palestinian factions, and probably knew
more about Hamas than anyone outside the organization. But he's also the intelligence chief for a dictatorship known for violations of human rights, the
man who keeps tabs on every dissident and democracy activist in the country,
and probably played a key role in the decision to prosecute Ayman Nour.

Rice had canceled her first planned visit to Egypt out of pique at how Nour
had been treated, and now Nour was facing a five-year prison term after being
convicted on bogus charges. Nour's party had been essentially destroyed because
of the schemes plotted by Suleiman and other Mubarak cronies. The ironies
were instantly and painfully apparent, but it didn't matter. Rice's planned hour-
and-a-quarter meeting stretched to nearly two hours. Abrams and Welch spent
even more time with Suleiman.

By contrast, Rice only spent a half hour with the Egyptian foreign minister,
Ahmed Aboul Gheit, running through the usual list of talking points. Aboul
Gheit was already miffed because Cheney had refused to meet with him on a
trip to Cairo a few weeks earlier—and because Rice had insisted that the Egyptian prime minister, not Aboul Gheit, be the host of that night's dinner.[45]

Rice thought Aboul Gheit was a nonentity, but their joint news conference
set the impression for her first day of the trip. Aboul Gheit quickly laid down
his marker: "We should give Hamas time. I'm sure Hamas will develop, will
evolve. We should not prejudge the issue."

Egypt, lacking the oil resources of its Arab neighbors, is not a big contribu-
tor to the Palestinians. But it is influential because of its peace treaty with
Israel—and because it is the heart of the Arab world. Every third Arab is an

Egyptian and Cairo is the cultural capital of the Arabs. Aboul Gheit mouthed the necessary diplomatic words that Hamas needed to "recognize the requirements" of seeking peace with Israel, but those words didn't make much of an impression. It was his emphatic plea to give Hamas more time—an undefined length of time—that stood in stark contrast to the American and Israeli position that action needed to be taken now.

Though Rice had discussed Nour's case in private with Aboul Gheit, she didn't mention it in public until she was asked about it—and even then she couldn't bring herself to say his name. A year ago, she had humiliated Aboul Gheit by publicly mentioning Nour's name even after Aboul Gheit had asked her not to do so. Now, she spoke vaguely of "disappointments and setbacks" in the past year, but also praised Mubarak as a visionary leader.[46] (Later in the trip, she even said Egypt "would never be the same.")[47]

In fact, Mubarak had manipulated the elections in the fall, eliminating any secular opposition to leave the Muslim Brotherhood as his only viable competitor—a neat bit of jujitsu in the American democracy campaign. Mubarak's message had been clear: If I go, you'll end up with Islamic radicals. In some ways, the ploy had backfired on him since the Muslim Brotherhood had done much better than anyone expected. The party would be strengthened even more by the victory by Hamas, which is an offshoot of the Muslim Brotherhood.

In the morning, Rice met with Mubarak for more than an hour, just the two of them with no aides present. In an effort to balance the unfortunate imagery, Rice also met with a small group of civil society activists, just as on her trip in June, but this time reporters were allowed to watch. Wilkinson had realized a closed session would just fuel stories that she was backsliding on the democracy push. So he overruled the U.S. ambassador's objections to allowing the press into the room.[48]

The open setting made for a livelier session, but the circumstances were much different. In June, she gave a speech that appeared to open the possibilities for political reform in Egypt, but now those possibilities were rapidly disappearing. The seven activists had a lot on their mind, and Rice took it in, writing her own notes but staying mostly silent during the one-hour meeting.

One prominent dissident, Saad Eddin Ibrahim, called the steps the regime had taken so far "window dressing" aimed at satisfying "foreign pressure." Hisham Kassem, a newspaper publisher and a vice president of Nour's Ghad Party, said that voters were not confident in the last election and "many wouldn't vote unless paid." He told Rice that "time is running short" and change must take place soon. There were only three years left of this administration, and "we don't know what the next administration will do, even if it's Republican."

Ibrahim was wary after the meeting. "There's a feeling that we're being betrayed by the Americans," Ibrahim said. The history shows that the United States, when faced with a choice, would ultimately let down democratic forces, he said, citing Hungary in 1956, Czechoslovakia in 1968, and China in 1989. "The record doesn't bode very well."[49]

Rice, meanwhile, sat for an interview with Egyptian Television's Mervat Mohsen. Her tough questions reflected the skepticism of the Arab world. "American calls for democracy have unwittingly brought unprecedented support for the Muslim Brotherhood, but you're not happy with the Muslim Brotherhood in power," she said. "Is this some kind of designer's democracy then, Dr. Rice?"

"No," Rice replied. "The United States is going to stand for the principle of democracy."[50]

By now, Rice and her aides had seen the news coverage from the day before. The headlines were pretty much the same—Rice was rebuffed or rejected by the Egyptians. Rice was furious, telling her aides that there was no divide between Egypt and the United States on Hamas—an assertion that left at least one official thinking Rice was deluding herself. McCormack blamed himself for the negative coverage, since he had made no effort to explain the news conference with Aboul Gheit. So, as the plane flew to Riyadh, Abrams and Welch were sent to the back of the plane to set the reporters straight. The officials urged them to focus on the fact that the Arabs were joining together to say Hamas had to accept Israel as a negotiating partner. This spin only served to deepen the skepticism of the reporters, who began to caustically joke about being on the right or wrong side of "freedom's divide" whenever the plane landed in another country.

Rice met with Foreign Minister Saud al-Faisal at the airport, again just to run through the talking points, and then went off to meet King Abdullah. The two of them were closeted for almost two and half hours with only their interpreters, while their aides waited outside. When Rice held the news conference with Saud, at close to 11 P.M., the same three female reporters from June, dressed head to toe in black abayas, were once again sitting there in the front row. The Saudis certainly weren't subtle. Neither was the query that one of the female reporters read from a piece of paper, which Rice's aides assumed was a planted question: "How is it possible to harmonize the U.S. position as a nation supporting freedom of expression and the right of people to practice democracy with your effort to curb the will of Hamas and put pressures on other countries?"

Rice said she was in Riyadh to talk about how the peace process could be continued. "That's the nature of the discussion," she said. "Different countries will have different modalities in how to deal with this." Of course, when it was his turn, Saud said Saudi Arabia would keep funding the Palestinians, noting that it was difficult to distinguish between humanitarian and nonhumanitarian aid.[51]

"She Was Very Polite"

The Arabs had the Americans trapped. The leverage the United States had hoped to use to prod greater freedoms was now dwindling, since the United States needed Arab help with Hamas.[52] Egypt made that clear by canceling local elections days before Rice arrived in Cairo. The headline in the UAE, *Gulf News* as Rice's trip ended reflected the Arab world's new bravado against the Americans: "America's Doomed Policy: Condoleezza Rice Has Allowed Herself to Be Drawn into a Battle She Cannot Win."

Mubarak certainly seemed pleased. The government newspaper *al-Gomhuria* published an interview a few days after Rice left the region, in which a preening Mubarak said he had won over Rice to his views on democracy. "She was very polite as she was listening to Egyptian opinions and points of view," Mubarak said. "She didn't bring up difficult issues or ask to change anything or to intervene in political reform, as some people say."

Mubarak added that Rice "was convinced by the way that political reform and the implementation of democracy is being done in Egypt. . . . She said that democracy in the Arab countries needed a generation." Rice, of course, had frequently said that democracy in the Middle East was a generational challenge for Americans—but Mubarak had figured out that that meant he had all the time in the world.[53]

The day after Rice left Egypt, Nour was slapped with seventeen new charges, including slander of Mubarak. His wife, Ismail, was accused of assaulting a police officer, which she denied. She said the regime was trying to "terrify real, secular opposition" and her family. "I don't want to be jailed. I have two children," she said. "I thought these people had enough of us already. But they haven't. If you are the opposition, they want to eat you. They don't have a ceiling. There is no common sense. I'm shocked, really, at what's happened to us."[54]

The same plea could have been made by democracy activists across the Middle East. By March 2007, Mubarak completed his dismantling of the democracy movement by pushing through constitutional amendments that limited opposition parties, suspended judicial supervision of elections, and enshrined draconian police powers. The vote on the referendum was held just after Rice visited Egypt during a drive to jump-start Middle East peace talks. For a year, even since the Hamas victory, Rice had muted her remarks on Egyptian democracy. But before departing Washington, she angered the Egyptian government by calling the amendments—billed by Mubarak as a reform measure—"a really disappointing outcome." She said she would raise the issue with the Egyptian president.[55]

Standing next to Aboul Gheit at a news conference on the bank of the Nile in Aswan two days later, Rice suddenly soft-pedaled the dispute. When a reporter asked her if her qualms had been met in the conversation with Mubarak, Rice's voice rose an octave, becoming thin and tense. "I have made my concerns known as well as my hopes for continued reform here in Egypt," she said, adding that the process of reform was going to have "its ups and downs."

Aboul Gheit, for his part, became almost poetic as he defended Egypt's version of democracy. Turning to Rice, he said, "If you look through the window of your suite here, you will see groups of granite rocks, a whole mountain of granite. That is the Egyptian spirit. The Egyptian spirit is as solid as granite. It's capable of going through the journey with solid steps forward in order to achieve the objective."

"I believe that very strongly," Rice replied.

"Thank you," Aboul Gheit said with a triumphal smile.[56]

A QUESTION IN KIEV

December 7, 2005

The small room set up for the news conference with Ukrainian president Viktor Yushchenko was plainly but appropriately decorated with a single oil painting of wheat fields, signifying the region's role as the onetime bread basket of the Soviet Union. As part of a European tour in early December 2005, Rice had traveled to Kiev to bolster the hero of the so called Orange Revolution, now somewhat tarnished by a faltering economy and squabbles with his former political allies. Ukrainian and American reporters stood, crammed behind a bank of cameras, as they waited for Rice and Yushchenko to emerge from a private discussion of the delicate political situation.

But the problems in Ukraine weren't really at the top of Rice's agenda that morning; it was the administration's troublesome policies on the detention and interrogation of terrorism suspects. She was in the midst of one of her trickiest diplomatic balancing acts, attempting simultaneously to placate angry European allies overseas and influence the White House back home. She was trying to do this without angering powerful opponents such as Vice President Cheney. And she wanted to make a dramatic move, using a few carefully phrased words at a news conference that ordinarily might never have touched on the issue she wanted to address.

So her staff, in effect, planted a question. It was a question that had been on reporters' minds ever since Rice had left for Europe a few days earlier, but she had stonewalled reporters and they had given up asking it. Now Rice was asking for a second chance. She had blown her answer the first time and she wanted to try again.

The administration's troubles had started a month earlier. Dana Priest of *The Washington Post* had written an article on November 2 exposing a secret CIA prison system for detainees suspected of links to terrorism.[1] Most surprisingly, she revealed that some prisons were located in several eastern European countries. The *Post,* however, honored a request from Bush administration officials not to name the countries. The officials, who included President Bush, argued that the disclosure could disrupt counterterrorism efforts and make the nations involved the targets of retaliation.[2]

This only heightened the mystery—and probably fueled the outrage in Europe. A series of investigations were launched, as the European media relentlessly examined whether new members of the European Union (such as Poland) or aspirants to the EU (such as Romania) might have secretly broken EU laws to help the Americans. The stakes were high: One senior European official warned that any EU country found to have hosted the CIA prisons would face "serious consequences," including losing its EU voting rights.[3]

For the European public, the prison furor was mainly a vehicle for expressing broad disgust at how the Bush administration had conducted the war on terrorism, especially at the detention facility at Guantánamo Bay. Anger had been smoldering beneath the surface for some time, and the prison story was the spark that lit a new fire—taking by surprise both the administration and the European elite, now reconciled to having to deal with Bush for another four years.

"Guantánamo Bay does terrible damage to America's image," explained Wolfgang Ischinger, the German ambassador to the United States at the time. "We who are friends and allies of the United States also suffer because of this problem. It is not something you can defend. It is so difficult to prevent real disappointment, frustration, and damage from being done to America's image from that issue."[4]

Rice privately agreed. Inside the administration, Rice, Zelikow, and State Department Legal Adviser John B. Bellinger III had worked quietly to shift the administration's policies on detainees so that it was no longer so damaging overseas.

During the first term, when Rice had been national security advisor, she had lost control of the process. Bush, with Cheney's prodding, had signed an executive order on November 13, 2001, that decided that terrorist captives should be barred from federal courts; instead, the military would have the power to imprison them indefinitely and convene special tribunals to prosecute them. This decision had been made without the input, or even the knowledge, of either the NSC or the State Department staff. Powell then largely lost a high-stakes battle over whether the United States would be bound by the Geneva Conventions in its treatment of detainees, and the State Department for the rest of Bush's first term found itself cut out of the loop on the administration's policymaking on detainees.[5] Rice now was trying to reopen these issues, but it had been a difficult and at times vexing challenge.[6]

A Very Public Challenge

Cheney and his top lawyer, David S. Addington, were absolutely opposed. Addington, probably one of the most influential and least known figures in the administration, had his fingerprints on many of the key policies in the war on terrorism. He even helped pick Guantánamo as the site for holding suspected terrorists. He ultimately became Cheney's chief of staff when Scooter Libby resigned after being charged with perjury in the investigation involving the outing of a CIA operative. In interagency meetings, Addington was especially scornful of arguments advanced by Bellinger, whom he seemed to view as weak and vacillating on issues of national security.[7]

Cheney believed that the president needs nearly unfettered power to deal with terrorists to protect Americans, including extreme interrogation methods, and he resisted any measure that might restrain the president's flexibility. But a growing number of administration officials supported Rice's view that the interrogation tactics, secret prisons, and prisoner abuse had come at a terrible cost to the U.S. image and had undermined U.S. efforts to promote human rights in other countries—and thus should cease.

Cheney had personally lobbied against an amendment proposed by Senator John McCain, an Arizona Republican, that would limit the military's interrogation and detention tactics to those described in the U.S. Army Field Manual; it would also prohibit all U.S. government employees from using cruel, inhuman, or degrading treatment as defined by international agreements. But ninety senators supported the proposal, forcing Cheney to offer an alternative that would have exempted the CIA from the prohibition. Despite the administration's insistence that the United States does not torture captives, Cheney's actions added to the growing suspicion overseas that the administration was just playing word games. A perception grew that the United States, which had long held itself as the paragon of human rights, was running torture facilities.

The dispute between Cheney and Rice in some ways resembled the struggles in the first term. Cheney's staff began to arrange meetings without key cabinet members, at one point forcing Rice to interrupt a trip to Canada to hold a secure video teleconference with Cheney so that she wouldn't be cut out of the decision-making loop. Cheney's office also made sure it automatically received internal memos and e-mail that were sent from the National Security Council staff to national security advisor Steve Hadley—sometimes even without the knowledge of the authors.[8]

Rice began to realize she would face a very public challenge over the furor: She was planning a weeklong trip to Europe in early December just at the moment the scandal over the prisons was at full boil. She had planned to meet the new German chancellor, Angelina Merkel, who had appeared more inclined to work with the administration than her Bush-bashing predecessor, Gerhard Schroeder. She would go to Romania to sign a long-term lease for the U.S. military to use an air base, coincidentally identified by Human Rights Watch to be one possible site for the secret prisons. She also planned to visit Ukraine, to hail the government brought to power by the Orange Revolution a year earlier, and then head to Brussels for NATO talks on Afghanistan.

In the eyes of Rice's media-conscious staff, it was all supposed to be a string of positive new stories—building a relationship with the new German government, winning access to an air base in the heart of the former Soviet empire, bolstering democratic forces in Ukraine, and expanding NATO's presence in Afghanistan. None of that really mattered now. Rice's yearlong efforts to repair relations with Europe were suddenly at risk. She realized that every day the storyline would be secret prisons, torture, and more secret prisons.

Jack Straw, the British foreign secretary, gave Rice an opening. Britain held the rotating presidency of the European Union, so the week before her trip he wrote her a letter seeking "clarification" about media reports that suggested "violations of international law."

The first impulse among many in the administration was to give Straw a polite brush-off. But Rice decided to give a full-throated response, believing that it was important to lay down some markers before she left for Europe—in other words, to get off defense and play some offense. She also wanted to demonstrate to Cheney and others that, unlike Powell, she was willing to be an effective and determined public defender of U.S. policies, even as she privately fought for changes in some of those policies within the administration. Addington even remarked to Bellinger how much he appreciated the tough defense Rice and her team were fielding.[9]

In a tactical decision, though, she delayed delivering the statement until the morning she left for Europe. It was a Monday, ensuring the issue did not dominate the Sunday morning public policy shows.

Rice at age five on her uncle's car. Birmingham, Alabama, was segregated in the early 1960s, but Rice grew up in a solidly middle-class environment.

COURTESY OF CONDOLEEZZA RICE

Rice with Santa Claus in an undated photo. Rice believes she was seven or eight years old at the time.

COURTESY OF CONDOLEEZZA RICE

Rice ice-skating with a
partner at age thirteen.
Long hours on the rink
helped make Rice the
consummate performer
as an adult.

COURTESY OF CONDOLEEZZA RICE

Rice with her parents,
Angelena and John Rice,
after she won the Outstanding
Senior Woman award at the
University of Denver in 1974.

COURTESY OF CONDOLEEZZA RICE

As national security advisor during President George W. Bush's first term, Rice often had to mediate between Secretary of State Colin L. Powell and Defense Secretary Donald H. Rumsfeld. Here, the two men debate a point in the Rose Garden in 2002 as Rice looks on uncomfortably.

© ROBERT A. REEDER/ *THE WASHINGTON POST*

Rice made a splash as soon as she became secretary of state, particularly with this appearance before U.S. troops in Germany in February 2005. A fashion writer commended Rice for her "attendant images of machismo, strength, and power." STATE DEPARTMENT PHOTO

Rice's speech in Cairo in June 2005 marked the high point of the administration's campaign for democracy in the Middle East. But events eventually turned against the White House.

Rice is filmed by an African Union soldier as she visits a refugee camp in Darfur, Sudan, in July 2005. Her brief visit did little to end the violence that has left as many as 450,000 dead.

Rice with British foreign secretary Jack Straw in Blackburn, England, in April 2006, shortly before they jointly made a surprise trip to Iraq. Rice and Straw worked well together, but he lost his post shortly after this high-profile trip.

Rice back in Iraq three weeks later with Rumsfeld and U.S. Ambassador Zalmay Khalilzad. Rumsfeld was unhappy to share the stage with Rice.

Rice with Russian foreign minister Sergey Lavrov during a meeting in South Korea in November 2005. Their difficult relationship largely guided policy toward Iran.
STATE DEPARTMENT PHOTO

Rice visiting sailors on the USS *Port Royal* during a trip to Australia in March 2006. Rice often wanted to see U.S. troops while overseas.   PHOTO BY JIM WILKINSON

Rice's staff carefully staged overseas events for maximum media impact. Rice visited an Islamic school in Indonesia in 2006, which included an appearance by *Sesame Street*'s Elmo. To the amusement of reporters, Rice seemed uncertain on why Elmo was there—or who he was.   PHOTO BY JOSIE DUCKETT

Rice speaking to reporters during a briefing on her Boeing 757 jet. Reporters often saw a different Rice, not the tightly controlled, on-message defender of the administration who appeared before the cameras.

PHOTO BY JAMES GREENE

Rice shares a light moment with reporters after they leave Iraq during a trip in 2006.

In February 2007, Rice arranged a meeting between Palestinian Authority president Mahmoud Abbas and Israeli prime minister Ehud Olmert. Despite huge obstacles, Rice decided that she would devote the rest of her tenure as secretary of state to making progress on creating a Palestinian state.

"A Vital Tool"

Rice's decision proved to be a smart move. Dana Priest had added to the furor with a second article, which was published in the *Post* on Sunday, the day before Rice was due to arrive in Berlin. She revealed that former German interior minister Otto Schily had been told by the U.S. ambassador to Germany of a bungled 2004 "rendition"—in which suspects are secretly transferred from countries without formal extradition proceedings—of a German citizen suspected of terrorist links.[10] The article said Schily had kept the case quiet at the request of the Americans, who had concluded that the German citizen, Khaled El-Masri, had done nothing wrong. The German media erupted. And now Merkel, who had wanted to show she could play nice with the Bush administration, was instead under pressure to show she could be tough.

The reporters traveling with Rice arrived very early that morning at Andrews Air Force Base. They were used to gathering at all hours for trips with the secretary, usually gossiping with staff and munching on hot chocolate-chip cookies made at the base. But now, at 7 A.M., they actually had to think and work. Rice's staff had put together an ersatz press conference area, with a podium and simple chairs, and the ten reporters sat down and listened as her words were beamed around the world. The reporters were only props, since she took no questions.

She read the text of the official reply she would send to Straw. But she looked like she was swallowing castor oil. The statement had been lawyered to death, appearing to the reporters to be little more than ten minutes of obfuscation and loopholes. Bellinger and Zelikow had led the fight for the State Department, though in some ways it was not as difficult as they might have expected. One technique they used was to pull together fragments of administration statements uttered on television and before congressional committees, trying to make the case that if it had been said once before it could be said again. Of course, it had never been said in one place, for the world to see, by such a senior U.S. official. Thus every phrase had been carefully vetted by teams of lawyers across the government. Hadley was surprised that it actually came together in time for Rice's departure. The result wasn't pretty.

Rice did not confirm or deny the existence of the prisons, saying, "We cannot discuss information that would compromise the success of intelligence, law enforcement, and military operations." But she defended U.S. actions in Europe as preventing terrorist attacks and dropped strong hints, in diplomatic code, that all operations on European soil had occurred only with the cooperation of European governments. The United States, she declared, "has fully respected the sovereignty of other countries that cooperate in these matters."[11] In other words, the Europeans knew what we were doing and we always got permission first before we did it.

Yet parts of the statement appeared misleading. She defended the practice of rendition as a "vital tool" that is recognized by international law and that has been used by many countries, including the United States, even before the September 11 attacks. U.S. renditions have sparked controversy and judicial probes in Germany, Italy, and Spain, but Rice noted that France used rendition in 1994 to remove the legendary terrorist "Carlos the Jackal" from Sudan for prosecution.

But these cases were not comparable. Carlos was put on trial after he was whisked away from Sudan, an authoritarian country that doesn't have any rule of law. The Bush administration was doing the opposite. The CIA was seizing prisoners from jurisdictions that respect the rule of law—as in the case of the poor German mistakenly nabbed in Macedonia—and transporting them to other less law-abiding jurisdictions so that they could be interrogated indefinitely without the interference of lawyers and judges.

There were other loopholes. Rice asserted that the United States does not transport terrorism suspects "for the purpose of interrogation using torture" and "will not transport anyone to a country when we believe he will be tortured." She added that "where appropriate, the United States seeks assurances that transferred persons will not be tortured." But that left open the possibility that the Bush administration did not try very hard to find out if suspects would be tortured—and in fact there were numerous cases in which suspects alleged that was exactly what had occurred.

The focus on "torture" was another red herring. The United States is a signatory to the UN Convention Against Torture, in which nations pledge to refuse to torture and pledge to prevent cruel, inhuman, and degrading treatment of prisoners. But the Bush administration had argued that the obligations concerning cruel, inhuman, and degrading treatment do not apply outside U.S. territory. Moreover, Priest had reported that CIA interrogators at the overseas sites have been permitted to use interrogation techniques prohibited by the UN convention or by U.S. military law.

It looked like another word game, the diplomatic version of three-card monte. It was easy for the administration to say it was against "torture" and most of the media reports focused on just that. But "torture" was just a ruse to avoid talking about other techniques that arguably fell short of torture but were also clearly illegal under international law.

"It Is Exceedingly Hard"

Rice planned to brief reporters shortly after her plane left for Berlin. Priest had written extensively about the contradiction between the text of the torture treaty and the administration's interpretation of it. She noted that the CIA had used the loophole about the treaty not applying outside the United States to conduct so-called enhanced interrogation techniques, including waterboarding (making suspects believe they are being drowned). Thus there was a logical first question: "Are you saying now that the administration believes that it does apply, that the language on CID [cruel, inhuman, and degrading treatment] applies outside the United States?"

Rice stiffened. And then she ducked the question completely. "The United States has obligations under the Convention Against Torture," she said. "Those obligations are determined by, and are interpreted and enforced by, U.S. law and by our Justice Department."[12]

Her answer was disappointing but also quite telling. Clearly, the policy had not changed. Peter Machler of Agence France-Presse picked up the theme, trying again to get some clarity: "Does the United States allow CID on other countries' territory?"

She gave another nonanswer. "Our people, wherever they are, are operating under U.S. law and U.S. international obligations." Again, she avoided the main issue: the Bush administration's interpretation of those laws that said they didn't apply overseas.

Every other reporter also tried to probe at some aspect of the prison issue. At one point, Rice spoke emotionally of appearing before the 9/11 Commission, using the anguish of that moment as a pointed example to her European counterparts. "It is exceedingly hard when you look at the families of people who lost their lives in a terrorist attack," she said. "You wonder to yourself: 'Did I do everything that I could?'"

Rice added that she would remind people in Europe—where the history of secret police under fascist and communist regimes has given the phrase "intelligence" a bad reputation—that intelligence is essential to battling shadowy terrorist networks. "Ultimately, if you want to stop attacks, you have to use intelligence to do it," she said.

The briefing ended, and Rice walked back to her cabin and reviewed the exchange with her staff. She knew she had a problem.

"We've got to find a way to answer the question" about whether the rules against torture apply overseas, she told her staff. Zelikow thought the statement had made the answer self-evident, and so did Rice. But they realized the press had clearly become so cynical about the word games the administration had played on this issue in the past that every statement was now considered a semantic artifice.

In fact, the Andrews statement had deliberately stopped short of clearly addressing the issue of overseas activities. Hadley and Rice had talked about it before she left, and they decided that they would leave this point vague—with the understanding that they would consider clarifying the issue publicly at a later date if necessary.[13]

"You Should Ask Your Question Again"

In Berlin, Rice's meeting with Merkel went well. The Americans had high hopes for the new relationship. As Assistant Secretary Dan Fried put it, Merkel "had nothing invested in this 'Europe as a counterweight to the United States' theory. She grew up in East Germany. She always thought, 'America, they're the ones that really stand for freedom.'"[14] Both governments were determined to make this new relationship work.

In their private meeting, Merkel, a fluent Russian speaker who had trained as a physical chemist in the former East Germany, teasingly tested Rice's rusty Russian.[15] But Merkel stumbled badly in the news conference afterward. It was such a mob scene—dozens of jostling reporters and twenty-seven television cameras—that it might have spooked the novice chancellor. Every question, as expected, was about the secret prisons and renditions. Rice turned them away easily with almost verbatim excerpts from her Andrews Air Force spiel. But then Merkel, speaking in German, declared that the Bush administration admitted it had mistakenly abducted the German citizen highlighted in Priest's article.

The clear implication was that Rice had privately conceded an error. This is an administration that doesn't admit error—and there were legal implications as well, since Masri had filed suit that day in U.S. District Court. Rice had said only that if mistakes are made, the U.S. government tries to quickly rectify them. Rice and her aides were appalled at Merkel's comment.

In an effort at damage control, one of Rice's top aides decided to brief reporters on the plane after she left Berlin. "We are not sure what was in her head" when Merkel said that, he declared. Rice did not discuss the case specifically with her, he said, though he acknowledged that other American officials had previously discussed it with the German government. He also hinted darkly that there was something disturbing about Masri's past. His remarks sent shock waves back to Berlin and threatened to rupture the relationship with Merkel even before it started.

In one of those dizzying days of diplomacy, Rice flew from Berlin to Bucharest, where she signed the base agreement during a three-hour stop, before landing very late in Kiev. Rice faced more questions in Bucharest about the prisons, a pattern that would continue all week. In fact, twenty-nine of the thirty-eight questions reporters asked Rice during her European stops concerned the U.S. treatment of detainees.

But when reporters woke up the next morning, Rice's traveling press corps felt the issue was played out. They had written about the prisons for days—the week before the trip, the day they left Andrews, in Berlin and Bucharest. There is a rhythm to these issues, and they all sensed the story was about to change. The Kiev stop provided the perfect opportunity, given the struggles in the Ukraine and the government's tense relations with its former patron, Russia.

Reporters covering the secretary of state always try to ask a question that yields new insight or breaks some news. Before any news conference with Rice, the reporters hone their questions carefully, trying to come with the perfect combination of words to put her on the spot. At news conferences overseas, when U.S. reporters might be able to ask at most two or three questions, they decide who will ask the questions and then together they work and rework each question until they think it's exactly right. There was any number of questions that could be posed that might generate a decent news story out of Kiev.

So it was surprising when Mindy Sofen, McCormack's assistant, walked up as reporters were milling about before the news conference with Yushchenko. "Sean says you should ask your question again," she said mysteriously, adding "if you want to."

"Let's Revisit It"

The reporters covering Rice thought this was an odd development. Rice and her aides were deliberately stepping on their opportunity to change the subject. The reporters huddled to discuss this request. There was concern that they shouldn't let Rice set the agenda—and skepticism that she would say anything new—but the curiosity about what she would say was too strong. When McCormack arrived, he wouldn't explain what was up, but he strongly suggested the reporters ask the question.

The reporters had already decided that Saul Hudson of Reuters would have a turn. He posed the query simply, knowing full well whatever he asked would get the same answer: "Madame Secretary, is the United States only obliged to prevent cruel, inhuman, and degrading treatment to its detainees on U.S. territory?"

Rice turned to Yushchenko and made a show of apologizing for the question, explaining that she'd been dogged by the issue on her trip. Then, she announced, "As a matter of U.S. policy, the United States obligations under the CAT, which prohibits, of course, cruel and inhuman and degrading treatment, those obligations extend to U.S. personnel wherever they are, whether they are in the United States or outside of the United States."[16]

It was an artful statement, appearing to directly address the issue she had ducked on the plane. In contrast to her earlier comments, she spoke not only of torture but also of the broader range of tough interrogation tactics—and then said the ban would apply universally.

Zelikow had written the language the night before, after arriving in Kiev. He was exhausted, but Rice pulled him aside and told him she was convinced they needed to settle this question once and for all. She asked him to draft a simple statement that he felt Washington could live with, and meanwhile she would call Hadley and let him know what she was planning to do. Before she had left for Europe, Hadley had agreed to consider addressing the issue if necessary. Now she was going to call in that chit.

"Well, let's revisit it," Rice said when she called. Hadley agreed—and even got clearance from Bush for her new language.[17]

An instant debate broke out among the reporters about whether Rice had said anything dramatically new. The news reports that day reflect the confusion, which was partially generated by McCormack's repeated refusal to provide much guidance. The early reports suggested a change in U.S. policy, but as the day went on, some of the reporters began to pull back a bit, especially when the White House denied there was anything new.

McCormack directed reporters to an obscure statement Attorney General Alberto Gonzales had submitted to Congress some months earlier that seemed to mirror Rice's new statement, suggesting this was already administration policy. (Gonzales had been asked to answer dozens of questions from lawmakers after an appearance on Capitol Hill, and this had been one of his answers to what are known in Washington as QFRs—"questions for the record"—which are submitted after a hearing and eventually made part of the formal record.)

But virtually no one had known about Gonzales's written statement—not even Zelikow when he drafted Rice's statement. He only found out about the QFR afterward, though it proved to be a convenient fiction that allowed the White House to claim there was nothing new. In reality, it had been a pitched battle within the administration on this very point—a battle that Zelikow felt the State Department already had fought and won. He would have written the statement the same way whether or not the QFR existed.[18]

For all its impact, Rice's statement left open some loopholes. It was unclear if the reference to "personnel" also applied to U.S. contractors or whether President Bush still asserted the right to selectively opt out of international obligations. She began her statement by saying "as a matter of policy"—the administration's traditional weasel words to signal that this was not a matter of legal obligation. The specific article of the Convention Against Torture relating to cruel, inhuman, or degrading treatment (article 16) applies only to territory within a state's jurisdiction—and the Justice Department had long argued that facilities in other countries are not within the United States' jurisdiction.

But these were matters of legal interpretation and Rice really was playing in the high-stakes arena of politics. In the public perception, Rice was breaking new ground. As Rice flew from Kiev to Brussels, many reporters sensed that Rice for the first time was flying solo from the White House. (Little did they know that she had obtained Bush's personal approval for this step, which made the White House's defensive public response even more bizarre.) Her statement seemed intended to box in Cheney and her opponents on the issue, to force them to surrender to the McCain amendment. As reporters suspected, the impact in Congress was immediate. Within hours, lawmakers hailed Rice's statement as evidence that the administration had caved.

Rice's remarks are "an important and very welcome change from their previous position, which I believe has cost us dearly in the world and does not reflect our nation's laws or our values," said Senator Carl M. Levin of Michigan, ranking Democrat on the Senate Armed Services Committee.

"Pure Speculation"

Rice's statement also changed the dynamic in Europe. Her remarks at Andrews Air Force Base had gone over like a lead balloon. Dutch foreign minister Ben Bot said it was unsatisfactory and he expected a "lively discussion" with Rice and thirty other European foreign ministers when they met for a private dinner in Brussels. Other officials also said that she hadn't done enough to ease concerns. But now, by the time she arrived at the dinner, every foreign minister would have seen the news reports suggesting she had changed U.S. policy while on the road, seeming to demonstrate both power and agility.

The stage was set for Rice to charm her counterparts. The dinner was an innovation Rice had promoted to encourage frank discussions among her European colleagues. A few months earlier, she had arranged for a lunch with

NATO and EU foreign ministers on the sidelines of the UN General Assembly. No staff, just three dozen or so foreign ministers. The idea, greeted skeptically by some, proved to be a hit. Now they were planning to try it a second time.

Rice raised the prison issue at the start of the meal, and the ministers spent about an hour discussing it before moving on to the problem of Kosovo. Not a single minister questioned Rice directly about the existence of secret CIA prisons. Even Bot, for all his bravado before the meeting, didn't press her hard. He emerged to say Rice "covered basically all of our concerns." He added that if the secret prisons existed—which he called "pure speculation"—Rice has made it quite clear that the United States did not violate international law in such facilities.[19]

Rice had laid the groundwork for a positive outcome earlier in the year, when she invested considerable effort in restoring transatlantic ties frayed by differences over the invasion of Iraq. Having experienced the gloomy postwar period and the era of good feelings with Rice, her counterparts had little appetite for letting the debate fester.

Rice also handled herself well. She needed to signal that U.S. policy had changed without directly saying so, since that would appear to confirm that the administration had once condoned repulsive interrogation techniques. She had put her reputation on the line, because if it ever emerged that she had misled Europeans about U.S. policy, it would come back to haunt her. And she had broken free of the restraints placed on her by the vice president's office. A week later, the White House essentially accepted a revised version of the McCain amendment.[20]

While Powell would always rush home after a NATO meeting, Rice decided to stay another night in Brussels simply because she wanted to have dinner with the traveling press corps. Her staff found a lovely small restaurant, which Rice and the reporters had to themselves for the evening. She candidly discussed the week's events and surveyed the various issues that were causing her concern. The reporters teased her about the fact that, in a meeting with Ukrainian students, she had claimed that the media had pegged her with the moniker "Warrior Princess." A little Internet research had discovered it was a name her staff had given her after the September 11 attacks—a play on Osama bin Laden's nickname, "Warrior Prince."

As Rice sipped her wine, she was relaxed and seemed very pleased with herself. The debate wasn't finished within the administration, but Rice, Bellinger, and Zelikow kept pressing. Their hands were strengthened in June 2006 when the Supreme Court ruled, in *Hamdan v. Rumsfeld,* that detainees must be put under the protections of the Geneva Conventions. In effect, the Court said, the CIA's program was illegal. At a climactic National Security Council meeting in August 2006, Rice told the president that it was important for the Bush administration to bring the issue to closure, both on foreign policy grounds and on moral grounds. She noted that the secret sites were having a corrosive effect on the nation's ability to win cooperation on a range of intelligence issues with its allies. Rice urged the president to resolve the issue rather than hand it off to his successor.[21] Within weeks, Bush officially acknowledged the prisons and announced that the remaining detainees had been transferred to Guantánamo Bay. But Rice's victory was short-lived. The president defended the program as a success and retained the right to reopen the prisons. To the anger of human rights groups, the CIA revealed in April 2007 that it had restarted the overseas detention program just three months after Bush's announcement.

CHAPTER 8

DOUBLE DATES IN BAGHDAD

March 31, 2006

It was a strange place for a major foreign policy speech: the skybox of an empty soccer stadium in a dreary town in northern England.

A small and rather skeptical crowd of British foreign policy dignitaries, most of whom had never set foot in the town of Blackburn, sat in uncomfortable chairs to hear Rice try to place the American experiment in the Middle East in a grand historical context: the centuries-old idea of liberal democracy. The speech was perhaps the fullest expression of Rice's belief that history would one day judge the Bush administration more kindly than the contemporary critics. Befitting the audience, it was learned and academic, full of historical references and nice turns of phrase.

But context is everything in diplomacy. Her speech was largely ignored by the audience and the reporters who gathered to listen to it. It would be remembered mostly for a poorly worded answer she gave to a question: "We've made tactical errors—thousands of them, I'm sure," in Iraq. Ironically, Rice made this statement—beamed instantly around the world in news reports—just as she was finally going to make a play to put her imprint on the disastrous Iraq policy, more than one year after becoming secretary of state.

In her first year as secretary, Rice had made a couple of quick trips to Iraq, testified before Congress about the war, appeared on television talk shows to defend it, and been deeply involved in the mechanics of the policy. A few days after she settled into her job, for instance, Phil Zelikow had traveled to Iraq as part of an exploratory team to assess the situation and then had helped draft a memo that declared that Iraq was in danger of becoming "a failed state." Rice considers Zelikow to be her intellectual soul mate, but she also feels he has a tendency toward hyperbole. She didn't take his warnings literally, but she acknowledged that the margin for fixing Iraq was narrowing. In the memo, Zelikow argued that the State Department's effort in Iraq was too focused on Baghdad, and that outside in the provinces there was poor coordination between military and diplomatic aims. Rice considers herself a problem solver, and this was a problem she quietly set out to fix early in her term.[1]

But, somehow, Rice as secretary avoided much public association with the war. In the public's eye, it was Bush's problem and Rumsfeld's fiasco. As national security advisor, Rice had been at the center of the decision making and a very public face in selling the invasion. But when she moved over to the State Department, the blame for the unfolding disaster didn't seem to follow her. This was a source of perverse pride for her staff. People wanted to like Rice, and so apparently did not want to believe she was one of the authors of the Iraq disaster.

One poll surveyed Americans on how much responsibility Rice bore for the way the war in Iraq had gone. The answers were astonishing. Only 10 percent answered she had "a lot" of responsibility, while 32 percent said "some." But 26 percent said "only a little," while, amazingly, 17 percent said "none at all."[2] This suggested that nearly 50 percent of Americans gave her a complete pass on Iraq. Only a tiny sliver remembered she had been on television making the public case for war with dubious assertions about Iraq's nuclear threat, such as "we don't want the smoking gun to be a mushroom cloud." Moreover, she had been constantly at Bush's side during the major decisions and, as national security advisor, was responsible for both the haphazard way the decision to attack Iraq was reached and the administration's failure to have a plan for the occupation. Belatedly, she had tried to insert herself and the NSC staff into the process of managing the war and the reconstruction, but she failed to make much of an impact.[3]

"The Most Unwelcome Visit"

Overseas, Rice's role wasn't as forgotten. As soon as British foreign secretary Jack Straw announced that he had invited Rice to spend the weekend at Blackburn, which he represents in Parliament, opponents to the war started organizing. They set up a "Stop Condi" Web site and promised to bring in busloads of protestors. A columnist for the *Liverpool Echo* put it bluntly: Rice's trip was "the most unwelcome visit to Liverpool since Oswald Mosley came here in the 1930s and got bricked in the head," referring to the notorious British fascist who traveled with a marauding black-shirted paramilitary corps.[4]

Straw knew Rice's visit would be controversial, but he thought it was a worthwhile gamble. In October, Rice had invited Straw to spend the weekend in her hometown of Birmingham, Alabama, part of an effort to take diplomacy outside capitals and build a personal bond with her counterparts. Straw, who brought along his wife, attended a college football game and saw the iconic sites of Rice's childhood and her experience with segregation. When Rice had made her first trip to Europe as secretary of state, Straw had been taken aback by a statement that Rice had made during a news conference in London: "When the Founding Fathers said, 'We the people,' they didn't mean me." After Straw saw Birmingham, the comment suddenly made sense to him.[5]

Straw already had a good working relationship with Powell, but he and Rice bonded during the Alabama trip. Despite a reputation in England as being a bit of a stiff, Straw excels at dry British wit and is personable and open with small groups. Rice would regularly pick up her phone and call Straw directly, not even bothering to go through the State Department's operations center, which is supposed to arrange diplomatic calls and keep records of them. Clearly, Straw had to return the favor and bring Rice to Blackburn.

Few people in Alabama knew or cared who Straw was when Rice brought him there, so his visit was not controversial. No such luck with Rice. As it happens, Blackburn has one of the largest concentrations of Muslims in England, about 25 percent of the population. Muslims had always been an important source of support for Straw—whites in the town who felt he kowtowed to Muslims derisively called him "Black Jack"—and many Muslims were angry about the Iraq War. Straw thought that perhaps the elegant and articulate Rice would be able rebut the criticism and put a human face on American policy. But he didn't underestimate the potential for conflict. He warned Rice she would face protestors.

From the start, the visuals of the two-day expedition fell flat. This was Beatles country, and Rice's staff had dearly wanted to arrange a meeting with Paul McCartney. He made himself unavailable. Rice had to be content with visiting the Paul McCartney Theater at a performing arts school McCartney had attended as a youth, where an almost all-white group tried to sing gospel music for her.

Straw also had originally timed the trip so they could attend a soccer game—in payback for that University of Alabama football game—but said he was disappointed to learn at the last minute that the Blackburn Rovers had moved their game from Saturday afternoon to a more lucrative television appearance on Monday night. (At least that was the public story. The real reason is that the British decided the soccer hooligans would give Rice too hard a time.)[6] So she just saw an empty stadium where some children kicked around a soccer ball. Rice had planned to visit a well-known mosque in Blackburn, but the prospect of protests unnerved the imam and the visit was canceled.

The weather was typically British: soggy skies, chilly rain, and an occasional glimmer of sunshine. The protestors never numbered more than a few hundred at any given location, but they were persistent and loud, dominating the news coverage. Many appeared to be Muslim. Everywhere Rice went, she heard chants recycled from the 1960s—"Hey, Condi, hey, how many kids did you kill today?"—and saw signs denouncing her as a war criminal. At the performing arts school, some students had hung a large sign on one of the windows: DON'T FUCK THE WHORE, FUCK THE WAR. Other students held red balloons—to signify the blood shed in Iraq—or wore black T-shirts declaring NO TORTURE, NO COMPROMISE. Just past the front door of the school, they stood silently, arms crossed, as Rice swept past them to tour the school.

The protestors had another effect. Many of the people Rice met—the mayor of Blackburn, the school's headmaster, Muslim leaders—made it clear that while they were happy to greet her, they also opposed the war. The Blackburn mayor, a Muslim named Yusuf Jan-Virmoni, said he merely hoped the visit would put his town on the map and boost the economy. The last notable visitor had been Mohandas Gandhi sixty years earlier; otherwise, Blackburn was best known for an odd mention in the Beatles song "A Day in the Life," concerning its pothole-ridden roads. (John Lennon sings: "I heard the news today, oh boy / 4,000 holes in Blackburn, Lancashire.")

Even when Rice and Straw lit candles at Blackburn Cathedral, the Very Reverend Christopher Armstrong called upon them to remember the victims of war. "We hold before God those who have a responsibility to make good and far-reaching decisions whilst listening to different views as to how peace and justice may be promoted," he intoned, his voice bouncing off the stone walls of the church. "We pray that in the counsel they take for the nations they may discern the still small voice of the One who calls each of us to light a candle for peace with our lives."

The British press had a field day, writing sharp and sometimes nasty stories that included speculation about why Straw kept touching Rice. The London *Times* even ran a series of photographs of Straw with his hands on Rice's arms and shoulders. The newspaper asked a body language expert to comment on what it all meant, eliciting the insight that they "share a very personal and intimate friendship . . . the fact Jack Straw is actively touching her is highly unusual; politicians tend to keep a suitable distance." The accompanying article said that Straw "hovered at Dr. Rice's elbow like a proud but anxious new boyfriend."[7] The coverage so embarrassed Straw that he became uncomfortable discussing his friendship with Rice with reporters.

At a cost of more than $500,000, helicopters hovered overhead, and nearly thirteen hundred British bobbies in yellow raincoats kept the protestors at bay.[8] Rice kept a smile on her face, shrugging off the protests with such aplomb that one British press wag dubbed her ability to turn on the charm "insta-Rice."[9]

"Tactical Errors—Thousands of Them"

The centerpiece of the visit came when Rice delivered her speech at Ewood Park, the soccer stadium. She strived mightily to place the American adventure in Iraq in the context of a grander idea—liberal democracy—and once again drew on her experience as a black woman growing up in the segregated South. For rhetorical purposes, it was a helpful coincidence that Liverpool had once prospered because of the slave trade with the American South—and that Blackburn textile mills had relied on the cotton picked by slaves. And she thought a British audience would appreciate a paeon to theorists like Thomas Hobbes, John Locke, and Adam Smith who had brought forth the notion of liberalism and helped create the American founding fathers' concept of democracy.

"It was even said, in my own lifetime, that blacks in America were 'unfit' for democracy—too 'childlike,' too 'unready,' too 'incapable,' too 'unwanting' of self-government," Rice said. "The criticism assumes that human beings are slaves to their culture, not the authors of it. Liberal democracy is unique because it is both principle and process, an end toward which people strive and the means by which they do so."

She spoke directly about the difficulties in Iraq—and the controversy over U.S. interrogation policies after the attacks of September 11. She celebrated "the daily work of negotiation, and cooperation, and compromise, the constant struggle to balance majority rule with individual rights." She acknowledged that "the appeal of liberal democracy is desirable, but its progress has not been even nor inevitable." She added that "for societies accustomed to thinking in zero-sum terms, or for diverse communities that have never shared power among themselves, liberal democracy can seem difficult and frustrating and even threatening."

The weakest part of her speech came when she sought to blame Saddam

Hussein for the sectarian violence engulfing Iraq, lamely arguing that he "took a society that was already rife with sectarian and religious divisions and drove it to the brink of the state of nature."[10] She ignored the American role in unleashing these tensions through a poorly managed and often ham-fisted occupation.

This audience, though polite, didn't buy her sales pitch. The gap between the United States and other countries, even England, was readily apparent. One of the hosts of the event was Chatham House, a British version of the Council on Foreign Relations, and it was represented on the dais by one of Britain's most famous foreign policy figures: former foreign secretary Douglas Hurd, a Conservative Party stalwart who served under Prime Minister Margaret Thatcher. With an elegant shock of white hair and a lanky frame, Hurd seemed the epitome of old-school England.

After Rice spoke, Hurd was scheduled to make a few brief remarks before she took questions from the audience. He acknowledged her efforts to improve U.S. diplomacy. But then in a few sentences he eviscerated her speech. "It is quite possible to believe" that democracy is necessary, he archly noted, but also to "believe that essentially the path must grow from the roots of its own society and that the killing of thousands of people, many of them innocent, is unacceptable whether committed by a domestic tyrant or for a good cause" by foreign invaders. In another sharp dig he added, "The world only works if the world's only superpower is bound by the rules like everyone else." His comments stung so much that they did not appear in the official State Department transcript of the event.[11]

During the question-and-answer period, Rosemary Hollis, the director of research at Chatham House, asked Rice for some reassurance that "some lessons have been learned from some of the mistakes made over the last three years." Rice answered with a well-worn refrain that of course they have made mistakes but the central strategy of getting rid of Hussein was right. "Yes, I know we've made tactical errors—thousands of them, I'm sure," Rice added.

For an administration that almost never admits error, it was a breathtaking statement. Rice didn't mention any specific mistakes and obviously the use of the word "thousands" was a number plucked out of thin air. She was drawing on history—there were many tactical mistakes made during the defeat and occupation of Germany that are all but forgotten now. But her point was debatable. Some might say fighting al-Qaeda was the right strategic decision but extending the war to Iraq was a strategic error that detracted from that central mission. Others might argue that there were many strategic blunders made during the course of the Iraq War, from an inadequate number of troops to the

failure to plan for the occupation or anticipate the insurgency, which could not be simply dismissed as "tactical" shortcomings.

In any case, the admission of "thousands" of errors generated the headlines and wiped away the intended impact of the speech. After seeing the wire stories on the remark, McCormack called a few reporters to stress that she meant it figuratively, not literally, but it was too late. All the reporters made her statement the central thrust of their stories, with the exception of the reporter for *The New York Times,* who mentioned them in the middle of a sharp-edged feature about her misbegotten day. But even then, the *Times* slapped this headline on the article for the final editions: "Rice, in England, Concedes U.S. 'Tactical Errors' in Iraq."[12]

After the speech, as the reporters took the one-hour drive back to Liverpool, they began to suspect something was up. Jim Wilkinson, who rarely travels in the same vehicle as the press corps, was on the press bus. He made small talk and insisted he simply wanted to see their hotel. But as soon as the bus arrived, he gathered the reporters into a room and dropped a bombshell: Under strict secrecy, Rice was flying to Iraq the next day. Moreover, she was bringing Straw along for the ride. The original schedule had Rice staying in England until Sunday and then going home, but she would slip out of Liverpool Saturday night and make a surprise appearance in Baghdad the next morning, before anyone noticed she was missing.

Wilkinson added that Rice would be sleeping overnight in Baghdad, which he said was intended to be a sign of confidence in Iraq. No secretary of state had done that since Powell in 2003, shortly after the invasion and before the insurgency had erupted in full force. But it was strange spin. Would Americans really feel more confident in the war effort because the secretary of state finally felt comfortable enough to stay a single night in the heavily guarded Green Zone? Would they even notice? Wilkinson couldn't stop talking about this, suggesting that it demonstrated Rice's bravery—which seemed to undercut the idea that things were getting better. It didn't strike the reporters as particularly newsworthy.

"Let Them Vent"

Rice had made two previous trips to Iraq. The first, in May 2005, was a lightning visit with just three wire service reporters; she had had to cancel a previous trip because it leaked and secrecy was broken, so her staff decided to sharply limit the press contingent for her first trip. She made the brief stop mainly to push the Iraqis to finish writing a constitution.

As her plane was taking off from Baghdad, Rice thought about what she had seen: the great rivers flowing through Iraq, the fertile green fields, the monuments with their sense of history. She compared that to Afghanistan, which seemed to her to be nothing but mountains and dirt. Iraq had oil, water, and people; Afghanistan had nothing. She decided to pick up the phone and call Bush.

"Mr. President, this is going to be a great country," she told him. He was very pleased to hear her enthusiasm.[13]

Then Rice returned in November with a larger press corps, just before the December elections, in an effort to get Sunni leaders engaged in the political process. On that trip, she announced one innovation: provincial reconstruction teams, or PRTs, which were intended to get diplomats and aid workers out of Baghdad and into the provinces. Rice developed this idea in response to Zelikow's memo at the start of her term. The teams would be staffed with political, economic, legal, and civil–military relations specialists who could help not only distribute aid but also advise regional Iraqi officials, thereby fortifying provincial governments that had had little authority under Saddam Hussein.

But the idea had been cobbled together quickly and without much support from the Pentagon. There were already three functional equivalents of consulates—in Mosul, Kirkuk, and Hilla. Rice simply relabeled them PRTs, suggesting at the time that there would soon be one in nearly every province. But the Pentagon, eager to reduce its military presence in Iraq, not expand it, balked at supplying soldiers to guard the new facilities. So the plan was stuck in a bureaucratic stalemate for months before the Pentagon relented and agreed to provide some security if the PRTs were placed near or on military bases.[14]

Now, nearly four months after the elections that were to finally usher in the permanent government, Rice was making a dramatic return to Iraq. She was coming to Baghdad to perform the diplomatic equivalent of shock therapy.

President Bush's approval rating was in the mid 30s, his lowest level ever. But the idea for the Rice-Straw trip had come from British prime minister Tony Blair, who knew Straw was planning a trip and asked Bush if Rice would consider going with him in an effort to convince the feuding Iraqi politicians to form a government before the country descended into civil war.[15] Bush readily agreed. The death toll had mounted as Shiites and Sunnis engaged in a deadly series of reprisal killings since the bombing of the revered gold-domed Shiite shrine in Samarra on February 22. Shiites and Sunnis who had coexisted for decades in the same towns were now fleeing their neighborhoods, the beginning signs of ethnic cleansing and internal displacement.

The interim prime minister, Ibrahim al-Jafari, had won a one-vote victory in the Shiite bloc—the largest in parliament—as their nominee for permanent prime minister. But he was fiercely opposed by Sunni and Kurdish leaders and had done little since his nomination to win their support. Now the country appeared leaderless and adrift. U.S. officials viewed Jafari as weak and ineffectual and made little secret of their desire that he step aside—though officially, of course, they would say Iraq was a sovereign country and any decision was up to the Iraqis. After the bombing of the Samarra shrine spawned a wave of sectarian violence between Shiites and Sunnis and Iraq appeared on the edge of civil war, the U.S. ambassador, Zalmay Khalilzad, had tried to get Jafari to do something about the violence.

"Zal, you've been here six months," Jafari replied. "How can you understand my country? Let them vent."[16]

Rice was under orders to deliver a blunt message that the Iraqis were losing patience—and, more important, so too were the countries that had expended blood and money ousting Saddam.

Adding Straw to the trip heightened the drama of Rice's trip. The British still had eight thousand troops in Iraq, by far the second largest amount, and the image of two foreign ministers arriving together to jawbone the Iraqis was a powerful one. Rice knew little about the mechanics of parliamentary democracy, so Straw also had a practical role: He planned to draw on his experience in parliamentary deal-making, explaining to the Iraqis how protracted negotiations on forming a government can disillusion citizens. He also wanted to share some examples of how several British prime ministers had put together their governments.

Straw thought the plan was a gamble that could backfire, but he decided it was worth it. Something had to be done. Despite the negative press, he also thought Rice's visit to Blackburn had worked out just fine. As one of Rice's aides joked, with the president's approval rating so low, how could the situation get worse?

Just before Rice departed Liverpool, Zelikow arrived to join the trip. Nick Burns, the undersecretary of state, had been with Rice before Liverpool, when she made quick stops in Berlin and Paris, so Zelikow could not resist telling reporters, "The A team has arrived." Zelikow, who had been in London coordinating the Baghdad visit with the British, had pushed hard within the administration for dramatic action to signal a new start in Iraq, having made a solo visit earlier in March as well as other trips.

Zelikow had asked for permission to carry a sidearm while in Iraq—a request that diplomatic security officials first thought was made in jest. But he was serious. Diplomatic security rejected the idea. "You can carry a gun, Philip, but you'll only get one bullet, which you'll have to carry in your pocket," cracked Wilkinson, referring to the constraints placed on Barney Fife, the bumbling deputy on *The Andy Griffith Show*.[17]

"Have a Good Trip"

As Rice's Boeing 757 jet flew through the night to Kuwait, where she would transfer to a military C-17 transport, Rice and Straw gathered the combined U.S. and British staffs in her flying office. Rice sat in her chair, Straw sat on her couch, and staff sat on the floor like their children. Rice and Straw told the staffers that they had decided that given the sensitivity of the discussions, Rice and Straw would do some of the meetings by themselves—and the rest of the staff could wait outside the doors.

When it came time to catch a few hours of sleep, Rice offered Straw the use of the foldout bed in her cabin. To his later regret, he didn't inquire about her own sleeping arrangements and she didn't offer an explanation, not wanting to get into a discussion about who slept where. So he gladly took the bed. He was shocked to discover in the morning that she had slept on the floor in the aisle, near the plane's garbage bag, on an exercise mat and rolled up in a sleeping bag and some blankets. The unusual sleeping arrangements might have remained a secret, but the reporters in the back of the plane found out when the flight attendants remarked they had trouble getting to the kitchen galley because Rice was blocking the way. The British tabloids, always eager to get in a dig, would later roast Straw for not being an English gentleman.

The Blackburn weather somehow had followed Rice. She arrived in Baghdad in a drenching rainstorm, on a chilly day when the temperatures, normally above 80 degrees in the spring, did not break 55 degrees. The downpour meant Rice's entourage couldn't use any of the fast and agile Black Hawk helicopters lined up on the airport tarmac.

On her previous visit, Rice had told reporters she looked forward to the day when she could drive into Baghdad and not have to take a low-flying helicopter twisting in the air to avoid enemy fire. Rice would now have her chance: She would travel to Baghdad on the once-notorious airport road, in a well-armed military convoy. Reporters, wearing body armor and helmets, rode in a Rhino—a large, heavily armored bus designed to withstand roadside bombs. The ugly Rhinos have gun ports for weapons and various ways to exit depending on whether it topples over or is struck by an attack. Rice, oddly, was placed in a less secure vehicle, a Chevrolet Suburban. (On her first trip, she had resisted wearing the unattractive desert-colored body armor over her stylish clothes but Mike Evanoff, her security chief, told her that she had no option.)[18]

After reporters boarded the Rhino, a remarkably chipper soldier gave these instructions: "This is a slippery road and the Rhino can tip over. If it tips over, climb through the exit in the roof. But if you are being shot at, don't leave. If a mortar or an IED hits the Rhino and it catches fire, you should leave, unless you are getting shot at. If you are on fire and getting shot at, don't leave. And if you feel the urge to stand up, don't. Have a good trip."

The Rhino holding Rice's staff didn't get the same spiel. Wilkinson mordantly wondered aloud if they'd be greeted by "flowers and sweets," self-consciously echoing Vice President Cheney's prediction before the invasion.

Before the war, the airport road had been pleasant, almost beautiful, lined by trees and flowering bushes. But they had all been bulldozed in an effort to deter insurgent ambushes, and now the way was strewn with garbage, rubble, and concrete Jersey barriers. Amazingly, Rice got stuck in a traffic jam and so the trip took nearly an hour. The airport road is protected by Iraqi soldiers, and for security reasons the Americans had not told them Rice was coming. An IED had gone off somewhere on the road and the Iraqis had set up a roadblock to check vehicles. So, along with forlorn-looking Iraqi drivers in battered and dusty vehicles, the secretary of state found she was stuck in traffic gridlock—at least until the U.S. military could untangle the mess and get her entourage into the safety of the Green Zone.

The Green Zone is another world, a funhouse version of America that happens to be in the center of the Middle East. Once intended to be temporary, the four-square-mile enclave in the heart of Baghdad had become more and more permanent—and increasingly separate from the reality of Iraq. Cafés and stores had sprung up to serve the Americans. The cafeteria had expanded dramatically, offering heaping portions of prime ribs, lobster tails, and Baskin-Robbins ice cream—and, with the exception of pita bread, nothing that remotely resembles Middle Eastern cuisine. Strangely, the walls of the cafeteria, which serves more than six thousand free meals a day, are decorated with mounted antique guns.

Largely immune to the turmoil outside the Green Zone, the soldiers and diplomats after hours have their choice of taking belly dancing and martial arts classes or sipping cocktails next to a huge pool. (NO DRINKING WHILE ARMED, warned a sign near the palm-fretted water.) Cuban cigars, banned in the United States, were on sale next to the appliance and clothing store for $6 each. One diplomat, on his second tour, said, semi-seriously, that he signed up again because he couldn't make it in the real world. "There's always beer in the refrigerator in my office," he said. "I don't know how it gets there but it's always there."

There was a booming business in T-shirts displaying grim humor—smiley faces with bloody bullet holes between the eyes or the signs on every military vehicle, warning people in English and Arabic to keep one hundred meters away "or you will be shot."

The soldiers and civilian workers live in small apartments carved out of eleven hundred sparsely furnished trailers. The reporters stayed in even smaller rooms, labeled "transient housing," each with a spongy bed, a small nightstand, and no running water. Showers are communal, with separate male and female facilities. (The buildings for the female showers carry a stern warning that the sign labeling them "female" should not be removed.)

The logistical support contract for the mission in Baghdad costs $200 million a year, dwarfing the $12 million in administrative expenses needed to run the State Department's second largest embassy, located in Cairo.[19]

Arabic is virtually useless in the Green Zone. The buildings are mostly guarded by soldiers from Latin American countries who speak little English, so anyone who gets lost needs to use Spanish to find their way back. The faux reality of the Green Zone was best typified by the signs stuck in bare patches of dirt, warning people: KEEP OFF THE GRASS!

The "Green" in the name means it is safe; the rest of Iraq is deemed by U.S. officials to be the "Red Zone." In fact, the rest of Baghdad had become so red that many Iraqi politicians have simply moved in the heavily guarded compound along with the Americans. (The compound was officially called "The International Zone.") By the time Rice arrived in early April 2006, the U.S. military had counted more than 2,500 violent incidents in the city so far that year, including more than 900 roadside bombings, 84 car bombs, 70 cases of people firing rocket-propelled grenades, 55 drive-by shootings, hundreds of small-arms attacks and political and sectarian assassinations, and dozens of mortar, grenade, and sniper attacks.[20]

Even inside the Green Zone, almost every street is lined with fifteen- or twenty-foot-high concrete blast walls. Every so often one can catch a glimpse of a hideous monument that Saddam Hussein had erected to celebrate a supposed military achievement. The American embassy is temporarily housed in a massive former presidential palace, itself a monument to bad taste, with ceilings soaring fifty feet or higher and clashing types of marble. The Republican Palace was the traditional presidential palace, which Saddam expanded after he seized power. The reporters were assigned to work out of a pale green room where Hussein had first taken the oath of office in 1979. The military had covered up a huge wall illustration of Hussein with cloth, but the room still had the feel of a new occupier replacing a former ruler. Around the corner from the press filing center, tucked into a massive dining room dominated by an ugly chandelier, an imitation Starbucks coffee shop served espresso, lattes, and frozen coffee drinks to the funky tunes of Putamayo CDs.

As if to accentuate the permanence of the American presence, a $600 million embassy complex rose nearby, comprising twenty-one buildings over 104 acres—about the size of Vatican City.[21]

"Count the Votes"

Immediately after arriving, Rice and Straw began to crisscross the Green Zone, meeting a succession of Iraqi officials in an effort to break the deadlock. Jafari is an awkward man, and the meeting, given Rice's desire to ease him out of office, was an appropriately awkward encounter. In the brief joint appearance before reporters, Rice appeared stiff and frosty. Support for Jafari's candidacy was rapidly beginning to crumble within Iraq, but he seemed to have little appreciation for his predicament.

Once the cameras left, Jafari made it clear to Rice and Straw that he was the nominee and he expected to serve as prime minister. He was entitled to his seat. Straw's feelings about Jafari had alternated over the months. Back in June, Straw decided Jafari was hopeless, but then on later trips he began to think maybe Jafari wasn't so bad after all. Now it was clear Jafari didn't have enough self-awareness to understand his dwindling political standing.

Rice and Straw couldn't really tell Jafari to step aside, but they came as close as possible to that line. Acting as a diplomatic tag team, they tried to make Jafari realize on his own that it was time to leave the political stage.

"I am not a politician," Rice began the meeting. "But I don't see how you get to a coalition that makes you prime minister." Then she turned to Straw, saying, "Jack here is a politician."

It was Straw's turn. He explained how he tried to round up support for votes in the British Parliament. "Sometimes, at some point, I have to go to the prime minister and say, 'The votes just aren't there.'"

Straw gently suggested, "You need to count the votes."

"We are trying to tell you that you are not going to be able to get there," Rice added.[22]

Jafari didn't get the hint, at least in that meeting. He replied that the Iraqi people wanted him to serve as prime minister.

In public, Rice again made her feelings clear. When Rice arrived at the residence of Adil Abdul Mahdi—who had lost the nomination to Jafari by just one vote—Rice was bubbling over with enthusiasm. "It's wonderful to see you," she gushed in front of the cameras. "It's wonderful to see you."

During their meetings, Rice and Straw were especially impressed with the transformation that had taken place with the Sunni leaders. For months, the allies had begged the Sunnis to get involved, but to little avail. Now they seemed to understand that they needed to be in the game. Straw told them they shouldn't fear democracy. After all, he had spent eighteen years in the opposition before coming to power. He felt his remarks seemed to resonate.

In an ominous sign that sectarian tensions were on the rise Sunni leaders emphasized to Rice and Straw that they wanted coalition forces to begin patrols in their neighborhoods. They had always resisted the idea before; now they acted like they had never had held any reservations.

That night, Rice and Straw had dinner with a mixed group of Iraqi leaders, one of whom was Saleh Mutlak, a Sunni politician who has long been accused of having ties to Iraqi insurgent groups. He told Rice that the sectarian tension between Iraqi Sunnis and Shiites had arrived with the U.S. invasion force in 2003, the direct opposite of what she had asserted in her speech in Blackburn. Mutlak wasn't sure if Rice believed him, but he was impressed that she appeared to listen. "When they came to Iraq, absolutely they were biased to the Shiites," he said. "I think they are being more evenhanded than what they were before. They realized they cannot solve the problems in Iraq without us."[23]

In the zero-sum game of Iraqi politics, however, if the Sunnis were feeling better about the Americans, the Shiites had to start feeling worse. As Rice had said two days earlier in Blackburn, "liberal democracy can seem difficult and frustrating and even threatening" to groups which had never shared power before. She understood that the Shiites, having finally achieved this great victory, were resentful that they were now being asked to give way to a unity government.

Rice tried to soften the blow by publicly lauding Ayatollah Ali al-Sistani, the Shiite cleric who held great sway over Iraqi politics but yet seemed determined to stand apart from the grubby day-to-day business of political deal-making. But her language seemed desperate. "I don't think there's anyone for whom we have greater respect than Ayatollah Sistani," Rice said. "He's been a voice of reason at difficult times for the Iraqi people."[24]

During the meal, insurgents fired off one of their nightly mortar rounds. Rice felt the vibrations and wondered what had happened. But as she looked around the table, she noticed her dinner companions seemed inured to it, much the way Californians barely feel the evening tremors of their fragile piece of earth.

Later that night, Rice met with Jafari alone at the ambassador's residence. The meeting confirmed everything that Rice disliked about Jafari—his nonstop complaining about his colleagues and his conviction that everything that was wrong in Iraq was someone else's fault. Rice became convinced there was no way he could be a leader of a nation. And she believed that the Iraqi people would conclude that democracy had failed if he was not held accountable for his poor leadership during the previous year.[25]

Nevertheless, Rice said she loved being in Baghdad, despite the massive flooding because the drainage system could not handle the rain, despite the garbage, despite the concrete barriers and the hideous monuments and the neo-fascist architecture. Privately and publicly, she claimed that the decrepit and dysfunctional city was actually inspirational. "When you look around, you realize that this is really a great Arab city," she told Libby Leist of NBC News. "It's a beautiful city and it's not just an Arab city. It's a city where different ethnic cultures come together."[26]

It was almost as if she willed herself to believe that so much blood had not been shed for so little. Yet even with her staff she seemed genuinely stimulated by Iraq. She never seemed demoralized or overwhelmed by the problems. In her mind, history was being made right before her eyes—and that was a good thing.

Rice and Straw made quite a pair, an elegantly dressed conservative woman and the plain blue-suit-and-tie former leftist student leader. By the time they returned to London, they had spent five straight days together, beginning with a meeting in Berlin on Iran, traveling to Blackburn, and now Baghdad. They clearly enjoyed each other's company. Rice good-naturedly teased Straw when he declared there needed to be a "Mr. A, Mr. B, or Mr. C" to run Iraq; to laughter she replied, "I'm sure we'd be all right with Miss A or Miss B or Miss C."[27] Straw's skillful turns of phrase even seemed to rub off on Rice, who as the trip wore on began to use simpler and more direct language than her usual mix of modifiers, caveats, and subordinate clauses.

But it proved to be the last hurrah for the Jack and Condi Show. After the trip, Straw blushed in Parliament when he was ruthlessly and publicly ribbed by the Tories for being the "Hugh Grant of the Cabinet."[28] A few weeks later, he was sacked as foreign minister by Tony Blair after Labour suffered losses in local elections. The British press speculated wildly on the reasons, with some suggesting that the Blackburn trip and Straw's closeness to Rice had been too much for Blair.

"The Enemy's Got a Brain"

After Rice and Straw returned home, Iraqi officials made predictable complaints about unseemly U.S. pressure. But Rice was also roasted by American critics for excessive meddling. *The Wall Street Journal,* normally a sympathetic voice, headlined its editorial "Condi's Iraq Stumble."[29] Marine Lieutenant General Greg Newbold, the Pentagon's former top operations officer, wrote a blistering column in *Time* magazine saying her comments on tactical errors were an outrage. "It reflects an effort to obscure gross errors in strategy by shifting the blame for failure to those who have been resolute in fighting," he said.[30]

In Blackburn, the day after Rice had spoken of thousands of errors, she was asked a cheeky question about her comment: "We're obviously very curious about which tactical mistakes would be at the top of your list. Is it the number of troops for the occupation, de-Baathification, disbanding the Iraqi army, the failure to anticipate the insurgency, or some other issue?"

Rice was irritated by the question and ducked it completely. In retrospect, she missed an opportunity to begin a discussion with the American people about the mistakes made in Iraq and how the administration hoped to learn from them. She could be brutally honest with her staff about those errors—and she recognized that time was running out to make a difference in Iraq. Many of the American and British officials flew to Baghdad reading the bestselling book *Cobra II,* the highly critical account of the poor planning before the invasion of Iraq. Rice's aides privately agreed that the devastating portrait in the book was correct, but she could not bring herself to have that discussion in the open. Instead, she would constantly sidestep it by making a brief acknowledgment: "I'm quite certain that there are things that, in retrospect, we would do differently." But, she'd add, that was the nature of "any big complicated operation" and it would be up to the historians to sort it out.[31] It was a clever rhetorical technique designed to shut down any substantive discussion of how and why the earlier decisions were made.

Then a strange thing happened. Rice's "thousands" of errors boomeranged to hit another target—Rumsfeld. He was asked about Rice's comment during an interview with South Dakota radio station WDAY. Interviewer Scott Hennen did a fine job of placing her remarks completely in context. Rice had "figuratively suggested recently we've made thousands of tactical errors" and "also suggested that the important test was making the right strategic decisions and that would be the test of history," Hennen told Rumsfeld. "Do you agree with that?"

"I don't know what she was talking about, to be perfectly honest," Rumsfeld replied. He said no war plan survives "first contact" with the enemy.

"Why? Because the enemy's got a brain. The enemy watches what you do and then adjusts to that, so you have to constantly adjust and change your tactics, your techniques, and your procedures," he said. "If someone says, well, that's a tactical mistake, then I guess it's a lack of understanding, at least my understanding, of what warfare is about."[32]

Rice's aides were appalled. Generally, despite their private tensions, Rice and Rumsfeld were civil to each other in public; the only other time Rumsfeld had so publicly bashed her was after she disclosed to *The New York Times* in late 2003 that she had set up a group in the White House to coordinate Iraq policy—a signal that the Defense Department wasn't doing the job. Rumsfeld acted then as if it was news to him, even though he had been part of the decision.

This was an even tougher shot at Rice—but it backfired. Within days, a half dozen senior retired generals called for Rumsfeld's resignation, forcing President Bush to issue a public declaration that he would retain Rumsfeld despite the public outcry.

Even Colin Powell came to Rice's defense. "We made some serious mistakes in the immediate aftermath of the fall of Baghdad," he said in a speech in Chicago four days after Rumsfeld's radio interview. "We didn't have enough troops on the ground," he said. "We didn't impose our will. And as a result, an insurgency got started, and . . . it got out of control."[33] Powell has been a four-star general and chairman of the Joint Chiefs of Staff; the clear implication was that he certainly had an understanding of the nature of warfare—and Rumsfeld was dead wrong.

Despite the criticism of the Rice-Straw visit, the payoff came three weeks later, partly prodded by a letter from Bush secretly transmitted to Sistani. Bush made it clear that the status quo was untenable and the problems of governance had to be fixed immediately. The president wanted to be sure Sistani understood that the United States, having invested so much blood and treasure, was willing to disengage from the effort if the meandering political course exemplified by Jafari was not abandoned. Rice had hinted at this publicly, but Bush's letter was intended to reinforce this stark reality.[34] Bush's back-channel correspondence with Sistani—who has refused to meet with Americans—has never been publicly acknowledged, in part because U.S. officials believe it would be embarrassing and potentially damaging for Sistani.

The old ayatollah quietly intervened and finally convinced Jafari to step aside.

"A Chance to Correct Our Mistakes"

Jafari's replacement was Nouri Kemal al-Maliki, who was a mystery to most of the senior officials in Washington, but immediately embraced as an "Iraqi patriot" who could save the American enterprise (the third such Iraqi leader in three years). Maliki, born in 1950 near the Shiite holy city of Karbala, had joined the Shiite-dominated Dawa Party in 1968. He fled Iraq in 1980, a year after Hussein rose to the presidency, and spent his years in exile in Iran and Syria. Though he opposed Hussein, Maliki also opposed the U.S. invasion. Since the toppling of Hussein, he had played a notable role in the committee that had written the Iraqi constitution, arguing against splitting Iraq along ethnic and sectarian lines.[35] Maliki had a reputation as a hard-line Shiite with little interest in reconciliation, but Ambassador Khalilzad was impressed by his performance during the government formation process. Critics would later charge that Khalilzad had persistently meddled in the formation of the national unity government and preferred Maliki because he was a weak leader who the hard-charging ambassador could easily manipulate.[36]

Though Rice had just been in Baghdad, she had not met, or even spoken, with Maliki—largely because of a strategy by the U.S. embassy to keep her away from many of the possible compromise candidates for fear that she would hinder their chances.

President Bush decided that Rice—along with Rumsfeld—had to go back to Iraq to take stock of Maliki and steer him in the right direction. This was the administration's last chance to save Iraq, and the joint appearance by the two top cabinet officials might have a galvanizing effect. The president's approval ratings had only gotten worse since Rice's trip with Straw three weeks earlier.

Rice had been scheduled to attend a NATO meeting in Sofia, Bulgaria, at the end of April, and was considering visiting Turkey and Greece as well. This provided the perfect opportunity to slip in another one of her surprise visits, a fact that was made clear to anyone studying her announced schedule: a five-day trip for three countries located next to each other. But there were no hints by her staff to reporters, or even warnings that speculation should be minimized. This was in part because the staff thought reporters by now knew the rules—and also because the decision had been made very late. Rice planned to leave on a Monday; Bush's principal foreign policy advisors had only agreed to add the Baghdad stop at a secret meeting the preceding Thursday. Coordination for the trip between State, the Defense Department, and the embassy only began in earnest on Saturday.

On Sunday morning, twenty-four hours before Rice's departure, Saul

Hudson of Reuters filed a story titled, "US's Rice to Visit Europe—and Maybe Beyond." Hudson noted that Rice at times has visited as many as four countries in a day and her aides were "willing to mislead about potential stops to dangerous countries." He openly speculated that "her apparently light schedule raises the possibility she could add a surprise stop in the Middle East such as Iraq."[37] He also listed Libya and Cyprus as potential surprise stops, but the damage was done. The possibility that Rice was going to Iraq was out in the open, on the Web, and in newspapers throughout the Muslim world.

Reuters has a large business clientele that might profit from news that Rice was going to Iraq, and unlike previous trips there had been no official gag order. But it was a potentially foolhardy story to write. Wilkinson and McCormack were furious and immediately booted Hudson off the trip. Mike Evanoff, the head of Rice's security detail, called the senior brass at Reuters and told them they had potentially put the lives of forty-two people at risk. (Later in the week, he would learn of at least one report that a terrorist group was overheard citing the Reuters story as part of a potential plot to target Rice.)

But as Rice flew to Athens on the first leg of the trip, Rice's aides said there was too much riding on this venture to cancel it. Rice gave her usual trip briefing, but even she seemed bored by the intricacies of Greek and Turkish politics. She stopped briefly in Athens—where three thousand protestors battled with riot police as they denounced Rice as a war criminal—and then flew off to Ankara for another round of pro forma meetings. The day had begun with a 3 A.M. arrival in Athens and didn't end until after the clock moved past midnight in Ankara, one of those exhausting periods when traveling with Rice seemed nothing but a never-ending succession of motorcades and news conferences—to little consequence.

The next morning, Rice flew early to Incirlik Air Base in southern Turkey and transferred to a C-17 cargo jet. As the plane flew to Baghdad, Rice's staff made it clear that this was a critical moment in the Iraq venture. The creation of a permanent government meant the United States would have increasingly less power to shape events. It was especially important that the State Department and the Defense Department work together well as the new government was established and began to build institutions of governance. Wilkinson walked up and down the plane, sitting down with groups of reporters to make this case over the screaming noise of the cargo jet. He spoke off the record at first but finally refined his pitch to a handful of on-the-record talking points, which notably included the word "mistakes."

"Clearly the new Iraqi government must perform on behalf of the Iraqi people," he said. "But the new government also gives us a chance to correct our mistakes and do our part to make Iraq work. This is an opportunity to be seized. The Iraqis must seize it, but the U.S. government must organize itself to help the Iraqis do so."

Among Rice's aides, there was a sense that if they didn't make the right decisions when the new government was formed, the odds that things would begin to work in Iraq would go way down. Zelikow and Wilkinson in particular believed that the administration needed to get ready for the new government with the same intensity as going to war, focusing especially on planning and execution. Rice agreed with them.

The subtext of the message was that the State Department—and Rice—was finally going to take control of Iraq policy. Before the war, Rumsfeld had demanded that the Defense Department take charge of postwar Iraq. Now, three years later, the problem would be largely handed over to State, which in any case needed to take charge of the political and economic problems strangling Iraq. As Rice put it after the trip, "The secretary of defense is the secretary of defense. He doesn't do foreign policy, and I would expect him to be worried about issues like, you know, militarily how are we dealing with issues."[38]

Zelikow envisioned Rice's two visits as the diplomatic equivalent of pounding the cue ball against a rack of balls at the start of a pool game. You hit the ball as hard as you can, and you have no idea what balls, if any, are going to end up in what pockets. But the balls are scattered, allowing you to set up better shots later in the game. (The problem with this analogy is that it was three years after the invasion of Iraq and the pool game was nearly over.)

Behind the scenes, there was a culture clash between the Defense Department and the State Department as aides tried to put together a schedule for the two high-powered personalities. The Pentagon first ran off and put together a largely separate schedule for Rumsfeld, even though the main point of the visit was that Rice and Rumsfeld were to be seen working together. The military also wanted a minute-by-minute plan—State is used to just blocking off chunks of time for meetings—and Rumsfeld's aides became quite concerned any time the meetings ran long and the carefully orchestrated plan was off schedule by a few minutes.

"The People Need Electricity"

Unlike the Straw trip, Rice landed in perfect weather in Baghdad—balmy but mild, almost like San Diego—allowing her to fly from the airport into the Green Zone, diplomatic security agents in each helicopter with their high-powered rifles at the ready.

But Rumsfeld's mood seemed as dark as the weather had been on the earlier trip. He was already in Baghdad, having unexpectedly moved up his schedule by six hours at the last minute—coincidentally giving him solo headlines in the late-edition newspapers. He appeared irritated at having to be there and at sharing the stage with Rice, not even bothering to speak to reporters who accompanied him on the thirteen-hour flight from Washington. While Rice courted the news media, racing through five television interviews in seventeen minutes, Rumsfeld gave no separate interviews. At one point, he arrived early for a meeting and saw an array of television cameras inside the room. He shook his head at the reporters and turned on his heel. He also became irritated at one of Rice's aides, Josie Duckett, as she took photographs before a meeting. He thought she was a journalist until Rice assured him Duckett was part of her entourage.

Rice and Rumsfeld first cochaired a lunch with about twenty-five top diplomatic and military personnel based in Iraq. The topic of the meeting sounded like a presidential campaign: "First 100 Days: Government Formation, Security, and Nonsecurity Priorities." Then Rice and Rumsfeld and their top aides shuttled back and forth across the Green Zone, essentially repeating the schedule that Rice and Straw had followed three weeks earlier.

The new person in the picture was Maliki, who impressed Rice's aides by being blunt and direct during a meeting held at the residence of Ambassador Khalilzad. He also eagerly shook hands with Rice, in contrast to some of the other Shiite leaders, such as Abdul Aziz al-Hakim, the head of the Supreme Council for the Islamic Revolution in Iraq, the powerful Shiite religious party. For religious reasons, Hakim would never shake hands with Rice, though he did ask her to write a note to his granddaughter.

Usually, Americans found, Iraqi officials spent a lot of time giving thanks for their liberation and avoiding specifics. Maliki proved to be different. Speaking in Arabic, he told Rice and Rumsfeld that his first challenge was to address the distrust between different elements in Iraq. While terror attacks were the biggest problem, he felt that if he succeeded at reducing sectarian tensions, then that would help with the terrorism questions. Second, he said, he needed to provide people with reliable and consistent electricity; the repeated blackouts were for many Iraqis the biggest symbol of American incompetence. With the stifling summer heat approaching, he said this would be a major priority. "The people need electricity," he declared, taking out his worry beads when he saw the Afghan-born Khalilzad begin to fiddle with his own set of beads.[39]

The biggest concern for the Americans was the Shiite-dominated Interior and Defense Ministries, said to be riddled with militias. Here again, Maliki mouthed all the right words, saying he wanted to hire technocrats—competent, substantive people. It was an impressive performance, at least to U.S. officials desperate for some sign that they could finally have a success story. They saw major differences in style between Maliki and the plodding Jafari; he spoke in short, clipped sentences and gave the appearance of being decisive. He cut off Rumsfeld when the defense secretary mentioned the Americans wanted at some point to reduce troop levels. The issue wasn't ready to be discussed, Maliki said.

But Maliki had never been in an executive role, having spent much of his political career as a legislator. He had virtually no inner circle and didn't even have a secretary to answer his phone. Rice assigned Wilkinson to stay behind for a few weeks and help Maliki set up an office, much as he had done for Palestinian leader Mahmoud Abbas before the unexpected victory of Hamas.

The experience would prove to be sobering to Wilkinson. He began to wonder why the American taxpayers had spent hundreds of billions of dollars in Iraq and yet the Iraqi prime minister couldn't begin work until Wilkinson personally brought paper and pens to his office. It just seemed absurd. One night, an insurgent rocket landed on the doorstep of Wilkinson's hut and he had no place to sleep, forcing him to learn chess out of sheer boredom. He became an obsessive chess player, but he also began to realize that Iraq was a disaster that the United States could never hope to fix.

In time, Maliki would prove to be as ineffectual as Jafari at ending the violence, rooting out corruption, and stemming the power of the militias. He would be simply overwhelmed by the job.

Before dinner that night with the Iraqi leadership, Rice and Rumsfeld came to the presidential palace to brief the traveling press. The session got off to a bad start when Bloomberg's Janine Zacharia, seated directly across from the two cabinet secretaries, asked what the intense secrecy and security surrounding their visit to Iraq signified about the stability of the country three years after the U.S.-led invasion. Rice turned to Rumsfeld to provide the answer. Rumsfeld stared at Zacharia with contempt, and a full ten seconds of silence passed as he seemed to contemplate how he could respond with the appropriate level of scorn.

"I guess I don't think it says anything about it," he snapped. He went on to say that President Bush had directed Rice and him to go to Iraq to "meet with the new leadership, and it happens that they are located here," a reference to the Green Zone. Rice broke in, calming the tension. "The security situation will continue to take our attention and the attention of the Iraqis," she said, adding, "The terrorists are ultimately going to be defeated by a political process here."

The mood was certainly different than Rice's chum-fest with Straw. Rumsfeld frequently doodled with a black felt-tip pen or stared absentmindedly at the ceiling when Rice spoke about the glories of Iraqi freedom. Rice would occasionally cast a nervous glance at Rumsfeld as he prepared to respond to a question. His answers were terse; hers were expansive. Asked about the flap over Rice's "thousands" of errors comment, Rumsfeld made no effort to smooth over the issue but pointed to Rice and said, "She's right here, and you can ask her." Rice was careful to note that her comment about tactical errors had been made "not in the military sense."

Most striking, Rumsfeld acted as if he were the last person in the Bush administration who still believed the president's 2000 campaign rhetoric denouncing nation building. Rice, in that briefing and a separate one with Iraqi journalists, eagerly cast the Iraqi transition as part of the administration's quest for democracy in the Middle East. She told the Iraqi journalists that differences were "being overcome by politics and compromise, not by violence and not by repression," making Iraq "a tremendous pillar of stability through the Middle East."

Rumsfeld, by contrast, did not display any enthusiasm for such notions of freedom and democracy, giving the impression that he was tired of the whole idea. He mentioned how it was he, not the Iraqis, who brought up the question of when U.S. troops might be able to leave. Asked how the Iraqi government should eliminate the militias that have terrorized the populace, Rumsfeld appeared to suggest it was a relatively easy task. "Other countries have dealt with these issues and done them in a reasonably orderly way and over a period of time in a manner that was, in many instances, without much violence," he said.[40]

That night, over a meal of fattoush salad and sayadieh fish (cooked with rice in an onion and tahina sauce), Rice and Rumsfeld met again with Maliki and six other Iraqi leaders. It was a festive evening. Barham Salih, the planning minister, made a detailed presentation on the government's action plan, saying "success depends on our competency." Tariq al-Hashimi, a Sunni politician who would continue as vice president in the permanent government, had only two weeks before lost a brother to an insurgent attack. But even he was enthusiastic. "I think we are about to open a new chapter in Iraq," he declared.[41]

The joy quickly evaporated. The next morning, as Rice and Rumsfeld were headed into their final round of meetings, two sedans loaded with gunmen sped through the streets of Baghdad, chasing a sport-utility vehicle carrying Hashimi's sixty-year-old sister. One of the attackers' cars cut off Maysoon al-Hashimi's vehicle and the other sprayed it with bullets, killing her instantly.

The attackers left behind a note: "This is a punishment for those who collaborate."[42]

CHAPTER 9

DIPLOMATIC WALTZ IN VIENNA

June 1, 2006

It was a chilly night on one of the coldest springs in Vienna's history. As the temperature fell below 40 degrees that evening, the more than fifty reporters sitting in the garden of the British ambassador began getting cold—and antsy. The news conference had been called for 8 p.m., and now the clock approached 10 p.m.

Inside the ambassador's residence, Rice met with her counterparts from Russia, China, Britain, France, and Germany. On the table was a critical document in the long effort to convince Iran not to use its nuclear program as a ruse to develop nuclear weapons. Finally, after months of bickering and uncertainty, an ungainly coalition appeared ready to decide on a strategy to push Iran to make a choice between cooperation and confrontation.

The ministers debated how to announce the deal to the media throng gathered outside—and the world—while keeping the details secret until European Union foreign policy chief Javier Solana could meet with Iranian officials and inform them directly of the choice that now confronted Iran. Russia's foreign minister, Sergey Lavrov, insisted on going through the brief draft statement word for word, prompting lengthy discussions about what the word "consider" or "is" might mean. The text was in English, but each nuance also had to be translated for the Chinese and the French.

Britain's foreign secretary, Margaret Beckett, who had replaced Jack Straw only three weeks earlier, felt it was important that an agreement be announced in some fashion. But the British had called the news conference too early. Sean

McCormack had warned them that the foreign ministers would likely want to fiddle with the draft statement. But the British went ahead and announced that the news conference would begin at 8 P.M.—and the reporters were required to arrive even earlier for security reasons.

For the Americans, this was a critical moment. Only the day before, Rice had announced a major shift in Bush administration policy: The United States, after more than a quarter century of shunning the Islamic Republic of Iran, would now be willing to join the negotiations that had been led by the Europeans for three years, thus far fruitlessly. The dramatic move was intended to jolt the Russians and Chinese into supporting the possibility of sanctions against Iran. U.S. officials now saw news of Rice's diplomatic victory fading as the media throng became angrier.

The British brought out glasses of wine, beer, and champagne to soothe the reporters. Then McCormack learned that the foreign ministers had decided to start dinner while they continued to work on the statement. He had had enough. The British had put together an elaborate security system, with special passes, blocking all but the two or three most senior officials in each delegation from entering the inner sanctum. But, cajoling and pleading his way past the guards, McCormack finally made it upstairs and told John Williams, the spokesman for the British Foreign Ministry, that there was a revolt going on outside. Williams said he knew, but they were having trouble getting Lavrov to leave the dinner.

Finally, Lavrov relented.

The ministers suddenly emerged into the garden, forcing reporters to drop their wine and beer glasses and rush back to their seats. Under the glare of more than a dozen television camera lights, the ministers assembled on either side of Beckett, who, as host, was designated to read the statement. "I feel like I am in the Bolshoi," Lavrov quipped to the other ministers.

Beckett spoke for barely more than a minute, as the statement the ministers had haggled over was only a few sentences long. "I am pleased to say that we have agreed on a set of far-reaching proposals as the basis for discussions with Iran," Beckett announced, saying that negotiations would resume and action in the Security Council would end if Iran suspended its enrichment of uranium. If Iran refused, she added vaguely, "further steps will have to be taken at the Security Council." She concluded: "So there are two paths ahead. We urge Iran to take the positive path and to consider seriously our substantive proposals, which would bring significant benefits to Iran."

The foreign ministers turned away and walked upstairs to finish their dinner, refusing to answer any questions from the shouting reporters. Lavrov, however, paused and asked the crowd with a smirk: "Was it worth it for you?"

A "Grand Bargain" Not Taken

In many ways, the confrontation with Iran over its nuclear program is Rice's biggest diplomatic test—and where the stakes are highest. If Iran acquires a nuclear weapon, the Middle East will be transformed. Tehran would suddenly be a fearsome regional power, likely unleashing a nuclear arms race in the region and making Israel more vulnerable.

As secretary of state, Rice has tried to forge a coalition that would thwart Iran's ability to build a nuclear weapon, but the chances of success are slim. History has shown that if a country is determined to build a nuclear weapon, it will succeed, no matter what the cost in terms of sanctions and international isolation. A military strike might only delay Tehran's ability to acquire a weapon, and without enough diplomatic groundwork, the United States would find itself isolated if it decides to act militarily. It is unclear how long such an attack would postpone Iran's acquisition of a nuclear bomb and also how much more it would make Iran defiant, determined, and anti-American. Rice's task is to keep the options open as long as possible for President Bush and his successors.

Like many other foreign policy challenges, this was a problem that Rice had only made worse through her tenure as national security advisor. The administration, paralyzed by disagreements on Iran and focused on Iraq, essentially had no policy on Iran during Bush's first term. Some officials wanted to test Iran to see if a nascent partnership that had formed on Afghanistan could be fostered; others were convinced the clerics' hold on power was fragile and the government would collapse with just enough pressure.

Instead, Iran is now in its strongest position in decades because of the inadvertent help of the Bush administration. Two of its enemies—the Taliban in Afghanistan and Saddam Hussein in Iraq—have been vanquished, and Iran now has allies and influence in both countries. The U.S. military presence in Iraq has given Tehran new leverage because it can easily respond to U.S. diplomatic pressure by having its Iraqi allies increase the violence there, including launching attacks on American troops and supply lines. Hezbollah in Lebanon, which receives at least $100 million in annual aid from Iran, became part of the Lebanese government. The rise of Shiite political power in Iraq and Lebanon has alarmed Iran's Sunni rivals, Saudi Arabia and Egypt, two of the United States' closest allies in the region. Iran has also been aided by the sharp rise in oil prices.

After the September 11 attacks, Colin Powell's State Department pushed the idea of accepting help from regimes like Iran in the fight against al-Qaeda, and then trying to leverage that cooperation into more positive relationships with the United States. Iranian officials proved to be cooperative in the war against the Taliban and key to building the new Afghan government at a conference in Bonn in late 2001. Iranian diplomats indicated to U.S. officials that there was real interest in Tehran in building on the experience to try to improve relationships between the two longtime antagonists.[1] But a few weeks later, Bush lumped Iran in the "axis of evil" with North Korea and Iraq in his 2002 State of the Union address, and Iranian cooperation largely ended.

But Bush's statement didn't actually amount to a policy, and there was little agreement over what to do next. When she was national security advisor, Rice repeatedly canceled high-level meetings that had been scheduled to formalize a presidential directive on Iran that would have set the administration's policy.

For much of Bush's first term, the most definitive statement of U.S. policy on Iran was a three-paragraph document written by a midlevel National Security Council aide and unexpectedly issued in Bush's name on July 12, 2002. In the statement, Bush said that "uncompromising, destructive policies have persisted" in Iran despite recent presidential and parliamentary elections that had brought some reform advocates to power. He accused Iranian leaders and their families of continuing "to obstruct reform while reaping unfair benefits" and demanded that the government listen to the Iranian people, who, he said, have "no better friend than the United States."[2]

Many U.S. officials suggested this was a sign that the United States had written off the government of President Mohammad Khatami, whom the Clinton administration had viewed as a reformer. The discussion within the administration turned from possible engagement to potential destabilization, though Iran largely became a back-burner issue as the administration focused on the looming war with Iraq.

In August 2002, an Iranian exile group held a news conference in Washington. They claimed that the Iranian government was secretly building two large nuclear facilities in Natanz and Arak that were near completion. The announcement attracted little attention at the time, in part because the National Council of Resistance of Iran was linked to the Mujahedin-e Khalq, an anti-regime militant group supported for years by Saddam Hussein and considered a terrorist organization by the State Department. But the MEK's announcement—which some State Department officials believe actually came from Israeli intelligence[3]—was one of the factors that led Iran to admit that it had spent eighteen years secretly developing the capability to produce fissile material for nuclear weapons. (Three months before the MEK news conference, U.S. officials also had secretly provided the geographical coordinates of the facilities to the International Atomic Energy Agency.)[4]

On the eve of the Iraq invasion, IAEA inspectors visited the Natanz site, about two hundred miles south of Tehran, and were stunned to see 160 centrifuges in neat rows, ready to begin spinning hot uranium gas into nuclear fuel.[5] While the United States was about to invade Iraq because of nonexistent weapons of mass destruction—and had been warning of Iran's nuclear intentions for years—it turned out that Iran was on the brink of a nuclear breakthrough.

On May 4, shortly after U.S. forces routed Iraqi troops and Baghdad fell, an unusual two-page document spewed out of a fax machine at the Near East bureau of the State Department. The fax was a proposal from Iran for a broad dialogue with the United States; it suggested that everything was on the table, including full cooperation on nuclear programs, acceptance of Israel, and the termination of Iranian support for Palestinian militant groups. The document listed a series of Iranian aims for the talks, such as ending sanctions, full access to peaceful nuclear technology, and a recognition of its "legitimate security interests." Iran agreed to put a series of U.S. aims on the agenda, including full cooperation on nuclear safeguards, "decisive action" against terrorists, coordination in Iraq, ending "material support" for Palestinian militias, and accepting a Saudi initiative to recognize Israel and create a Palestinian state. The document also laid out an agenda for negotiations, with possible steps to be achieved at a first meeting and the development of negotiating road maps on disarmament, terrorism, and economic cooperation.[6]

The unexpected fax was primarily the work of Sadegh Kharazi, Iran's ambassador to France and the nephew of Iran's foreign minister, Kamal Kharazi; it had been passed on by the Swiss ambassador to Tehran, Tim Guldimann. The Swiss government is a diplomatic channel for communications between Tehran and Washington because the two countries broke off relations after the 1979 seizure of U.S. embassy personnel. In a cover letter, Guldimann certified that the document was a genuine proposal supported by key power centers in Iran, including Iran's supreme religious leader, Ayatollah Ali Khamenei.

State Department officials wanted to test Iran's unorthodox approach. Hillary Mann, a senior State Department policy-planning official who until March had handled the Iran portfolio at the National Security Council, drafted a six-page memo to Powell calling for "grand bargain" with Iran. In the memo, Mann argued that the Iranians were scared by the U.S. victory and the United States could strike a deal on a number of issues, including terrorism and nuclear weapons. She attached to the memo a copy of the Swiss fax. She also included a copy of a report that her husband, former NSC official Flynt Leverett, had written to Rice and CIA director George Tenet about an unusual encounter he had had with General Mohsen Reza'i in Europe. Reza'i, a key player in Iranian politics who had once headed the Revolutionary Guards, had also emphasized Iran was interested in a deal that would allow it to move in a different direction.

A few weeks later, Powell told Mann that she had written a "great memo," but it was something he could never sell to the White House.

Rice has no recollection of seeing the Swiss fax or reading Leverett's report.[7] (With Mann's departure from the White House, there was a bureaucratic vacuum at the NSC in terms of Iran policy.) In any case, the Bush administration was not interested in any sort of "grand bargain" at the time. Officials ignored the Iranian initiative—except to formally complain that Guldimann had exceeded his authority in sending along the fax.[8]

In retrospect, it might have been a missed opportunity. The United States appeared to be at the height of its power; Iran, shaken by how quickly the United States had vanquished a foe that Iran had failed to defeat in a grinding eight-year war, still had not mastered the nuclear fuel cycle. Bush administration officials dismiss the fax as largely the invention of the Swiss ambassador. But some analysts believe the administration's failure to respond positively to the fax emboldened more conservative elements in Iran's political system to seek a confrontation with the United States.

Within the administration, some Pentagon officials even began to press for an aggressive campaign against Iran, using the remnants of MEK forces located in Iraq as a vanguard working for the United States. The Iranians suggested they would be willing to trade the MEK for al-Qaeda figures they had seized in Iran, promising to allow the Red Cross into Iranian jails for the first time to keep tabs on the treatment of MEK prisoners. There was briefly a debate over whether it was moral to give up the MEK, but the Pentagon moved quickly to protect their status in Iraq, making a deal impossible.

"We'll Have Nothing Left"

With the Bush administration still contemplating how to engineer the fall of the Iranian mullahs, three European countries—Britain, France, and Germany—in 2003 took the lead in trying to restrain Iran's nuclear ambitions. Bush administration officials were skeptical, essentially telling the Europeans that they didn't think it would work and were not sure if they even wanted it to work. The three European countries, who became known as the EU-3, wanted to offer Iran a choice of suspending its program or facing sanctions at the UN Security Council. The Americans spoke of isolating Iran with sanctions and the threat of regime change, but that bravado became hollow as the United States became mired in Iraq. Repeated American efforts to get the thirty-five-member board of the IAEA to report Iran to the Security Council failed. By pushing too hard too soon, the Americans seemed to confirm that they were acting out of animus toward Iran rather than nonproliferation concerns.

The European-Iranian negotiations were fitful, though Iran at several points pledged to suspend its activities while the negotiations continued. For both the Europeans and the Iranians, the negotiations were mainly a route for eventually getting the Americans to the table. At one point, when the Europeans were pressing Iran to give up uranium conversion, one senior Iranian official candidly told John Sawers, a senior British diplomat: "Look, John, that's what we are saving up for negotiating with the Americans. We can't spend all our possible concessions in negotiating with you. We'll have nothing left."

Meanwhile, the IAEA investigated Iran's program, conducting hundreds of inspections and uncovering numerous examples of how Iran has misled the agency about its activities, including a secret relationship between Iran and Pakistani nuclear scientists. They could neither confirm that the Iranian program was peaceful nor find smoking-gun evidence of a nuclear weapons program. (The IAEA is supposed to detect the diversion of nuclear material regardless of the purpose, so finding a "smoking gun" is technically not essential, but the Iranians have milked it diplomatically.)

Shortly after the 2004 presidential election, the EU-3 and Iran resumed negotiations. Iran agreed to suspend uranium enrichment in exchange for restarting talks on an Iran-EU trade agreement, support for Iran's application to join the World Trade Organization, and other benefits. As was discussed earlier, one of the first decisions Rice made after becoming secretary was to convince President Bush for the first time to explicitly back the EU-3 talks by dropping objections to Iran's WTO application and considering sales of civilian aircraft parts to Tehran. Rice had few illusions that the EU-3 talks would actually succeed, but she correctly perceived that the United States had to demonstrate it was willing to exhaust every diplomatic opportunity if it ever hoped to win support for tough sanctions at the UN Security Council. The Iraq experience and U.S. tactics on Iran at the IAEA had made U.S. motives suspect to the rest of the world—that a path to sanctions was merely a ruse for a path to war.

There were other, more subtle shifts. During the first term, the Bush administration had taken a tough line on Iran's nuclear program, even protesting a Russian project to build an $800 million nuclear power plant in Bushehr. The administration argued that Iran, with its vast oil and gas reserves, had no need for a nuclear program. But as a signatory to the nuclear Non-Proliferation Treaty, Iran had a right to a peaceful program that met the nonproliferation obligations of the treaty. (Developing the program in secret, however, was a violation of the NPT.) At the request of the Europeans, Rice dropped that language and began to acknowledge Iran's right to nuclear power. This significant shift in U.S. policy was never formally announced or acknowledged.

Though U.S. intelligence judged Iran was about ten years from actually acquiring a nuclear weapon, experts believed Iran would soon cross the threshold of mastering the fuel cycle, giving it the technical capacity to produce weapons. In the June 2005 elections, a new hard-line government led by Mahmoud Ahmadinejad came to power. Even the reformist politicians in Iran supported the development of Iran's nuclear program, but Iran's negotiating stance became significantly tougher. Iran rejected the EU's final offer for a deal, and subsequently broke the IAEA seals on its uranium-conversion equipment and began enrichment. A senior Iranian official bragged that the Iranians had hoodwinked the Europeans, using the negotiations as a ruse to master key stages in the nuclear fuel process, and so Iran was prepared to act when the talks finally broke down. He noted that when the secret sites were discovered in 2002, the United States was at "the height of its arrogance," so Iran had seized any tactic that would delay consideration of the matter at the Security Council at the time.[9]

As part of the agreement to support the EU-3 negotiations with Iran, Rice believed she had extracted a promise that if the negotiations failed, Britain, France, and Germany would support referral to the Security Council—though European officials say this was always their strategy so it was easy to make this commitment. Outrageous statements by Ahmadinejad, such as a pledge to wipe Israel off the map, made it easier to keep that coalition together. Germany had been considered the weak sister of the group, but after Ahmadinejad's comments about Israel, the historical burden of the Holocaust made it difficult for Germany to appear too sympathetic to Iran. But Rice and European officials understood that real success at the Security Council depended on Russia and, to a lesser extent, China—which could both cast vetoes against any resolution concerning Iran.

In August 2005, the European talks with Iran collapsed. Then, in mid-September, Rice and Ahmadinejad made speeches before the UN General Assembly within an hour of each other. It was the Iranian president's first visit to the United States, and he made the most of the moment, gleefully tossing out anti-American rhetoric with abandon in the grand UN General Assembly Hall. He defiantly declared Iran would never give up its nuclear enrichment program and would not "cave in to the excessive demands of certain powers."

Rice was not in the room when Ahmadinejad spoke, but Nick Burns, who as undersecretary for political affairs ran the Iran policy on a day-to-day basis, got a report from the U.S. mission. He broke free from a diplomatic session on

Haiti to call Rice and warn her before she encountered reporters after meeting with the Libyan foreign minister. Forewarned, Rice shrugged off the inevitable question. She said she had not read the speech, adding that "everyone understands what Iran needs to do: Iran needs to return to negotiations."[10]

But Ahmadinejad's language made a deep impression on Rice, and she became even more alarmed when he denied the existence of the Holocaust. Iran was flexing its muscles and she knew the United States needed to contain it. She came back from New York with a directive for her staff: This is really serious; we need to fire on all pistons on this. Diplomacy would be emphasized, but Rice hedged her bets in case the process failed. She unveiled a $75 million program to promote democratic reforms in Iran, established a "listening post" in Dubai where diplomats were specifically assigned to watch Tehran, and worked with the Treasury Department to target banks and Iranian entities suspected of funneling aid to militant groups and bankrolling the nuclear program.

"What Does That Mean?"

The first step was to draw the Russians into the diplomacy.

Bush's pledge to promote democracy in the second term had made relations with Russia increasingly difficult. Vladimir Putin's dismantling of democratic institutions and his crackdown on the media was suddenly harder to ignore. Putin's interference in Ukraine's elections—and then his decision to briefly cut off natural gas to Ukraine in a pricing dispute after his favored candidate lost—forced a much broader reassessment of relations with Russia. Moscow is the world's largest gas supplier and dominates many European markets. Rice unleashed a diplomatic effort to promote a planned pipeline from Azerbaijan that would weaken Russia's tight grip on European energy supply. Ironically, the effort to box in the Russians forced the administration to set aside its concerns about poor human rights records and limited democracy in such energy-rich countries as Azerbaijan and Kazakhstan.

While Rice had trained as a Soviet specialist and still practices Russian once a week with a State Department interpreter, Russian diplomats are privately contemptuous of her knowledge of contemporary Russia, believing she is stuck in a time warp and doesn't understand the country.[11] Russian foreign minister Sergey Lavrov, who honed his negotiating skills during a ten-year stint as Russia's UN ambassador, is a proud and frequently effective diplomat—a showman who doesn't hesitate to use a diplomatic stiletto. One diplomat said that Lavrov has basically two demeanors during negotiations: horrible or merely unpleasant.

Lavrov, in fact, put Rice on the spot during their very first meeting after she became secretary of state. On her first trip, she stopped in Ankara, Turkey, and Lavrov flew in to meet her. He had a long list of complaints, beginning with extremely minor consular issues involving people who couldn't get U.S. visas. Rice was taken aback by the smallness of his performance; he was acting almost like a low-level diplomat rather than a foreign minister.

But Rice came to appreciate Lavrov's straightforward and serious approach. She concluded that if he says he will do something, he will—and if he says he will not do it, he won't. She thought her style was much like his—blunt and to the point—and she was amused to notice that other foreign ministers tried hard to smooth things over when Rice and Lavrov debated policies.[12]

Several diplomats who have been in meetings with Lavrov and Rice say Rice is kidding herself if she thinks they have a good relationship. Some sensed a sexist, possibly even a racist, tinge in Lavrov's treatment of Rice. Diplomats said Lavrov has perfected the art of irritating Rice—so much so that she often responds in a very sharp, acerbic, and even emotional way. Rice's reaction is so shrill that she begins to lose her natural allies in the room, in contrast to the calmer and more menacing Lavrov. He frequently exploits that dynamic to his advantage.

Asked about the Lavrov-Rice tensions, French foreign minister Philippe Douste-Blazy made an exasperated expression and then turned to his interpreter, remarking, "It is obvious." His interpreter nodded that she had noticed the fireworks herself.[13]

During a meeting in Moscow in 2006, Russian technicians by accident piped the private lunchtime conversation to reporters, allowing them to hear Rice and Lavrov bicker over Iraq. With increasing irritation, Rice sometimes cut Lavrov off in midsentence with tart comments, at one point demanding, "What does that mean?" After a long pause, Lavrov said, "I think you understand." Rice shot back, "No, I don't."[14]

At one news conference, Lavrov couldn't resist taking a shot at Rice when she offered a backhanded compliment of how far Russia had come from the Soviet days, despite slippage on democracy. "I was first in the Soviet Union in 1979," Rice said. "I assure you that there have been massive changes in this country since that time and since the Russian Federation was born in 1991."

Lavrov jabbed: "By not coincidence, I also first visited the U.S.A. in 1979, and I have been taking note of changes, many of which we strive to discuss with our American counterparts."

Rice looked startled by his comment and, turning to Lavrov, demanded, "Sergey, when did you go and where did you go in the United States in 1979 that you saw so much change?" Lavrov said he visited Manhattan, and Rice sneered, "Oh, in New York. Now I understand."[15]

The undercurrent of tension between the United States and Russia, reflective of the relationship between Rice and Lavrov, would dominate the diplomacy on Iran. Step by step, Rice sought to draw the Russians deeper into supporting sanctions—and they resisted, fearing a repeat of Iraq. They did not want to give carte blanche to the Americans. The Russians wanted to drag the Americans into talks with Iran—and ultimately to get them to accept Iran's right to nuclear power. Russia has huge economic and political investments in Iran and will not easily give them up.

"No One Can Predict the Consequences"

In September 2005, after the collapse of the Iran-EU agreement, the IAEA board found that Iran had not complied with its treaty negotiations on nuclear power. But Russia and China had abstained—a huge problem if the Europeans and Americans ever hoped to bring the issue to the Security Council. The IAEA board normally decides by consensus, as it had in virtually all previous decisions to find countries in noncompliance with their NPT "safeguards" agreements.[16] The departure from consensus—and in particular the lack of unity among the five permanent members of the Security Council—was a bad omen.

After touring Central Asia in October 2005, Rice unexpectedly added a stop in Moscow for a one-hour discussion with Putin and Lavrov on Iran, accompanied only by William Burns, the U.S. ambassador to Russia. They met in Putin's dacha, about a forty-five-minute drive from central Moscow, and sipped tea as they gathered around Putin's dining table. Rice and Burns are both fluent in Russian, while Putin and Lavrov speak English very well, so both sides spoke in their native tongues, only using an interpreter every so often to clarify a technical point. Rice and Lavrov also followed up the discussion with a ten-minute private meeting.

Reporters traveling with Rice thought the mission was a failure because Lavrov emerged saying he still saw no need to transfer the issue to the Security Council. He said it was preferable for the IAEA to continue to keep the Iran dossier. He argued that Iran, under international law, had the right to enrich uranium, while Rice reiterated that Iran had no need for a civil nuclear power program. But behind the public display of division, the meeting marked an important turning point. It was a sober, practical discussion, and Rice began to see the glimmerings of a diplomatic process on Iran that would include Russia, and ultimately China.

Putin said that he understood the strategic problem posed by Iran's nuclear program and the possibility that Tehran could acquire a nuclear weapon. In an earlier private conversation with Bush, Putin had expressed such sentiments but never in such a formal setting had he been so straightforward with the Americans about the Iranian threat. He even noted that Russia had amended its agreement on Bushehr so that Iran would have to return the spent fuel because he didn't trust what the Iranians would do with it.

Putin added that diplomatic cooperation was important and he wanted to work with the United States and the Europeans. He noted the important role played by the IAEA. But he said he was very skeptical that sanctions, as a general proposition, would work, and he emphasized that use of force was a very bad idea.

"No one can predict the consequences, especially given the volatility of the region," Putin said.

"The United States is trying to achieve a diplomatic solution," Rice responded, adding that the administration did not intend to use military force at this stage. She wanted Russia to be part of the diplomatic effort. Rice also indicated that she understood Iran's need for nuclear energy—something she had never said publicly—and was willing to accommodate that. (As noted earlier, this language eventually would become part of her public statements.)

But, she emphasized repeatedly, "Iran can't be permitted to obtain nuclear weapons."

Putin and Lavrov told Rice that they had a new idea: The Russians wanted to offer the Iranians a deal. They could enrich uranium, but the sensitive part of the process would be done on Russian soil. Essentially, Iran would have only an administrative role, but not have access to the technical knowledge. Rice was intrigued and said she would report back to President Bush on this concept, which would mean a reversal in the administration's long campaign to prevent Iran from ever having access to nuclear power. U.S. officials hoped that if Iran rejected the idea, Russia would finally support bringing the matter to the UN Security Council. Bush publicly endorsed the idea a month later, after a meeting with Putin.[17]

But the Iranians never really accepted the Russian proposal, setting the stage for a British innovation that would change the dynamics of the negotiations.

"We Are the Perm Five"

Knowing that Rice liked to conduct diplomacy in informal, senior-level settings, in January 2006 British foreign secretary Jack Straw invited the foreign ministers of the other four permanent members of the Security Council—the United

States, Russia, China, and France—and Germany to dinner when they came to London for a conference on Afghanistan. (Javier Solana, the EU foreign policy chief, was also included.) They met on the second floor of One Carlton Gardens, the official residence of the British foreign secretary, set in a cul-de-sac in the historic St. James district of the city. Each minister was permitted to bring one aide; Rice was accompanied by Nick Burns. In the middle of the winter, the four-story white building, built in the 1830s and briefly home to the exiled Louis Napoleon (later Napoleon III of France), felt overheated and stuffy.[18]

Burns and his counterparts from the other countries had held several meetings on Iran, but Straw recognized the issue had become too difficult and needed the intervention of the foreign ministers. Lavrov and Rice had had a phone conversation on January 10, in which for the first time Lavrov said Russia would not block a Security Council resolution but "we need a Security Council strategy."[19] The dinner started late, at about 9 P.M., and for the first two hours the ministers ate privately in one room while the political directors supped in the room next door.

Working with Burns and his European counterparts, Straw's senior policy aide, John Sawers, had put together a statement before the dinner that would say the group had decided to report Iran to the Security Council. As dessert was being cleared, Straw brought out the document and announced that he thought it summed up the discussion they had just had. Lavrov protested rather vehemently, and everyone took a ten-minute break to study the document. Then the political directors joined the ministers in the smoky dining room, crowding around a small table as they drank coffee and tea and munched on chocolate. Both Rice and Burns were jet-lagged and exhausted.

The next two hours were dominated by an intense debate between Rice and Lavrov, focused on how long to give the Iranians to comply with demands it suspend its program and how best to accomplish that goal. Rice pressed to finally bring Iran to the Security Council, but Lavrov was fiercely opposed. The United States would have the presidency of the Security Council in February, giving John Bolton, the strong-willed U.S. ambassador to the United Nations and long an advocate of action against Iran, a golden opportunity to set the agenda.

Rice made her case by speaking in Great Power terms, appealing to the national vanity of the countries at the table. "We are the Perm Five," she said, meaning the five permanent members of the Security Council, with veto power. "We are responsible for global stability." She argued that the IAEA is not the place where such decisions are made; it is the Security Council that passes judgments and imposes sanctions. Thus, if sanctions were ever to be considered a possibility, they had to take Iran to the Security Council.

"This discussion is premature because the IAEA has not finished its work," Lavrov shot back.

Since Russia had abstained from the IAEA board resolution in September, Lavrov distanced himself from that decision. He felt strongly that nothing should happen until after the director general of the IAEA, Mohamed El-Baradei, delivered a report on Iran's compliance in March. The report was expected to confirm that Iran had not met its safeguards obligations and was preparing to begin pilot-scale enrichment. At that point, he insisted, it would be the moment to decide whether to report Iran to the Security Council.

As the clock passed midnight, Burns watched the two skilled diplomats lob shots at each other and feared that the evening would end in failure. Neither appeared willing to give ground. The French, the Germans, and the Chinese were basically spectators, but Straw played an important moderating role in the debate, backing Rice up but softening some of her sharp edges as Lavrov increasingly needled her. Straw focused on finding a common position so that the Europeans could move the Russians and Chinese off the sidelines and into the game.

Rice finally conceded Lavrov's point on waiting for the IAEA report, but she didn't want Iran to drag out the discussions. The ministers agreed they would announce that the IAEA board should report to the Security Council what was expected of Iran, along with associated reports—in effect, transferring the dossier from the IAEA to the Security Council. But the Security Council would be instructed not take any action until March, after it received ElBaradei's report and only if Iran failed to respond to the IAEA board's request. In other words, Iran would have thirty days to demonstrate it was willing to negotiate.

It was a bit of a gamble on Rice's part, but she essentially incorporated Lavrov's concerns within a proposal she could live with. Rice and Straw got the headline they were looking for: Iran would be referred to the Security Council. But it also meant the ministers had deliberately leapfrogged over the month when the United States would be president of the Council. The Russians didn't want the hard-nosed Bolton in charge of the process that month, and Rice was more than willing to sacrifice his moment in the sun.

The six ministers then spent another hour, working until past 1:30 A.M., arguing over the statement Straw would issue to reporters announcing the tenuous agreement.[20]

Then, everything started unraveling.

"They're Pinging Us"

The deal struck in London set in motion a long and complicated series of diplomatic moves by all sides—crisis negotiations, efforts to revive the Russian proposal, apparent breakthroughs, and then sudden failures—that only highlighted the fact that the Russians and the Americans were still at odds over Iran. Once the Security Council received the IAEA referral, it took three difficult weeks to produce a bland Security Council presidential statement that said almost nothing—even though presidential statements have no real force.

When the six ministers met again, this time in Berlin on March 30, the divisions were apparent. Rice and Burns had thought getting a presidential statement would be easy, and now they sat through a dispiriting conversation with the other ministers that showed how naive they had been. Rice privately raised the idea of sanctions but could not even get a commitment from Lavrov to keep the process going at the Security Council. He wanted the IAEA to once again take charge of the issue. Three weeks earlier, in a private dinner with Rice and Hadley in Washington on March 6, he had warned that Iran could throw out IAEA inspectors and leave the nonproliferation treaty, much like North Korea had, thus removing the entire Iranian program from scrutiny. He didn't want to take that chance.

The Berlin meeting was badly organized by the Germans, with lots of formality (microphones, interpretation booths, a massive table in a large auditorium) rather than the informal discussion around a small table in Carlton Gardens. Rice could feel the steam coming out of the effort—as did reporters, despite energetic spin by Burns after the meeting. At a news conference, Lavrov and the Chinese representative emphatically rejected the idea of sanctions. "There has already been enough turmoil in the Middle East," China's deputy foreign minister, Dai Bingguo, bluntly stated. "We do not want to see new turmoil being introduced to the region."[21]

Rice returned to Washington knowing that the coalition was about to collapse. The Iranians knew it, too. On April 11, Ahmadinejad proclaimed in a nationwide live broadcast that Iran had succeeded at enriching uranium to new levels. "I'm announcing officially that Iran has now joined the countries that have nuclear technology," Ahmadinejad said, standing before a backdrop featuring doves around an Iranian flag. "This is a very historic moment, and it's because of the Iranian people and their belief. And this is the start of the progress of this country." He added that "the nuclear technology is only for the purpose of peace and nothing else."

Despite the sense of confrontation, the Americans had been getting lots of signals that the Iranians wanted to talk. Rice was curious about this, and she wanted to understand what the Iranians were thinking. There had been a stream of back-channel messages from Tehran asking for a dialogue. "They're pinging us," she told aides. When she raised this with Zoellick, he had one piece of advice: Do it with the Europeans, not alone.[22]

Rice decided to seek Bush's approval for a plan that would finally bring the United States to the negotiating table. Rice will generally tip off Bush when she is considering a policy shift. "I'm thinking about this, but I'm not prepared to make a recommendation yet," she said. Bush gave her an encouraging reply.

Rice had known that this moment would eventually come—it was the biggest diplomatic card the United States could play. Some of the administration's closest allies, like German chancellor Angela Merkel, had long requested it—and there was a growing chorus of opinion articles by foreign policy heavyweights also urging this step. The question in Rice's mind was: When do you play this card for maximum leverage?

There had already been hints that the Americans were preparing a change of course. A month earlier, Sawers had sent Burns and his European counterparts a confidential memo that raised the possibility of more concessions, including the United States joining the talks, as a way of luring Russian and Chinese support for a Security Council resolution on Iran. The memo leaked almost immediately. Burns spoke to Sawers every day, calling him as he drove to work in the morning, and the memo accurately reflected ideas that had been forming in his own mind. But he was horrified it leaked, and he darkly suspected it came from within the Bush administration. He publicly and loudly dismissed the idea, saying the United States would not consider joining the talks.[23]

The Sawers memo demonstrates how much of the policy toward Iran at this point was really dictated out of London and Paris, with the Americans along for the ride. The Europeans tried to coordinate their policies, along with the Americans, and hoped to spring traps for the Russians and Chinese. The Russians milked the disclosure of the memo for all it was worth. Sergey Kislyak, a Russian deputy foreign minister, called Sawers once a day for two weeks demanding an attachment to the memo that had not leaked before Sawers finally relented and gave it to him.

Rice knew that the president did not want any dialogue with Iran to turn into one-on-one negotiations with the United States. Bush feared such talks would allow Iran to balk at U.S. terms—and then the United States would get blamed for failure. But Rice was in a powerful position in the administration. Unlike the first term, Cheney and Rumsfeld had much less power and influence. They knew that Rice had the trust of the president. For all the boldness of Rice's proposal, Cheney was not much of an obstacle and largely embraced it. His main caution was that the shift should not lead the administration down a "slippery slope," in which U.S. officials end up retreating from their core red line: an end to Iranian enrichment and reprocessing—the two paths toward fissile material.

Bush told Rice he was interested in seeing a time line for the diplomacy on Iran. On Easter Sunday, April 16, Rice drafted a two-page plan for a new approach. It combined the threat of sanctions from the Security Council, the possibility of negotiations that provided real incentives for Iran to cooperate, and then unilateral steps the United States and other nations could take if the Security Council effort collapsed. Sunday afternoons are generally Rice's only time for relaxation—playing golf or tennis or watching a football game in the fall. But this day, she gave up her few hours of spare time and worked alone in her Watergate apartment. It was quiet; Rice can't concentrate when music is playing.

Rice wrote the plan out in longhand and then typed it up on her computer. She also marked the tracks and key dates in different colors—green, pink, yellow, and orange—on an Outlook calendar she had had one of her aides print off the computer. In the memo, Rice made the case that the United States had one last card to play—and they couldn't play it too soon or too late. She also warned the coalition was falling apart.

A critical date was the G-8 meeting in July; for the first time Russia was the host of the annual summit of the world's leading industrial powers. Rice believed Putin would be more willing to bend if he could ensure a successful summit. There was another crucial date: At the end of the year, the Iranians had announced, they hoped to have built a three-thousand-centrifuge cascade for enriching uranium. Time was running short.

"What Is the Strategy?"

Rice gave the proposal to Hadley and then discussed it privately with Bush over breakfast on May 5. Bush thought her plan had merit, but he warned he hadn't made up his mind. Neither Hadley nor Bush could understand her color-coded calendar no matter how much she tried to explain it.

During a May 8 lunch that also included Cheney, Hadley, and White House chief of staff Josh Bolten, Rice noted that she was going to New York later that day for yet another meeting of the foreign ministers. "I want to start to talk about this with the other foreign ministers," she told Bush.

"I haven't made up my mind," he said.

"I'm not trying to force a decision but part of your decision making will be influenced by the response of the others," Rice said. Bush acknowledged she had a point and gave his permission.

Suddenly, Ahmadinejad sent an eighteen-page letter to Bush, which the Iranian president even posted on his Web site. The rambling letter attacked the United States, but it also appeared to be a plea for dialogue. When Rice arrived at Andrews Air Force Base for her flight to New York, Burns handed her the Ahmadinejad letter, which he had just received from the Swiss embassy. She took the letter and then said, "I've got something for you." She handed him the proposal for talks and the color-coded calendar. Burns looked at the document in shock.

"Who did this for you?" Burns asked. This is the kind of staff work on Iran he would ordinarily do, and it looked like he had just been cut out of the bureaucratic loop.

"I did it," Rice said.

"You did it?" Burns said, puzzled. Then she explained her color code and how to read her complex, somewhat confusing calendar.

Seeing the proposal on paper took Burns's breath away.

The idea had been informally discussed, of course. The allies, especially the British, brought it up constantly. Someday, Straw or Sawers would say, you need to join us at the table. Everyone knew that any deal the Iranians made with the Europeans would be meaningless unless the United States was part of that agreement. When pressed, Burns had always given the same answer: "Yes, but at the right time and under the right conditions. We haven't talked to them in twenty-seven years. We can't just show up and give them a gift. There has to be something that we get."

Now, here it was—on paper. Within the administration, there were so many taboos about Iran; the United States doesn't talk to the Iranians, doesn't meet with them, and doesn't do them any favors. If anyone at Burns's level or below had suggested the idea, it would have been strangled in its infancy, probably through a leak like the disclosure of the Sawers memo. But now Rice was going to break that dynamic, overturning a quarter century of silence.

As Rice flew to New York, she read Ahmadinejad's letter, dismissing it as not serious. She arrived at the meeting at the Waldorf-Astoria carrying a secret: U.S. policy was on a verge of a major turn. But when she got there, despite Bush's permission, she decided not to reveal it. The mood of the group had turned dark and uncertain, in part because of the Ahmadinejad letter.

The session lasted well into the night. The ministers had planned to have cocktails for forty-five minutes, but that stretched to two hours; their meal of sea bass shriveled while Lavrov and Rice had an increasingly difficult conversation.

Lavrov had arrived in a foul mood, angry over a speech Cheney had given the week before that blasted Russia's crumbling democracy and its growing monopoly of European energy supply lines. To rub salt in the wound, Cheney had given the speech in Lithuania, once part of the Soviet Union. Lavrov was also smarting over comments by Burns that Russia should stop a $700 million sale of an air-defense system to Iran and possibly end cooperation on the Bushehr nuclear plant.

The ministers had spent enough time together that they no longer relied on talking points and just plunged into debate. The Iranian letter had had an impact, not just on the Russians but on others as well. Several ministers wondered whether the Iranian outreach should be tested.

"What is the strategy?" Lavrov asked Rice. "You ask for a resolution, but what happens after the second, the third, or the fourth resolution? What is the plan?"

Rice replied, "We want to be on a diplomatic track. But in order for that track to work, it has to have some teeth."

Lavrov shot back: "It can't be all sticks, there have to be some carrots."

Backed by the Chinese representative, Lavrov said Russia was not ready to do more at the United Nations. "Iran has to be given a chance," he said. "You can't just give them negative signals. You have to give them positive signals."

Rice acknowledged that Lavrov had a point. She asked, "If the Iranians want to move, do they know what they would get if they agreed to negotiations?" The other ministers agreed that it wasn't very clear—an earlier European proposal known as the Paris Agreement was rather out-of-date.

Before the ministers met, the political directors had felt they were on track to reach an agreement on a new Security Council resolution that would have made Iran's suspension of enrichment activities mandatory under international law—though everyone expected Lavrov would be a tough bargainer. But during the discussion over drinks, Rice unexpectedly gave up on seeking an immediate resolution, stunning the political directors when the ministers finally emerged for the meal. Even Burns, whose close working relationship with Rice won admiration from other participants, told at least two officials that he was surprised by Rice's backtracking in the face of Lavrov's offensive.

Rice's change in tactics would delay the eventual resolution for two months. But it also had the effect of shaping the diplomacy to best showcase the announcement she would soon make about American participation in the talks.

After the ministers and the political directors sat down for their meal of overcooked fish, Lavrov suddenly launched an aggressive attack on Cheney and Burns. He pointed four times at Burns, seated next to Rice, and denounced him. "We are totally opposed to what Cheney and Burns are saying," he said "They are creating a problem and they will divide us."

Lavrov probably focused more on Burns simply because he was there—and Cheney was not—but Rice defended Burns and asked him to reiterate why Russia should end its air-defense sale. She noted that everything Burns had said had been personally authorized by her.

Finally, Beckett, the new British foreign secretary, spoke up. It was only her first day on the job, but in her schoolmarm's voice she said Lavrov's behavior was disgraceful.

"I've never heard such a personalized attack on an official who is simply doing the job of representing his government," she said. "All these political directors, yours and mine and Nick Burns, these are all career officials, they are serving at our pleasure. You should assume that what they say represents the views of government."

Rice chimed in. "Nick was speaking for our government when he spoke about ending Russian arms sales to Iran. That's our position and that will remain our position."

Lavrov shut up. But the dinner conversation continued to be difficult.

Burns wished Rice had decided to reveal their secret. Burns wanted to burst out, "Look, guys, just give us something, play a little ball with us, and it will allow us to move forward." He gritted his teeth mostly in silence—though he whispered to his friend John Sawers, "We're brewing something big but I can't tell you about it." The British immediately guessed the Americans would bend on talking with the Iranians.

Despite Beckett's intervention supporting Burns, it was clear that Rice was left shorthanded without Jack Straw at her side. Rice and Straw were so close that they spoke at least three times a week, and Iran had always been the main issue they discussed. Beckett had barely settled into her new post, she was jet-lagged, and she was not able to give Rice the moderating support that Straw had provided so ably at the London meeting. Beckett also did not yet have the personal standing to intervene in the discussion and influence her peers. By all appearances, Lavrov got the better of Rice that evening. The Russians were thrilled that the resolution had suddenly been pushed to the side, even though some officials present believed they had been prepared to agree to it if Rice had pushed hard enough.[24]

Instead, the ministers told the political directors, there would be an interim step: an effort to lay out two paths, one positive and one negative. The foreign ministers assigned the political directors to come up with a list of proposals that would sharpen the choice for Iran, with particular instructions to be bold with the positive path. "If they don't take this, we'll know they aren't serious," Rice told the other ministers.

Lavrov would explain the approach in a confusing but oddly evocative manner, emphasizing the incentives over the possibility of sanctions: "Sometimes a big carrot could serve as a stick."[25]

"We Need to Be Careful"

The New York meeting reinforced Rice's conviction that the United States needed to join the talks. The Europeans could no longer carry the burden of the negotiations by themselves. During this period, the administration had supported the negotiations but had never been a player. Burns and Rice would get briefings on the talks, and consulted with the Europeans, but their influence was limited. So the United States didn't have the weight it normally has in such high-stakes diplomatic crises. Now the United States would have leverage to influence the talks—it would no longer be a passenger on the train but would now be in the conductor's seat.

Of course, this was the moment the Europeans had long sought. At every stage during the talks, when Rice asked the Europeans whether they were serious about sanctions, they would ask if she was serious about engagement. The French and the Germans, in particular, had been as skeptical about the United States' willingness to engage as the Americans were about European willingness to impose sanctions. "We felt we could achieve a real result only with American involvement," a European diplomat said.

Thus a key part of the European strategy was to bring the Americans into the tent, in part because they were fearful of a rogue United States unleashing unilateral sanctions. That would be bad for business—and possibly sting European companies that were rapidly investing in Iran. After all, U.S. trade with Iran amounted to a few hundred million dollars a year—Iran sold nuts and rugs and the Americans provided cigarettes and wood pulp—but Germany, France, Russia, and China sold steel, cars, weapons, air conditioners, and other durable goods. The total trade of the other Security Council members with Iran kept rising even as potential sanctions against Iran were discussed, going from $18 billion in 2005 to an estimated $22 billion in 2006.[26]

With the Americans on board, the incentives for Iran could be greater, too. During the August 2005 talks, the French refused to permit any reference to European countries participating in nuclear cooperation with Iran because French companies did not want to be penalized in the American market. But, now, the United States could provide legally binding exemptions that would open the Iranian nuclear business to anyone.

The Iranians were also eager for the Americans to finally join the talks.

Another European diplomat said the EU-3 negotiations with Iran felt like being at a cocktail party, talking to someone, and realizing he is looking over your shoulder at the person he really wants to talk to.

During the week of May 13, under strict secrecy, Rice formed a small group of her closest aides to decide how to structure and package the announcement. The group included Burns, McCormack, Robert Joseph, Philip Zelikow, Jim Wilkinson, and Brian Gunderson. They were instructed to inform none of their aides and make no photocopies of documents. Meetings of the group in Rice's office were obscured on Rice's calendar by listing them under the vague title of "security issues."

When asked about talks with Iran, McCormack subtly changed his answers at the daily press briefing. He dropped the standard language that the United States did not need to be at the table because Iran knows what is expected of it. Then he battled away questions by pretending, in his answers, that reporters had asked about direct negotiations between the two countries, not whether the United States would join the talks. Reporters were fooled.

Joseph was assigned to write Rice's statement. Gunderson, a former Capitol Hill staffer, focused on selling the policy shift to key Republican lawmakers, while McCormack and Wilkinson developed a strategy on how to showcase the announcement and how to reach out to conservative opinion leaders. Officials wanted the Iranians to understand that this was a genuine offer, not a propaganda stunt, so it was decided that Rice would speak in the ornate Benjamin Franklin Room on the eighth floor of the State Department, not the press briefing room. The event was structured to give it a presidential feel, including having Rice make a long walk to the podium before the cameras.

When Prime Minister Blair visited Washington on Thursday, May 29, Bush let him know that the United States was strongly considering joining the talks. Blair then told Merkel, who had pressed Bush to consider joining the talks when she visited Washington earlier in the year. Blair also called President Jacques Chirac.

The weekend before the announcement, Rice went to Camp David to make the final pitch to President Bush for the decision. Her team had worked up answers for Rice in order to address questions from Bush about the wisdom of the move. Bush and Rice discussed the initiative at some length, walking through various scenarios and questioning whether the Europeans could be trusted to stick with the Americans if Iran balked at the terms. Bush finally gave his approval—though Rice double-checked with him again the morning of the announcement.

On Memorial Day, Rice's team went to her Watergate apartment to make the final preparations; they were joined by Hadley, Zoellick, Karen Hughes, deputy national security advisors J. D. Crouch and Elliott Abrams, and White House counselor Dan Bartlett.

On Tuesday, the day before the announcement, Rice let Ambassador Bolton—long a skeptic about dealing with Iran—in on the secret. Clearly, he was among the last to know because she was afraid of leaks. Bolton was then invited to join Rice, Hadley, Burns, and Joseph over dinner to discuss the initiative. During the meal, Bush called Hadley, and the group passed around the phone to individually speak to the president. "We need to be careful," Bush warned. "We don't want to be seen as weak and caving in to Iran."

Bolton, who had deep misgivings about the decision, was given the assignment of calling conservative commentators such as Charles Krauthammer of *The Washington Post,* William Kristol of *The Weekly Standard,* and Paul Gigot of *The Wall Street Journal* and praising Rice's gambit. He made it clear at the beginning of each call that he was calling at the behest of the secretary of state—a way of signaling to his friends that he was only following orders.

The final piece fell into place when Bush called Putin and came away believing he had extracted a commitment from the Russian president to support an escalating series of sanctions if Iran did not come back to the negotiating table.

Because Switzerland represents U.S. interests in Iran, on the morning of the announcement Burns called the Swiss ambassador to his office and asked him to transmit Rice's statement to the Iranian Foreign Ministry. Bolton, meanwhile, tried to make the first public U.S.-to-Iran communication in more than a quarter century. He called the Iranian ambassador, Javad Zarif, to request a meeting, but Zarif said he was under instructions not to meet with Bolton. Mark Groombridge, one of Bolton's top aides, was then dispatched to hand-deliver Rice's statement to the Iranian mission to the United Nations.

Minutes later, Rice strolled into the packed Benjamin Franklin Room and made the historic announcement—that "as soon as Iran fully and verifiably suspends its enrichment and reprocessing activities, the United States will come to the table with our EU-3 colleagues and meet with Iran's representatives." In an effort to sugarcoat the radical nature of the proposal, her statement began with some red meat for the conservatives that reminded listeners of the threat posed by an Iranian government possessing nuclear weapons. But she also emphasized the positive: She acknowledged Iran's right to have nuclear energy and spoke of the administration's interest in "a beneficial relationship of increased contacts in education and cultural exchange, in sports, in travel, in trade, and in investment."[27] The skillful presentation and the groundwork prepared by her staff kept the potential conservative backlash silent—at least at first.

Playing Solitaire, Not Poker

Rice flew to Vienna that afternoon to seal the deal with the other foreign ministers. Her plane was filled with reporters, but the only policy people on board were Burns, Wilkinson, and McCormack. Burns, in fact, would be the only person in the room with her when she met with the ministers, while Wilkinson and McCormack were there mainly to tend to the media. The tiny entourage underscored how much of the diplomacy was done at Rice's level—and how irrelevant the rest of the State Department seemed to her team.

The negotiations certainly weren't over. Besides endless discussion about the precise wording in the press statement, the final details of the incentive package needed to be nailed down. Rice may have delivered U.S. participation in the talks, but the Europeans and the Russians wanted to give the Iranians something else: hope that one day they could enrich uranium on their own soil. In their August 2005 proposal, the Europeans had quietly suggested a review period after ten years, despite strong American resistance. They realized Iran would not sign away its rights to enrichment forever, and they wanted to make essentially the same offer, but without a defined time period. Lavrov opposed the idea of making the review subject to a Security Council vote, arguing that Iranians would never agree because they would believe the Americans would veto it unless there was regime change. The ministers agreed to fudge the issue by saying the review would be made by "relevant bodies"—which the Americans interpreted as the Security Council. Rice made sure to get Lavrov's verbal commitment that Russia would not disagree with that interpretation.

The ministers also had a long conceptual debate about the framework for considering the sanctions. They agreed sanctions would be introduced incrementally, proportionate to Iranian actions and commensurate with the pressure needed to persuade Iran to take the steps required of it. The list of sanctions represented a Chinese menu of sorts, largely drawn from previous Security Council resolutions, but they were deliberately constrained to show that the countries were pursuing a path of economic pressure and not a path to potential war. An oil and gas embargo, for instance, was not on the list.[28]

None of this was publicly disclosed at the time. Rice and her aides wouldn't even use the word "sanctions" in Vienna, even off the record, and when Solana took the package to Tehran he did not even bring a printed list of the sanctions. The incentives were the focus of his presentation. Besides dangling in front of Iran the right to one day enrich uranium on its own soil, Rice agreed to sign onto a list that included joint international projects to build nuclear reactors, nuclear fuel guarantees, international investment, energy partnerships, and a long list of potential deals on civil aviation, telecommunications, high technology, and agriculture.

However, as the Iranians quickly noticed, the proposal that now included the Americans dropped language from the 2005 European proposal that provided a commitment not to use or threaten to use force "against the territorial integrity or political independence" of any state, including Iran, and commitment to "an expanded dialogue and relationship" on regional security issues. Instead, it merely substituted a vague reference to supporting a conference on regional security, which might not even be an official government-sponsored event. Rice felt such commitments on paper would cause real problems with Saudi Arabia and other Persian Gulf countries. It was easy for the Europeans to offer such proposals because they did not have the same close ties—though she felt the discussion might have expanded to regional security if the Iranians had taken a chance and accepted the offer.[29]

Still, as the details emerged, Rice came under fierce attack from some on the right. Richard Perle, the former Reagan administration official with close ties to Rumsfeld, thundered that Rice had maneuvered Bush into an "ignominious retreat" and had come to represent "a diplomatic establishment that is driven to accommodate its allies even when (or, it seems, especially when) such allies counsel the appeasement of our adversaries."[30] Within the Republican Party, those were fighting words.

Over the course of a few months, Rice had made an extraordinary series of concessions in order to prod the Iranians back to the negotiating table. She accepted Iran's right to have a civil nuclear program. In theory, she even accepted Iran's right to enrich uranium. She offered to negotiate with the Iranians—and put on the table an economic package that fell just short of bribery. She had maneuvered the administration from being on the sidelines of the Iran diplomacy to the center of the action. She did this from a position of weakness—the United States had little choice because it was so bogged down in Iraq—and yet often managed to make it appear as if the United States was making these moves from a position of strength.

Yet, in the end, it may have been too late. As one U.S. official put it, for years the Americans had been playing solitaire while the Iranians were playing poker. Rice's shift had been a tactical move—another card in play—but it was not accompanied by any broader strategic reexamination of the relationship with Iran. The Iranian government toyed with the idea of sitting at the table with the Americans. But now that Iran felt it was on the cusp of joining the nuclear club, it could not get past Rice's bottom-line demand that it first halt enrichment.

CHAPTER 10

BLOWUP OVER BEIRUT

July 26, 2006

French foreign minister Philippe Douste-Blazy glanced over at Rice. He could see he was in trouble.

Rice had "that look," a rigid countenance that appeared to reveal nothing but anger and disdain. But he plunged ahead, demanding an immediate cease-fire in the devastating summer war between Israel and Hezbollah—even though he knew it might result in a diplomatic blowup at a meeting in Rome attended by more than a dozen foreign ministers.

Rice was annoyed. Ever since she had arrived in Rome after shuttle diplomacy between Jerusalem and Beirut, she had maneuvered behind closed doors to prevent this from happening. She had first spoken to the Italian foreign minister, Massimo D'Alema, who was the host of the conference, and warned him that she couldn't agree to an immediate cease-fire.

"If you push for that, the conference will blow up," Rice told him. "That would be bad for you, bad for the prime minister, and bad for peace." D'Alema agreed. She thought he had skillfully tried to bridge the gaps in the positions, offering language calling for a cease-fire—but not an immediate cease-fire—in the draft statement.

Rice had also met in her hotel suite the night before the conference with Secretary-General Kofi Annan, European Union foreign policy chief Javier Solana, and the Lebanese prime minister, Fouad Siniora. "Look, calling for an immediate cease-fire makes no sense because it's not going to happen, we're all going to look weak, and, Fouad, you're going to look like the international community didn't support you," Rice said. Siniora said he had to call for a cease-fire when, for fifteen days, Israeli bombs had rained across southern Lebanon and even Beirut, killing more than four hundred people. But he said he understood her position.

Then, that morning, Rice had had breakfast with Douste-Blazy and the British foreign secretary, Margaret Beckett. She wanted to make sure they also agreed not to call for an immediate cease-fire. Douste-Blazy is generally pretty straightforward, but he wouldn't quite commit to Rice's game plan. She walked into the conference worried about Douste-Blazy's intentions, but her concerns eased when he kept his mouth shut through most of the meeting.

Then Siniora shook the private gathering of ministers with a moving statement, warning that only "pain, frustration, financial ruin, and fanaticism" would emerge from Lebanon's rubble. He accused Israel of war crimes and pleaded for an "immediate and comprehensive cease-fire."

"Is the value of human life less in Lebanon than that of citizens elsewhere? Are we children of a lesser god?" Siniora asked. "Is an Israeli teardrop worth more than a drop of Lebanese blood?" He quoted Roman historian Tacitus, applying a nearly two-thousand-year-old saying to Israeli attacks on Lebanon during the past two weeks of fighting: "They created a desolation and call it peace."

Suddenly, Douste-Blazy also demanded an immediate cease-fire.

Rice muttered to NSC aide Elliott Abrams, seated next to her, that she didn't understand why Douste-Blazy was engaging in what she considered grandstanding. "There isn't going to be an immediate cease-fire," she whispered. "What does it do to our credibility to call for an immediate cease-fire when there will not be an immediate cease-fire?"

Then, Rice repeated her comment to Abrams out loud to the rest of the foreign ministers. "When will we learn?" she added. "The fields of the Middle East are littered with broken cease-fires and every time there's a broken cease-fire, people die, there is destruction, and there is misery."

Douste-Blazy received support from a number of foreign ministers, especially Finland's foreign minister, Erkki Tuomioja, for a statement calling for "urgent work on an immediate cease-fire." Yet the foreign ministers from Saudi Arabia, Jordan, and Egypt—all of whom disliked Hezbollah and were concerned about the spread of Shiite influence in the region—remained silent. Beckett, who supported Rice, tried to offer a compromise, as did Spanish foreign minister Miguel Moratinos. But by then the battle lines had been drawn.

The ministers spent nearly an hour arguing over the words, producing diplomatic gobbledygook that made it clear there was no agreement. The ministers issued a statement expressing their "determination to work immediately to reach with the utmost urgency a cease-fire that puts an end to the current violence and hostilities."[1]

When Rice, Annan, D'Alema, and Siniora met with the media afterward, she was stunned by the heat in the room. The Italians had packed hundreds of reporters into a small room without any chairs; the reporters had been waiting for hours in sweltering temperatures, tempers flaring. As the ministers haggled over the text, the Rome fire department had even made an emergency visit to remove the doors, but the heat had barely abated. During the news conference, the normally poised Rice found herself wiping beads of sweat from her forehead. Sixty television cameras and dozens of still photographers recorded the moment.

The next day's *New York Times* spread the photo across half of the front page, showing a bedraggled Rice appearing to hold her forehead in distress over her diplomatic struggles—after, as the photo caption put it, "15 nations failed to reach accord on ending the fighting." It was not an image that Jim Wilkinson would have kept stuffed in his office drawer. Rice did not look strong or in control; she looked in over her head.

"Let's Help Lebanon, and That Will Punish Syria"

Lebanon started out as a success story for the Bush administration. It had become a symbol of democracy sweeping the Middle East, a moment when the United States and France—antagonists over Iraq—worked closely together to achieve diplomatic victory. The Israeli-Hezbollah war changed all that. Rice's handling of the conflict earned her some of the toughest criticism of her tenure, threatening to tarnish the image of competence and steely decision making that she had sought to convey.

President Chirac had gotten the ball rolling in mid-2004 when Bush visited France for the sixtieth anniversary of the Normandy invasion. "You're always talking about democracy in the Middle East," Chirac said to Bush. "There's one true democracy in the Middle East that's occupied by foreign forces. We ought to be doing something about that."[2]

Chirac was referring to Lebanon, a fragile Arab country with substantial Christian, Muslim, and Druze populations—a total of eighteen religious sects—that had been a French protectorate after World War I, when it was split off from Syria. Lebanon had suffered through a devastating fifteen-year civil war that began in 1975 and Israeli invasions in 1978 and 1982 targeting Palestinian refugee camps and other havens for anti-Israeli activity. Militias were largely dissolved after a 1989 peace agreement, and the Israeli army withdrew from southern Lebanon in 2000, but Lebanon barely existed as an independent political entity. As a measure of Lebanon's weakness, its army had not been deployed in the south for nearly three decades.

The anti-Israeli militia Hezbollah, funded largely by Iran, kept its arms and essentially controlled the southern part of the country. Syrian forces, which had intervened in the civil war, helped keep the peace elsewhere. The 1978 Israeli invasion, in fact, had started a population transfer of poor Shiite farmers from the border hills to the southern Beirut suburbs, creating a pool of support for Hezbollah. Syria wielded influence through twenty thousand troops on the ground and a network of intelligence operatives throughout the country. Ever since the French had left, Lebanon's constitution reflected the country's delicate religious balance, distributing power among a Christian (Maronite) president, a Sunni Muslim prime minister, and a Shiite Muslim speaker of the parliament. But the hard power in Lebanon was in Maronite hands. The army commander and intelligence chief are required to be Maronite, even though the demographics of the country had begun to tilt radically toward the Shiites. This was a source of instability in the country.

Bush and Chirac discussed the situation in Lebanon, and Bush agreed with Chirac. They should seize an opportunity to make a stand there. Chirac's proposal found a receptive audience in Washington, where hard-liners at the National Security Council, Vice President Cheney's office, and the Defense Department had long toyed with the idea of using Lebanon as a way to pressure the Syrian government.

Within weeks, the ruler of Syria, Bashir Assad, opened the door for action. He demanded the Lebanese parliament ignore the constitution and extend the six-year presidential term of his ally, Emile Lahoud, for three more years. He even summoned Lebanon's parliamentary leaders to Damascus in August and instructed them to change the constitution immediately—and told them Syrian forces would be doubled in Lebanon by the end of the year. In a brief meeting intended to show Syria was issuing an order, Assad gave a warning to Prime Minster Rafiq Hariri, a personal friend of Chirac: "Lahoud is me. If you and Chirac want me out of Lebanon, I will break Lebanon."[3]

Quietly urged on by Hariri, the United States and France in September responded by convincing the UN Security Council to approve Resolution 1559, which demanded the withdrawal of all foreign forces and the "disbanding and disarmament" of all armed groups, meaning Hezbollah. It was a stinging rebuke of Syria, and encouraged political opposition to Syrian rule. In October, Hariri, a billionaire who played a leading role in the postwar reconstruction of Lebanon, resigned after Syria ordered him to step aside. Hariri began organizing for parliamentary elections, boldly refusing to allow any Syrian-nominated members on his election list. It appeared that the opposition might win enough seats to deny Lahoud the presidency.

On February 14, barely two weeks after Rice became secretary, Hariri was assassinated when a massive car bomb targeted his motorcade as it passed through downtown Beirut. Rice responded by immediately recalling the U.S. ambassador to Syria. There was tremendous pressure within Congress and the administration to take other actions to destabilize Syria.

Again, a conversation between Chirac and Bush proved crucial. Seven days after the assassination, Bush met Chirac in Brussels for dinner. Bush wanted to discuss ways to punish Syria, which clearly had a role in Hariri's death. He was also angry that Syria appeared to be allowing insurgents to easily cross the border into Iraq. But Chirac argued for another approach: "Let's help Lebanon, and that will punish Syria." Chirac noted that Syrian power was exercised in large part through Lebanon. So, he said, if you severed Syria's base of power in Lebanon, then you would transform the relationship between Lebanon and Syria—and that would be a blow to the Syrian regime.[4]

Bush agreed to this idea, which resulted in a well-coordinated U.S.-French effort to promote Lebanese aspirations for independence from Syria. The Hariri assassination sparked a wave of protests and demonstrations that led to the withdrawal of Syrian forces by April 27, ending its twenty-nine-year military presence. Anti-Syrian politicians—an alliance largely made up of Sunni, Christian, and Druze parties—swept to victory. Representatives of Hezbollah also won fourteen seats—and received one seat in the cabinet.

"Any who doubt the appeal of freedom in the Middle East can look to Lebanon," Bush declared.[5]

"I've Met with Him"

A few months later, on July 23, Rice made a surprise eight-hour visit to Beirut in the middle of a trip to Israel. Wilkinson and other Rice aides kept the reporters in the dark about the Beirut stop up until the last minute. Rice planned to visit Israeli prime minister Ariel Sharon at his ranch, and reporters were told to expect a 6:30 A.M. call about whether there would be room in the helicopters to accompany her there. Instead, they learned Rice was headed to Beirut under extremely tight security.

Once Rice arrived, her motorcade of bulletproof SUVs, tires squealing, screamed through Beirut, with diplomatic security personnel leaning out of the windows with their weapons and the cars shifting position every thirty seconds.

Rice's vehicle was always boxed in by four cars so that some other poor souls would take the brunt of any attack.

The visit was mostly symbolic, designed to show support for the new government. Syria had tightened controls on the border, hurting Lebanon's fragile economy by blocking Lebanese exports so that agricultural products rotted at the border. Rice raised the problem in a tense meeting with Lahoud, who claimed that he was trying to resolve the problem but also laid out Syria's rationale for the border closure, including a claim that explosives were found on Lebanese trucks. Rice responded that it was curious Syria could so effectively halt traffic on Lebanon's border but not on Iraq's border, a reference to the insurgents entering Iraq from Syria.[6]

Rice also visited Saad Hariri, a member of parliament and son of the slain former prime minister. The massive five-story building in the Hariri family compound where the meeting took place was festooned with huge photos and banners dedicated to his father. Rice met with the son in a room as large as the White House East Room with windows twenty feet high; an adjacent dining room had seating for more than a hundred people.

Rice paid homage to Hariri at his grave site, near the waterfront between a huge blue-domed mosque and a Virgin megastore. Accompanied by his son, she silently placed a white-flowered wreath on the grave and then visited the nearby graves of seven bodyguards who were also killed. "We love you, Condoleezza," a woman in the crowd shouted. Her motorcade crawled slowly past the site of the killing and, next to it, the hulk of the St. George Hotel, which had been attacked and set ablaze during the initial fighting in 1975 and had not yet been rebuilt at the time of Hariri's killing.

Rice had an extremely difficult meeting with Nabih Berri, a Shiite who is speaker of the parliament, pro-Syrian, and close to Hezbollah. He was in a bad mood in part because he was annoyed at having to interrupt his daughter's wedding to meet with Rice. Though Berri had once been a lawyer for General Motors and had lived in Detroit in the 1970s, he seemed to some of Rice's aides to be a "dinosaur," unaware of the democracy that was sweeping his country.[7]

Rice primarily wanted to bolster Prime Minister Siniora, an economist and banker by training and someone whom she considered a potential reformer. Siniora is a pleasant man who wears a tie and speaks fine English, certain to appeal to Americans, though he headed a government that did not democratically reflect the population. She ignored the microphones set up by local media at every location, except for when she met Siniora at the Grand Serail, the Ottoman-era military barracks that houses his office. Though the State Department considers

Hezbollah a terrorist group—and UN Security Council Resolution 1559 demanded the disarming of militia groups—Rice indicated she would not push the government hard to break with Hezbollah. Rice said Hezbollah had a "history of blood" but "there is a process of political reconciliation that is underway in Lebanon" that was important to support now.[8]

Rice returned to Beirut for another surprise visit on February 23, 2006. Wilkinson again pulled a fast one on reporters, letting them believe that when Rice left Riyadh, Saudi Arabia, that day, she would be headed to the United Arab Emirates, the next scheduled stop of a Mideast tour. Instead, Rice made a six-hour detour to Beirut—with special Saudi permission to let the plane fly through Israeli airspace. (Planes going to and from Saudi Arabia ordinarily are prohibited from traversing Israeli airspace.) The secrecy by now seemed a bit much, part of a scam to keep alive Rice's image as an international woman of mystery.

In fact, the night before the news that Rice was coming to Beirut had already leaked to a Hezbollah newspaper. The report had prompted a midnight consultation between Rice and her security chief, Mike Evanoff. Rice asked plaintively if she could still go to Beirut. Evanoff held up his right hand as if he were going to swear an oath. "I'm trying to imagine the testimony I would have to give Congress if you died in a terrorist attack," he half-joked. But he relented and approved the trip.[9]

Once again, the tires of Rice's motorcade often squealed as the vehicles veered through traffic to avoid potential attacks. Reporters based in Beirut thought the security was excessive, with one saying the "Americans are stuck in the 1970s." The city was especially beautiful that day—sparkling oceanfront resorts overlooked by snowcapped mountains, warm sunshine with a slight breeze, chic shops filled with buyers—that it seemed difficult to imagine danger in the dark corners.

The main point of this four-hour visit was to insult Lahoud as the one-year anniversary of the withdrawal of Syrian forces approached. No meeting with Lahoud was planned, even though he was president of the country. Rice had met with him seven months earlier, but when reporters asked her why he wasn't on the schedule this time, she shrugged and said, "I've met with him."[10]

Rice had even designed a kind of netherworld between snubbing Lahoud and meeting with the acceptable officials: placing a phone call. Because Berri had been nasty and brusque with Rice in July, Rice only planned to call him. But while she was on the phone with Berri while traveling forty-five minutes north of Beirut to see Cardinal Nasrallah Sfeir—the patriarch of the Maronite Catholic Church and an influential figure in the debate over Lahoud's fate—Berri decided to put on a charm offensive. He convinced her to stop by his palatial home in west Beirut, replete with marble floors and hallways, on the way back to the airport. She agreed, and Berri was off probation. That left only Lahoud dangling without an invitation. The Lebanese reporters were convinced Rice had a favorite in the presidency race, but she denied it.

Rice also visited the home of Druze leader Walid Jumblatt—a meeting rich with irony. Jumblatt had long been a Syrian supporter but had recently switched sides. "This process of change" to democracy "has started because of the American invasion of Iraq," he said. "I was cynical about Iraq. But when I saw the Iraqi people voting, eight million of them, it was the start of a new Arab world."[11]

Jumblatt's new tone had only come after years of insults hurled at administration officials, including labeling Rice as "oil-colored." In 2003, after insurgent rockets missed the then deputy secretary of defense Paul D. Wolfowitz in Baghdad, Jumblatt said, "We hope that next time the rockets will be more accurate and effective in getting rid of this virus and his like, who wreak corruption in Arab lands." He said he felt "great joy" at the 2002 space shuttle disaster because an Israeli astronaut died in it; in 2004, he declared "the killing of U.S. soldiers in Iraq is legitimate and obligatory." He also said that the real axis of evil is one of "oil and Jews" and called Bush a "mad emperor."[12] None of these wild and anti-Semitic comments seemed to matter now—though Jumblatt apologized for them when he met with Rice privately.[13]

Rice's two trips to Beirut amounted to little more than drive-by diplomacy. She was preoccupied with Iraq, Iran, the Hamas victory, and other foreign policy issues, and she didn't keep her focus on the nascent democracy in Lebanon that the administration had celebrated as a great success. Despite her snubbing of Lahoud, the effort to remove him fizzled and he remained in power. Shiite cabinet ministers began to refuse to attend cabinet meetings and the government ground to a halt. Rice saw the cables from U.S. ambassador Jeffrey Feltman and read the news stories about the situation in Lebanon; she realized that things were beginning to fall apart. The administration, despite paying lip service to Resolution 1559, had not pressed hard enough to have it implemented. Now Hezbollah was gaining political strength in the country. Rice understood that Lebanon was a problem—but it wasn't yet a crisis that could grab her attention.[14]

"The Birth Pangs of a New Middle East"

On July 12, 2006, while on a trip to Paris to deal with the Iranian nuclear crisis, Rice received an unexpected call from Israeli foreign minister Tzipi Livni. She told Rice that Hezbollah commandos in Lebanon had attacked across the blue line—the northern border of Israel—and had abducted two Israeli soldiers and killed four others. "We are going to react," Livni said, not saying anything more. The Israelis tend not to provide much detail about their plans, even to the U.S. government.

Rice immediately called National Security Advisor Steve Hadley. "This could get really bad," she told him, noting it had been a long time since Hezbollah had seized Israeli soldiers.[15]

By coincidence, David Welch, the assistant secretary for Near Eastern affairs, was in Cairo. As soon as he learned of the seizure, he called Omar Suleiman, the Egyptian intelligence chief, to give him the news. "We have a big problem," Suleiman said.

"Yes, we sure do," Welch replied.

The two-month-old government of Israeli prime minister Ehud Olmert was already facing another crisis when Hezbollah struck: Radical Palestinians associated with Hamas had captured another Israeli soldier outside the Gaza Strip two and a half weeks earlier. The situation in Gaza had deteriorated dramatically since the Hamas victory five months earlier. International aid had been cut off and Israel had rounded up many Hamas legislators.

Olmert was actually meeting with the parents of the first soldier when he received a note that there was also "Hannibal" in the north—Israeli army code for a captured soldier.[16] The attack came as a complete surprise to the Americans and the Israelis, though after the kidnapping of the soldier near Gaza, U.S. officials had quietly warned Lebanon and Syria—and by extension, Hezbollah—not to escalate the situation.[17]

Livni's call set in motion the most intense four-week period of U.S. diplomacy since Rice became secretary of state. When the war was over, it would become clear that all sides had miscalculated. Hezbollah did not anticipate the massive Israeli response, apparently believing that the seizure of a few soldiers would provide bargaining chips for a few Lebanese prisoners languishing in Israeli jails. The Israeli government went to war without clear goals, causing a painful split between Olmert and Livni. The Bush administration was unsure how to respond, caught between its support for Israel and its desire to preserve Lebanon's democracy. In the end the U.S. response damaged both governments, while inspiring anger and revulsion in the Arab world and hurting the nascent partnership with France.

After the meetings in Paris, Rice was planning to join Bush as he first visited Germany and then flew to the annual summit of the G-8 industrial powers in St. Petersburg. A day after the Hezbollah seizure, Rice had another conversation with Livni—a much tougher one.

Rice was concerned that the Israeli government kept saying it was attacking Lebanon, so she warned Livni to avoid doing anything that would destabilize the Lebanese government. The Israelis felt strongly that it was important to raise the cost to all the Lebanese for the actions of a few—so people in Beirut would not wink at the actions of Hezbollah in the south—an approach that made Rice and U.S. officials uncomfortable. Rice thought the fight was with Hezbollah, not the Siniora government, which had not launched the attack. Rice also noted that Arabs were not rushing to defend Hezbollah's actions. "You need a Lebanese partner if you aren't going to end up with Lebanon falling into civil war again," Rice told Livni.[18]

Bush, at a news conference with German chancellor Angela Merkel, publicly echoed Rice's private warning. "Israel has a right to defend herself," Bush said. "Whatever Israel does, though, should not weaken the Siniora government in Lebanon. We're concerned about the fragile democracy in Lebanon."[19]

Flying to Russia, Bush worked the phones from his cabin, telling moderate Arab leaders to not just condemn Israel but also keep the focus on Hezbollah's actions. With Hadley and Rice listening in on headsets, Bush told leaders such as President Hosni Mubarak of Egypt and King Abdullah II of Jordan that he was trying to calm the situation by warning Israel not to topple the government in Beirut, but "the real culprit in this case is the militant wing of Hamas and Hezbollah." Bush noted there are other risks: Iran was trying to control the region and Syria might take back Lebanon. The calls seemed to go well, earning Bush a thumbs-up from Hadley and a grin from Rice.[20]

The Saudi government issued an unusually tough statement, saying "it is necessary to make a distinction between legitimate resistance and irresponsible adventurism adopted by certain elements within the state and taken without its knowledge, without legitimate authority or coordination and consultation with Arab countries." The statement, without mentioning Hezbollah by name, said "it comes down to them to put an end to a crisis that they created."[21]

In St. Petersburg, the world leaders haggled over a statement that, when issued on July 16, laid out the parameters for ending the fighting and creating "the conditions for a cessation of violence that will be sustainable." The statement called for return of the Israeli soldiers, the end of shelling of Israeli territory, an end to Israeli military operations, and the release of arrested Palestinian ministers and parliamentarians.

Unbeknown to the leaders, Rice had stayed up until midnight in her hotel room the night before, typing out a draft statement on her computer. The Russians, as conference chair, had offered a statement that the Americans had considered unacceptably weak. In the morning, Undersecretary Nick Burns presented Rice's version as an alternative. (He did not disclose that it was the secretary of state's handiwork because that would raise the diplomatic stakes for getting it approved.) Lower-level officials negotiated over the draft all day, but the Russians kept balking, to the increasing consternation of Bush. At 5 P.M., he became tired of waiting and announced to the other leaders: "I'm going home. I'm going to get a shower. I'm just about meeting'd out."

Prime Minister Blair then intervened, going into a back room with President Putin. Rice and Russian foreign minister Sergey Lavrov joined them, and Rice took Putin point by point through the statement. Putin approved it once Rice agreed to remove a direct reference to Iran and Syria as supporters of terrorism.[22]

Welch, after quick visits to Israel and Jordan, by now was in Libya on a previously scheduled trip; he consulted on the statement via telephone, usually over an open line because communications were so poor. There was nothing Welch could do about that. When one Libyan official noted that Welch had seemed rather busy, he shrugged and said, "You guys have learned more about how our Middle East policy is made from my two days here than you could in two years" of intelligence reports.

Up until this point, the Bush administration had handled the diplomacy well. The blame for the crisis was placed on Hezbollah, and the tacit support of some Arab governments for Israel's response was an achievement. But then the administration let the situation spiral out of control.

In St. Petersburg, Bush told Rice that she really had to go to the region to deal with the crisis. She agreed in principle, but told him she was reticent because she didn't know what she could really do. Blair then spoke to Bush, asking bluntly when Rice was going to go to the Middle East. She began to realize she had to make a trip—that this was the sort of Middle East test that every secretary of state faced. But she would not leave for seven crucial days, as the Israeli bombardment continued unabated.[23]

Olmert, a novice prime minister who, unlike many of his predecessors, had not risen high in the Israeli military, was buoyed by the popular support the war initially generated in Israel. But Livni was opposed to continuing the operation for more than a few days, believing a diplomatic process was necessary to secure gains for Israel after Hezbollah's long-range missiles were attacked. She was also influenced by a secret report by Israel's military intelligence that a heavy bombing campaign and small ground offensive would show diminishing returns within days and not achieve the government's goals.[24]

On July 16, the same day as the G-8 statement, Livni presented Olmert with a "diplomatic exit" strategy, but he rejected the idea in favor of continuing the war. The dispute caused a deep rift between Olmert and Livni, who not only was foreign minister but also held the title of deputy prime minister. The G-8 statement called for the return of Israeli soldiers, and Olmert made that his bottom-line public demand for ending the fighting. "Only the return of the abducted soldiers will stop the operation," he declared on July 18.[25] However, in private meetings with U.S. officials, Olmert said he had no intention of negotiating for the return of the prisoners.[26]

Rice and other U.S. officials were completely unaware of the serious differences between Olmert and Livni; in fact, Rice was very surprised to learn of the split after the war was over.[27] So the Americans watched and waited, in part because they wanted to give the Israelis as much time as possible to wage a successful military campaign. They kept getting inconsistent reports from the Israelis about how much damage was being done to Hezbollah, but it appeared to some officials that Israel had a chance to strike a terrible blow against the militant group. Bush, for instance, was convinced that the Israeli effort would be seen as successful because Hezbollah would no longer be able to control southern Lebanon after Israel finished with it.

Rice's top advisors were split. NSC aide Elliott Abrams tended to believe Israel was doing more damage to Hezbollah than Welch did, and he was not receptive to suggestions that Israel needed to realize the limitations of its operation. But Welch wasn't urging U.S. intervention, either. He was deeply skeptical that Israel could achieve its aims, but he thought his skepticism wouldn't matter. He thought Israel would go ahead no matter what, until either they learned they were not able to get all they wanted or the circumstances changed. The best the United States could do, he thought, was to help the Israelis rethink their calculations.[28]

As Rice discussed a possible trip with her aides, Welch said the United States needed to be involved in finding a solution to the problem.

"We can't allow this to unfold with no vision about what might happen afterward," he argued. "We have to insert ourselves on our terms into this discussion. Otherwise we will be pulled into the aftermath on someone else's terms." As an example, he pointed to the U.S. crisis diplomacy that was necessary in 1996 after the Israelis shelled Qana, a village in southern Lebanon, killing 106 people.

Rice finally agreed to go to the Middle East. She had been scheduled to travel to Asia to focus on North Korea before attending a conference in Malaysia, so she scrubbed the first part of the trip. In the Middle East, she hoped to come up with a statement of principles that both Lebanon and Israel could support as a basis for a cease-fire that would be enshrined in a UN resolution.

Before Rice left, she held a news conference in Washington. She wanted to lay out her line that she would not be going to the region to reestablish "the status quo ante," but would aim for a more permanent solution to the problem of Hezbollah. Yet her enviable skill at communications failed her when ABC's Jonathan Karl asked her why she had not left earlier on her mission.

"I could have gotten on a plane and rushed over and started shuttling and it wouldn't have been clear what I was shuttling to do," Rice bristled. Now, she said she could perceive "the outlines of a political framework that might allow the cessation of violence in a more sustainable way." The carnage and destruction, she added, represented "the birth pangs of a new Middle East—and whatever we do we have to be certain that we're pushing forward to the new Middle East, not going back to the old one."[29]

Her statement about "birth pangs" spawned ridicule and derision throughout the Arab world. One Palestinian newspaper printed a cartoon that depicted her pregnant with an armed monkey. The comment would prove to be an albatross she carried throughout her journey.

"A State, Not a Charity"

Just before Rice left Washington, there was a sign that the unspoken support of moderate Arabs for Israel's military action was crumbling. In an Oval Office meeting, Saudi foreign minister Saud al-Faisal delivered a letter to Bush from King Abdullah asking for U.S. help in arranging an immediate cease-fire. The war had now gone on for nearly two weeks. After taking a risk by issuing their unusual statement condemning Hezbollah's actions, the Saudis publicly had to signal that they could not tolerate a continuation of the Israeli response. Hezbollah haphazardly launched hundreds of rockets at Israeli population centers, eventually killing more than 40 civilians, but more than 1,100 Lebanese civilians would also die from Israeli attacks.

"You've got to stop this right now," Saud privately warned Bush and Rice. "Israel will not destroy Hezbollah but Hezbollah is now in a corner. We will squeeze them. But if this goes on, public sentiment will shift—against Israel and also against the United States."[30]

As her first stop, Rice flew directly into Beirut, again under great secrecy. She transferred from her plane in Cyprus and then swooped into the city on a Marine helicopter because Israel had bombed Beirut's international airport. Hydraulic oil dripped from the rotor of Rice's helicopter, splattering her expensive beige suit. Black smoke from Israeli attacks rose from the distance as Rice traversed at high speed through the strangely quiet city.

Siniora greeted Rice with a kiss on each cheek before asking for her help in arranging an immediate cease-fire—an image that Hezbollah would later seize as an example of how Siniora was beholden to the Americans.

"Thank you for your courage and steadfastness," Rice told Siniora before their two hours of closed-door talks began. Though the meeting was cordial, she told him she could not accept an immediate cease-fire, insisting peace would only come with a comprehensive settlement that disarmed Hezbollah. She had a much tougher meeting with Nabih Berri, the speaker for the parliament whom she had nearly spurned on her last trip but who now emerged as a significant power broker. He had just won the public endorsement of Hezbollah leader Hassan Nasrallah to negotiate on behalf of Hezbollah in the crisis. Berri told Rice there could be no solution unless Israel agreed to exchange Lebanese prisoners for the two abducted Israeli soldiers.[31]

Angry demonstrators followed Rice around the city. "This is not a war against Hezbollah that is being waged, this is a war against Lebanon and its people," said Shereen Sadeq, one demonstrator. 500,000 REFUGEES: AMERICA'S TAX DOLLARS AT WORK, said one demonstrator's sign. BE OUTRAGED, said another.[32]

The Lebanese could not understand why Rice said a cease-fire was not possible or "sustainable," believing her stance was simply a ruse to give Israel as much time as necessary to destroy Hezbollah. Rice said she wanted to support Lebanese democracy, but at the same time described Hezbollah as a challenge to democracy. In fact, Hezbollah had broad support in Lebanon for its argument that pursuing democracy meant much greater Hezbollah representation in the government. Hezbollah even argued that in waging a war against Israel, it—and not the government—was truly representing the people of Lebanon. In a revealing comment that showed Rice's mind-set two weeks before the war broke out, she was overheard telling Russian foreign minister Sergey Lavrov that Iraq was "the only legitimately elected government in the Middle East with a possible exception of Lebanon, which was a peculiar election." Rice thought the election was peculiar because Hezbollah had gained seats.[33]

Within the Francophilic Lebanese elite, Rice became derisively known as "Condi Candide," after Voltaire's naive character who clings to the nostrum that "All is for the best in this, the best of all possible worlds," even in the face of disaster after disaster. Rami G. Khouri, the influential editor-at-large of Beirut's *Daily Star* newspaper, ridiculed her statements, saying she was traveling to "a diplomatic Disneyland of her own imagination." He described her "birth pangs" comment as the result of an "American orgy of diplomatic intoxication with the enticements of pro-Israeli politics." He also expressed a wish that she had read a modern history of the Middle East on her flight to the region so that "she can cut through the haze of her long political drunken stupor."[34]

After the meetings in Lebanon Rice flew to Israel for consultations with Livni and Olmert before heading to Rome for the ill-fated conference. Olmert candidly told Rice that he was having trouble with his military—that they only wanted to conduct the operation in certain ways. (Israel at first limited itself largely to an air campaign.) To some American officials, the Israelis were quickly losing credibility. They would claim they were harming Hezbollah— and then a hundred more rockets would be launched at Israeli cities. Every so often, U.S. officials would raise questions about the Israeli approach. Hadley, for instance, called Olmert's chief of staff, Yoram Turbowicz, several times to complain about bombings in Beirut or on bridges north of the city.

Despite Olmert's public stance on the return of the soldiers, he told Rice he would not negotiate for their return. Rice agreed, noting that in wartime you may sometimes have prisoners of war, but the United States did not negotiate for soldiers.

One thing that was striking about her itinerary was that she made no plans to go to Damascus, one of the key sources of the problem. Syria still played a hidden role in Lebanon's affairs, and it was through Syria's porous border that Hezbollah was able to build up its cache of weapons and rockets. Assad, to the annoyance of Sunni leaders in Egypt, Saudi Arabia, and Jordan, appeared to have agreed to a temporary marriage of convenience with the Shiite Hezbollah, if only to retain his influence in Lebanon. (For public relations purposes, the administration also strongly suggested that Iran and Syria had coordinated the Hezbollah attack in order to relieve the pressure on Iran in the dispute over its nuclear program, but Rice didn't really believe that.)[35]

The last time war broke out between Israel and Hezbollah, in 1996, Warren Christopher, who was then secretary of state, shuttled for a week between Damascus and Jerusalem to produce an agreement that lasted for a decade. But Rice was determined to shun Damascus. The U.S. ambassador had never returned after the Hariri killing. Rice arranged for the chargé d'affaires to deliver a démarche—a stern diplomatic message—to the Foreign Ministry saying Syria should not allow more weapons to enter Lebanon and should not interfere with a potential deployment of the Lebanese army to the south. But she repeatedly batted away reporters' inquiries about why she was not trying every diplomatic lever at her disposal. "Syria knows what it needs to do," she said.[36]

Former deputy secretary of state Richard Armitage, who held the last high-level talks with Assad in January 2005, just before the Hariri assassination, publicly ridiculed her stance. "We get a little lazy, I think, when we spend all our time as diplomats talking to our friends and not to our enemies," he said.[37]

In fact, a year earlier, after Syrian troops were withdrawn from Lebanon, there had been an intense debate within the Bush administration about whether a dialogue should be pursued. Vice President Cheney was strongly opposed, believing talks were useless; he also retained the hope that the Syrian government was weak and might collapse. But Robert Zoellick thought it was worth exploring whether the United States could take advantage of Assad's weakness and thus turn him to be more supportive on Lebanon and Iraq. The risk was that the approach would fail and Assad would end up strengthened, but in Zoellick's analysis even though Assad had his back to the wall, in the end he would survive. Ever the realist, Zoellick looked upon Syria as part of the global chess game. After all, in 1991 intense diplomacy by Secretary of State James Baker had resulted in Syria (then ruled by Assad's father) joining the coalition that ousted Iraq from Kuwait and then becoming the first country to accept the U.S. invitation to join an Arab-Israeli peace conference in Madrid. He thought there was nothing wrong with trying to play that chess piece again.

But Rice wouldn't push back against Cheney's tough stance. She worried about the cost of engaging with Syria, particularly whether Assad would demand relief from the UN investigation into Hariri's assassination as the price of doing business. Assad had made it clear that he was tired of receiving lectures from visiting American diplomats. Syria is "a state, not a charity," Assad told one visitor. "If it is going to give something up, it must know what it will get in return."[38]

But that debate was over now. Welch was among those who had found the administration's discussion on Syria extremely tortured. He certainly didn't think it was a display of weakness to talk to adversaries. But, in the current crisis, he and other officials agreed that Damascus was not necessary for ending the war; instead, the diplomacy needed to focus on Beirut, which had a government that simply needed to function better. For all the criticism of the administration by outsiders for the refusal to talk to Syria during the current crisis, there was little debate inside about the wisdom of Rice's choice.[39]

"CNN Says Rome Is a Failure"

Rice arrived in Rome for the ministerial conference believing she had made good progress in both Lebanon and Israel on a statement of principles for a UN resolution, including deploying an international force to southern Lebanon. In essence, Rice wanted to empower the Lebanese government to take control of its territory and remove the threat to Israel from its northern border. But Israel and Lebanon were still stuck on issues like the timing of a cease-fire and the disposition of a ten-square-mile plot of land and villages known as Shebaa Farms.

Shebaa Farms is one of those symbolic issues that so often dominate disputes in the Middle East. Israel had occupied the land when it seized the Golan Heights from Syria during the 1967 war; Lebanon laid claim to it, though the United Nations had cast serious doubt on Lebanon's assertions. Though Israeli forces in 2000 had left Lebanon, Hezbollah justified continued attacks on Israel on the grounds that Israel had not fully withdrawn from Lebanese territory. In the months before the war, in response to feelers from a senior Israeli official, Rice had held very quiet talks with Israeli and Lebanese officials—which had never leaked—about finding a solution to Shebaa Farms as a way of eliminating the issue for Hezbollah.[40] But the war made such diplomacy very difficult. Now Siniora, in a seven-point plan, wanted to place the area under UN jurisdiction until border delineation and Lebanese sovereignty over them were fully settled, believing it would deprive Hezbollah of an issue. Rice told Siniora that he would not get any agreement from the Israelis in the current crisis, but she agreed to push as hard as she could to test the Israeli response.

Despite the progress, Rice was cautious and directed Welch to be very careful when briefing reporters before the Rome conference. She forbade him from describing the elements of the draft statement, believing that if he publicly explained where they had reached agreement, both the Israelis and the Lebanese would pull back. In any case, Welch thought the conference was already obsolete and wouldn't be able to advance the debate beyond the statement issued at St. Petersburg. He would later blame himself for the disastrous coverage of the Rome meeting.

Rice was hamstrung in other ways. Wilkinson, her press-savvy aide-de-camp with an unerring instinct for avoiding impending disaster, had recently left State to become chief of staff to incoming Treasury secretary Hank Paulson. Sean McCormack, her spokesman, had stayed in Washington because his wife was about to give birth. Rice brought along Karen Hughes and Sean's deputy, Adam Ereli, as replacements, but for once, the smooth-running Rice public relations machine was not evident during the trip. Unlike Wilkinson, Hughes barely mingled with reporters to find out what was on their minds.

Ereli, who had never traveled with Rice before, was impressed at how often Rice made snap decisions on the road—while at the same time keeping in constant contact with Hadley or Bush, providing a running commentary on what she was doing. The bad press did not seem to concern her, not even the growing anger in the Arab world. She shrugged it off, telling aides that the Arabs "are paranoid and there is nothing we can do about that until the situation on the ground changes."

Officials in Washington were worried, though. After the Rome conference ended, as reporters were scrambling to finish their stories before Rice's plane took off for Malaysia, Ereli got a call from White House spokesman Tony Snow. He wanted to know what was going on in Rome before he began the "morning gaggle" for White House reporters. Ereli began to run down a list of accomplishments, when Snow interrupted, "Well, CNN says Rome is a failure."

Ereli looked at the television and saw the headline: "Rome Talks Fail to Reach Agreement." Correspondent John King gave a grim report: "The mood was described as tense, frustrating. Secretary of State Rice was said to be under constant siege, viewed by many at the Rome emergency summit as the obstacle to a cease-fire." Ereli knew the CNN producer was not in the filing center and could not be reached, so he announced an impromptu background briefing in a desperate attempt to turn the other reporters away from that storyline. "There is consensus," he insisted, annoying reporters who had heard the opposite from officials from other countries.[41]

"Fail" was not a word that was supposed to be associated with Rice.

After Rome, Rice flew halfway around the world to Kuala Lumpur for the annual meeting of Southeast Asian nations—a diplomatic conclave she had skipped in her first year, dispatching Zoellick instead. The diplomatic blowback for snubbing the meeting had been intense and Zoellick had just quit the department as well. So she was stuck.

Rice had avoided the Southeast Asian gathering in her first year largely because she had little interest in participating in the frivolous highlight of the annual event: song-and-dance routines by the foreign ministers. Colin Powell had danced to "Y.M.C.A.," and Madeleine Albright performed an Eva Peron impersonation, while Zoellick had worn jeans and a bandana to sing "Oh My Darling, Clementine." That night, Japanese foreign minister Taro Aso planned a Humphrey Bogart impersonation, New Zealand's Winston Peters would sing like Johnny Cash, China's Li Zhaoxing would lead a choir, and South Korea's Ban Ki-moon planned to strut the stage in green sequins.

Rice, in a flowing red batik silk dress and pearls, refused to join in the fun, striking a somber note by performing a pair of Brahms pieces, accompanied by famed Malaysian violinist Mustafa Fuzer Nawi. "It's a serious time. It's not a time that is frivolous," Rice told reporters, saying she wanted to play "something that is in accordance with my mood."[42]

"Boss, You Have to Take a Look at This"

Rice flew back to Israel on July 29. Welch and Abrams had stayed behind in Jerusalem, while Phil Zelikow was bouncing around European capitals trying to arrange an agreement for an international force. Rice thought she might be able to strike a deal on a framework for a UN resolution relatively quickly, but when she arrived, Olmert told her he still needed ten to fourteen days to achieve his objectives against Hezbollah.[43]

In meetings with the Israelis, Rice took a hard stance on Shebaa Farms, as part of her plan to test the Israeli response. Olmert forcefully rejected any return of Shebaa Farms in the current circumstances, saying to Rice, "Israel was attacked and its sovereignty was infringed, and now it is being asked to give land to the aggressor?"[44] But she wasn't really looking for return of the land; she wanted a diplomatic formula that would give Siniora some political cover while not actually requiring Israel to do anything immediately. She wanted to put the onus back on Syria to give up claim on the land.

Rice and her aides had dinner with Olmert, and after the meal they were sitting in his living room when Welch received a disturbing message on his BlackBerry. It was the text of a French resolution that was being floated at the United Nations, calling for an immediate cease-fire. He passed the BlackBerry to Rice, who then read the French text out loud to Olmert. The French move diverged significantly from the track that Rice had been pursuing, which was to create a political settlement as part of the cease-fire. Welch realized that Rice's diplomatic efforts were likely for naught; the French resolution would make it extremely difficult for her to cinch a deal in the next couple of days.

In the morning, it became impossible. Rice was meeting alone with Israeli defense minister Amir Peretz while Welch and other aides waited outside in the hallway. Welch got a BlackBerry message from Ambassador Feltman in Beirut: Lebanese television was showing scenes of devastation from an Israeli missile attack on an apartment building in Qana. "I'm watching pictures of people being pulled out and the casualty toll is going to be high," Feltman reported. Welch couldn't believe it. Another Israeli-Lebanese war, and Qana was again the site of a disaster. He walked over to Brigadier General Eitan Dangot, a former artillery commander and the defense minister's liaison to the military. Welch had known Dangot for years and had worked closely with him on the Rafah accord. Now he angrily confronted him.

"How come you didn't tell us?" Welch demanded. Dangot replied that they were still checking it out, but he thought Israel was responsible for the deaths.

"I'm going in there and I'm going to tell her," Welch said. "This is not good news."

Welch interrupted the meeting and handed Rice the BlackBerry. "Boss, you have to take a look at this," he said.

Rice read Feltman's message. She realized they had a mess on their hands. She asked Peretz what had happened. He gave the same explanation: We think we made a mistake, but we're not sure and we are investigating. The meeting ended quickly.

Welch was furious with the Israelis, believing they should have given a warning about the problem. But Rice was more philosophical, thinking she would have done the same thing if she had been in Peretz's shoes. She would have wanted to know what had happened before she began a conversation about it with outsiders.[45]

Rice gathered her staff. She had planned to take a helicopter into Beirut that afternoon for a final round of talks, but she said it was obvious she couldn't go to Beirut and the diplomatic mission was over. There was no way Siniora could meet with her.[46] They debated whether she should issue a written statement or immediately speak to the reporters. Hughes, who had become increasingly riled by the images of the war that flashed on CNN, ended the debate by forcefully saying Rice had to appear before the media. "We refused to call for an immediate cease-fire," said Hughes, a former television journalist. "They are going to ask if this would have happened if we had called for an immediate cease-fire." She said Rice had to knock that down quickly.[47]

Rice also ordered Welch and Abrams to tell the Israelis that they had to do something to indicate they understood the magnitude of the event. She was already annoyed that the Israelis had been dragging their feet on easing the humanitarian situation—thousands of foreign nationals had been trapped trying to flee the country and now there was a growing refugee problem in southern Lebanon. Hughes also believed it was important that the Israelis do more on the humanitarian front.

The Americans approached the Israelis with the idea of considering a brief pause in aerial attacks, perhaps twenty-four to forty-eight hours, under the guise of investigating the incident at Qana. The initial reports were sketchy, but at first it appeared that at least fifty-six people, including thirty-two children, had been killed. Various Israeli officials gave different explanations about what could have happened, strengthening the American argument for a pause. (A week later, Human Rights Watch concluded the death toll was actually twenty-eight, including sixteen children.)

When Rice came down to the filing center to speak to reporters shortly after noon, she seemed shaken and drained as she read a statement, drafted by Hughes and Ereli, that said she was "deeply saddened by the terrible loss of innocent life."

The inevitable questions came about how much responsibility the United States had for this tragedy. "The United States has been working harder and harder and harder," Rice said. "I would put our efforts beside anyone's efforts to deal with the current situation." She added: "I would have wanted to have a cease-fire yesterday, if possible."[48]

Under pressure from the Americans, the Israelis agreed to a forty-eight-hour halt in air strikes, which would also include a twenty-four-hour period of safe passage for refugees. But Rice's team was so eager to claim some sort of diplomatic achievement, in an effort to change the tenor of the stories, that Ereli called a news conference at midnight to commend the Israeli government for its decision—before the Israeli government had made its own announcement.

The next day, before leaving for Washington, Rice announced that she glimpsed "an emerging consensus on what is necessary for both an urgent cease-fire and a lasting settlement," including an immediate deployment of an international force to southern Lebanon. A solution, she predicted, could be reached "this week."[49]

She was wrong. It would take another twelve days—the length of time that Olmert had sought before the Qana tragedy—as Hezbollah continued to launch a daily barrage of more than a hundred rockets into Israel and the Israeli military pounded targets across Lebanon.

"The French Draft Is Horrible"

As Rice flew home, reporters questioned her about her mood and the unusual amount of criticism she had received for her diplomatic efforts. Rice claimed to be unperturbed. "I hate to disappoint you," she said. "I haven't had much time to read the columns back home. So you can read them to me later." One reporter, Andrea Stone of *USA Today,* especially laid it on the line. "You looked really bad at several times during this trip. I mean, you always look fabulously, but you looked tense. I mean, tell us what you were feeling."

Rice wouldn't bite. "Maybe I'm just not as self-reflective as you think I am," she answered, before veering back into policy: "Guys, I have a particularly strong sense of commitment to Lebanon itself. This is a place—these are wonderful people, it's a beautiful place. And it's had such trouble and such misery for such a long time."[50] The fact that the Lebanese had greeted her with protests and anger did not seem to factor into the equation.

That night, Rice had dinner with Bush and briefed him on the trip. The United States had hoped to end the war with a single UN resolution. But given that the French had offered a resolution calling for an immediate cease-fire, she told the president, it seemed clear that there would need to be two resolutions—one establishing a political framework and then a second authorizing an international force. "We're going to have a rough several more days," Rice said. "It's going to be a while before we can get a cease-fire in place."[51]

Many Israeli and Lebanese officials are convinced Rice was so angry over Qana that she returned to Washington determined to end the war, but then Bush calmed her down over dinner and convinced her to let Israel keep going. Within the Middle East, the Rice-Bush dinner achieved a certain mythology as yet another opportunity lost. But, from Rice's perspective, the dinner was only a trip report, while a far more important meeting took place a few days later at Bush's ranch in Crawford, Texas. There, on August 6, Bush, Rice, and other aides debated whether they needed to pressure Israel to halt its offensive and whether the UN route was still effective. In the end, Bush decided to stick with the same strategy—give Israel the leeway to harm Hezbollah while the United States focused on getting the two UN resolutions.[52]

Yet, in the wake of Qana, the dynamic had changed. No longer was the administration trying to define the acceptable conditions for a cease-fire. Rice and her aides wanted to end the fighting immediately, even though other officials had deep misgivings. But the complaints were muted. Abrams simply left to go on vacation, while Cheney's office was content to complain about the overall direction but rarely intervened.

For most U.S. officials, that period of diplomacy became a blur. The French did not want to organize a force, which they were expected to head, until there was a political framework in place. But it turned out that neither the Israelis nor the Lebanese wanted two resolutions. The Israelis did not want to agree to a cease-fire, only to have their forces sit in place, waiting for an international force to arrive. And the Lebanese did not want the Israelis in Lebanon for an indeterminate period, either.

Communications between the French and the Americans began to break down. It was now August, the traditional vacation time for France. Many senior officials were becoming unreachable. Burns canceled his plans for a two-week vacation with his family in New Hampshire, and now he found that his French counterparts were off at their country homes. Once he got their telephone numbers, sometimes six hours would pass before his calls were returned. On top of that, Chirac in effect became the Lebanese desk officer for the French government, so agreements made with lower-level officials were later overruled by the president.

At one point, on August 5, the United States and France announced they had agreed on a resolution that would halt the fighting, ask an existing UN force known as Unifil to monitor the border, and lay out a plan for a permanent cease-fire and political settlement. A second resolution to follow in a few weeks would create a new international force.

But the Lebanese almost immediately rejected it. The Arab League sent a delegation to New York to deliver a tough message to the French and American ambassadors: This is an imperialistic resolution that defends Israel at the expense of Arab lands. Bolton called Rice after the meeting to warn that the French, who considered themselves pro-Arab, were jumping ship. The Israelis, meanwhile, had been continually surprised by the resilience of Hezbollah— and now Olmert laid the groundwork for a military ground offensive deep into Lebanon. Columns of Israeli troops thrust into Lebanon, some transported by helicopter to the hills just below the Litani River, setting off some of the fiercest fighting of the war and resulting in heavy Israeli casualties.

Rice, normally a sound sleeper, kept waking at night, opening her eyes like clockwork at 1 A.M., 2 A.M., 3 A.M. Each time, the same thought crossed her mind: "How are we going to get ourselves out of this mess?"[53]

All hands were mobilized at the State Department, with Zelikow working on the French, another team trying to build an international force, and, over at the White House, Hadley talking constantly to the Israelis, the French, and the Russians. Welch was in Lebanon, shuttling between Siniora and Berri. Siniora had laid down Lebanon's bottom-line demands in a seven-point plan that the Lebanese cabinet had approved, including the Hezbollah representatives. Berri would keep a sheet of the seven points in front of him when he met with Welch, saying they would not do anything more or less. He was especially concerned about ensuring the return of internally displaced people.

The Americans, of course, could not talk to Hezbollah—and Hezbollah would never talk to the Americans. In a diplomatic dance, Berri never directly said that he was bringing Hezbollah along. "You have to convince me, and if I am convinced then I may play my other role, which is convince them," Berri told Welch. "First you have to convince me, and I am not convinced." Berri would later describe Welch as a decent diplomat but "the icing on a bad cake."

For several days, the French bolted from an agreement with the Americans, offering a new resolution to calm the concerns of the Arabs. In a sign of the tensions within the administration, Cheney's chief foreign policy aide, John Hannah, sent Burns a terse e-mail on August 8: "UN draft is progressively going from bad to worse. Please keep us informed."

Burns told him not to worry: "The French draft is horrible. We are going to reject it."[54] Suddenly, officials began to discuss the possibility of the United States having to use its veto against a French resolution. But it would be a 14-to-1 vote, and terribly damaging for U.S.-French relations, not to mention the battered U.S. image in the Arab world.

On Thursday, UN ambassador John Bolton told Rice that he thought the talks would go on through the weekend. Rice was appalled. "John, this can't go on," she said. She knew that if the Israelis launched a full-scale ground offensive, everything would unravel once again.

"I don't see any way to get it into blue and get it done," he replied, using UN lingo for the twenty-four-hour period when a proposed resolution is supposed to be considered by capitals. This period is a courtesy that can be easily waived, but this was Bolton's way of telling Rice that the decisions could no longer be made by the envoys in New York; it was now up to the foreign ministers and the heads of state. Bolton privately thought Rice was a poor negotiator, and so he dreaded the moment when the text passed into her hands.

Rice then had to decide whether to travel to New York on Friday even though the resolution was not finished. As a general rule, a secretary of state does not show up for a vote on a Security Council resolution unless the deal is fixed. Rice called Beckett, who said she was trying to get to New York even though flights had been canceled because of a terrorist threat. "A lot of people think we'll look foolish sitting there," Rice noted.

"We can look foolish sitting at home or we can look foolish sitting in New York," Beckett replied. "It doesn't seem to matter to me." Beckett's bravado cheered Rice and convinced her to make the trip.[55]

With so many drafts flying around, there was a major break in the negotiations between the Americans and Israelis. Livni thought she had reached clear understandings with Welch on Thursday, but Friday morning, Israeli time, she saw a draft resolution that reflected French thinking, including Israel entrusting Shebaa Farms to the United Nations. "We can't live with this," Livni told Rice by phone. (Olmert had forbidden her to travel to the United Nations to deny her credit for ending the war.) Israel announced it was expanding its ground operation.[56]

In Lebanon, Siniora also was not happy. He wanted more references to Shebaa Farms, not fewer. "The State Department has brought me nothing," he told Welch bitterly. "They have not successfully addressed a single one of my issues."

Welch, taken aback, scolded Siniora. "The secretary of state is the single most devoted person to solving this problem and one of the most popular people in the United States," he shot back. "If you don't think the State Department is helping you, then tell me now. I can leave and go to North Carolina on my vacation."

At the United Nations, Rice personally reworked the language to find compromises between the Lebanese and Israeli positions, juggling such issues as the number of references to Shebaa Farms. She won Siniora's agreement but couldn't get a definitive answer from the Israelis. Livni asked her to wait until 5 P.M. EST but Rice said that Bolton had to present the resolution at 3 P.M. "Give me until three thirty or four o'clock," Livni said. "Three thirty," Rice said. Bolton then had to do a slow stall at the Security Council until Livni reported back the news at 3:53 P.M.: Israel agreed. The expanded ground offensive would not take place

The resolution passed unanimously, bringing an end to a conflict that had killed more than 1,100 Lebanese and nearly 160 Israelis. It called on Israel to begin withdrawing all its forces from Lebanon "in parallel" with the deployment of UN peacekeepers and fifteen thousand additional Lebanese troops. The international force had a mandate to use firepower—but no explicit role in disarming Hezbollah. Under the resolution, it could take "all necessary action" in areas where it was deployed to ensure that those areas were "not utilized for hostile activities of any kind," and "to resist attempts by forceful means to prevent it from discharging its duties." UN troops were also authorized to use force to protect civilians and ensure the flow of humanitarian assistance.

The administration immediately hailed the passage of the resolution as a diplomatic victory, but insiders understood it was a bundle of compromises that left much open to interpretation. Some Americans suspected the French finally gave in because their UN diplomats were desperate to begin their August vacations. "It's a pile of crap," Bolton told his aides. He refused a request from Rice's office to go on television to defend the resolution.[57]

Made in the USA

Rice went immediately on vacation to the Greenbrier but for the first two days spent most of her time on the phone with Siniora and other officials trying to work out the details of the Israeli withdrawal.

From the perspective of Rice and her aides, she had successfully handled a difficult diplomatic assignment. She was out there largely alone, making many of the key decisions; Bush did not even speak to Olmert from the time the war started until after the resolution passed. She had won unanimous passage of a Security Council resolution that finally brought the Lebanese army—and an enhanced international force—back to southern Lebanon. She even managed to strike a deal with Siniora without ever involving Syria. And though publicly many nations assailed the continuation of the war, some foreign officials privately told Rice they did not mind if Israel's attacks damaged Hezbollah. As Rice flew to New York to forge the final agreement, Zelikow remarked to her how, no matter what, the burden always fell on U.S. shoulders—the rest of the world looked to the United States to carry the weight and do the hard work of resolving any major crisis.

But from a broader strategic perspective, the war may have marked an ominous turning point—the decline of American power in the region. Some eight hundred thousand people under the protection of Hezbollah in southern Lebanon may have fled their homes because of its ill-considered seizure of Israeli soldiers, but the militia's ability to remain standing against the feared Israeli military gave the movement a tremendous boost in the eyes of the Arab world. Moderate Arab nations now had to tread very carefully in dealing with Hezbollah.

Rice's unwillingness to prod Israel to end the conflict sooner made it appear as if Israel was acting as the U.S. proxy against Hezbollah, just as Hezbollah was seen as a proxy of Iran. Arab promoters of democracy felt betrayed, believing that Rice, when faced with a choice between Israel and an elected Arab government, had blatantly sided with Israel. In the final analysis, many in the region thought the final cease-fire deal did not look that much different than the cease-fire proposals Rice had rejected at Rome—except that hundreds more Lebanese had died and Hezbollah had gained enhanced status within Lebanon and the Arab world. Hezbollah, in fact, decorated the mountains of rubble across south Beirut that were created by Israeli bombs with giant red-and-white banners that mockingly declared, in English and Arabic, MADE IN USA, THE NEW MIDDLE BEAST, and SMART BOMBS FOR DUMB MINDS.[58]

Thus, Israeli weakness made the United States seem weaker—and this was on top of the American failure to control the spiraling violence in Iraq. In contrast to Rice's grand aims of a "new Middle East," the truce took effect without having achieved the U.S. goal of eliminating Hezbollah's threat to Israel, and the resolution offered no guarantee that Hezbollah would finally be disarmed. Hezbollah immediately began to challenge the badly weakened Siniora government, bringing hundreds of thousands of protestors into central Beirut. At one point, organizers displayed a banner along the side of a building, showing Siniora kissing Rice beneath an image of dead children. THANKS, CONDY, the banner said in English.[59]

The war in Lebanon had other consequences. Iran was emboldened to resist the international effort to restrain its nuclear program; it soon turned down

Rice's offer to join the European-led talks in exchange for suspending nuclear enrichment. The British and the Americans began to notice that the French, once stalwart allies on the issue, seemed less enthusiastic about confronting Iran now that thousands of French troops were in southern Lebanon, cheek-by-jowl with Hezbollah forces. Moreover, the war, combined with the seizure of the Israeli soldier by Hamas, forced Olmert to abandon his plan to withdraw from large parts of the West Bank. Rice once had hoped the plan would help lead to a breakthrough on a Palestinian state, but Olmert's opponents claimed that Israel clearly had achieved no peace by unilaterally leaving southern Lebanon and Gaza.

Ironically, in the two most liberal societies in the Middle East—the Palestinian territories and Lebanon—militia groups had been voted into the governments. The influence and rise of Hamas and Hezbollah directly affected the way the United States was seen in the region: on the defensive and in decline.

That was the true nature of Rice's "new Middle East."

BACK TO BEIJING—AND BEYOND

Rice was exhausted.

She had just returned from a weeklong trip to the Middle East and, after dinner with friends, was resting in her apartment when she got a call from Nick Burns via the State Department operations center at around 9 P.M. He had rather shocking news: The Chinese had informed the U.S. embassy in Beijing that North Korea would test a nuclear weapon within minutes. Officials in Pyongyang had given their patrons in Beijing only two hours' notice.

All Rice could do was wait. About an hour later she got a call from the operations center. The U.S. Geological Survey had confirmed that a seismic event had taken place about two hundred miles northeast of Pyongyang, near the city of Kilju, indicating an underground nuclear test. Then she began another round of late-night telephone diplomacy, calling foreign ministers on the other side of the globe about the latest crisis to occur on her watch. At one point, she had to decide whether to stay up and wait for a call at 1:30 A.M. with the Chinese foreign minister or try to sleep a little bit. She chose sleep. Then after that conversation, she had to get up again at 4 A.M. to take another call.

Within days, Rice flew to Asia, trying to build a united front against the North Koreans. The Chinese were embarrassed that they had failed to prevent their client state from testing a nuclear weapon, giving the Americans hope that, finally, Beijing would put some pressure on Pyongyang. One of the Chinese officials she met with was none other than state councilor Tang Jiaxuan, who had given her so much grief when she visited China in 2004. He had just returned from a meeting in Pyongyang with North Korean leader Kim Jong Il, and he once again had a stack of five-by-eight cards by his side when he met with Rice.

Tang spoke in a forty-minute monologue about his trip before Rice could ask a question. But this time there was little she could do about that; Tang literally held all of the cards.[1] The Chinese were engaged, but despite certain international sanctions the North Koreans had gained tremendous leverage because of their test. It was time to make a deal.

"Nothing's Working"

The North Korean nuclear test came just as Rice neared the end of her first two years as secretary of state—when nothing seemed to go right for her or the Bush administration.

Rice had begun her tenure as secretary by humiliating the Egyptian foreign minister over the case of political activist Ayman Nour. Now it was Ahmed Aboul Gheit's turn to humiliate her. When Rice had traveled to Egypt on her Middle East trip, just before the North Korea test, she was asked by a reporter the inevitable question about Nour, who still languished in prison.

"I've spoken about Ayman Nour at each time that I meet with my Egyptian counterparts," Rice said.

"You didn't raise it today," Aboul Gheit gleefully interjected.[2]

Meanwhile, the war in Iraq was by now an acknowledged disaster, even by many in the administration. Hezbollah had gained power and strength in Lebanon, largely because of the perception that it had stood firm against the Israelis while the government simply acted as a tool of the Americans. Iran had refused the offer of talks with the Americans, and it took months of tense talks with the Russians for the Security Council to impose relatively weak sanctions. The nascent government in Afghanistan was increasingly fragile and under siege from a resurgent Taliban. The democracy effort in the Middle East had faltered. The peace deal in Darfur had failed to take root and the Sudanese government refused to accept a UN-led force. As Palestinian factions openly attacked each other in the streets, the prospect of a Palestinian state seemed ever more distant. The Republican-controlled Congress, in one of its last acts, approved legislation to implement Rice's nuclear deal with India, but set conditions that snagged talks with New Delhi.

One poll, surveying twenty-six thousand people in twenty-five countries in Europe, Africa, Asia, South America, and the Middle East, found that in the two years Rice had been secretary of state, global opinion of U.S. foreign policy had sharply deteriorated. Nearly half of those polled said the United States was playing mostly a negative role in the world.[3]

"These are scary times we live in," one senior Rice aide confided. "Nothing's working. We can blame Iran, we can blame North Korea, and we can blame Hezbollah. You can blame them all because they are all terrible people. But at some point you have to ask yourself, are you going about this right? We are big, we are powerful, and we should be able to prevail. But ultimately we are finding ourselves more isolated than at any time in our history."

Americans sensed that, too, and responded by sweeping the Republicans out of power in the midterm elections. Rice, who had been a political junkie since childhood, stayed up until midnight watching the returns. She had generally ignored the Republican-led Congress, but now she would have to deal with Democrats who had very different ideas about foreign policy. That night she had also learned of another secret: The president would announce in the morning that Defense Secretary Rumsfeld was being replaced by former CIA director Robert Gates, whom Rice had once unsuccessfully sought as her deputy.[4]

On the personnel front at the State Department, Phil Zelikow also announced his departure shortly after the election, depriving Rice of a valuable resource. Zelikow had annoyed many powerful figures in the administration, especially since too many references to his private memos seemed to turn up in news reports. The final straw appeared to be a *New York Times* profile that portrayed Zelikow as a realist truth-teller in an administration stocked with starry-eyed idealists.[5] Rice detests such articles because she thinks they make her job tougher in her dealings with the vice president's office and the Defense Department. Zelikow was replaced by Eliot A. Cohen, a neoconservative professor who had backed the Iraq invasion but who had turned sharply critical of the administration's mismanagement of the occupation.

UN ambassador John Bolton also resigned once his recess appointment expired and it became clear that he could not be confirmed by the Senate. The White House was not willing to risk a fight with the new Democrat-controlled Congress by pulling a questionably legal end run around the law concerning recess appointments. That opened up another hole in her foreign policy team. She had failed to quickly replace Zoellick, and by year's end she had been without a deputy for six months—a new record for a job that is critical to the running of the State Department. A series of potential candidates turned her down, including General James L. Jones, the NATO supreme commander. Finally, in January, with an assist from Bush, she was able to lure career diplomat John D. Negroponte, the director of national intelligence, back to State as her deputy.

Among the rank and file of the State Department, Rice was an increasingly unpopular leader, appearing to be indifferent to their concerns. While this book has focused mostly on her diplomatic initiatives, her personnel policies were controversial at Foggy Bottom. Her agenda of "transformational diplomacy" began an overdue shift to send more diplomats to countries such as China and India while reducing posts in Europe. But under relentless pressure to fill jobs in Iraq, Afghanistan, and other hot spots, Rice ordered that hardship posts needed to be filled first, before more attractive positions were filled. For older foreign service officers, who had done the hardship tours in their youth but now had family obligations, the shift in policies was too much. As a result there was significant brain drain as experienced employees fled to retirement, especially those with expertise in Asia.

After the election, attention turned to a report on Iraq being prepared by a bipartisan panel of elder statesmen headed by former secretary of state James Baker and former congressman Lee Hamilton. The group had labored in obscurity for months, but now suddenly it was perceived as a way for the Bush administration to change course on Iraq. When the group was first proposed, Rice had insisted that it focus on the future, not rehash debates about whether the invasion made sense in the first place.

Just before the Iraq Study Group report was released in early December, Rice and Bush met with Iraqi prime minister Nouri al-Maliki in Amman, an encounter made awkward by a highly critical memo by Steve Hadley on Maliki's failings that had just surfaced in the media. Rice left the meeting to go immediately in her motorcade to the West Bank, for a rather aimless afternoon of going from Amman to Jericho to Jerusalem and then back to Jordan. She spent more time traveling in her motorcade than in meetings as she tried to nurture a fledgling truce in the Gaza Strip. Rice had specifically sought Bush's commitment to a Palestinian state when she agreed to become secretary of state, and she would gamely insist that the "fundamentals are now better" for a Palestinian state than at any time in history.[6] Yet she had little to show for her efforts. Demanding a "two-state solution" made for a good slogan, but in the region, many Arabs had long perceived an inattention to detail and a general message of indifference from the administration.

When the Iraq Study Group report was released, it was another blow. Baker may have been secretary of state for Bush's father, but the bipartisan report of five Democrats and five Republicans was harsh and critical of the Bush administration's handling of its Iraq venture. In fact, far more of the report was devoted to diplomatic strategy than military matters, which in itself appeared to be an implicit rebuke of Rice and her handling of foreign policy.

The administration's effort to spread democracy to Arab lands was not mentioned in the report, except to note briefly that most countries in the region are wary of it. The report urged direct talks with Iran and Syria, both of which the administration had largely shunned. It also called for placing new emphasis on resolving the Israeli-Arab conflict, including pressing Israel to reach a peace deal with Syria, on the grounds that the issue shapes regional attitudes about U.S. involvement in Iraq.

Without mentioning Rice by name, the report urged what it called a "new diplomatic offensive." In effect, it said that her approach to building a regional "compact for Iraq" was too narrow, that her efforts to engage moderate Arab states lacked ambition, and that her pursuit of Israeli-Palestinian peace needed to be reinvigorated. It was quite a slap. Baker, widely considered to be an effective secretary of state, seemed to be telling Rice that she didn't know how to do her job.

In many ways, the Iraq Study Group report was a compilation of the many complaints that traditional foreign policy experts—the so-called realist school of which Rice had once been a member—had long had about the Bush administration's approach to the Middle East. But, even if the recommendations were adopted, the chances for a sudden breakthrough were slim. Iran and Syria might have been more amenable to serious negotiations a few years ago, when the United States seemed triumphant after the fall of Hussein. But that moment has probably passed, and now Iran and Syria were convinced the United States was on the ropes. U.S. officials "are gradually sinking in this swamp and now they cannot help themselves out," said senior Iranian cleric Akbar Hashemi Rafsanjani in a sermon. "It would take us a lot of efforts now to help them out of the bottom of the swamp."[7]

The administration largely rejected the Baker-Hamilton approach as it crafted its own new Iraq policy. In January, the day after Bush announced the plan—which called for an increase in troops, not a decrease—Rice appeared before the Senate Foreign Relations Committee. In a surreal scene, Republican senator after Republican senator denounced the plan. Senator Chuck Hagel of Nebraska called the president's speech "the most dangerous foreign policy blunder in this country since Vietnam." Senator George Voinovich, an Ohio Republican, lectured Rice: "I've gone along with the president on this, and I bought into his dream, and at this stage of the game, I don't think it's going to happen."[8]

There have been few congressional hearings held the day after a major presidential speech in which not a single lawmaker from either party defended the president's proposals.

"It Is Not Deal-Making"

Behind the scenes, Rice plotted to salvage the remainder of her time in office. She was greatly aided by Rumsfeld's departure and Gates's arrival. The new defense secretary wanted to focus mostly on Iraq and he told his staff to leave foreign policy to the State Department. He joined forces with Rice on a number of issues, including arguing to finally close the detainee facility at Guantánamo.[9] Cheney's influence also began to dwindle, as he was deprived of his compatriot at the Pentagon and wounded by the trial—and conviction—of his former top aide Scooter Libby on perjury charges.

In January, Rice huddled with her top aides and decided that she would focus on three key issues in her final two years: ensuring a nuclear deal with North Korea, resolving the conflict with Iran over its nuclear program, and making progress on creating a Palestinian state. Negroponte could handle the rest of the globe. There was a sense of desperation in her moves, particularly as she repeatedly drew on the ideas and approaches of the Clinton administration—almost as if she was trying to erase the previous six years. On the Middle East, she spent Christmas vacation in 2006 reading through a three-foot-high stack of reports from the State Department historian's office, trying to glean lessons from Clinton's intensive efforts in the waning days of his presidency.[10]

Rice's new pragmatism is best illustrated by the turnabout on North Korea. Rice dates the beginning of the new policy from Bush's lunch with Chinese president Hu Jintao in April 2006, when Bush directly raised the idea of completing a peace treaty with North Korea.[11] But the nuclear test spurred her to act.

A few weeks after the October 2006 nuclear test, the North Koreans said they would return to the six-nation disarmament talks. Christopher Hill, the chief U.S. negotiator who in July 2005 had to ignore Rice's instructions in order to have dinner with Kim Gye Gwan, his North Korean counterpart, was finally authorized to begin meeting with Kim to reach an understanding on how to dismantle Pyongyang's programs. He thought North Korea would be willing to bargain, but then the North Koreans stiffed him when the six-party talks were finally held in December 2006. The North Koreans only wanted to talk about Treasury's investigation of illicit North Korean activities, which had resulted in a freeze of $25 million in North Korean accounts at a bank in Macao.

The Americans blinked. Hill received permission to meet with Kim in Berlin in January 2007—the first time such a meeting had been held outside Asia, away from the watchful eyes of the Chinese. After a Middle East trip,

Rice flew into Berlin in the midst of Hill's talks to get an update. She then called Bush directly to make a pitch for accepting a tentative deal reached by Hill—bypassing layers of bureaucracy potentially hostile to an accord. Without saying so publicly, Hill had engaged in bilateral negotiations to reach a preagreement that would then be blessed by the other nations at the talks—exactly the approach long urged by advocates of engagement.

A month later, Pyongyang agreed to shut down its nuclear reactor in exchange for resolving the Treasury probe in Macao and a provision of fuel oil. Until the deal was announced, Rice and Bush left most of the government officials hostile to an agreement in the dark about the details. During the negotiations, Rice called Hill constantly in Beijing—seven times on the final day—and at one point she urged him not to thwart a deal by being too stingy on how much fuel oil North Korea would ultimately receive.[12]

Moreover, the administration completely caved on the issue of the Macao bank and the $25 million in frozen funds, agreeing to settle the matter even before the nuclear reactor was disabled. Rice convinced Treasury secretary Hank Paulson to return all of North Korea's money even though Treasury investigators were convinced a significant percentage stemmed from illicit activities the administration had previously condemned. Rice wanted a success story. With only months left in Bush's presidency term, she was not going to let a measly $25 million stand in the way of a possible nuclear deal. North Korea eagerly exploited the abrupt shift in policy, humiliating the administration by refusing to begin serious implementation talks until the money was actually transferred. Rice even let Hill visit Pyongyang before a final reactor deal.

Absent regime change, North Korea clearly was not going to give up its weapons unless the United States paid a much higher price than if the administration had actually engaged in real diplomacy in 2002, when the administration first raised alarms (now considered possibly overhyped) about Pyongyang's alleged uranium enrichment program. In other words, the North Koreans would need to be rewarded for their "bad behavior"—precisely the outcome that Bush said he would always avoid. Rice's embrace of engagement with North Korea, after years of vacillation, infuriated many conservatives. Undersecretary of State Robert Joseph had worked for Rice for six years but felt marginalized in the debates over North Korea and Iran. He resigned in February 2007, shortly after the deal was announced, because he was so angry at the concessions that Rice had made.

On Iran, Rice was pleasantly surprised that the Security Council resolution, passed with difficulty in December 2006, turned out to pinch Tehran after all. The Treasury Department was unleashed to convince banks and corporations to stop doing business with Tehran, and the pitch was effective because the resolution had been passed under Chapter 7 of the UN Charter, reserved for the gravest offenses. The U.S. Navy also dispatched a second aircraft carrier group to the Persian Gulf. Rice upped the pressure by winning passage of a second Security Council resolution in March 2007. This time, the process was easier because she decided to negotiate the parameters of a resolution with Russian foreign minister Sergey Lavrov first, only bringing the Europeans into the discussions after Russia and the United States had reached an understanding.

But Rice also opened the door to cooperation with Iran, agreeing to join discussions on stabilizing Iraq that in May 2007 put her at the same table as the Iranian foreign minister. The move suggested that if Rice felt she could operate from a position of strength, she would be much bolder in her dealings with the Islamic Republic.

Finally, on the Israeli-Palestinian front, Rice began making near monthly trips to Israel and the West Bank, seeking to prod the Israelis and Palestinians to begin making nascent steps toward creating a Palestinian state. Both Israeli prime minister Ehud Olmert and Palestinian Authority president Mahmoud Abbas were politically weakened and seemed in no position to make a deal. But in a reversal of the administration's previous policy, Rice pushed them to begin discussing the contours of a Palestinian state. Previously, under the road map peace plan, such issues as the status of Jerusalem were not to be discussed until after a long series of incremental steps. The move seemed at least three years too late; the Europeans had been calling for this ever since the road map process collapsed in September 2003, but Rice had maneuvered to sidetrack that discussion by pushing for the Israeli withdrawal from Gaza.

Rice also pushed Israel's Arab neighbors to reaffirm a peace offer made to Israel in 2002—something all but ignored by the Bush administration at the time. Rice even said she would not rule out offering her own ideas for settling the conflict, just as Clinton had done shortly before he left office.[13]

Rice dates her efforts on Middle East peace back to her Camp David conversations with Bush about whether she should become secretary of state.[14] But outsiders, especially in the Arab world, wondered if her many trips were really aimed at winning Arab support for the struggling Iraqi government and for a possible showdown with Iran. Before he left the State Department, Zelikow had hinted at such a strategy. "For the Arab moderates and for the Europeans, some sense of progress and momentum on the Arab-Israeli dispute is just a sine qua non for their ability to cooperate actively with the United States on a lot of other things that we care about," he told a foreign policy conference.[15]

Despite skepticism at home and abroad, Rice insisted there are opportunities for a breakthrough. "The strategic context is very different and it's in transition, so it's difficult and it's hard and it's somewhat turbulent, but it has real advantages for the United States," she said. She viewed it as "a kind of clarifying moment between extremism and mainstream" in the Arab world that she intended to exploit and shape with extensive travel to the region in her remaining months as secretary of state.[16]

Many Arab and European diplomats found this notion of "extremism" versus "mainstream" to be a misguided concept for the maelstrom of the Middle East, where alliances shift as often as the desert sands. (Rice, in fact, had borrowed this language from Israeli foreign minister Tzipi Livni.) Abbas demonstrated this when, under prodding from Saudi Arabia, he struck an accord in February 2007 with Hamas to create a unity government. Abbas's decision surprised Rice and infuriated the Israelis, setting back her efforts. The Saudis, who sweetened the deal by reportedly pledging $1 billion to the Palestinians, were unapologetic for ruining Rice's tentative efforts at peacemaking. Rice suffered another setback when in June 2007 Hamas used its increasing power to seize control of Gaza, leaving Abbas in charge of only the West Bank.

During one of her 2007 Middle East trips, Rice conducted a running tutorial on her view of history and diplomacy with the reporters traveling with her. Drawing mostly from examples she knew well concerning Germany and the Soviet Union, she argued that diplomacy was not about making deals. "You aren't going to be successful as a diplomat if you don't understand the strategic context in which you are actually negotiating," she said. "It is not deal-making. It's not." Instead, she said, it was a matter of waiting until the underlying conditions were right, and then acting.[17]

Many reporters found her argument strange. It appeared to be an all-purpose excuse for why talks with Iran and Syria were not necessary and also why progress had been slow on so many foreign policy fronts.

Rice's series of speeches when she first became secretary—combined with Jim Wilkinson's stylish image-making—had obscured the fact that Rice fundamentally lacks a strategic vision. Her approach has been largely tactical, a series of ad hoc efforts designed to deal with an unfolding series of crises that stemmed from decisions she had helped make in the first term. Her closeness to the president gave her tremendous clout within the administration, making her a far more powerful figure than Colin Powell, but she did not use it to force a fundamental rethinking of the administration's approach to the world. As a result, Iraq sank even deeper into a morass, so much so that Congress and the American public had turned to the retired officials of the Iraq Study Group to try to force a change in policy.

As President Bush's confidante for more than seven years, Rice has failed to provide him with a coherent foreign policy vision. The president appears to be the idea generator; after all, he shifted Rice from her roots in foreign policy realism and infused her with a desire to spread democracy through the Middle East. In both presidential terms, Rice was at the center of the decision making and often responsible for crafting and implementing presidential directives. Yet the results have been disappointing—and sometimes devastating to U.S. interests.

Nowhere is Rice's failure of vision more apparent than in the Middle East. The ambition of bringing democracy to the region is a notable goal, but the administration never seemed to connect that goal with a real plan for achieving it. When elections went the wrong way, from the administration's perspective, as in the Palestinian territories or Lebanon, Rice's response was to judge the election an aberration, not an exercise in free expression. Hezbollah's rise, some might argue, is the result of an authentic yearning for a greater say in the country's affairs by the country's growing Shiite population. Yet the administration found itself joined with autocrats like Egypt's Hosni Mubarak in expressing concern that the pro-Western Lebanese government could be toppled. Mubarak was worried that a successful campaign by Hezbollah would foment demands for more freedom in his own country—which presumably was the goal of U.S. policy. Increasingly, the whole democracy effort seemed to be a farce, especially as the United States constantly looked to Egypt and Saudi Arabia to rescue it from Iraq and foster progress in the Israeli-Palestinian conflict. In a striking and worrisome development, Egypt's best-known democracy movement, Kifaya ("Enough"), shifted its focus after the Lebanon war from attacking Mubarak to demanding an end to the country's peace treaty with Israel.[18]

Rice studiously ignores any contradictions in her approach. The invasion of Iraq had been promoted in part as a way to bring democracy to the region and help Israel. Now she argued that because the turmoil in Iraq had led to the rise of Iran, the collective fear of the Sunni world would make Arabs more willing to strike a deal with Israel. Similarly, the administration had sought to prevent North Korea from testing a nuclear bomb. But now that it had happened, Rice spun it a different way—this made the world more united in dealing with the North Korean threat. Rice even managed to claim that Hamas's unexpected electoral victory, which was such a blow at the time, was actually a potential boost for peace.

"I'm enough of an historian to know that my reputation will be what my reputation is. It might be different in five months from five years to fifty years, and so I'm simply not going to worry about that," Rice said, when asked about her legacy. "I suppose, when people look back and they say, now what does the Middle East look like, ten years from now or twenty years from now or thirty years from now, the policies will be judged on whether or not democracy has moved forward in the Middle East and whether or not extremists have been pushed out."[19]

Despite her diplomatic setbacks, Rice remains personally popular with Americans. Wilkinson's public relations efforts to forge a strong image for Rice continued to pay dividends, even though she no longer conducted the media-friendly excursions that had marked the beginning of her tenure. She now rushed as quickly from meeting to meeting as Powell did, skipping any opportunities to savor a country's culture or make a connection with its people. When she is done with her meetings for the day, Rice doesn't even flip the local television channels. She will call back to Washington, usually to Steve Hadley, read a few pages in a book, and then go to sleep.

After the midterm elections, the Quinnipiac Poll asked registered voters to rate their feelings for twenty U.S. leaders on a scale of 0 to 100. Rice placed fourth, with a rating of 56.1, after former New York City mayor Rudolph Giuliani (64.2), Illinois senator Barack Obama (58.8), and Arizona senator John McCain (57.7). She edged out Bill Clinton (55.8) and was far ahead of Hillary Clinton (49.0) and President Bush (43.8). The poll also found that by a wide margin, Americans regarded her as the most powerful woman in the United States, followed by Clinton and House Speaker Nancy Pelosi.[20]

Even though Rice became more of a lightning rod for Iraq after Rumsfeld resigned, a *Washington Post* poll in early 2007 found her approval rating was still at 58 percent, the highest of any administration official and 22 percentage points higher than Bush.[21] On a personal level, Rice is an exceedingly friendly and gracious individual—even to reporters whose articles have displeased her. These qualities, apparent to the general public, would make her a formidable political candidate. One of her advisors, in fact, believes she is increasingly interested in running for governor of California.

Some of Rice's friends harbored the fantasy that Bush, desperate to secure his legacy, would find some medical reason to replace Cheney with Rice, making her the front-runner for the Republican presidential nomination in 2008. Rice insists she has no interest in being president or vice president, but such a move would be in keeping with her entire life. She never really sought out jobs like provost of Stanford University, national security advisor, or secretary of state, but found herself plucked for them by powerful patrons.

While Rice speaks fondly of returning to Stanford and teaching, by the time the Bush administration ends she will not have dealt with students full time for some fifteen years. She is also not a popular figure on campus, both because of her stormy tenure as provost and because of a general liberal revulsion of Bush administration policies. Some Stanford colleagues predict she will flee Stanford for other opportunities within a year after she returns to Palo Alto. Certainly, with her youth, talent, and intelligence, Rice could easily run a major corporation or fulfill her dream of running the National Football League— and still have at least two decades to decide whether she wants to return to public life as a politician.

Her youth affords her another opportunity. At the moment, she is the confidante of a president widely considered a failure. The judgment of history may be harsh on the Bush-Rice partnership. Or the pendulum could swing, depending on the outcome in Iraq and what historians discover when the administration's secrets are declassified. Assuming she retains her good health and vigor, Rice will only be in her seventies when those judgments will begin to be formed. She will learn whether her hope that she might be considered the next Acheson was prescient—or merely the result of the same blind optimism that led the nation into Iraq in the first place.

without hesitation dozens of administration officials consented to repeated interviews, sometimes hours at a time, that were conducted exclusively for this book. Not a single request for an interview was turned down.

I have previously covered national politics, Congress, and the White House, so I am not exaggerating when I say that some of the hardest-working and most professional reporters in Washington cover the State Department. I have benefited tremendously from the advice and counsel of a number of my fellow travelers, especially Anne Gearan, Libby Leist, Cam Simpson, and Janine Zacharia.

A number of people who are experts in specific issues covered in this book took the time to carefully read individual chapters as I was writing and offer thoughtful comments, including Aluf Benn, Ed Cody, Kate Hunt, and William Rich. A close friend, Ianthe Dugan, also read and commented on several chapters. I especially want to thank a career government official who closely read the chapters on India, North Korea, and Iran, making more than a hundred suggestions for improving the text. He wishes to remain anonymous. Thanks also to my readers of the full manuscript once it was completed. I alone am responsible for the text and any possible errors of fact or judgment.

The Hoover Institution at Stanford University allowed me to come there twice as a media fellow, permitting me to spend valuable time on campus in an effort to better understand Rice's pre-Washington life. Thanks to Mandy Mac-Calla and Dave Brady for giving me the opportunity.

In 2001, Dale Russakoff of *The Washington Post* wrote what I believe is still the best single article on Rice's background and history. She generously provided me with the transcripts and notes of her interviews with Rice and Rice's family and friends, as well as other material she had collected.

I never would have thought of writing a book without the persistent prodding of Robin Wright, my *Post* colleague on the foreign policy beat. Every day that I came into the office, she would tell me I needed to write a book. One day, she thrust a piece of paper at me with the name and phone number of a book agent and insisted I call him. Out of sheer desperation, I finally gave in. Robin's persistence and determination show up every day in her reporting.

Rafe Sagalyn, my agent, was rather dubious when I came up with my first book idea, and he pushed me to come up with something better. He then took pity on a first-time book writer and guided me though the proposal-writing process, even though my first drafts showed I had little clue about the book business.

Michael Flamini, my skillful and enthusiastic editor, his assistant, Vicki Lame, and the rest of the team at St. Martin's Press expertly guided the book to publication.

ACKNOWLEDGMENTS

I have a rare job that allows me to be in Beijing's Tiananmen Square in the morning and then in Moscow's Red Square in the afternoon. This book would never have been possible without *The Washington Post*'s dedication to serious coverage of national and international issues. Even in difficult economic times for the newspaper industry, the *Post* gave me—and its readers—a front-row seat as Condoleezza Rice embarked on the most active travel schedule of any secretary of state since Henry Kissinger.

I am grateful for the farsighted leadership of Donald Graham. Having worked at another newspaper that was crippled by the corporation's desire to please the stock market, I know it makes a difference to be able to see the primary owner and manager regularly walk through the newsroom, intensely interested in the work of reporters. I want to thank publisher Boisfeuillet Jones, executive editor Len Downie, and managing editor Phil Bennett for their support and encouragement over the years. Also at the *Post*, I am grateful to Liz Spayd, at the time the assistant managing editor for national news; Mike Abramowitz, then the national editor; and my direct editors, Scott Vance and later Greg Schneider, for their encouragement of this book. Many *Post* reporters who have previously written books provided helpful advice.

This book would have been much more difficult to write without the co-operation of Secretary Rice and her top aides. They never asked me for details about my project—indeed, some may disagree with my conclusions—but

I owe a lot to my family. My oldest son, Andre, was an avid reader as the chapters were completed, while my younger children, Hugo and Mara, kept me company in the basement while quietly playing on their own computer or tiptoeing around my stacks of papers and notes.

This book is dedicated to my wife, Cindy Rich. She has had to endure far too many of my lengthy absences while juggling her own career and the raising of our three children. She had to deal with illnesses, broken limbs, and a flooded kitchen while I called home on a poor cell phone connection from places like Fallujah or Darfur (or, perhaps more annoying, from exotic resort locations like Phuket or the Dead Sea). Writing this book only added to my time away from family life. For nearly a quarter century, Cindy has been my best friend and partner, and I will always be sustained by her love and support.

NOTES

Above my desk at *The Washington Post,* left behind by a previous diplomatic correspondent, hangs a wonderful statement uttered decades ago by Gamal Abdel Nasser, the onetime Egyptian president and father of Arab nationalism: "The genius of you Americans is that you never make clear-cut stupid moves, only complicated stupid moves, which make us wonder at the possibility that there may be something to them—which we are missing."

This is a work of contemporary history, and thus it is limited by the nature of that genre. In reporting and writing this book, I always worried that there was something that I might be missing as I tried to understand the decisions made by Rice and her advisors. Unfortunately, many of the memorandums outlining their thinking and the records of conversations between Rice and foreign officials will remain classified for decades. I conducted scores of interviews exclusively for this book with key participants in the events described here. Whenever possible, I relied on contemporary notes and documents. But memories can be faulty, selective, or hazy—and people sometimes disagree about what exactly transpired. I hope I have provided a rough guide for historians of the future as they puzzle out this period in U.S. foreign policy.

Most of these interviews were conducted on "deep background," meaning the information could be used but not attributed to any particular individual. In the text, I used direct quotes from private conversations only if I could obtain reasonable assurance that the quote was accurate as cited to me, such as checking with as many other people as were in the room at the time. I found that people remember what they said better than what others may have said, so in most cases I have tried to verify the quote with the speaker and have used the words that the speaker recalls. (There are a couple of instances in which several people remember precisely the words of the speaker, while the speaker claims to have no memory of that conversation, so then I have used the majority view of the conversation.) Still, readers should realize that sometimes I am summarizing several hours of conversation into a handful of quotes.

I have tried to provide sourcing for much of the information in this book, but I understand that some readers will be frustrated that so much material is attributed merely to "administration officials." Unfortunately, such is the nature of modern Washington, particularly when writing about events that took place as recently as this year. "Administration officials" always means two or more sources. For a few crucial conversations detailed in this book, I have tried to identify the precise number of sources.

I traveled with Rice on many of the overseas trips described in this book. I do not source events I witnessed with my own eyes. (The State Department Web site maintains an excellent inventory of every public comment uttered by Rice, so I do provide references for all of her public statements cited in the book.) For the few trips I missed, I reconstructed scenes from newspaper and magazine articles (cited in the notes) and interviews with people on Rice's plane, including other reporters.

There are many ways to translate Arab names into English. I followed the style used by the foreign desk of *The Washington Post.*

Introduction: From Birmingham to Beijing

1. Interviews with administration officials, April–May 2006.
2. Interviews with administration officials, September–October 2006. Albright also displayed a portrait of Acheson, who was instrumental in granting her father asylum.
3. Philip D. Zelikow, "Practical Idealism: Present Policy in Historical Perspective," speech given at the Stanford University Institute for International Studies, May 6, 2005. Neither Cheney nor Rumsfeld are true neoconservatives. They care more about the projection of American power. But they surrounded themselves with many neoconservative aides who worked the levers of power within the bureaucracy.
4. Sylvia Carter, "Raising a Glass to the Cocktail," *Newsday,* May 17, 2006, p. B12.
5. George Rush and Joanna Molloy, "As South Drowns, Rice Soaks in N.Y.," *Daily News,* September 2, 2005, p. 32.
6. Ben Widdicombe, "Condoleezza Displeaza Spike," *Daily News,* March 4, 2006, p. 14.
7. Interview with a senior State Department official, December 20, 2006.
8. Interview with Régis Le Sommier, reporter for *Paris Match,* December 7, 2004. Le Sommier recorded the exchange before sitting down for an interview with Bush. He also reported Bush's comments in an article for *Paris Match.*
9. Interviews with administration officials, April–May 2006.
10. Interview with an administration official who heard Bush speak, September 19, 2006.
11. Interview with a senior State Department official, October 17, 2006.
12. Peter Stothard and Nick Danziger, "What Condi Did First," *The Times* (London), April 1, 2006.
13. Condoleezza Rice, "Interview with the NBC Editorial Board," New York City, May 8, 2006. www.state.gov/secretary/rm/2006/66020.htm.
14. Interviews with administration officials, April–May 2006.
15. Ron Suskind, *The Price of Loyalty: George W. Bush, the White House and the Education of Paul O'Neill* (New York: Simon & Schuster, 2004), p. 27.

16. "The National Security Strategy of the United States of America." www.whitehouse .gov/nsc/nss.html.

17. Interviews with U.S. and Japanese officials, June 2005.

18. Interview with a senior State Department official, December 15, 2006.

19. This comparison between Powell and Rice is based on interviews with U.S. officials who traveled with both of them and remarked on the different styles.

20. Interview with Wolfgang Ischinger, March 8, 2006.

21. Interview with Coit D. Blacker, October 3, 2006.

22. Unpublished Rice interview with *Washington Post* reporter Dale Russakoff, June 22, 2001.

23. Interviews with Coit D. Blacker and David Kennedy, October 3, 2006.

24. Michael Getler, "Putting 'The Boondocks' in the Dock," *The Washington Post,* October 19, 2003, p. B6.

25. George Rush and Joanna Molloy, "Steamed Rice: Russian Pol Unleashes Rant," *Daily News,* January 13, 2006, p. 32.

26. Daniel Williams, "In Egyptian Movies, Curses! We're the Heavies," *The Washington Post,* March 20, 2006, p. C1.

27. Condoleezza Rice, "Interview with James Rosen of Fox News," Vilnius, Lithuania, April 21, 2005. www.state.gov/secretary/rm/2005/44976.htm.

28. Dale Russakoff, "Lessons of Might and Right," *The Washington Post* magazine, September 9, 2001. Rice called the reporter a day later to elaborate that she didn't set out to not have a family, but "I couldn't pass on some of the opportunities."

29. Interview with Randy Bean, October 5, 2006.

30. Records of the purchase, Blacker's sale of his one-third share, and the line of credit showing Rice's signature are on file at the Santa Clara County Assessor's Office, San Jose, California. The single-story home, built in 1938, was purchased for $550,000, with a mortgage of $412,000. Bean's full name is Lee Randolph Bean.

31. Interview with Michael McFaul, October 5, 2006.

32. Russakoff, "Lessons."

33. Kathy Olmstead, "Soviet-Studies Expert at Stanford Following an Unconventional Path," *The Boston Globe,* December 19, 1984, p. 2.

34. Bloomberg reporter Janine Zacharia called Rice's office to let them know Barber would be her guest at the White House Correspondents Association dinner in 2006 and wondered if Rice could stop by the Bloomberg table. Within an hour, Zacharia got a call asking if Barber and Zacharia could have lunch with Rice at the State Department, a meal that consisted of balsamic-glazed sirloin atop an arugula salad. Rice asked Barber to autograph the menu for Randy Bean, who is also a football fanatic and lifelong Giants booster. Rice "really studies college and pro football," Zacharia said in a memo recounting the lunch for this book. "It is not a passing fancy. She speaks in great detail."

35. Russakoff, "Lessons."

36. Condoleezza Rice, "Interview with *Essence* Magazine," Washington, D.C., May 25, 2006. www.state.gov/secretary/rm/2006/71813.htm. The photo of John Rice and McNair appeared in Stothard and Danziger, "What Condi Did First." In the unpublished Russakoff interview Rice made it clear that McNair was not a playmate. "I can

remember going to her birthday parties. Denise was just enough older that she wasn't a playmate."

37. Rice's father patrolling with a shotgun has appeared in numerous profiles. Her mother buying Girl Scout cookies is from Ann Reilly Dowd, "What Makes Condi Run," *AARP: The Magazine,* September–October 2005.

38. Wil Haygood, "Honored to Have the Chance," *The Boston Globe,* December 21, 2000, p. A1. In the interview with *Essence* Rice said it was ridiculous.

39. Russakoff, "Lessons."

40. Olmstead, "Soviet-Studies Expert."

41. "To murder Beethoven" quote appeared in Bob Cuddihy, "Steps to la Dolce Vita," *The Scotsman,* August 4, 2000. The $13,000 piano is from Sheryl Henderson Brunt, "The Unflappable Condi Rice," *Christianity Today,* August 22, 2003. "Love at first sight" quote appears in Michael Dobbs, "Josef Korbel's Enduring Foreign Policy Legacy," *The Washington Post,* December 28, 2000, p. A05.

42. Jay Nordlinger, "Star-in-Waiting," *National Review,* August 30, 1999, LI, no. 16.

43. Hans Morgenthau and Kenneth Thompson, *Politics Among Nations,* 6th ed. (New York: McGraw-Hill, 1985), p. 165.

44. Interview with Dennis Ross, August 31, 2006.

45. Norman Kempster, "Mixed Success in Mideast, Africa," *Los Angeles Times,* August 30, 1988, p. 1.

46. Interviews with McFaul and Ross. Rice said she decided she would not feel comfortable in Congress because she is a "strong executive-prerogatives person," in Phil McCombs, "Secret Weapon at the NSC," *The Washington Post,* March 17, 1987, p. D1.

47. Interviews with Ross and other officials at the time. The same point is made in James Mann, *Rise of the Vulcans: The History of Bush's War Cabinet* (New York: Viking, 2004).

48. Jacob Heilbrunn, "Condoleezza Rice: George W's Realist," *World Policy Journal,* Winter 1999/2000, p. 49.

49. Alexander Dallin and Condoleezza Rice, eds., *The Gorbachev Era* (Stanford, Calif.: Stanford Alumni Association, 1986).

50. Casper was quoted saying this was a factor in Nicholas Lemann, "Without a Doubt," *The New Yorker,* October 14, 2002, p. 164.

51. Interview with Kennedy.

52. Interviews with Blacker and other Stanford officials.

53. Interview with Kennedy.

54. Interviews with Blacker and Bean.

55. Condoleezza Rice, "Promoting the National Interest," *Foreign Affairs,* January/February 2000, p. 45.

56. Interview with Kennedy.

57. The Stanford colleague declined to be identified.

58. Lawrence Wilkerson, "Boon or Danger to American Democracy," speech given to the New America Foundation, October 19, 2005.

59. Interview with Blacker.

60. Ibid.

Chapter 1: Rebirth in Paris

1. Cam Simpson, "Rice Trip Focuses on Détente, Discipline, Details," *Chicago Tribune,* February 11, 2005, p. 5; Anne Gearan, "Rice Gives Europe a New Stylish, Intellectual Image of the United States," Associated Press, February 9, 2005. Some details also came from interviews with observers of the event, conducted in August of 2006.

2. Interviews with administration officials, June 2006.

3. Powell would not officially be informed he had lost his job until November 10, five days after Bush's first conversation with Rice, according to Karen DeYoung, *Soldier: The Life of Colin Powell* (New York: Knopf, 2006), p. 6. The account of Rice's decision to accept the job is based on interviews with Bean, Blacker, and administration officials, conducted in September and October of 2006.

4. "President and Prime Minister Blair Discussed Iraq, Middle East," White House news conference transcript. www.whitehouse.gov/news/releases/2004/11/20041112-5.html.

5. Interviews with people who attended the briefings, April–June 2006.

6. The one political appointee to head a regional bureau was Jendayi Frazer, who had been Rice's student at Stanford, as assistant secretary of state for Africa. Frazer is also the only African American that Rice has named to a senior position at the State Department.

7. Interview with an administration official, October 1, 2006.

8. Interview with an administration official who witnessed Rice's outburst, March 2, 2005. The article in question was David Sanger, "U.S. Is Shaping Plan to Pressure North Koreans," *The New York Times,* February 14, 2005, p. 1.

9. Interviews with administration officials, April–October 2006. The account of Rice's decisions in hiring her staff—and the histories of those staffers—is based on more than fifteen interviews and official biographies.

10. Wilkinson's name is on the news release issued by Armey's office calling attention to Gore's comments.

11. After eighteen months, Wilkinson achieved his dream, becoming chief of staff to incoming Treasury secretary Hank Paulson, partly on the recommendation of Zoellick.

12. J. Anthony Holmes, "The Rhetoric and the Reality," *Foreign Service Journal,* September 2005, p. 5.

13. Another key member of that team had been Dennis Ross, head of policy planning under Baker. He later gained fame as Middle East envoy in the Clinton administration.

14. Interview with a senior State Department official, October 17, 2006.

15. Zoellick's role in Sudan policy is covered in a later chapter, but unfortunately his equally important role in China policy does not easily fit in this book. He initiated a high-level dialogue with the Chinese, and, in a critical speech on September 21, 2005, he raised the idea of China becoming a "responsible stakeholder" in the world. The term "stakeholder" does not easily translate into Chinese, and Zoellick's speech prompted an intense debate within China over its meaning. Zoellick developed the speech with little input from other members of the administration—Rice privately thought the stakeholder concept was a little odd—but the Chinese government ultimately came to see it as an important moment in U.S.-China relations.

16. Philip D. Zelikow and Condoleezza Rice, *Germany Unified and Europe Transformed: A Study in Statecraft* (Boston: Harvard University Press, 1995). Zelikow originally wrote the book as a classified history for the State Department.

17. Rice also selected a colleague from Stanford, Stephen D. Krasner, to head the policy planning bureau, an important post. Krasner played a key role in Rice's efforts to overhaul foreign aid. Before selecting Zelikow, Rice asked Bellinger for a memo on the role of the counselor and whether it would conflict with the policy planning bureau.

18. Robert Novak, "Who Runs Our State Department?" *Chicago Sun-Times,* April 10, 2006, p. 35.

19. "John Kerry's State Department," *The New York Sun,* November 21, 2005.

20. Interview with French ambassador Jean-David Levitte, June 16, 2006.

21. One of Hughes's innovations was a campaign-style rapid-response unit that monitored Arabic newscasts and then distributed early-morning summaries. Previously, the government produced fourteen disjointed, stale reports, which came out twenty-four to forty-eight hours after news appeared overseas. Hughes put together a team of people who spoke Arabic and other languages to monitor news reports by computer and on large flat-screen TVs, producing an instant report on the "hot issues" overseas and suggesting messages to counter the bad news. She also created regional spokesperson offices in Dubai and London to handle inquiries from Arab media.

22. Besides Rice's core aides listed earlier, the cheese-and-Coke group included NSC aide Elliott Abrams, future assistant secretary for Europe Daniel Fried, and State Department executive secretary Karl W. Hofmann.

23. Condoleezza Rice, "Opening Remarks," Senate Foreign Relations Committee, Washington, D.C., January 18, 2005. www.state.gov/secretary/rm/2005/40991.htm.

24. John Lewis Gaddis, "Grand Strategy in the Second Term," *Foreign Affairs,* January/February 2005, p. 2. Administration officials explained the significance of the article on Rice's thinking.

25. Interview with Wolfgang Ischinger, March 8, 2006.

26. Interviews with administration officials, August 2006.

27. Condoleezza Rice, "Remarks to the Press En Route London," February 3, 2005. www.state.gov/secretary/rm/2005/41785.htm.

28. Ibid.

29. Condoleezza Rice, "Remarks with British Foreign Secretary Jack Straw," London, United Kingdom, February 4, 2005. www.state.gov/secretary/rm/2005/41834.htm.

30. Condoleezza Rice, "Remarks with German Chancellor Gerhard Schroeder," Berlin, Germany, February 4, 2005. www.state.gov/secretary/rm/2005/41845.htm.

31. Condoleezza Rice, "Remarks at the Institut d'Etudes Politiques de Paris," Paris, France, February 8, 2005. www.state.gov/secretary/rm/2005/41973.htm.

32. Interview with Levitte.

33. Elaine Sciolino, "The French Are Charmed and Jarred by 'Chère Condi,'" *The New York Times,* February 10, 2005, p. A6.

34. Interviews with administration officials, May 2006.

35. Gearan, "Rice Gives Europe."

36. Simpson, "Rice Trip."

37. Condoleezza Rice, "Interview with James Rosen of Fox News," Paris, France, February 9, 2005. www.state.gov/secretary/rm/2005/42032.htm.
38. "Rice Declares New Page with EU Despite Iran Strains," Agence France-Presse, February 9, 2005.
39. Interviews with administration officials, April 2006. Rice officially announced the shift on March 11, 2005.
40. Interviews with U.S. and European officials, April–September 2006.
41. Robin Givhan, "Condoleezza Rice's Commanding Clothes," *The Washington Post,* February 25, 2006, p. C1.
42. Interview with Ischinger.
43. Interview with an administration official, May 26, 2006.
44. Interviews with Bill Sammon and other *Washington Times* personnel present at the meeting, December 2006. Blankley was seated between Sammon and Wilkinson, and Sammon saw Wilkinson pass the note to Blankley during the interview. Sammon said Blankley told him about Wilkinson's note suggesting the presidential question after he popped his question. Sammon said he was "a little bit shocked" to learn of the note after Rice had answered so demurely. Another *Washington Times* reporter confirmed he saw the note. Both Blankley and Wilkinson said they have no memory of the incident. A *Washington Times* editor graciously listened to a tape of the interview to identify Sammon as the questioner.
45. Condoleezza Rice, "Interview with *Washington Times* Editorial Board," Washington, D.C., March 11, 2005. www.state.gov/secretary/rm/2005/43341.htm. Her comments did not reflect the fact that she once considered running for Congress.

Chapter 2: Passage to New Delhi

1. Wilkinson added another innovation: cultural airport greeters. Instead of Rice being met by protocol chiefs or foreign ministers, he requested that the secretary be greeted by a country's pop culture heroes, especially sports or music stars, guaranteeing extensive coverage by the local media. Because Rice tended to arrive at night, this also ensured that she was already on the front page of the morning newspapers when she arrived for meetings with top officials, which in its own way was a form of intimidation. Not every country agreed to this scheme: Middle Eastern countries flatly refused to allow it, but it was successful elsewhere. In Romania, she was met by Olympic legend Nadia Comaneci, young Romanian Olympic gymnasts, and Special Olympians. In Belgium, the media widely covered her meeting with cyclist Eddy Merckx, who won the Tour de France five times. And in Tokyo, Rice was greeted at the airport by Konishiki, a sumo champion clad in a black kimono. A photo of the six-hundred-pound wrestler hugging the much smaller Rice even appeared on the front page of the *Financial Times.* The next day, Wilkinson paraded through the press cabin of Rice's plane, holding up the newspaper, and declared: "You laugh because you do not understand." The program ended after Wilkinson left the State Department.
2. Condoleezza Rice, "Promoting the National Interest," *Foreign Affairs,* January/February 2000, p. 45.
3. Interview with a senior State Department official, October 17, 2006.
4. Interviews with administration officials, April–May 2006.

5. Interviews with administration officials, March–April 2006.

6. Interview with Ashley Tellis, former aide to Blackwill, March 28, 2006.

7. Robert D. Blackwill, "The India Imperative," *The National Interest,* Summer 2005, pp. 9–17.

8. Colin L. Powell, "Interview with Glenn Kessler and Peter Slevin of *The Washington Post,*" Washington, D.C., October 3, 2003. www.state.gov/secretary/former/powell/remarks/2003/25139.htm.

9. The National Security Strategy of the United States of America. www.whitehouse.gov/nsc/nss.html.

10. The Gilpatric Report on Nuclear Proliferation, January 1965, National Security Archive Electronic Briefing Book No. 1, "The United States, China, and the Bomb." www.gwu.edu/~nsarchiv/NSAEBB/NSAEBB1/nsaebb1.htm.

11. Interview with Indian ambassador Ronen Sen, March 24, 2006.

12. "Just after the NPT India became a nuclear power and got left out of the nuclear club. That's really what happened. You know, the five who are so-called grandfathered into the NPT—the United States, Russia, China, France, and Great Britain—it's almost an accident of history that they were in, you got the NPT and you were grandfathered in." Condoleezza Rice, "Interview with the *New York Post* Editorial Board," New York City, September 25, 2006. www.state.gov/secretary/rm/2006/73107.htm. Her comments minimized the fact that India tested a nuclear device six years after the NPT was negotiated.

13. The preceding three paragraphs are based on interviews with administration officials involved in the discussions, March–May 2006.

14. Interview with a senior State Department official, October 17, 2006.

15. Condoleezza Rice, "Remarks En Route to India," March 15, 2005. www.state.gov/secretary/rm/2005/43465.htm.

16. Condoleezza Rice, "Remarks with Indian Foreign Minister Natwar Singh, New Delhi, India," March 16, 2005. www.state.gov/secretary/rm/2005/43490.htm.

17. C. Raja Mohan, *Impossible Allies: Nuclear India, United States and the Global Order* (New Delhi: Indian Research Press, 2006), pp. 57–60. In interviews, Indian officials confirmed this account.

18. Interview with Indian foreign secretary Shyam Saran, March 28, 2006.

19. The memo was described by administration officials, May 2006.

20. Interview with a senior State Department official, October 17, 2006.

21. Interviews with administration officials, March–April 2006.

22. "Background Briefing by Administration Officials on U.S.–South Asia Relations," March 25, 2005. www.state.gov/r/pa/prs/ps/2005/43853.htm. Mohan first disclosed that Zelikow was "administration official number one."

23. Mohan, *Impossible Allies,* pp. 71–72.

24. Interview with an administration official, March 24, 2006.

25. The merger had been recommended by the State Department's inspector general, but Joseph left it the hands of political appointees, who used the consolidation to settle ideological scores. See Glenn Kessler, "Administration Critics Chafe at State Dept. Shuffle," *The Washington Post,* February 21, 2006, p. A4. Zelikow looked into the merger after he read a Knight-Ridder article about the fallout (Warren Strobel, "State

Department Sees Exodus of Weapons Experts," Knight-Ridder, February 8, 2006). He sent a memo to Rice saying that he had concluded it had been handled poorly.

26. Interviews with administration officials. The account of the deliberations leading up to the July 2005 agreement is based on interviews with more than twenty U.S. and Indian officials in March 2006, including some conducted by or with my *Washington Post* colleague Dafna Lizner. She contributed reporting to an article I wrote on the agreement: Glenn Kessler, "India Nuclear Deal May Face Hard Sell," *The Washington Post,* April 3, 2006, p. A1

27. The United States cut off the supply for the Tarapur reactors after India's 1974 nuclear test, which India viewed as a violation of U.S. obligations made when it built the plants. The French, the Chinese, and the Russians had occasionally provided a new supply of fuel, but Tarapur was running out again in 2006–2007.

28. Alex Perry, "Why Bush Is Courting India," *Time,* February 28, 2006. The article attributed this anecdote to Singh press advisor Sanjaya Baru, p. 28.

29. This is the view of U.S. officials. Indian officials suggest they convinced Rice to make another stab at reaching a deal. Mohan, *Impossible Allies,* pp. 150–51.

30. The term India wanted to use—"voluntary safeguards"—was a reference to the "voluntary offer" safeguards agreements of the five recognized nuclear-weapon states, which permit but do not require the IAEA to apply safeguards to designated facilities. They also allow the recognized nuclear states to modify the list of facilities designated as eligible for safeguards.

31. George W. Bush, "President, Indian Prime Minister Singh Exchange Toasts," Washington, D.C., July 18, 2005. www.whitehouse.gov/news/releases/2005/07/20050718-12 .html.

32. Interview with Saran.

33. The memo was described by an administration official who read it, March 16, 2006.

34. Interview with a senior State Department official, October 17, 2006.

35. The official asked not to be identified.

36. Interview with Sen.

37. The "nonpaper" was described by administration officials.

38. Interviews with U.S. and Indian officials, March–May 2006.

39. "Text of Indian Premier's Address to Parliament," February 27, 2006. www.pmindia .gov.in/speeches.htm.

40. Condoleezza Rice, "Briefing by Secretary Rice and National Security Adviser Hadley Aboard Air Force One," Shannon, Ireland, February 28, 2006. www.state.gov/r/pa/ ei/wh/rem/62271.htm.

41. Interviews with U.S. and Indian officials, September–October 2006.

42. Interviews with administration officials, March 2006.

43. After the House approved legislation supporting the deal in July 2006, lawmakers were stunned to learn that the administration planned to impose sanctions on two Indian firms for selling missile parts to Iran. The congressionally mandated report on the sanctions was late, and the sanctions decision undercut administration claims that India had a stellar nonproliferation record. Administration officials claim they briefed two staff members the morning of the vote about the pending sanctions, but they acknowledge that most House members were unaware of the action. House International

Relations Committee chairman Henry Hyde (R-Ill.) was so angry that he drafted a letter recommending a criminal investigation of the State Department's handling of the report, according to a congressional official who saw the letter. But the letter was never sent.

Chapter 3: Showdown near Seoul

1. The display screen only showed the State Department seal when reporters were permitted in the room. It was described by an administration official.
2. Condoleezza Rice, "Remarks to Troops at Command Post Tango, Command Post Tango Operations Center, Republic of Korea," March 19, 2005. www.state.gov/secretary/rm/2005/43652.htm.
3. Condoleezza Rice, "Remarks at Sophia University, Tokyo, Japan," March 19, 2005. www.state.gov/secretary/rm/2005/43655.htm.
4. Interviews with administration officials, April–May 2006.
5. Interviews with Clinton administration officials at the meeting, November 2003.
6. Interviews with administration officials, April–May 2006.
7. Interviews with Powell aides, January 2003.
8. Interviews with administration officials, November 2003. They suggested they had plotted other ways of killing the agreement. Thus, even if intelligence analysts had not concluded North Korean had a uranium enrichment program, this crisis over its nuclear program would have taken place—though perhaps the death of the Agreed Framework would have been more gradual.
9. The preceding two paragraphs are based on interviews with several administration officials, November 2003.
10. Interview with David Straub, Korea desk official at the time and one of the officials who met with the North Koreans in New York, June 23, 2006. Speaking to reporters on April 28, 2003, Powell said it was "nonsense" that State had tried to deceive others in the administration and asserted the North Korean reprocessing claim was not "particularly new or newsworthy."
11. See, for instance, Glenn Kessler, "Bush Signals Patience on North Korea Is Waning," *The Washington Post*, March 4, 2004, p. A14, and Glenn Kessler, "Impact from the Shadows," *The Washington Post*, October 5, 2004, p. A1.
12. Interviews with administration officials conducted in 2003 for an article on Rice's management of the National Security Council, though this quote does not appear in the article. Glenn Kessler and Peter Slevin, "Rice Fails to Repair Rifts, Officials Say," *The Washington Post*, October 12, 2003, p. A1. Straub, an advocate of diplomacy, went public with this criticism of Rice in a speech in Arlington, Virginia, on June 21, 2006.
13. Interviews with administration officials, May 2006.
14. Condoleezza Rice, "Remarks to the Press in China, Beijing," March 21, 2005. www.state.gov/secretary/rm/2005/43678.htm.
15. Interviews with administration officials, May 2006.
16. Glenn Kessler, "China Rejected U.S. Suggestion to Cut Off Oil to Pressure North Korea," *The Washington Post*, May 7, 2005, p. A11. There have long been rumors that China had shut down an oil pipeline to pressure the North Koreans. In March 2003, unnamed diplomats in Seoul were quoted in news reports as saying that China had

shut down its pipeline for three days, supposedly to convince North Korea to attend the three-way talks in Beijing. But many U.S officials now doubt that the reported shutdown was related to nuclear diplomacy.

17. The conversation was described by three administration officials in the room at the time; a fourth official said he had no memory of it. Interviews conducted May–October 2006.

18. Korean Central News Agency, July 9, 2005.

19. The account of Hill's meeting with the North Koreans and Rice's conversation with Li is based on interviews with five administration officials, May–October 2006. After North Korea tested a nuclear bomb in 2006 and the administration was criticized for not having held bilateral talks with North Korea, Rice would frequently cite Hill's dinner with Kim as evidence that the administration allowed bilateral contacts. She did not mention that Hill ignored his instructions or that she had been angry with the Chinese.

20. Congressional Research Service, "North Korean Counterfeiting of U.S. Currency," March 22, 2006. www.fas.org/sgp/crs/row/RL33324.pdf.

21. Interviews with Treasury Department officials, November 2005.

22. Interviews with administration officials, May 2006.

23. Interview on CNN broadcast, July 25, 2005.

24. Interview with an administration official involved in the call, August 16, 2005.

25. C. Kenneth Quinones, a former State Department official who held unofficial back-channel talks with the North Koreans during this period, said that from the start of the crisis the North Koreans consistently wanted light-water reactors. "If father could get two, son's got to have two," he was told. See "Speech at the U.S.-Korea Institute of Johns Hopkins–SAIS," Washington, D.C., November 2, 2006.

26. Saul Hudson, "U.S. Says N. Korean Right to Nuke Power No Deal-Breaker," Reuters, August 23, 2005.

27. In the fourth draft, a key sentence read: "The United States stated that it recognizes and respects the sovereignty of the DPRK, and that it undertakes to take steps to normalize its relations with the DPRK, subject to bilateral policies and dialogue." But, at the insistence of Washington, that sentence was changed to: "The DPRK and the United States undertook to respect each other's sovereignty, exist peacefully together, and take steps to normalize their relations subject to their respective bilateral policies." Such differences speak volumes in diplomacy, since any reference to bilateral dialogue was removed and the onus was shifted from just the United States to both countries. The fourth draft was obtained from a confidential source.

28. Interviews with U.S. and Asian diplomats, May–October 2006.

29. The incident about "peaceful coexistence" was described by five administration officials and two diplomats from other countries. Interviews conducted October–December 2006.

30. Interviews with administration officials, April–May 2006. During Rood's confirmation hearings to be assistant secretary of state for international security, he told the Senate Foreign Relations Committee on August 2, 2006, that he had a role in preparing the statement, but that the "final calls" on its content were made "at pay grades above mine."

31. Korean Central News Agency, September 20, 2005.
32. David L. Asher, "The North Korean Criminal State, Its Ties to Organized Crime, and the Possibility of WMD Proliferation," Nautilus Institute Policy Forum, November 15, 2005. www.nautilus.org/force/security/0592Asher.html.
33. Interviews with administration officials, May–October 2006.
34. The conversation between Hu and Bush was described by three administration officials, August–October 2006.

Chapter 4: Exposed in Riyadh

1. Administration officials in interviews described the gift of the abaya and Rice's reaction to it, March–April 2006.
2. Robin Wright and Glenn Kessler, "Bush Aims for 'Greater Mideast' Plan," *The Washington Post*, February 9, 2004, p. A1.
3. Peter Slevin, "Bush to Cast War as Part of Regional Strategy," *The Washington Post*, February 26, 2003, p. A19.
4. George W. Bush, "Second Inaugural Address," January 20, 2005. www.whitehouse.gov/news/releases/2005/01/20050120-1.html. Peter Baker of *The Washington Post* counted the number of Bush's references to freedom for an article in the *Post*.
5. Aluf Benn, "Israel and Arab Democracy," *The National Interest*, Summer 2005, pp. 44–48.
6. Interview with a senior State Department official, December 15, 2006.
7. See Jeffrey Goldberg, "Breaking Ranks," *The New Yorker*, October 31, 2005, and Glenn Kessler, "Rice Goes from the Inside to the Front," *The Washington Post*, January 17, 2005, p. A1.
8. Goldberg, "Breaking Ranks."
9. Interviews with administration officials, June 2005.
10. Rice's intervention in the Nour case was first reported in Jonathan Karl, "Condiplomacy," *The Weekly Standard*, April 4, 2005. It was confirmed by administration officials.
11. Condoleezza Rice, "Remarks with Egyptian Foreign Minister Ahmed Aboul Gheit," Washington, D.C., February 15, 2006. www.state.gov/secretary/rm/2005/42325.htm.
12. Interviews with administration officials, June 2006–January 2007. Wilkinson's e-mail was provided by an administration official.
13. Rice's approach was described by a senior State Department official, October 31, 2006.
14. Condoleezza Rice, "Joint Press Availability with Egyptian Foreign Minister Ahmed Aboul Gheit," Sharm el-Sheikh, Egypt, June 20, 2005. www.state.gov/secretary/rm/2005/48325.htm.
15. Condoleezza Rice, "Remarks at the American University," Cairo, Egypt, June 20, 2005. www.state.gov/secretary/rm/2005/48328.htm.
16. Condoleezza Rice, "Remarks En Route to Brussels, Belgium," June 21, 2005. www.state.gov/secretary/rm/2005/48430.htm.
17. Condoleezza Rice, "Interview on ABC News with Jonathan Karl," Cairo, Egypt, June 20, 2005. www.state.gov/secretary/rm/2005/48369.htm.

18. Interviews with administration officials, May–June 2006.
19. Condoleezza Rice, "Joint Press Availability with Saudi Foreign Minister Saud al-Faisal," Riyadh, Saudi Arabia, June 20, 2005. www.state.gov/secretary/rm/2005/48390.htm.
20. Turki's quotes are from the notes of a source who attended the dinner.
21. Rice, "Remarks En Route to Brussels, Belgium."
22. Condoleezza Rice, "Roundtable with Saudi Media," Riyadh, Saudi Arabia, June 21, 2005. www.state.gov/secretary/rm/2005/48401.htm.

Chapter 5: Rumble in Khartoum

1. Interviews with administration officials in the meeting, July 2005.
2. *The Washington Post* reporter Nora Bousany translated Bashir's remarks for this book after watching a videotape of the incident.
3. Interviews with administration officials, July 2005.
4. Colin L. Powell, "Press Briefing En Route to Kenya, Nairobi," Kenya, October 21, 2003. www.state.gov/secretary/former/powell/remarks/2003/25501.htm. His offer to the leaders was described by administration officials, November 2003.
5. This conclusion is widely accepted by analysts. Two excellent overviews are Marisa Katz's "A Very Long Engagement," *The New Republic,* May 15, 2006, and Samantha Power's "Dying in Darfur," *The New Yorker,* August 20, 2004.
6. This was UN Security Council Resolution 1593.
7. Interviews with administration officials, June–August 2006.
8. Alex de Waal, "Tragedy in Darfur," *Boston Review,* October/November 2004.
9. Interviews with administration officials, July 2005.
10. Jonathan Karl, "The Darfur Disaster," *The Weekly Standard,* May 2, 2005.
11. After Garang's death, the capital was moved to Juba by his successor and the United States opened a consulate there.
12. Condoleezza Rice, "Remarks at the Independent Women's Forum upon Receiving Woman of Valor Award," Washington, D.C., May 10, 2006. www.state.gov/secretary/rm/2006/66139.htm.
13. Condoleezza Rice, "Address to the Africa Society of the National Summit on Africa," Washington, D.C., September 27, 2006. www.state.gov/secretary/rm/2006/73259.htm.
14. Interview with a senior State Department official, October 22, 2006.
15. Ibrahim Ali Suleiman, "African Union Accuses Government, Janjaweed of Combined Attacks on Civilians," Associated Press, October 1, 2005.
16. Emily Wax, "U.S. Envoy Scolds, Warns Squabbling Sudan Rebels," *The Washington Post,* November 8, 2006, p. A26.
17. Jonathan Karl, "Dead End in Darfur," *The Weekly Standard,* December 12, 2005.
18. Joel Brinkley, "Darfur Crisis Defies Even Redoubled U.S. Peace Efforts," *The New York Times,* November 13, 2005, p. A14.
19. Interviews with administration officials, March 2006.
20. The account of the Abuja negotiations is based on interviews with Zoellick, UK development minister Hilary Benn, EU representative Pekka Haavisto, African Union consultant Alex de Waal, and two rebel officials, conducted in May 2006. Zoellick

and de Waal quoted from notes they took during meetings. I also relied on a confidential report written by an international diplomat present at the talks.

21. Both de Waal and Haavisto provided accounts of Zoellick's comments before I interviewed Zoellick. De Waal took extensive notes. Zoellick spoke without notes, but confirmed his remarks to Minnawi.

22. This exchange is from Zoellick's notes.

23. I obtained a copy of the eleven-paragraph confidential cable, which had been circulated by Cameron Hume, the chargé d'affaires in Khartoum.

Chapter 6: Sleepless in Jerusalem

1. The Forum for the Future was created at the G-8 meeting of industrial democracies hosted by President Bush at Sea Island, Georgia, in 2004. It was part of Bush's effort to promote democracy in the Middle East, but since it was created at the G-8, responsibility for cohosting the annual conference rotates among the G-8 countries.

2. The account of Cheney's visit to Iraq is based on interviews with four administration officials, September–December 2006.

3. The conversation in the car is based on interviews with four administration officials, June–October 2006.

4. Bush publicly never backed off that statement, but in 2002 he privately rebuked Sharon when the Israeli leader began to repeat the comment to the president. Bush interrupted Sharon when he began to say he was a "man of peace and security," according to a witness to the exchange. "I know you are a man of security," Bush said. "I want you to work harder on the peace part." Then, adding a bit of colloquial language that at first seemed to baffle Sharon, Bush jabbed: "I said you were a man of peace. I want you to know I took immense crap for that."

5. Interviews with administration officials, June 2002.

6. Interviews with U.S. and Jordanian officials, October 2003. Bush made the private remarks to the king in September 2003.

7. Interview with former Sharon chief of staff Dov Weissglas, January 20, 2007.

8. Karen DeYoung, *Soldier: The Life of Colin Powell* (New York: Knopf, 2006), p. 358.

9. Ibid., p. 383.

10. Interviews with administration officials, January–July 2006.

11. Interview with Weissglas. One U.S. official who witnessed the Rice-Weissglas exchange regarded it as one of her finest moments as national security advisor. In an interview in April 2003, the official recalled that Rice told Weissglas: "If we have the same conversation one week from now, you will have serious problems in this building and you will have it with me." Weissglas does not recall that specific comment, but he said that Rice's controlled anger was the main reason for the quick Israeli withdrawal.

12. The Quartet was a Bush administration innovation designed to coordinate policy and avoid public spats with the Europeans and the United Nations over Palestinian issues by giving them a formal role in the peace process.

13. Interview with Weissglas.

14. For an excellent reconstruction of Sharon's decision making on Gaza, see Aluf Benn, "The Silent Partner," *Haaretz*, December 30, 2006.

15. Interview with Weissglas.
16. Weissglas said that in response to the Americans, the Israelis produced three West Bank withdrawal options—four settlements, seventeen settlements, and all settlements that would not be included in a peace deal. They only shared the first two options with the Americans. To the Israelis' surprise, Rice and her aides argued Israel should only abandon four small settlements, not seventeen, on the theory that leaving Gaza was difficult enough.
17. Daniel Dombey, "Scowcroft Lambasts Bush's Unilateralism," *Financial Times,* October 14, 2004; Jeffrey Goldberg, "Breaking Ranks."
18. Interview with Weissglas.
19. Interviews with administration officials, August 2006.
20. The Abrams and Welch profiles are based on interviews and official biographies.
21. Interviews with Palestinian officials, November 2006.
22. George W. Bush, "President Welcomes Palestinian President Abbas to the White House," May 26, 2005. www.whitehouse.gov/news/releases/2005/05/20050526 .html.
23. Interviews with administration officials, September–October 2006.
24. According to Weissglas, Abbas privately told the Israelis he had deep misgivings about holding elections and did not want them to take place, but he could not resist the pressure of the Americans.
25. Andy Newman, "How Old Friends of Israel Gave $14 Million to Help the Palestinians," *The New York Times,* August 18, 2005, p. B1.
26. Interviews with Palestinian officials, September 2006.
27. Interview with a senior State Department official, October 22, 2006.
28. The account of the Rafah negotiations is based on interviews with U.S., Israeli, and Palestinian officials, September 2006–January 2007.
29. Interview with Weissglas.
30. Interview with a senior State Department official, October 22, 2006.
31. Interviews with administration officials, September–November 2006. Asked about this account, Wolfensohn said "it is not impossible" he made the comment about never being "treated this way in seventy-two years," but he does not specifically recall saying it. He confirmed the rest of his remarks.
32. Anne Gearan, "Top Mideast Envoy Expresses Frustration as Israeli-Palestinian Talks Drag On," Associated Press, November 14, 2005.
33. Condoleezza Rice, "Joint Press Availability with European Union High Representative Javier Solana and Quartet Special Envoy Jim Wolfensohn," Jerusalem, November 15, 2005. www.state.gov/secretary/rm/2005/56890.htm.
34. "Periodic Report, Office of the Special Envoy for Disengagement," April 2006.
35. Interviews with U.S. and Israeli officials, September–October 2006. In the wake of the 2006 Lebanon war prompted by Hezbollah, U.S. officials recall their response to Livni with bitter irony and say, in retrospect, she was right.
36. Interview with Weissglas.
37. Interviews with U.S. and Palestinian officials, November 2006.
38. Interviews with Palestinian officials, November 2006. Palestinian officials later ruefully said they never realized that the political types like Wilkinson and Hughes had

the real clout in the administration, not careerists like Welch, and that they should have paid more attention to them.

39. Interviews with administration officials, May 2006.

40. Scott Wilson and Glenn Kessler, "U.S. Funds Enter Fray in Palestinian Elections," *The Washington Post,* January 22, 2006, p. A1.

41. Interviews with administration officials, October–December 2006.

42. The account of Rice's morning is based largely on an interview with a senior State Department official, with supplemental material from other administration officials, October 2006.

43. Rice's quotes come from the notes of an administration official present for the phone calls and staff discussion, interview conducted September 2006.

44. Henry Hyde, opening remarks at the International Affairs Budget Request for Fiscal Year 2007, Committee on International Relations, House of Representatives, February 16, 2006.

45. Interviews with administration officials, February 2006.

46. Condoleezza Rice, "Remarks with Egyptian Foreign Minister Ahmed Aboul Gheit," Cairo, Egypt, February 21, 2006. www.state.gov/secretary/rm/2006/61811.htm.

47. Condolezza Rice, "Remarks with Saudi Foreign Minister Saud al-Faysal bin Abd al-Aziz Al Saud, After Meeting," Riyadh, Saudi Arabia, February 22, 2006. www.state.gov/secretary/rm/2006/61910.htm.

48. Interviews with administration officials, February 2006.

49. Interview with Saad Eddin Ibrahim, February 22, 2006.

50. Condoleezza Rice, "Interview on Egyptian Television with Mervat Mohsen," Cairo, Egypt, February 22, 2006. www.state.gov/secretary/rm/2006/61837.htm.

51. Rice, "Remarks with Saudi Foreign Minister."

52. Under threat of Treasury Department action, Arab banks became reluctant to directly transfer tens of millions of dollars to the Hamas-led government, ultimately allowing for a relatively effective embargo at first. But European officials successfully pressed to provide funds directly to the Palestinians through a "temporary" mechanism that became increasingly permanent.

53. "Mubarak Says Egypt Won Over Rice on Democracy," Reuters, March 1, 2006.

54. Christine Spolar, "In Interview, Jailed Politician Says He's Egypt's 'Model of Repression,'" *Chicago Tribune,* March 5, 2006.

55. Condoleezza Rice, "Press Roundtable Interview," Washington, D.C., March 23, 2007. www.state.gov/secretary/rm/2007/mar/82158.htm.

56. Condoleezza Rice, "Remarks with Egyptian Foreign Minister Aboul Gheit," Aswan, Egypt, March 25, 2007. www.state.gov/secretary/rm/2007/mar/82166.htm. The official transcript does not record Aboul Gheit's "thank you," but I witnessed the exchange and transcribed it.

Chapter 7: A Question in Kiev

1. Dana Priest, "CIA Holds Terror Suspects in Secret Prisons," *The Washington Post,* November 2, 2005, p. A1. Priest would win a Pulitzer Prize for beat reporting for this article and others on CIA activities.

2. Howard Kurtz, "Bush Presses Editors on Security," *The Washington Post,* December 26, 2005, p. C1.
3. "EU Warning to States Hosting CIA Prisons," *The Guardian Weekly,* December 2, 2005.
4. Interview with Wolfgang Ischinger, March 8, 2006.
5. An excellent history of the first-term debate over detainees appears in Karen De-Young, *Soldier: The Life of Colin Powell* (New York: Knopf, 2006), pp. 364–72.
6. In June 2005, for instance, Zelikow and acting deputy defense secretary Gordon R. England had written a joint memo calling on the administration to seek congressional approval for its detention policies, for a return to the minimum standards of treatment in the Geneva Conventions, and for eventually closing the Guantánamo detention facility. Defense Secretary Rumsfeld was so angered by the proposal that he ordered all copies of the memo destroyed. See Tim Golden, "Detainee Memo Created Divide in White House," *The New York Times,* October 1, 2006, p. A1.
7. Interviews with administration officials, May–June 2006. See also Daniel Klaidman, Stuart Taylor, Jr., and Evan Thomas, "Palace Revolt," *Newsweek,* February 6, 2006, and Chitra Ragavan, "Cheney's Guy," *U.S. News & World Report,* May 29, 2006.
8. Dana Priest and Robin Wright, "Cheney Fights for Detainee Policy," *The Washington Post,* November 7, 2005, p. A1.
9. Interviews with administration officials, May 2006.
10. Dana Priest, "Wrongful Imprisonment: Anatomy of a CIA Mistake," *The Washington Post,* December 4, 2004, p. A1.
11. Condoleezza Rice, "Remarks upon Her Departure for Europe," Andrews Air Force Base, December 5, 2005. www.state.gov/secretary/rm/2005/57602.htm.
12. Condoleezza Rice, "Remarks En Route to Germany," Berlin, Germany, December 5, 2005. www.state.gov/secretary/rm/2005/57643.htm.
13. Interviews with administration officials, October 2006.
14. Daniel Fried, "Remarks at the National Conference of Editorial Writers," Washington, D.C., May 2, 2006. Released by the State Department.
15. Interview with Ischinger.
16. Condoleezza Rice, "Press Availability with Ukrainian President Viktor Yushchenko," Kiev, Ukraine, December 7, 2005. www.state.gov/secretary/rm/2005/57723.htm.
17. Interviews with three administration officials, October 2006.
18. Interviews with administration officials, June 2006.
19. Interview with Ben Bot, December 8, 2006.
20. When President Bush signs bills, he often issues "signing statements" that suggest he does not entirely accept the legislation. His signing statement on the McCain amendment was no exception, raising questions about whether he truly accepted it. Some scholars have suggested that the McCain amendment was carefully worded to allow some agencies to delegate the dirty work of CID to foreign governments or private contractors.
21. Dafna Linzer and Glenn Kessler, "Decision to Move Detainees Resolved Two-Year Debate Among Bush Advisers," *The Washington Post,* September 8, 2006, p. A1. Bush's decision resolved the initial use of the secret prisons, but the debate over the

administration's detainee policies would continue both inside and outside the administration, with an aggressive stance continually pushed by Cheney's office in opposition to the State Department.

Chapter 8: Double Dates in Baghdad

1. Interview with a senior State Department official, October 22, 2006.
2. *The Washington Post* poll, June 7–11, 2006, among one thousand randomly selected adults nationwide. The margin of error for overall results is plus or minus three percentage points. The poll also found that 52 percent had a favorable view of Rice and 27 percent had an unfavorable view, a far better ratio than any other senior Bush administration official. Of the people with a favorable impression of Rice, 58 percent said it was mostly based on their view of her professional abilities.
3. The full history of Rice's involvement in the Iraq War decisions as national security advisor has been carefully documented in such works as Bob Woodward's *Plan of Attack* (New York: Simon & Schuster, 2004) and *State of Denial* (New York: Simon & Schuster, 2006). The administration's failures in the occupation of Iraq have been well described in such books as Thomas E. Ricks's *Fiasco* (New York: Penguin, 2006) and Rajiv Chandrasekaran's *Imperial Life in the Emerald City* (New York: Knopf, 2006). An excellent account of Rice's poor management of the war and its aftermath as national security advisor is Chitra Ragavan, "Who Lost Iraq?" *U.S. News & World Report,* November 27, 2006. My aim in this chapter is not to repeat this fine reporting but to illustrate a key period in Rice's engagement in Iraq as secretary of state.
4. Adrian Butler, "Bring Back Kids' Rail Warnings," *Liverpool Echo,* March 22, 2006, p. 12.
5. Jack Straw, UK foreign secretary, "Remarks at the Blackburn Institute's Frank A. Nix Lecture, University of Alabama," Tuscaloosa, Alabama, October 21, 2005. www .state.gov/secretary/rm/2005/55423.htm.
6. Interview with an administration official, May 2006.
7. Ben MacIntyre, "4,000 Cops in Blackburn, Lancashire. Oh Boy, What a Second Date," *The Times* (London), April 1, 2006.
8. Sam Lister, "Policing Condoleezza Visit Costs 300,000 Pounds," *Daily Post* (Liverpool), April 27, 2006.
9. MacIntyre, "4,000 Cops."
10. Condoleezza Rice, "Remarks at BBC Today—Chatham House Lecture," Ewood Park, Blackburn, United Kingdom, March 31, 2006. www.state.gov/secretary/rm/ 2006/63969.htm.
11. I recorded Hurd's comments.
12. Joel Brinkley, "Rice, in England, Concedes U.S. 'Tactical Errors' in Iraq," *The New York Times,* April 1, 2006, p. A9. The early edition headline was "Rice Faces Cancellations and Catcalls on British Visit."
13. Interview with a senior State Department official, December 15, 2006.
14. See, for instance, Glenn Kessler and Bradley Graham, "Rice's Rebuilding Plan Hits Snags," *The Washington Post,* January 15, 2006, p. A24, and Bradley Graham and Glenn Kessler, "Iraq Security for U.S. Teams Uncertain," *The Washington Post,* March 3, 2006, p. A11.

15. Interviews with administration officials, December 2006.

16. Interviews with administration officials, September 2006.

17. Interviews with administration officials, May–October 2006.

18. Interviews with administration officials, April 2006.

19. Statistics provided by an administration official, April 2006.

20. John Ward Anderson and Jonathan Finer, "The Battle for Baghdad's Future," *The Washington Post,* April 9, 2006, p. A17.

21. Charles J. Hanley, "U.S. Building Its Largest Embassy in Iraq," Associated Press, April 14, 2006.

22. Interviews with British and U.S. officials, April–September 2006.

23. Jonathan Finer, "Pressure on Shiites Is Giving the U.S. New Ally in Sunnis," *The Washington Post,* April 13, 2006, p. A17.

24. Condoleezza Rice, "Remarks with British Foreign Secretary Jack Straw En Route to Baghdad," Iraq, April 2, 2006. www.state.gov/secretary/rm/2006/63990.htm.

25. Details on the dinner and Rice's meeting with Jafari were provided through interviews with administration officials, April 26, 2006, and October 22, 2006.

26. Condoleezza Rice, "Interview with Libby Leist of NBC," Baghdad, Iraq, April 2, 2006. www.state.gov/secretary/rm/2006/63995.htm. The NBC Baghdad bureau thought Rice's comment about Baghdad's beauty was so funny that they blew up the quote on a banner that was strung across the wall of the office.

27. Condoleezza Rice, "Remarks with British Foreign Secretary Jack Straw," Baghdad, Iraq, April 3, 2006. www.state.gov/secretary/rm/2006/64036.htm.

28. Ann Treneman, "Just a Minute, Isn't That Hugh Grant," *The Times* (London), April 26, 2006, p. 14.

29. Editorial, "Condi's Iraq Stumble," *The Wall Street Journal,* April 6, 2006.

30. Lieutenant General Greg Newbold, "Why Iraq Was a Mistake," *Time,* April 17, 2006, p. 42.

31. Condoleezza Rice, "Interview on CBS *Face the Nation* with Bob Schieffer," April 30, 2006. www.state.gov/secretary/rm/2006/65493.htm.

32. Donald H. Rumsfeld, "Radio Interview with Scott Hennen, WDAY Radio, Fargo, N.D.," April 4, 2006. www.defenselink.mil/transcripts/2006/tr20060404-12766 .html.

33. Monifa Thomas, "Powell: U.S. Made 'Serious Mistakes' in Iraq," *Chicago Sun-Times,* April 9, 2006.

34. The letter was described by administration officials, June–October 2006.

35. Nelson Hernandez and K. I. Ibrahim, "Top Shiites Nominate a Premier for Iraq," *The Washington Post,* April 22, 2006, p. A1.

36. Khalilzad was installed ambassador in June 2005 largely because when he was envoy to Afghanistan he demonstrated that he could work behind the scenes and prod warring tribes to work together. Often officials in Washington did not want to know the details of the midnight deals he was reaching. But he is also an undisciplined showman. Zoellick was heavily involved in Iraq policy at first but then dropped the portfolio after he complained to Rice that Khalilzad was deliberately ignoring his instructions.

37. Saul Hudson, "US's Rice to Visit Europe—and Maybe Beyond," Reuters, April 23, 2006.

38. Condoleezza Rice, "Remarks at the National Conference of Editorial Writers," Washington, D.C., May 1, 2006. www.state.gov/secretary/rm/2006/65572.htm.

39. The meeting was described by an administration official who took notes during it, April 26, 2006.

40. Condoleezza Rice, "Joint Roundtable with Secretary of Defense Donald Rumsfeld," Baghdad, Iraq, April 26, 2006. www.state.gov/secretary/rm/2006/65317.htm. Rumsfeld fiercely disputed my characterization of the differences in tone after I wrote a feature for the *Post* on what I had observed. The day the article appeared, radio host Laura Ingraham asked him about the article's assertion that he and Rice seemed in "separate orbits," and he responded: "Oh, absolutely not. What nonsense. It's just fairly typical *Washington Post* stuff." www.defenselink.mil/transcripts/2006/tr20060428-12921.html.

41. The dinner was described by an administration official who took notes during the meal, April 26, 2006.

42. Nelson Hernandez, "Gunmen in Baghdad Kill Sister of Iraqi Vice President," *The Washington Post,* April 28, 2006, p. A12. Hashimi would lose another brother to insurgents a few months later.

Chapter 9: Diplomatic Waltz in Vienna

1. Flynt Leverett, "Illusion and Reality," *The American Prospect,* September 2006, pp. 29–33. Leverett served on the State Department's policy planning staff and was a senior director at the National Security Council in 2001–2003, focused on Middle East issues. He says he voted for Bush in 2000 but has since become a critic.

2. "Statement by the President," White House news release, July 12, 2002. www.whitehouse.gov/news/releases/2002/07/20020712-9.html.

3. Israeli and MEK officials consistently deny this, but from personal experience I found that information from the MEK and the Israelis was often similar. They could derive their information from similar sources.

4. Mark Hibbs, "U.S. Briefed Suppliers Group in October on Suspected Iranian Enrichment Plant," *Nuclear Fuel,* December 23, 2002, p. 1.

5. Joby Warrick and Glenn Kessler, "Iran's Nuclear Program Speeds Ahead," *The Washington Post,* March 10, 2003, p. A1.

6. The document and cover letter were provided by a confidential source. They are posted on the Web at www.washingtonpost.com/wp-srv/world/documents/us_iran_/roadmap.pdf and verified by U.S. and Iranian officials.

7. Interviews with a senior State Department official, October 22 and October 31, 2006. Leverett, in an e-mail to the author, said he faxed a copy of his report to Rice's West Wing office and received confirmation from her executive assistant that it had been received and taken into her office. He never heard from Rice but was later told that a senior NSC staff director was furious he had held the "unauthorized" meeting with Reza'i, indicating his report had been read by at least someone on Rice's staff.

8. Interviews with Leverett and other former administration officials, June 2006.

9. Hassan Rohani, "Beyond the Challenges Facing Iran and the IAEA Concerning the Nuclear Dossier," text of speech given to the Supreme Cultural Revolution Council, September 30, 2005, published in *Rahbord,* pp. 7–38. FBIS-IAP20060113336001.

10. Condoleezza Rice, "Remarks with Libyan Foreign Minister Abd al-Rahman Shal-gam," New York, September 17, 2005. www.state.gov/secretary/rm/2005/53378.htm.
11. Interviews with foreign diplomats, May–June 2006.
12. The account of the Ankara meeting and Rice's feelings about Lavrov are from inter-views with a senior State Department official (October 22, 2006) and other adminis-tration officials.
13. Interview with Foreign Minister Philippe Douste-Blazy of France, September 21, 2006.
14. Glenn Kessler, "A Spat over Iraq Revealed on Tape," *The Washington Post,* June 30, 2006, p. A20.
15. Condoleezza Rice, "Remarks with Foreign Ministers at the G-8 Ministerial," Moscow, June 29, 2006. www.state.gov/secretary/rm/2006/68443.htm.
16. In February 2003, consensus also could not be reached on North Korea's decision to leave the NPT and restart its nuclear reactor—and then no action was taken by the UN Security Council. The failure to reach an agreement on North Korea was also considered a bad sign for working together on Iran.
17. The account of the Putin-Rice meeting is based on interviews with administration officials, August–September 2006.
18. No diplomatic grouping is complete without some sort of algebraic shorthand. From the European perspective, the United States, Russia, and China were now at the table with the EU-3 discussing Iran, so European officials called the meeting the "EU-3 plus Three." But that suggested history had started before the Americans arrived. The Americans preferred to call the group the "P5 plus One"—a reference to the five per-manent members of the UN Security Council. The Germans—the "one" without veto status—were immensely annoyed by this nomenclature.
19. Interview with an administration official who kept notes of the conversation, No-vember 16, 2006.
20. The account of the January meeting is based on interviews with six U.S. and Euro-pean officials, conducted June 2006–February 2007.
21. Condoleezza Rice, "Press Availability After the P5+1 Meeting," Berlin, March 30, 2006. www.state.gov/secretary/rm/2006/63864.htm.
22. The following account of the decision to agree to talks with the Iranians is based on interviews with seven administration officials, as well as several European officials, June–October 2006.
23. Sawers, according to a copy of the March 16 memo, noted "the period running up to the G8 Summit [hosted by Putin] will be when our influence on Russia will be at its maximum, and we need to plan accordingly." Burns's denial appeared in Colum Lynch, "Security Council Fails to Reach Accord on Iran," *The Washington Post,* March 21, 2006, p. A12.
24. The account of the May meeting is based on interviews with seven U.S. and Euro-pean officials, June 2006–February 2007.
25. Michele Kelemen, "U.S. Adapts to Setbacks in Middle East Policy," *All Things Con-sidered,* National Public Radio, May 12, 2006.
26. Neil King, Jr., and Marc Champion, "Nations' Rich Trade with Iran Is Hurdle for Sanctions Plan," *The Wall Street Journal,* September 20, 2006, p. A1.

27. Condoleezza Rice, "Press Conference on Iran," Washington D.C., May 31, 2006. www.state.gov/secretary/rm/2006/67103.htm. The State Department posted a translation of the statement in Persian on its Web site.
28. Interviews with U.S. and European officials, August–September 2006.
29. Interview with a senior State Department official, December 15, 2006.
30. Richard Perle, "Why Did Bush Blink on Iran? (Ask Condi)," *The Washington Post*, June 25, 2006, p. B1.

Chapter 10: Blowup over Beirut

1. The account of the debate between Douste-Blazy and Rice is based on interviews with Douste-Blazy and five administration officials who were at the Rome conference, August–October 2006. Siniora's remarks to the conference are from Cam Simpson, "Summit Ends Without Cease-Fire Call," *Chicago Tribune*, July 27, 2006, p. 16.
2. Interviews with French and U.S. officials, June–October 2006.
3. Neil MacFarquhar, "Behind Lebanon Upheaval, 2 Men's Fateful Clash," *The New York Times*, March 20, 2005, p. A1.
4. Interviews with French and U.S. officials, June–October 2006.
5. George W. Bush, "President Discusses War on Terror," National Defense University, Fort Lesley J. McNair, March 8, 2005. www.whitehouse.gov/news/releases/2005/03/20050308-3.html.
6. Interviews with administration officials, February 2006.
7. Berri's background is from Andrew Lee Butters, "Hizballah's Unlikely Rep at the Bargaining Table," *Time*, July 25, 2006.
8. Condoleezza Rice, "Press Availability with Lebanese Prime Minister Siniora," Beirut, Lebanon, July 22, 2005. www.state.gov/secretary/rm/2005/49959.htm.
9. Interviews with administration officials, February 2006.
10. Condoleezza Rice, "Briefing En Route Beirut, Lebanon," February 23, 2006. www .state.gov/secretary/rm/2006/61949.htm.
11. David Ignatius, "Beirut's Berlin Wall," *The Washington Post*, February 23, 2005, p. A19.
12. Al Kamen, "U.S. Envoy at Home with a Gun and a Plane," *The Washington Post*, March 3, 2006, p. A15.
13. Interviews with administration officials, March 2006.
14. Interview with a senior State Department official, October 31, 2006.
15. Interview with a senior State Department official, October 31, 2006, and December 15, 2006. Much of the account of Rice's diplomacy in this period is based on interviews with six administration officials, conducted August–December 2006. One official consulted his notes of key meetings with Israeli and Lebanese officials.
16. Scott Wilson, "Israeli War Plan Had No Exit Strategy," *The Washington Post*, October 21, 2006, p. A1.
17. Interviews with administration officials, August–September 2006. The warnings were passed through the U.S. embassy in Damascus and through Siniora's office. Welch also spoke directly to Saad Hariri, who reported that he had been assured that Hezbollah had no intention of escalating the situation. After the attack, Welch went

back to Hariri and told him there was a rumor that Hariri himself had approved the operation. Hariri denied that, saying that in an act of bad faith Hezbollah had lied to him.

18. Interviews with U.S. and Israeli officials, September–October 2006.

19. President Bush, "Press Availability with German Chancellor Merkel," Stralsund, Germany, July 13, 2006. www.state.gov/p/eur/rls/rm/69067.htm.

20. Richard Wolffe, "Backstage at the Crisis," *Newsweek,* July 31, 2006, p. 30. Wolffe was given unusual access to Bush and other administration officials during the G-8 summit.

21. "Saudi Accuses Hezbollah of 'Adventurism,'" Agence France-Presse, July 14, 2006.

22. Wolffe, "Backstage," and interviews with administration officials.

23. Interview with a senior State Department official, October 31, 2006.

24. Wilson, "Israeli War."

25. Aluf Benn and Akiva Elder, "Looking for the Endgame," *Haaretz,* October 1, 2006, p. B1.

26. Interviews with administration officials, December 2006.

27. Interview with a senior State Department official, December 15, 2006.

28. Interviews with administration officials, August–September 2006.

29. Condoleezza Rice, "Special Briefing on Travel to the Middle East and Europe," Washington, D.C., July 21, 2006. www.state.gov/secretary/rm/2006/69331.htm.

30. Interview with an Arab diplomat, March 19, 2007.

31. Liz Sly and Cam Simpson, "Rice Visits Beirut, Doesn't Endorse Immediate Cease-Fire," *Chicago Tribune,* July 24, 2006.

32. Helene Cooper and Jad Mouawad, "In First Stop, Rice Confers with Leaders of Lebanon," *The New York Times,* p. A13.

33. Russian technicians had failed to turn off a sound feed of a ministers lunch that included sharp sparring between Rice and Lavrov. I made a transcript of the Lavrov-Rice conversation, which took place on June 29, 2006, two weeks before the war started. Rice's comment was explained by a senior State Department official, October 31, 2006.

34. Rami G. Khouri, "A New Middle East, or Rice's Fantasy Ride?" *Daily Star* (Beirut), July 23, 2006. The Lebanese description of Rice as Candide was provided by *The Washington Post* correspondent Edward Cody.

35. Interview with a senior State Department official, October 31, 2006. A reconstruction of Hezbollah's actions suggests that Nasrallah was mainly motivated to win the release of Lebanese prisoners in Israeli hands, something that senior State Department officials privately suspected from the beginning. See Anthony Shadid, "Inside Hezbollah, Big Miscalculations," *The Washington Post,* October 8, 2006, p. A1.

36. Rice, "Special Briefing."

37. Renne Montagne, "Armitage: U.S. Must Talk to Syria," *Morning Edition,* National Public Radio, July 26, 2006.

38. Flynt Leverett, *Inheriting Syria: Bashar's Trial by Fire* (Washington, D.C.: Brookings Institution Press, 2006), p. 145.

39. The internal debate on Syria was described by administration officials, August–September 2006. Rice would refuse to meet the Syrians until May 2007.

40. Interview with an administration official, March 7, 2007.

41. CNN transcript, July 26, 2006, and interviews with administration officials, August 2006.

42. Al Kamen, "Sonata Cease-Fire," *The Washington Post*, July 28, 2006, p. A23; Mark Bendeich, "ASEAN Dinner Dishes Whimsy," Reuters, July 28, 2006.

43. "Israel Seeks 10–14 Days for Offensive—PM Office," Reuters, July 30, 2006.

44. Benn and Elder, "Looking for the Endgame."

45. Interviews with administration officials, August–October 2006.

46. Four administration officials in the room at the time agreed in separate interviews that Rice had decided not to go to Beirut before she spoke to Siniora, though some news reports at the time said he told her not to come. The administration account is that she told him she should not come and he readily agreed.

47. Interviews with administration officials, August–October 2006.

48. Condoleezza Rice, "Briefing on Efforts to Stop Violence in Lebanon," Jerusalem, July 30, 2006. www.state.gov/secretary/rm/2006/69720.htm.

49. Condoleezza Rice, "Statement on Three-Part Comprehensive Settlement," Jerusalem, July 31, 2006. www.state.gov/secretary/rm/2006/69726.htm.

50. Condoleezza Rice, "Briefing En Route Ireland," Shannon, Ireland, July 31, 2006. www.state.gov/secretary/rm/2006/69732.htm.

51. Interview with a senior State Department official, October 31, 2006.

52. Interview with a senior State Department official, March 27, 2007.

53. Interview with a senior State Department official, October 31, 2006.

54. An administration official supplied a copy of the e-mail exchange.

55. Interview with a senior State Department official, October 31, 2006.

56. Interviews with administration officials and Benn and Elder, "Looking for the Endgame."

57. Interviews with administration officials, August 2006.

58. Mohamad Bazzi, "Turning Rubble into Rhetoric," *Newsday*, September 3, 2006, p. A36.

59. Michael Slackman, "As Crowd Demands Change, Lebanese Premier Is Puzzled," *The New York Times*, December 11, 2006, p. A3.

Conclusion: Back to Beijing—and Beyond

1. Interviews with administration officials, October 2006.

2. Condoleezza Rice, "Remarks with Egyptian Foreign Minister Ahmed Aboul Gheit," Cairo, Egypt, October 3, 2006. www.state.gov/secretary/rm/2006/73525.htm.

3. Kevin Sullivan, "Views on U.S. Drop Sharply in Worldwide Opinion Poll," *The Washington Post*, January 23, 2007, p. A14. The survey was done for the BBC by GlobeScan, an international polling company.

4. Interview with a senior State Department official, December 15, 2006.

5. Helene Cooper and David Sanger, "Rice's Counselor Gives Advice Others May Not Want to Hear," *The New York Times*, October 28, 2006, p. A1.

6. Condoleezza Rice, "Interview with Agence France-Presse," Washington, D.C., December 11, 2006. www.state.gov/secretary/rm/2006/77627.htm.

7. "Iran Needs 'Practical' Moves by U.S. Before Talks over Iran," Agence France-Presse, November 17, 2006.

8. Dana Milbank, "The Secretary vs. the Senators," *The Washington Post,* January 12, 2007, p. A01.

9. Thom Shanker and David E. Sanger, "New to Pentagon, Gates Argued for Closing Guantánamo Prison," *The New York Times,* March 23, 2007, p. 1.

10. Interview with a senior State Department official, February 19, 2007.

11. Interview with a senior State Department official, March 27, 2007.

12. Interviews with administration officials, February 2007.

13. Condoleezza Rice, "Press Roundtable Interview," Washington, D.C., March 23, 2007. www.state.gov/secretary/rm/2007/mar/82158.htm.

14. Interview with a senior State Department official, March 27, 2007.

15. Philip D. Zelikow, "Building Security in the Broader Middle East," Weinberg Founders Conference, the Washington Institute for Near East Policy, September 15, 2006. www.washingtoninstitute.org/html/pdf/Zelikow091506.pdf.

16. Condoleezza Rice, "Interview with *The Washington Post* Editorial Board," Washington, D.C., December 14, 2006. www.state.gov/secretary/rm/2006/77856.htm.

17. Condoleezza Rice, "Roundtable with Traveling Press," Kuwait City, January 16, 2007. www.state.gov/secretary/rm/2007/78930.htm.

18. Hamza Hendawi, "Egyptian Activists Turn from Democracy Campaign to Bitterness at Israel and U.S.," Associated Press, September 14, 2006.

19. Condoleezza Rice, "Roundtable with Traveling Press," London, January 18, 2007. www.state.gov/secretary/rm/2007/79038.htm.

20. The Quinnipiac Poll, survey of 1,623 registered voters taken from November 13 to November 19, 2006, with a sampling error margin of plus or minus 2.4 percentage points. The survey on most powerful women was released on November 22, 2006, and one on U.S. leaders was released on November 27, 2006.

21. *The Washington Post*–ABC News poll, conducted February 22–25, 2007, using a random sample of 1,082 adults, with a sampling error of plus or minus three percentage points.

INDEX

Abbas, Mahmoud, 93, 125, 127–29,
    133, 240–41, 263n24. *See also*
    Fatah
  Bush, conversation with, 135
  Rice's disappointment in, 130,
    131–32, 137–38
  Welch, conversation with, 130
ABC News, 108
Abdullah (Jordanian king), 124, 215
Abdullah (Saudi king), 90, 94, 100,
    101, 142, 218
  abaya, gift to Rice from, 88–89
Aboul Gheit, Ahmed, 92–96, 140–44,
    234
Abrams, Elliott, 92, 121, 130–36, 140,
    142, 203, 217, 224, 225, 254n22
  background of, 128–29
  Wolfensohn, confrontation with, 133
Abu Ghraib prison scandal, 96
Abuja peace accord, 119, 261n20
Acheson, Dean, 3, 4
Addington, David S., 147, 148

advisors, of Rice, 27–29
Afghanistan, 27, 90, 148, 183, 236. *See
    also* Khalilzad
Africa. *See* Sudan
Agence France-Presse, 44, 151
Agreed Framework, 68, 81, 84, 258n8
Ahmadinejad, Mahmoud, 188, 189,
    195, 198
Albright, Madeleine, 29, 32, 88, 223,
    250n2
American Foreign Service Association,
    29
Ankara, 269n12
Annan, Kofi, 35, 108, 137, 206, 208
Anton, Michael, 37
Aquino, Corazon, 89
Al Arabiya television, 36
Arafat, Yasir, 23, 93, 123–24, 127
Armey, Richard, 27
Armitage, Richard, 42, 69, 80, 220
Armstrong, Christopher, 161
Ashrawi, Hanan, 136

Assad, Bashir, 209, 220
Asselborn, Jean, 45
Atomic Energy Commission, 60
Austria, 181–205
axis of evil, 67–68, 71, 184
Azerbaijan, 189

Baghdad. *See* Iraq
Bahrain, 121
Baker, James A., 6, 16, 26, 27, 29, 30,
    31, 221, 236, 237
Banco Delta Asia (Macao), 79–80,
    84–87, 238, 239
Ban Ki-moon, 223
Bartlett, Dan, 203
Bashir, Omar Hassan, 102–6, 109,
    116–18
Bean, Lee Randolph (Randy), 11, 12,
    16, 18, 22, 251*n*30, 251*n*34
Beckett, Margaret, 181, 182, 200, 207,
    229
Beirut. *See* Lebanon
Belarus, 72, 99
Bellinger, John B., 24–27, 28, 49,
    146–49, 156, 254*n*17
Benn, Hilary, 114, 261*n*20
Berlin meeting, Iran, 195
Berlioz, Hector, 20
Berri, Nabih, 211, 212, 213, 219, 228
Biden, Joseph, 35
bilateral talks, 69, 70, 74, 82
bin Laden, Osama, 105, 156
Bishop, Nina, 22
Blackburn Cathedral, 161
Blacker, Coit D., 9, 10, 11, 12, 15, 17,
    18, 19, 24, 251*n*30
Blackwill, Robert D., 32, 51, 91
Blair, Tony, 24, 125, 165, 172, 202,
    216
Blankley, Tony, 46, 255*n*44
bluntness, of Rice, 9

body language, of Straw and Rice,
    161–62
Bolten, Josh, 197
Bolton, John R., 57, 112, 193, 203,
    229, 235
    Lebanon resolution, dislike of, 230
    Rice's nomination of, 34–35
Bosnian War, 72
Boston Globe, 13
Boston Review, 107
Bot, Ben, 155, 156
Boucher, Richard, 29, 44
Boxer, Barbara, 38
Britain, 41–42, 59, 62, 181, 186
Brose, Christian D., 37, 94, 97
Brown v. Board of Education of Topeka,
    Kansas, 12
Brussels, 148, 155
Brzezinski, Zbigniew, 7, 18
Bureau 39, 85
Burma, 72, 99
Burns, R. Nicholas, 23, 27, 57, 59, 81,
    188, 193, 202, 204, 215, 228–29
    background of, 33–34
    Lavrov's anger at, 199–200
    Rice's Iran memo, surprise at, 198
Burns, William, 25, 129, 191
Bush, George H. W., 3, 6, 10, 12, 16,
    27, 30, 32, 50, 51, 67, 91, 129,
    236
Bush, George W./Bush administration,
    4, 32, 39, 80, 94, 119, 189, 222,
    243
    Abbas delegation meeting with, 135
    approval ratings of, 165, 175
    Arafat and, 123–24
    Bashir letter from, 116–17
    bilateral talk refusal of, 70
    Bolton appointment and, 35
    Chirac and, 208–10
    Clinton, Bill, skepticism of, 122–23
    counterterrorism efforts of, 146

CVID of, 81–82
Darfur atrocities response of, 107
funds for Palestinian reform of,
    129–30
G-8 hosted by, 262n1
Gaza funds, 136
German citizen abduction admitted
    by, 152
on Hamas victory, 137
Hughes connection with, 36
India nuclear power and, 48–64
Iran and, 45, 182–83, 184, 192
Iraq War and, 21, 159
Israel and, 39, 125
Lebanon as success story for, 208
Middle East democracy push from,
    89–92
Minnawi's visit with, 118
North Korea and, 66, 67–68
nuclear weapon development during,
    67
opting out of international
    obligations, 155
Palestinian state promise of, 122
peace treaty offer to North Korea,
    86–87
Quartet of, 125, 262n12
reelection of, 22–24
Rice as campaign advisor to, 17–18
Rice, close association with, 2–3,
    5–9, 242–44
Rice nominated as secretary of state
    by, 21
second inaugural address of, 90
secret prisons defended by, 157
Sharon and, 124, 127, 262n4
Sistani, secret letter from, 174
State of the Union address, 40, 67,
    71, 129
Sudan critical of, 105
terrorist captives executive order,
    146–47

torture law interpretation, 151
undiplomatic language of, 75
Zoellick irritating, 30
Bush, Laura, 6, 58, 98

Canada, 2
Capps, Ron, 119
Card, Andrew, 7, 23
Carlos the Jackal, 150
Carter, Jimmy, 15
The Case for Democracy: The Power of
    Freedom to Overcome Tyranny and
    Terror (Sharansky), 89
Cash, Johnny, 223
Casper, Gerard, 17
Cedar revolution, 93
Charles, Robert, 27
Cheney, Dick, 4, 7, 8, 31, 34, 35, 70,
    80, 85, 145, 148, 155, 168, 196,
    197, 199, 209, 221, 227, 228,
    238, 243, 250n3, 262n2
    Aboul Gheit meeting refused by,
        140
    on Arafat and peace, 123–24
    Lavrov, anger at, 199–200
    Rice, dispute with, 147–48
    terrorist captives executive order,
        146–47
Cheney, Elizabeth, 120–21, 136
Chen Shui-bian, 1
China, 1, 10, 45, 54, 59, 62, 73–74,
    76, 80, 82, 119, 142, 182, 188,
    191, 193, 236, 238, 253n15
    human rights abuse in, 91
    Iran's trade with, 201
    Nixon and, 49
    North Korea and oil from, 73–74,
        233–34, 258n16
    Rice angry with, 77, 259n19
    six-party talks, 71–74
    UN supported by, 87

Chirac, Jacques, 42–45, 202, 208–10, 227
Christopher, Warren M., 25, 29, 32, 220
CID. *See* cruel, inhuman, and degrading treatment
Clinton, Bill/Clinton administration, 11, 32, 69, 72, 77, 122–23, 184, 238, 243, 253*n*13. *See also* Agreed Framework
  Bush, George W., skeptical of, 122–23
  China's human rights and, 10
  India's nuclear weapon program and, 51
  nuclear facility in North Korea during, 67
  Rice scornful of, 18
Clinton, Hillary, 243
clothes, of Rice, 45–46
CNN, 124, 223, 225
Cobra II, 173
Cohen, Eliot A., 235
Comaneci, Nadia, 255*n*1
Command Post Tango, 65, 66
complete, verifiable, irreversible dismantling of nuclear programs (CVID), 81–82
Condiriceisangry.com, 9
confirmation hearings, of Rice, 38, 40, 71–72
congressional race, Rice's consideration of, 16, 252*n*46
Congressional Research Service, 78
Congress, Rice's relationship with, 60, 64, 139, 158, 241
Control Room, 28
Convention Against Torture (CAT), 150, 155
counterfeit money, of North Korea, 78–80, 84–87
Crouch, J. D., 81, 84, 203

cruel, inhuman, or degrading treatment, 150, 151, 153, 155
Cuba, 72, 99
cultural airport greeters, 255*n*1
CVID. *See* complete, verifiable, irreversible dismantling of nuclear programs
Czechoslovakia, 15, 142

Dahlan, Mohammed, 133. *See also* Fatah
Dai Bingguo, 195
Daily Star, 219
D'Alema, Massimo, 206, 208
Dallin, Alexander, 10
Danforth, John, 105
Dangot, Eitan, 224
Darfur, 105–19, 234
Defense Department, 177
democracy, 92, 208, 215, 234, 242
  Aboul Gheit and, 96, 144
  Bush, George W., promoting, 90–91, 262*n*1
  Hurd on, 163
  Hyde on, 139
  Iraq invasion and, 98
  liberal, 158, 162, 171
  Rice on, 91–92, 96
  U.S. standing for, 142
Deng Xiaoping, 86
DeTrani, Joseph, 75
de Waal, Alex, 107, 117, 261*n*20, 262*n*21
diplomacy, 36–40, 42, 189, 191, 192, 197, 204, 216, 217, 227, 239, 241. *See also* transformational diplomacy
Diskin, Yuval, 133
Douste-Blazy, Philippe, 190, 206, 207, 270*n*1
Duckett, Josie, 178

Egypt, 2, 18, 88, 98, 120, 125, 183, 207, 220. *See also* Mubarak, Hosni; Nour, Amyan
  election canceling in, 143
  human rights abuse in, 91
  Rice respecting laws of, 99
  Rice's visit to, 95–99, 139–40, 144
ElBaradei, Mohamed, 194
elections, equaling freedom, 101
England, 159–62, 166, 173
England, Gordon R., 265*n*6
Ereli, Adam, 222, 223, 226
EU-3, 187, 188, 202, 203
  plus Three, 269*n*18
Europe. *See specific countries*
Evanoff, Mike, 167, 176, 212

F-16 deals, 50–51, 54, 56
Fahd (King), 100
al-Faisal, Saud (Prince), 88, 100–1, 142–43, 218
al-Faisal, Turki (Prince), 101
Fatah, 130, 131, 135
Fayyad, Salam, 136
Federal Register, 79
Feith, Douglas, 81
Feltman, Jeffrey, 213, 225
Financial Times, 255*n*1
Foreign Affairs, 18, 38, 50
Forum for the Future, 120, 262*n*1
Foster, Jim, 84
"four plus two" process, 86
Fox News, 44
France, 41–42, 59, 62, 181, 186, 193, 201, 213, 224, 227, 229
  Iran's trade with, 201
  rendition in, 150
  Rice's visit to, 20–22, 42–45
Frazer, Jendayi, 118, 253*n*6
Freedom House, 99

Fried, Daniel, 152, 254*n*22
friendships, of Rice, 10–12
Fur tribe, 108, 118–19

Gaddis, John Lewis, 38
Gandhi, Mohandas, 161
Garang, John, 105–11
Gates, Robert, 235, 238
Gaza, 126, 131–35, 214, 236
  Rice's role in Israeli departure from, 125–27, 263*n*16
G-8. *See* Group of Eight
Geneva Conventions, 147, 157, 265*n*6
genocide, 106, 107, 119
Germany, 16, 30, 41–42, 53, 152, 181, 186, 193, 201, 214, 239
Gerson, Michael, 94, 118
Ghad Party, 141
Gigot, Paul, 203
Gilpatric Committee, 52
Gingrich, Newt, 37
Giuliani, Rudolph, 243
Givhan, Robin, 46
Global Equity Initiative, 117
global warming, 38
Golan Heights, 222
al-Gomhuria, 143
Gonzales, Alberto, 154
Gorbachev, Mikhail, 16
Gordon, Charles, 108
Gore, Al, 4, 11, 28, 253*n*10
GQ magazine, 36
Green, Grant, 25
Green, Michael J., 56, 60, 66, 83
Green Zone, 164, 168–70, 177
Groombridge, Mark, 203
Group of Eight (G-8), 90, 214, 216, 262*n*1
Guantánamo detention facility, 146, 147, 157, 265*n*6

Gulf News, 143
Gunderson, Brian, 27, 37, 202
    Rice's selection of, 28–29

Haavisto, Pekka, 114, 117, 261*n*20,
    261*n*21
Hadley, Stephen, 8, 36, 50, 57, 59, 72,
    80, 83, 129, 148, 154, 195, 197,
    203, 214, 215, 222, 228
Hagel, Chuck, 237
al-Hakim, Abdul Aziz, 178
Hamas, 122, 130–43, 214, 215, 232,
    264*n*52
Hamdan v. Rumsfeld, 156–57
Hamilton, Lee, 236
Hannah, John, 228
Hariri, Rafiq, 93, 209, 210, 211, 220,
    221
Hariri, Saad, 211, 270*n*17
Hart, Gary, 15
al-Hashimi, Maysoon, 180
al-Hashimi, Tariq, 180
Hastert, Dennis, 27
Helal, Gemal, 102
Helsinki Accords, 89, 90
Hennen, Scott, 173
Hezbollah, 183, 234, 240, 242,
    270*n*17, 271*n*35
    Israel-, War, 206–32
Hilal, Sheikh Musa, 108
Hill, Christopher R., 66, 72–73, 78–86,
    238, 239, 259*n*19
    background of, 72
    bilateral talks, desire for, 74, 85
    North Korean dinner of, 76–77
    "peaceful coexistence," distress over,
        82–83
Hobbes, Thomas, 162
Hofman, Karl W., 254*n*22
Holbrooke, Richard, 72, 80
Hollis, Rosemary, 163

House International Relations
    Committee, 139
Hudson, Saul, 96, 153–54,
    175–76
Hughes, Karen, 35–36, 135, 203,
    222, 254*n*21
Hu Jintao, 1, 78, 86, 238
human rights, 10, 89, 91, 140, 147
Human Rights Watch, 148, 225
Humayuns' Tomb, 48–49
Hume, Cameron, 113, 261*n*23
hundred-day plan, 37–40
Hungary, 142
Hurd, Douglas, 163
Hurricane Katrina, 5
Hussein, Saddam, 102, 162–63, 165,
    169, 183, 184, 237
Hyde, Henry, 139, 258*n*43

IAEA. *See* International Atomic Energy
    Agency
Ibrahim, Saad Eddin, 141–42
image-making, of Rice, 4–5
India, 48–64, 59, 234
    Bolton on, 35
    Hyde's anger over, 257*n*43
    -Iran natural gas pipeline deal,
        54
    nuclear power of, 256*n*12, 257*n*27,
        257*n*30, 257*n*43
    Pakistan's relations with, 53
Ingraham, Laura, 268*n*40
Institut d'Études Politiques de Paris,
    42
intellectual transformation, of Rice,
    18–20
International Atomic Energy Agency
    (IAEA), 58, 61, 184–85, 187, 191,
    193, 195
International Criminal Court, 106
intifada, second, 123

Iran, 3, 41–42, 58, 72, 98, 99, 118, 181, 236, 237. *See also* Shiites; Sunnis
  Bolton on, 35
  EU-3 discussing, 269*n*18
  IAEA investigating, 187
  incentives presented to, 204–5
  India-, natural gas pipeline deal, 54
  media questions about, 45–47
  noncompliance with treaty negotiations, 191
  nuclear technology in, 187–97
  Rice and 2003 offer, 185–86, 268*n*6, 268*n*7
  Russia's investments in, 191
  sanctions against, 192–94
  Taliban war cooperation, 183–84
  U.S. negotiations with, 43, 45–47, 182–83, 188, 196, 197–203, 199, 203
Iraq, 3, 41, 102, 109, 158–80, 183, 184, 236
  Cheney, Elizabeth, visiting, 120–21
  Green Zone, 121
  invasion, 28, 68, 89, 98
  nonexistent weapons of mass destruction, 185
  Rice and, 173, 177
  Rice, conversation with Bush about, 165
Iraq Study Group, 236, 237, 241
Iraq War, 38, 42, 68, 90, 105, 125, 266*n*3
  Bush, George W., association with, 159
  Rice not getting responsibility for, 159
  U.S. blunders, 163–64
Ischinger, Wolfgang, 9, 39–40, 46, 146
Islamic radicalism, 90
Israel, 39, 59, 90, 109, 120–42, 208, 214, 224–25, 240, 263*n*16, 268*n*3. *See also* Sharon, Ariel
  Gaza, pull out of, 131
  Hamas election participation, 134–36
  -Hezbollah War, 206–32
  negotiation breakthrough with, 97
  -Palestinian relations, 120–43
  U.S. funds for, 129–30

al-Jafari, Ibrahim, 165–66, 170, 172, 174
Janjaweed, 106, 108, 109, 111, 113, 115
Jan-Virmoni, Yusuf, 161
Japan, 8, 53, 70, 74, 82, 83, 91
Al Jazeera, 28
Jefferson, Thomas, 3
JEM, 115
jihad, 101
Jim Crow Democrats, 15
Joint Chiefs of Staff, 7
Jones, Elizabeth, 25
Jones, James L., 235
Jordan, 125, 129, 132, 207, 220
Joseph, Robert G., 50, 57, 58, 71, 202, 203, 239, 256*n*25
Jumblatt, Walid, 213

Kadima, 136
Karl, Jonathan, 99, 101, 108
Kassem, Hisham, 141
Kazakhstan, 189
KCNA (news service), 71
Kelly, James, 68–74, 80
Kennedy, David, 10, 17, 18
Kerry, John, 25, 32, 38, 71, 72
Khalilzad, Zalmay (Ambassador), 166, 175, 178–79, 267*n*36
Khamenei, Ali (Ayatollah), 185
Kharazi, Kamal, 185
Kharazi, Sadegh, 185

Khartoum. *See* Sudan
Khatami, Mohammad, 184
Khouri, Rami G., 219
Kiev. *See* Ukraine
Kifaya, 242
Kim Gye Gwan, 76, 85, 238
Kim Il Sung, 77
Kim Jong Il, 69, 77, 86, 87, 234
Kingibe, Baba Gana, 111
King, John, 223
Kislyak, Sergey, 196
Kissinger, Henry, 3, 7, 100
Konishiki, 255n1
Korbel, Josef, 14, 15
Kosovo, 72
Krasner, Stephen D., 254n17
Krauthammer, Charles, 203
Kristol, William, 203
Kwan, Michelle, 86

Lahoud, Emile, 209, 211, 212, 213
LaPorte, Leon J., 66
Lavrov, Sergey, 34, 181, 182, 189–99,
    204, 216, 219, 240, 269n12,
    271n33
  anger at Cheney and Burns,
    199–200
  skill at irritating Rice, 189–91
Lawless, Richard, 77–78
Le Figaro, 44
leaks, 26–27
Lebanon, 183, 206–32, 212, 221, 242.
    See also Hezbollah
Lee, Spike, 5
Lefkowitz, Jay, 85
Leist, Libby, 172
Leverett, Flynt, 185, 186, 268n1,
    268n7
Levin, Carl M., 155
Levitte, Jean-David, 43
Li Zhaoxing, 2, 77, 223, 259n19

Libby, I. Lewis ("Scooter"), 8, 81, 147,
    238
Libya, 115
light-water reactors (LWRs), 83, 84
Lineberry, Liz, 102
Lithuania, 199
Liverpool. *See* England
Liverpool Echo, 159–60
Livni, Tzipi, 134, 137, 213–14, 215,
    217, 220, 229, 241
Locke, John, 162
London meeting, Iran, 192–93
London *Times,* 161
Lugar, Richard, 37
LWRs. *See* light-water reactors

Macedonia, 72
Machler, Peter, 151
Mahdi, Adil Abdul, 170
al-Maliki, Nouri Kemal, 175, 178, 180,
    236
Mann, Hillary, 185–86
Marcos, Ferdinand, 89
Marshall, George C., 3, 4
El-Masri, Khaled, 149, 152–53
McCain amendment, 147, 156,
    265n20
McCartney, Paul, 160
McCormack, Sean, 29, 41, 77, 103,
    121, 153, 154, 164, 176, 181–82,
    202, 204, 222
McFaul, Michael, 12
McNair, Denise, 13, 251n36
McPhatter, Genoa, 24
media, 33–34, 37, 66, 95–97, 101, 108,
    149, 152, 172, 226
  anger of, 182–83
  on Austria trip, 204
  in Baghdad, 168
  Bush, George W., and Merkel with,
    215

female journalists in abayas, 100, 142
Hill talking to, 72
Iran questions of, impacting Rice, 45–47
Iraqi, 180
Israel's meetings watched by, 141
in Korea, 65–66
"outposts of tyranny" unnoticed by, 72
prison questions of, 153
Rice's relationship with, 40–42, 44, 46, 49, 62–63, 144
Rice's trip leaked by, 176
Rice using names of, 99
in Rome, 222
in Sudan, 103–4
torture reporting of, 150
in Ukraine, 145
on U.S. relations with India, 54
Zoellick and, 31, 111–12
MEK. *See* Mujahedin-e Khalq
Merckx, Eddy, 255*n*1
Merkel, Angela, 148, 149, 152, 202, 215
Middle East, 3, 88–101, 124, 217–20, 240–41, 243. *See also* new Middle East; *specific locations*
Milosevic, Slobodan, 73
Minnawi, Minni Arko, 111, 115–18, 261*n*21
Mishra, Brajesh, 50
Mitchell, Andrea, 104
Mofaz, Shaul, 133
Mohsen, Mervat, 142
money laundering. *See* counterfeit money, of North Korea
Moratinos, Miguel, 207
Morgenthau, Hans, 15, 18
Mosley, Oswald, 160
Moynihan, Daniel Patrick, 128–29
Mubarak, Hosni, 90, 92, 94, 98, 140, 141, 143, 215, 242

Muhammad (Prophet), 138
Mujahedin-e Khalq (MEK), 184, 186, 268*n*3
Musharraf, Pervez, 50, 55
Muslim Brotherhood, 99, 141, 142
Mutlak, Saleh, 171

Nasrallah, Hassan, 219, 271*n*35
Nasser, Gamal Abdel, 249
National Council of Resistance of Iran, 184
National Rifle Association, 27
National Security Council (NSC), Rice joining, 16
NATO, 108, 109, 112, 148, 175
Natsios, Andrew, 119
Nawi, Mustafa Fuzer, 223
NBC, 104, 172
Negroponte, John D., 235, 238
neoconservatives, 4
Newman, Connie, 25
new Middle East, 231, 232
New York meeting, Iran, 197–201
New York Sun, 32
New York Times, 40, 164, 174, 208, 235
Newbold, Greg, 173
Next Steps in Strategic Partnership (NSSP), 52, 55, 56
The Night Baghdad Fell, 11
9/11 Commission, 32, 151
Nixon, Richard, 49, 86
nonproliferation policy, 52–53, 57
Non-Proliferation Treaty (NPT), 52, 59, 187–88, 256*n*12
Noriega, Roger, 25
North Korea, 35, 54, 58, 65–87, 99, 118, 184, 238, 239, 258*n*8
China and, 73–74, 258*n*16
criminal activities of, 78–80, 84–87
drafts of September 19 statement, 259*n*27

North Korea (*continued*)
    Hill and, 80–81, 259*n*19
    NPT left by, 269*n*16
    nuclear power of, 233–34, 269*n*16
    Rice and, 66, 70–71, 87
    South Korea and, 75
    Treasury crackdown reaction of, 86
North-South Comprehensive Peace
    Agreement, 106–7
Nour, Amyan, 24, 92–94, 99, 140, 143,
    234
Nour, Ismail, 143
Novak, Robert, 32
NPT. *See* Non-Proliferation Treaty
NSC. *See* National Security Council
NSSP. *See* Next Steps in Strategic
    Partnership
nuclear programs, 51, 181, 183,
    213–14
    CVID, 81–82
    Germany, 53
    India, 48–64, 256*n*12, 257*n*27,
        257*n*30, 257*n*43
    Iran, 184–97, 231–32
    North Korea, 65–87, 233–34,
        269*n*16
Nuclear Suppliers Group, 52
al-Nur, Abdel Wahid, 111, 115–18

Obama, Barack, 243
Obasanjo, Olusegun, 114–15,
    116–17
Odierno, Raymond, 102
Olmert, Ehud, 136, 214, 216, 217,
    220, 232
al-Omari, Ghaith, 135
O'Neill, Paul, 7
Orange Revolution, 145, 148
"outposts of tyranny" remark, 66,
    71–73, 74, 77, 99

P5 plus One, 269*n*18
Padilla, Chris, 116
Pakistan, 53, 55, 59, 91, 129, 187
Palestinians, 23–24, 120–42, 215, 234,
    240
Paris Agreement, 199
Paulson, Hank, 222, 253*n*11
"peaceful coexistence" terminology,
    82–84
Pelosi, Nancy, 243
Peretz, Amir, 224
Perle, Richard, 205
Peron, Eva, 223
Peters, Winston, 223
Philippines, 89
plutonium, 69
Poland, 72, 146
political reconstruction teams (PRTs),
    165
Politics Among Nations (Morgenthau),
    15
Powell, Colin L., 4, 7, 19, 24, 26, 29,
    31, 32, 34, 36, 37, 38, 69, 70, 80,
    90, 110, 119, 183, 223, 243
    Arafat and, 124
    detainee treatment battle, 147
    "grand bargain" memo to, 185–86
    North Korea briefing of, 67
    nuclear policies and, 51
    resignation of, 23, 24, 253*n*3
    Rice compared to, 3, 8–9, 25, 40, 42,
        44, 48–49, 51, 77–78, 92, 148,
        156, 241, 251*n*19
    Rice defended by, 174
    Sudan sanctions and, 105
Powell, Dina, 27, 36
practical idealism, 4
Present at the Creation (Acheson), 3
presidential bid, of Rice, 46–47, 243
Priest, Dana, 146, 149, 151
Prince Saud. *See* al-Faisal, Saud

prisons, 186
  CIA scandal, 146–48, 150
  secret, 3, 146, 149–50, 151, 152,
    156, 157, 265n21
PRTs. See political reconstruction teams
Putin, Vladimir, 91, 189, 191, 192,
    197, 203, 216, 269n17

al-Qaeda, 18, 105, 163, 183, 186
Qana incident (1996), 217
Qana incident (2007), 224, 225, 227
QFRs. See questions for the record
Quartet, 125, 262n12
questions for the record (QFRs),
    154–55
Quinnipiac Poll, 243
Quinones, C. Kenneth, 259n25

Rabin, Yitzhak, 132
racism, 13–14
Rafah agreement, 133–34, 224
rapid-response unit, 254n21
Reagan, Ronald, 15, 25, 89, 129, 205
realism, of Rice, 15, 18–19, 91–92
Red Zone, 169
rendition, practice of, 150, 152
Republican National Convention
    (1992), 10
Republican National Convention
    (2000), 19
Resolution 1559, 209, 212, 213
Reuters, 96, 153, 176
Reza'i, Mohsen, 185–86
Rice, Angelena, 10
Rice-Bush Black Box, 6–9
Rice, John, 14, 22, 251n36, 252n37
Rocca, Christina, 56
Rock, Allan, 114
Romania, 146, 148, 153

Rood, John D., 57, 58, 59, 84, 259n30
Rosen, James, 44
Ross, Dennis, 15, 16, 253n13
Rove, Karl, 29
Rumsfeld, Donald, 7, 34, 159, 173,
    177, 178, 196, 235, 238, 243,
    250n3, 265n6
  Rice's relationship with, 8, 173–74,
    179–80, 268n40
Russia, 11, 37, 59, 62, 63, 82, 181,
    182, 187–95, 216, 234. See also
    Lavrov, Sergey
  Iran and, 191, 201
  Rice's love for, 14
  U.S. tension with, 190–91

Salih, Barham, 180
Salim, Salim Ahmed, 112–13, 113–14
Sammon, Bill, 47, 255n44
Saran, Shyam, 55, 58, 59, 60
Saudi Arabia, 18, 88, 91, 94, 98, 99,
    129, 139, 183, 205, 207, 220
Sawers, John, 187, 193, 196, 198, 200,
    269n23
Schily, Otto, 149
Schroeder, Gerhard, 42, 45, 148
Science Po, 42
Scowcroft, Brent, 16, 18, 91–92, 126
secrecy. See also prisons
  of Iraq visit, 179
  of nuclear weapons in North Korea,
    68
  of Rice, 26–27, 60, 202, 212, 218
segregation, 12–13
Sen, Ronen, 52, 61
September 11 attacks, 18, 19, 22, 24,
    30, 37, 89, 91, 105, 123, 150,
    162, 183. See also 9/11
    Commission
Sfeir, Nasrallah, 212
Sharansky, Natan, 89, 90–91

Sharon, Ariel, 39, 90, 123, 129, 130, 134–36
  Abbas contact cut off by, 132
  Bush, George W., and, 124, 127, 262n4
  Gaza plan of, 126
  Rice and, 127–28, 210
  siege ended by, 125
Shebaa Farms, 222, 224, 229, 230
Shiites, 165, 166, 171, 207
Shultz, George, 17–18, 25, 26
signing statements, 265n20
Singh, Manmohan (Prime Minister), 55, 56, 58, 59–60, 62–63
Singh, Natwar, (Foreign Minister), 54, 56, 59
Siniora, Fouad, 206–7, 208, 211, 219, 222, 228, 229, 230, 270n17, 272n46
al-Sistani, Ayatollah Ali, 171, 174
six-party talks, 71–74, 82, 86
slavery, 12–13, 96, 98, 162
Smith, Adam, 162
Smoking Dragon and Royal Charm, 79
Snow, Tony, 223
Sofen, Mindy, 153
Solana, Javier, 45, 113, 117, 132, 137, 181, 193, 204, 206
South Korea, 72, 75, 82
South Sudan, 106, 109
Spamalot, 5
Stanford University, 7, 9, 10, 11, 12, 15, 16, 17, 35, 243–44
"statement of principles," 80–81
stereotypes, of Rice, 21–22
Stillman College, 14
Stone, Andrea, 226
Straw, Jack, 45, 148, 159–61, 166–67, 172, 181, 192, 198, 200
  conversation with al-Jafari, 170
  diplomatic assistance of, 192–94, 200

  relationship with Rice, 160, 162, 172
  sleeping arrangements with, 167
Sudan, 102–19, 253n15
Sudanese Liberation Army, 111
Suleiman, Omar, 140
Sunnis, 165–66, 171, 183, 242
Syria, 98, 99, 118, 129, 209, 220, 221, 237, 241

Tacitus, 207
tactical errors, Rice admitting, 158, 173, 180
Taha, Ali Uthman Muhammad, 107–8, 113
Taliban, 183, 234
Tang Jiaxuan, 1, 2, 233–34
Team Rice, 27
The Ten Commandments, 96
Tenet, George, 185
terrorism, 18, 91, 123, 126, 130, 132, 145–50, 179, 184, 216. *See also* Hamas
Thatcher, Margaret, 163
"thousands of errors" comment. *See* tactical errors, Rice admitting
three-nation talks, 69
Tiananmen Square, 45
Time magazine, 173
torture, 150, 151
transformational diplomacy, 3, 60–61, 236
transition team, of Rice, 24–27
Treiki, Ali, 115
Truman, Harry S., 3, 53
Tuomioja, Erkki, 207
Turkey, 176

Ukraine, 145–57, 148, 189
United Nations (UN), 35, 119, 222, 228, 229, 230, 240

Bush, George W., speech to, 123
Convention Against Torture, 150
Darfur peacekeeping by, 112
Genocide Conventions, 106
International Criminal Court,
    106
United States (U.S.), 59, 62, 142. *See
    also* Bush, George H. W.; Bush,
    George W./Bush administration;
    Iraq War
Arabs trapping, 143
autocratic leaders, reliance by,
    89–90
carrying weight of major world crisis,
    231
credibility of, 98–99, 127
crisis diplomacy of, 217
Darfur and, 106, 119
double standards of, 96
foreign policy of, deteriorating, 235
-French relations, 229
Hamas victory influencing, 137–43,
    140
India's nuclear power and, 48–64,
    257n27
Iran's negotiations with, 182–83,
    186, 196–206
nonexistent weapons of mass
    destruction and, 185
nonproliferation policy of, 52
North Korean counterfeiting and,
    78–80
offering money for Palestinian
    reforms, 129–30
powerlessness at negotiations, 70
Qana incident and, 226
rendition of, 150
Rice defending policies of, 148
Russia, tension with, 190–91
Salim backed by, 113
Sudan sanctions by, 103
torture and, 147–52

upbringing, of Rice, 12–15
USA Today, 226
Uzbekistan, 91

Vienna. *See* Austria
Voinovich, George, 237
Voltaire, 219
Voting Rights Act (1965), 96
Vulcans, 30

walk-ups, 22
Walles, Jacob, 137
Wall Street Journal, 173, 203
war crimes, 108, 207
Ward, William, 128, 130
"Warrior Princess," 156
Washington Post, 40, 46, 146, 149, 203,
    243, 249, 250, 257n26
Washington Times, 46
WDAY, 173
weapons of mass destruction,
    nonexistent, 185
Weekly Standard, 203
Weissglas, Dov (Dubi), 124–26,
    132–36, 262n11, 263n16
Welch, C. David, 92, 101, 121,
    128–33, 136, 137, 140, 142, 217,
    221, 222, 224, 225, 228, 229,
    270n17
    Abbas, tough talk with, 130
    background of, 129
    White House Correspondents
        Association dinner (2006), 251n34
Wilkerson, Lawrence, 19
Wilkinson, Jim, 20, 24–27, 35, 37, 43,
    49, 66, 92, 94, 102, 103, 120–21,
    167, 168, 177, 202, 204, 212,
    222, 241, 243, 253n10, 253n11,
    255n44
    background of, 27–29

Wilkinson, Jim (*continued*)
  cultural airport greeters of, 255*n*1
  Gaza work of, 135
  on Iraq, 176, 179
  media and, 40–41
  Rice stereotypes eliminated by,
    21–22
  on secretary of state's travel, 40
Williams, John, 182
Wolfensohn, James R., 122, 131, 133
Wolf, John S., 125
Wolfowitz, Paul, 31, 89, 213
women's rights, 88, 94, 98, 101, 111
World Trade Organization, 45, 114

Yugoslavia, 72
Yushchenko, Viktor, 145, 153, 154

Zacharia, Janine, 179, 251*n*34
Zaghawa, 118
Zagoria, Donald, 75

Zarif, Javad, 203
Zelikow, Philip, 27, 30, 56, 66, 94,
    149, 152, 156, 158, 165, 166–67,
    202, 224, 228, 240, 254*n*17,
    256*n*25, 265*n*6
  background of, 31–33
  on Egypt, 97
  India deal, role in, 50–51, 53
  on Iraq policy, 159, 177
  Kiev statement, role in, 154
  Rice's thoughts on, 32, 159, 235
Zimbabwe, 72, 99
Zoellick, Robert B., 27, 34, 38, 50–51,
    91, 203, 221, 223, 235, 253*n*11,
    261*n*20, 261*n*21
  Abuja talks and, 112–18
  background of, 30–31
  China policy, role in, 253*n*15
  on Iran/U.S. meeting, 196
  Iraq policy, role in, 267*n*36
  Sudan policy, role in, 104–5, 107–9,
    111–12, 253*n*15
  on Ward mission, 128